# ENVIRONMENTAL PRINCIPLES AND
## OF ENVIRONMENTAL L.

Environmental principles—from the polluter pays an͏       ͏ationary principles to the principles of integration and sustainability—proliferate in domestic
international legal and policy discourse, reflecting key goals of environmental
protection and sustainable development on which there is apparent political consensus. Environmental principles also have a high profile in environmental law,
beyond their popularity as policy and political concepts, as ideas that might unify
the subject and provide it with conceptual foundations or boost its delivery of
environmental outcomes. However, environmental principles are elusive legal
concepts. This book deepens the legal understanding of environmental principles in light of recent legal developments. It analyses the increasing legal effects of
environmental principles in different jurisdictions and demonstrates how they are
shaping and revealing innovative and evolving bodies of environmental law. This
analysis is a step forward in understanding a key feature of modern environmental
law and presents a robust methodology for dealing with novel legal concepts in the
subject. It also makes a contribution to environmental policy debates and discussions internationally that rely heavily on environmental principles, including their
supposed legal effects.

# Environmental Principles and the Evolution of Environmental Law

Eloise Scotford

·HART·
OXFORD · LONDON · NEW YORK · NEW DELHI · SYDNEY

HART PUBLISHING
Bloomsbury Publishing Plc
Kemp House, Chawley Park, Cumnor Hill, Oxford, OX2 9PH, UK

HART PUBLISHING, the Hart/Stag logo, BLOOMSBURY and the Diana logo are
trademarks of Bloomsbury Publishing Plc

First published in hardback, 2017
Paperback edition, 2019

A catalogue record for this book is available from the British Library.

Library of Congress Cataloging-in-Publication Data

Names: Scotford, Eloise, 1978– author.

Title: Environmental principles and the evolution of environmental law / Eloise Scotford.

Description: Oxford [UK] ; Portland, Oregon : Hart Publishing, 2017.   |   Includes bibliographical
references and index.

Identifiers: LCCN 2016046230 (print)   |   LCCN 2016046773 (ebook)   |   ISBN 9781849462976
(hardback) | ISBN 9781782252900 (Epub)

Subjects: LCSH: Environmental law.   |   Environmental policy.   |   Environmental law—European Union
countries.   |   Environmental law—Australia—New South Wales.   |   Sustainable development—
Law and legislation—Australia—New South Wales

Classification: LCC K3585 .S425 2017 (print)   |   LCC K3585 (ebook)   |   DDC 344.04/6—dc23

LC record available at https://lccn.loc.gov/2016046230

ISBN: HB: 978-1-84946-297-6
PB: 978-1-50993-010-4
ePDF: 978-1-78225-289-4
ePub: 978-1-78225-290-0

Typeset by Compuscript Ltd, Shannon

To find out more about our authors and books visit www.hartpublishing.co.uk.
Here you will find extracts, author information, details of forthcoming events and
the option to sign up for our newsletters.

To Liz and Michael, with thanks

… we are condemned to toil in the dimmest light as we feel our way toward the evolution of our conceptions and ideals of the natural order.[1]

[1] Lawrence Tribe, 'Ways Not To Think About Plastic Trees: New Foundations for Environmental Law' (1974) 83(7) *Yale LJ* 1315, 1341.

# ACKNOWLEDGEMENTS

This book has had a long gestation and there are many people to thank, for teaching me, for their support and for their patience. The research for this book began during my postgraduate study at Magdalen College, Oxford, and the book is largely based on my DPhil thesis submitted to the University in 2010. Since then, the legal landscape involving environmental principles has only spread and deepened, providing even more territory to chart. The work for the book in fact began when writing a BCL dissertation in 2006–7, when I was trying to make sense of the knotty body of European Court of Justice cases relating to the regulatory control of waste materials. In that work, my assumptions about the predictable nature of legal doctrine came seriously into question. In her subtle and effective way, my supervisor Liz Fisher (now Professor of Law, Corpus Christi College, Faculty of Law, University of Oxford) guided me in finding a path to conduct interesting, imaginative and rigorous legal research. She helped me to see that my intellectual insecurity when faced with an uncharted and complex body of law was in fact an interesting legal question. She taught me to see the stories and arguments behind legal doctrine, and to understand how legal ideas, preconceptions and methods meet the complicated world of real world environmental problems. Liz supported me in every step of the process of writing this book, particularly during her time as my doctoral supervisor, and gave me time, space and encouragement to write (and rewrite, think and write again). Without Liz and her approach to research and to life, I would not have found the intellectual strength or depth to write this book or to develop my career as a scholar of environmental law. I have dedicated this book to her and to my husband Michael—the dream team of support and inspiration.

The list of acknowledgements only begins there. I would like to thank the following for their support during the process in writing this book, in roughly chronological order: Karen Yeung (for her early supervision as temporary BCL dissertation supervisor when she was Fellow of St Anne's College, Oxford, and for her support and guidance since then as Professor of Law at King's); William Heath (BCL colleague and a big supporter of 'principles'); Laura Treacy (BCL colleague and a dear friend); Sanja Bogojevic (DPhil colleague and fellow explorer of environmental law); Benjamin Spagnolo (DPhil colleague, excellent meadow-walking companion, and the best proofreader in town); Brian Preston (Chief Judge of the New South Wales Land and Environment Court) for his encouragement and intellectual generosity in relation to this project; Sandy Steel and Rachael Walsh (KCL colleagues and new lecturer support group 2010–14); Tanya

Aplin and Maria Lee (invaluable mentors for London University life and more inspiring female academics); Sonam Gordon and Mubarak Waseem (wonderful legal research assistants and students from King's); and James Lee and Natasha Simonsen (invaluable KCL colleagues who went the extra mile to encourage and support me across the finish line). I would also like to thank Rachel Turner and Emily Braggins at Hart Publishing. These two editors oversaw the development of this book over many years, and were endlessly supportive and patient. I am hugely grateful to Hart, including Richard Hart who originally supported this book project, for seeing the potential of this book and for prioritising its quality above all else.

Life is very good at getting in the way of legal research and the time during which this book was created was full of exciting and challenging life events. My mother Jenni died in 2007 when the first seeds of this book had already been planted. My mum always wanted to write a book (there is a manuscript in a green bag that I need to look at properly one day…) and her involvement in my education at a young age gave me a deep commitment to learning. She also questioned everything, which could be pretty irritating but drilled into my subconscious the habit and importance of independent critical thinking. I think Mum would be proud of this book although she might find it a bit boring. She was more into direct action, saving Sydney foreshores and bushland from development, and that kind of thing. Together with my mother, my father Tony also provided me with excellent educational opportunities. I am enormously grateful for all of these. My Dad is a lawyer and so he might enjoy reading the book slightly more than Mum would have done. This book is really a hybrid product of my parental influences— independent critical thinking about environmental issues and the law. On parental influences, I have one other important mention—my godmother Nicki. Nicki is my English family and has provided me with a huge amount of love and support as an immigrant to the United Kingdom and through the life events that have accompanied the writing of this book. In the final stages of writing the book, I spent many Thursdays in Nicki's attic study being inspired by the view of her beautiful garden whilst my young daughter Rose enjoyed playing with Nicki and her happy dogs, BB and Razzle Dazzle.

Last but not least, one of the exciting life events that accompanied the gestation of this book was meeting my now husband Michael in 2011. Michael is not an academic or a lawyer but he has a sharp critical eye and kindly read many draft chapters of this book with enthusiasm and gave helpful feedback and support. Michael and I met fleetingly in Australia and embarked on an adventurous journey of travels, discovery and relocation to end up building a life together in London. So at least a wedding and baby (Rose—thank you for being an angel whilst Mummy 'wrote the book'!) delayed the completion of this book but they also enriched it in untold ways. Life has gotten in the way but it has given me time to think more, to see more, to learn more and to become more confident about what I want to say. The lonely genesis of this book is in stark contrast to the life-filled times of its completion. Finally, thank goodness it is done!

# CONTENTS

# TABLE OF CASES

**Table of Cases (European)**

**A**

# TABLE OF LEGISLATION

**United Nations Materials**

**Other Materials**

# 1

# Principles Principles Everywhere: Making Sense of Environmental Principles as Legal Concepts

## I. Introduction

This book started from a creeping sense that there was something going on with environmental principles and legal reasoning. In reading decisions of the European Court of Justice (as it then was), I noticed the Court relying on the precautionary principle and the principle of prevention to reach their conclusions on some very knotty and significant legal points.[1] That got me thinking and digging and it soon became apparent that environmental principles seemed to be everywhere—whether it was the polluter pays principle, the precautionary principle or the 'principle' of sustainable development. They were found in different legal systems, and at different jurisdictional levels—rooted in international law and policy in some respects, but also manifesting in national and regional statutes and case law. They were also prevalent in environmental law scholarship,[2] and in policy and political debate relating to environmental issues and sustainability. It proved difficult to narrow down the focus for analysis. What were these popular pithy principles? Why were they becoming so commonplace in policy debate and legal argument? How on earth was a lawyer to make sense of them? Clearly there was something interesting going on from a legal perspective but isolating that amongst the policy and politics was a challenge, and to an extent is impossible.[3]

---

[1] eg Joined Cases C-418/97 and C-419/97 *ARCO Chemie Nederland v Minister Van Volkshuisvesting* [2000] ECR I-4475 (relying on the precautionary and preventive principles to interpret the fraught definition of waste in EU law); Case C-127/02 *Landelijke Vereniging tot Behoud van de Waddenzee and Nederlandse Vereniging tot Bescherming van Vogels* [2004] ECR I-7405 (relying on the precautionary principle to interpret the requirement for appropriate assessment in relation to proposed development that was to affect special areas of conservation in the EU Natura 2000 network).

[2] I am indebted to Liz Fisher for many reasons (see the Acknowledgments) but also for the title of this chapter. Liz wrote an inspiring piece on 'precaution spotting' by environmental law scholars that similarly noted the preponderance of references to the precautionary principle in EU law: Elizabeth Fisher, 'Precaution, Precaution Everywhere: Developing a "Common Understanding" of the Precautionary Principle in the European Community' (2002) 9(1) *MJ* 7.

[3] Elizabeth Fisher, Bettina Lange and Eloise Scotford, *Environmental Law: Text, Cases and Materials* (OUP 2013) ch 11; Martin Shapiro and Alec Stone Sweet, *On Law, Politics, and Judicialization*

This book aims to show what is legally interesting about environmental principles, at the date of writing. In essence, it shows two things. First, it demonstrates how environmental principles are being used by some judges to develop legal reasoning, facilitating steps in the evolution of legal doctrine relating to environmental problems that might not otherwise have been possible. Second, it shows how environmental principles are significant and highly charged concepts for scholars in thinking about the nature of environmental law as a discipline. Environmental principles carry high hopes for environmental law scholars, relating not simply to the roles and impact of environmental principles in legal reasoning, but also to the coherent structure and legitimacy of environmental law as a subject. In both these senses—concerning doctrinal development and subject identity—environmental principles are becoming important concepts in the evolution of environmental law.

These two evolutionary paths are intertwined, in a way that can generate a 'fuzzy' analytical focus, obscuring clear thinking about environmental principles as legal ideas. This is because the broader scholarly ambitions for environmental principles in environmental law can obfuscate the fine-grained detail of their legal impacts. Tseming Yang and Robert Percival struggle with this challenge in their exposition of 'global environmental law':[4]

> Global environmental law is the set of legal principles developed by national, international and transnational environmental regulatory systems to protect the environment and manage natural resources. As a body of law, it is made up of a distinct set of substantive principles and procedural methods that are specifically important or unique to governance of the environment across the world … We cannot set out in detail the substantive governing principles of global environmental law … Describing [this emergent system of legal principles] would be no easier a task than setting out the governing principles of national, international, and transnational environmental law.

One reason for this difficulty in seeing environmental principles in detail, whilst they also occupy a global stage, is that environmental principles are expected to achieve many things. It is suggested, often concurrently, that environmental principles will provide solutions to *environmental problems* and that they will provide solutions to *legal problems* in environmental law. In the latter sense, there are a number of suggested roles for environmental principles: that they are universal and foundational legal concepts that bring coherence and moral legitimacy to the disorganised, multi-jurisdictional bundle of regulation and decisions that constitute environmental law; that they might make environmental law look like other

---

(OUP 2002). If we see environmental principles as an example of transnational law, then the blurred line between formal state-based law and political rhetoric reflects 'the way legal rules are being formed and applied in today's world': Paul Schiff Berman, 'From International Law to Law and Globalisation' (2005) 43 *Colum J Transnat'l L* 485, 537.

[4] Tseming Yang and Robert V Percival, 'The Emergence of Global Environmental Law' (2009) 36 *Ecology LQ* 615, 616–617.

established legal subjects (including through the role of principles in judicial reasoning); or that they might otherwise overcome the considerable challenges of methodology in environmental law scholarship.[5] This final point is significant because environmental law is a discipline beset by methodological challenges—particularly due to its multi-jurisdictional, interdisciplinary, novel and reactive nature.[6] It has no long-standing legal tradition in which to frame and analyse its legal developments. To the contrary, environmental law deals with environmental problems that are, by their very nature, often legally disruptive.[7]

This book aims to show that, far from being a solution to these kinds of methodological challenges, environmental principles are affected by them in the same way as are other legal developments in environmental law. In particular, there is no way to define legally what an environmental principle is in the abstract. This is not simply because there is no universal doctrinal tradition of 'environmental principles' in environmental law,[8] but because such a singular theoretical tradition is not possible, considering the ambiguous and open-ended nature of environmental principles and the multiple jurisdictions in which, increasingly, they have legal roles. Further, environmental principles are inconsistently labelled, defined and grouped, and they are adopted and applied in a wide range of legal as well as non-legal contexts. This ambiguity in definition and application is in fact what makes environmental principles such powerful symbols, which can carry many meanings and have many potential roles. Legal confusion is further generated by the fact that environmental principles are, first and foremost, statements of policy. Environmental principles, such as the precautionary principle and polluter pays principle, represent goals of environmental protection and sustainable development. All of this represents a significant challenge for the legal study of environmental principles. Indeed it raises the question whether they are appropriate subjects of legal study at all.

This book argues that environmental principles are appropriate subjects of legal study, but only with a clearly framed methodology, appreciating both their open-ended nature and symbolic significance in environmental law. Its central contention is that there is no getting away from the detail when trying to understand the legal roles of environmental principles. Whilst it can be argued that environmental principles represent a new kind of high-level transnational legal norm and ethic in relation to environmental issues, the meanings and application of specific principles are only made concrete within discrete legal settings. The book thus examines

---

[5] These high hopes for environmental principles and the reasons for their proliferation in environmental law scholarship are examined in ch 2.
[6] Elizabeth Fisher, Bettina Lange, Eloise Scotford and Cinnamon Carlarne, 'Maturity and Methodology: Starting a Debate about Environmental Law Scholarship' (2009) 21(2) *JEL* 213.
[7] Elizabeth Fisher, 'Environmental Law as "Hot Law"' (2013) 25(3) *JEL* 347; Elizabeth Fisher, Eloise Scotford and Emily Barritt, 'The Legally Disruptive Nature of Climate Change' (2017) 80 *MLR* (in press).
[8] *cf* Sands and Peel who suggest that certain environmental principles have become accepted principles of international law through extensive state practice: Philippe Sands and Jacqueline Peel, *Principles of International Environmental Law* (3rd edn, CUP 2012) 188.

judicial reasoning in two jurisdictions in which a growing body of case law involving environmental principles has been developing: the European Union ('EU') and New South Wales ('NSW'). By mapping the doctrinal treatment of environmental principles in two sets of courts in these jurisdictions—the Court of Justice of the European Union ('CJEU'),[9] and the New South Wales Land and Environment Court ('NSWLEC')—the book analyses the evolving roles of environmental principles comparatively. This approach tests scholarly assumptions that environmental principles are or can be universal, in a manner that focuses in detail on the legal frameworks in which environmental principles are employed.

These close contextual analyses of environmental principles in EU and NSW law are found in Chapters Four and Five. They show that environmental principles perform very different legal roles in these different jurisdictional settings, albeit that they are implicated in novel and interesting doctrinal developments in both jurisdictions. The resulting maps of these two terrains of environmental law reinforce that there are no analytical shortcuts in appraising the evolution of environmental law, particularly not in the form of environmental principles. Environmental principles do not neatly unify environmental law as a universal body of law, legitimise it as a scholarly subject, solve its methodological problems, or otherwise provide quick solutions to environmental problems. Rather, environmental principles are significant focal points for determining the nuanced evolution of environmental law within discrete legal systems, in terms of their own legal frameworks, doctrines and cultures, which can reflect changing environmental policy priorities to the extent that such priorities inform legal reasoning. Further, the connections and cross-references between similarly named principles across jurisdictions can trigger and reinforce doctrinal developments within particular jurisdictions, but they do not indicate equivalent legal developments across jurisdictions. This approach, and conclusion, is one for environmental law scholarship generally—novel legal concepts are to be fundamentally understood within the complexities of the legal systems in which they operate, even if those systems are open to external legal influences.[10] A comparative analysis of judicial reasoning involving environmental principles is thus significant in relation to both of the book's aims—in elaborating the legal roles of principles within particular legal systems, and in examining their broader role within environmental law and environmental law scholarship.

---

[9] The CJEU is comprised of the Court of Justice ('CJ'), formerly the European Court of Justice ('ECJ'), and the General Court, formerly the Court of First Instance ('CFI'). See further n 75.

[10] This reflects a systems theory understanding of legal systems that are normatively closed but cognitively open, acting as self-referential systems that respond to external change through their own normative logics: see Gunther Teubner, 'Autopoiesis in Law and Society: A Rejoinder to Blankenburg' (1984) 18 *Law and Society Review* 291: *cf* the earlier work of Philippe Nonet and Philip Selznick, *Law and Society in Transition: Toward Responsive Law* (Harper 1978) ('responsive' legal systems are self-referential but responsive to external social influences, which are filtered through systems' internal frames of normative development).

This chapter introduces the project of the book by setting out its methodology and scope, showing that precise analytical steps are required to appraise developments concerning environmental principles in different legal cultures, whilst recognising that environmental principles can also have a transnational character. Chapters Two and Three then develop the argument for the importance of the book's comparative analysis, both in the context of environmental law scholarship and across different legal spaces in which environmental principles have been developing (often ambiguous) meanings and roles. Chapter Two examines the scholarly motivations for, and methodological approaches to, analysing environmental principles to date; while Chapter Three examines the evolution of environmental principles at both international and domestic/regional levels, focusing on the particular legal contexts mapped in this book. This deeper examination of environmental principles within legal contexts, and their role in environmental law scholarship, shows that environmental principles are not universal or autonomous legal concepts for which there is an obvious legal analytical framework. Rather, environmental principles look very different, despite similar names, in different jurisdictions. At the same time, environmental principles are playing important legal roles in these different legal settings and there is increasing and shared enthusiasm for their use across jurisdictions, although any commonality rests in their symbolism and ability to stimulate legal change rather than in their legal equivalence. The challenge in studying environmental principles as legal ideas is thus primarily a methodological one—how to make sense of principles that have some transnational connections but which are taking on different and prominent legal roles within particular jurisdictions.

As a brief introduction, Part II identifies the environmental principles with which this book is concerned and the extent of their high profile in environmental law. The deep scholarly interest in environmental principles is elaborated critically in Chapter Two, but a quick sketch here of the wide legal interest in environmental principles establishes that environmental principles are increasingly prominent legal phenomena globally. Even this brief outline highlights that environmental lawyers need to make sense of environmental principles and to take them seriously in appreciating how environmental law is evolving across jurisdictions.

## II. Environmental Principles and Their High Profile in Environmental Law

There is no definitive and universal catalogue of environmental principles.[11] Further, it is not possible to state definitively what an 'environmental principle' is

---

[11] In environmental law scholarship, there is an extensive but inconsistent group of identified 'environmental principles': see eg Nicolas de Sadeleer, *Environmental Principles: From Political Slogans to*

or means. As indicated above, environmental principles are primarily policy ideas concerning how environmental protection and sustainable development ought to be pursued.[12] They are 'policies' in the broad sense that environmental principles reflect courses of action adopted to secure, or that tend to secure, a state of affairs conceived to be desirable.[13] Further, they are policies in the Dworkinian sense of 'collective goal[s] of the community as a whole'.[14] This raises an immediate question about whether environmental principles have any legal identity at all.[15] Certainly, environmental principles have no pre-programmed legal identities as generally expressed ideas of policy. This Part explains how environmental principles have come to have a high legal profile, despite their policy roots, through legal instruments, legal scholarship and judicial reasoning. More broadly, the book argues that it is fundamentally through their legal roles and treatment in particular legal settings, such as in EU and NSW law, that environmental principles develop focused legal identities and (marginal) legal meanings.

This Part introduces the environmental principles examined in this book by name and a brief description to orient the discussion, focusing on those principles that have become prominent in the case law of the European courts and NSWLEC. The general descriptions given here belie a wide range of often-conflicting definitions given for environmental principles, which reflect their open-textured formulation. These definitional conflicts are further examined in Chapter Three, and mean that, in legal terms, environmental principles fall within a 'category of concealed multiple reference'.[16]

*Legal Rules* (OUP 2002) 1–2 (examining the precautionary principle, principle of prevention and polluter pays principle as the 'three foremost environmental principles' amongst a number of principles whose 'disparity leads to perplexity'); *cf* Alhaji B M Marong, 'From Rio to Johannesburg: Reflections on the Role of International Legal Norms in Sustainable Development' (2003) 16 *Geo Int'l Envtl L Rev* 21, 59–64 (identifying a variety of groupings of principles said to constitute 'legal principles of sustainable development'). This variety of groupings reflects developments in a range of legal and policy contexts: see ch 3.

[12] Environmental protection and sustainable development are not the same goals: Mary Pat Williams Silveira, 'International Legal Instruments and Sustainable Development: Principles, Requirements, and Restructuring' (1995) 31 *Willamette L Rev* 239, 241–2.

[13] Neil MacCormick, *Legal Reasoning and Legal Theory* (Clarendon Press 1994) 261; Leonor Moral Soriano, 'A Modest Notion of Coherence in Legal Reasoning: A Model for the European Court of Justice' (2003) 16(3) *Ratio Juris* 296, 308–9.

[14] Ronald Dworkin, *Taking Rights Seriously* (rev edn, Duckworth 1978) 82.

[15] There is extensive jurisprudential debate on the role of policy in law, including Dworkin's concern about the proper distinction between policy and law in judicial reasoning, which is examined in ch 2 to the extent that it has influenced environmental law scholarship on environmental principles: see ch 2(II)(D)(i). Environmental law scholars however recognise that policy plays an important, if doctrinally challenging, place in environmental law: Fisher, Lange and Scotford, *Environmental Law: Text, Cases and Materials* (n 3) 439–459; D E Fisher, *Australian Environmental Law: Norms, Principles and Rules* (Thomson Reuters 2014) 125.

[16] Julius Stone, *Legal System and Lawyers' Reasonings* (Stanford University Press 1964) 246. The connection between amorphous ideas like environmental principles and Stone's legal categories of 'illusory reference' was made by the editors in their introduction to Paul Martin and others (eds), *The Search for Environmental Justice* (Edward Elgar 2015) 2.

In the case law of the European courts, six environmental principles can be identified. These are the *preventive principle* (that pollution or other environmental harm should be prevented, as opposed to remedied once generated), the *principle of rectification at source* (that environmental harm should be prevented at its source), the *precautionary principle* (that lack of full scientific knowledge should not be a reason for postponing preventive action where there is a risk of serious environmental harm), the *polluter pays principle* (that polluters should pay for the environmental harm they cause), the *integration principle* (that environmental protection requirements should be integrated into other policy areas), and the *principle of sustainable development* (generally reflecting some balancing of environmental, economic and social factors, or as 'development that meets the needs of the present without compromising the ability of future generations to meet their own needs').[17]

In the case law of the NSWLEC, there is some overlap with these EU law environmental principles, although they are referred to as *principles of 'ecologically sustainable development'* in NSW law. Thus there are identifiable versions of the precautionary principle, the polluter pays principle and the integration principle, although the latter two have explicitly different manifestations in this context. The polluter pays principle is contained within a broader '*principle of internalisation of environmental costs*', and the integration principle in this legal context refers to the idea that economic and environmental (and sometimes social) considerations should be integrated in public decision-making. Two other environmental principles also feature prominently in NSWLEC reasoning—the *principle of intergenerational equity* (that current generations owe duties to future generations to conserve environmental resources), and the *principle of conservation of biological diversity and ecological integrity* (as it suggests, that biodiversity should be conserved and ecological integrity maintained).

All these environmental principles, and others,[18] now have a high profile in environmental law and policy internationally, and in environmental law

---

[17] There is extensive debate over the concept of sustainable development, including its elusive definition: see ch 3, text accompanying nn 75–91. The definition quoted here is the often-cited one from the Brundtland Report: World Commission on Environment and Development, *Our Common Future* (OUP 1987) 43 ('Brundtland Report').

[18] eg the principle of intra-generational equity, the principle of sustainability, the principle of sustainable use, the principle of substitution, the proximity principle and the principle of self-sufficiency. These are discussed in chs 3, 4 and 5, as they arise as principles at the fringe of judicial reasoning in EU and NSW law, or otherwise in environmental policy and legal scholarship. There are also other 'environmental principles' that have been suggested by scholars as emerging norms of environmental law, such as the non-regression principle (Michel Prieur, 'Le Nouveau Principe de «Non Régression» en Droit de l'Environnement' in Michel Prieur and Gonzalo Sozzo (eds), *La Non Régression en Droit de l'Environnement* (Bruylant 2012), the principle of resilience (Nicholas A Robinson, 'Evolved Norms: A Canon for the Anthropocene' in Christina Voigt (ed) *Rule of Law for Nature: New Dimensions and Ideas in Environmental Law* (CUP 2013), and the principle of ecological proportionality (Gerd Winter, 'Ecological Proportionality: An Emerging Principle of Law for Nature?' in Christina Voigt (ed) *Rule of Law for Nature: New Dimensions and Ideas in Environmental Law* (CUP 2013)). See also the various 'principles' of sustainable development discussed in ch 3(II)(B).

scholarship. As indicated above, they constitute a seemingly amorphous group of policy catchphrases.[19] They are designated as 'principles' by their name, by the instruments in which they are found,[20] or by commentators by way of shorthand. It is in this third sense particularly that the study and profile of 'environmental principles' in environmental law has flourished, in particular since the early 1990s. Thus environmental law textbooks now have chapters or sections on 'principles' of environmental law and policy,[21] serious scholarly works on environmental principles in law have been written,[22] legal conferences and judicial symposia concerning environmental principles have been held,[23] and legal academic articles and book chapters on environmental principles proliferate.[24] In addition, interdisciplinary and 'transdisciplinary' works include legal appraisal of environmental principles.[25]

---

[19] *cf* Stephen Tromans, 'High Talk and Low Cunning: Putting Environmental Principles into Legal Practice' [1995] *JPEL* 779, 780.

[20] eg Brundtland Report (n 17) annexe 1; the Rio Declaration also sets out its agreed environmental protection proclamations as 'principles': United Nations Conference on Environment and Development, 'Rio Declaration on Environment and Development' (14 June 1992) UN Doc A/CONF.151/26 (Vol. I), 31 ILM 874 (1992); Treaty on the Functioning of the European Union (Lisbon Treaty) ('TFEU') arts 11, 191; Protection of the Environment Administration Act 1991 (NSW) ('POEA Act') s 6(2).

[21] eg Stuart Bell, Donald McGillivray and Ole Pedersen, *Environmental Law* (8th edn, OUP 2013) 56–75; Fisher, Lange and Scotford, *Environmental Law: Text, Cases and Materials* (n 3) ch 11; Susan Wolf and Neil Stanley, *Wolf and Stanley on Environmental Law* (6th ed, Routeledge-Cavendish 2014) [1.8]; Jan H Jans and Hans HB Vedder, *EU Environmental Law*, 4th edn (Europa Law Publishing 2012) 13–31; Sands and Peel, *Principles of International Environmental Law* (n 8) ch 6; Maria Lee, *EU Environmental Law, Governance and Decision-Making* (2nd edn, Hart 2014) 4–15; Maurice Evans, *Principles of Environmental and Heritage Law* (Prospect Media 2000) chs 5–9; Fisher, *Australian Environmental Law: Norms, Principles and Rules* (n 15) chs 5–7.

[22] In particular, de Sadeleer, *Environmental Principles* (n 11). See also Richard Macrory, Ian Havercroft and Ray Purdy (eds), *Principles of European Environmental Law* (Europa Law Publishing 2004).

[23] eg M Sheridan and L Lavrysen (eds), *Environmental Law Principles in Practice* (Bruylant 2002); UNEP, 'Johannesburg Principles on the Role of Law and Sustainable Development', Global Judges Symposium, Johannesburg, South Africa, 18–20 August 2002. Interdisciplinary conferences have also been held on environmental principles, including their legal appraisal, eg Timothy O'Riordan and James Cameron (eds), *Interpreting the Precautionary Principle* (Cameron May 1994); Ronnie Harding, Michael Young and Elizabeth Fisher, 'Interpretation of Principles' (Fenner Conference on the Environment—Sustainability: Principles to Practice 1994).

[24] eg Tromans, 'High Talk' (n 19); Ben Boer, 'Institutionalising Ecologically Sustainably Development: The Roles of National, State, and Local Governments in Translating Grand Strategy into Action' (1995) 31 *Willamette L Rev* 307; Paul Stein, 'Turning Soft Law into Hard—An Australian Experience with ESD Principles in Practice' (1997) 3(2) *The Judicial Review* 91; Michael G Doherty, 'Hard Cases and Environmental Principles: An Aid to Interpretation?' (2004) 3 *YEEL* 57; Gerd Winter, 'The Legal Nature of Environmental Principles in International, EC and German Law' in R Macrory, I Havercroft and R Purdy (eds), *Principles of European Environmental Law* (Europa Law Publishing 2004); Astrid Epiney, 'Environmental Principles' in R Macrory (ed) *Reflections on 30 Years of EU Environmental Law* (Europa Law Publishing 2006); Eloise Scotford, 'Mapping the Article 174(2) Case Law: A First Step to Analysing Community Environmental Law Principles' (2008) 8 *YEEL* 1; Brian Preston, 'Sustainable Development Law in the Courts: The Polluter Pays Principle' (2009) 26 *EPLJ* 257; Andrew Edgar, 'Institutions and Sustainability: Merits Review Tribunals and the Precautionary Principle' (2013) 16(1) *Australasian Journal of Natural Resources Law and Policy* 61; Brian Preston, 'The Judicial Development of Ecologically Sustainable Development' in Douglas Fisher (ed), *Research Handbook on Fundamental Concepts of Environmental Law* (Edward Elgar 2016).

[25] eg Sharon Beder, *Environmental Principles and Policies: An Interdisciplinary Introduction* (Earthscan, 2006); Andreas Philippopoulos-Mihalopoulos, *Absent Environments: Theorising*

The profile of environmental principles in environmental law has particularly grown internationally in recent decades because of their increasing presence in international treaties and soft law agreements, binding regional agreements, and domestic legislation.[26] The wide range of 'environmental principles' that have been formulated in international soft law agreements concerning sustainable development are of particular significance, since these provide an apparent basis on which to build a universal understanding of environmental principles as legal concepts.[27]

Environmental principles also have a high profile in case law across jurisdictions. They have been judicially recognised in at least three ways. First, judicial reasoning has considered environmental principles contained in legal instruments that a court is interpreting or applying—this is seen in both the European judgments and NSWLEC decisions analysed in Chapters Four and Five, in relation to the Treaty on the Functioning of the European Union ('TFEU') and NSW statutes, which respectively contain references to certain environmental principles. Second, judicial reasoning has also been innovative in its recognition and treatment of such principles. Judges of the NSWLEC recognised environmental principles and employed them in judicial reasoning before they were included in NSW legislation,[28] and, in public international law, Judge Weeramantry delivered (often dissenting) opinions in the International Court of Justice declaring various environmental principles to be 'important and rapidly developing principle[s] of contemporary environmental law',[29] and important legal principles that must be recognised.[30] The Indian courts have also been particularly progressive in reading environmental principles into their constitutional jurisprudence.[31]

Third, judicial reasoning in particular jurisdictions has promoted the profile of environmental principles by cross-referring to judgments concerning

---

*Environmental Law and the City* (Routeledge-Cavendish, 2007); Robinson, 'Evolved Norms: A Canon for the Anthropocene' (n 18).

[26] On how environmental principles are appearing and evolving at different jurisdictional levels, see ch 3.

[27] See ch 3(II)(A).

[28] See ch 3(IV)(C)(i).

[29] In relation to the precautionary principle and principle of intergenerational equity: *Nuclear Tests Case (New Zealand v France)* [1995] ICJ Rep 288, 341 (dissenting opinion).

[30] Judge Weeramantry has identified the precautionary principle as 'gaining increasing support as part of the international law of the environment': ibid 342. In a subsequent case, he found that the principle of sustainable development is a legal 'principle of reconciliation' between the needs of development and the need to protect the environment: *Gabčikovo-Nagymaros Project (Hungary v Slovakia)* [1997] ICJ Rep 7, 90 (separate opinion). The majority judgment in *Pulp Mills (Argentina v Uruguay)* [2010] ICJ Rep 14 supported this approach, finding that the concept of sustainable development informed a key treaty provision (at [178]).

[31] See eg *Vellore Citizens' Welfare Forum v Union of India* AIR 1996 SC 2715, 2721-2 (the precautionary principle and polluter pays principle applied as rules of law by relying on constitutional provisions); *AP Pollution Control Board v Nayudu* AIR 1999 SC 812, 821 (principle of intergenerational equity); *Samaj Parivartana Samudaya v State of Karnataka* AIR 2013 SC 3217 (principle of intergenerational equity). The Pakistani courts have been similarly progressive in adopting the precautionary principle as a legal rule in interpreting the Pakistan constitution: *Zia v WAPAD* PLD 1994 SC 693 [8].

environmental principles in other jurisdictions, building what looks like global, or transnational, jurisprudence on environmental principles independent of the legal context in which they are being used.[32] Examples of this are seen in NSWLEC reasoning,[33] as well as in other jurisdictions such as India and Canada,[34] although this kind of transnational judicial discussion is notably absent from European decisions involving environmental principles. All this judicial activity has been developed partly through networks of judges,[35] who have a 'sense of shared purpose and values, and willingness to learn from the experiences of each other'.[36] This cross-fertilisation of judicial reasoning has also informed, and been informed by, legal scholarly developments with respect to environmental principles. Together, these authoritative discussions have progressively built a mutually reinforcing footing for the high profile of environmental principles in environmental law generally. In short, environmental principles are now part of the 'lingua franca' of environmental lawyers across jurisdictions internationally.[37] This high profile suggests that environmental principles are concepts that environmental lawyers need to understand and analyse.

The following Part sets out the distinctive methodology of the book, which is designed for such lawyerly analysis. In particular, it is designed to analyse environmental principles as novel legal concepts in environmental law, by avoiding generalisations or assumptions about the legal nature of environmental principles and, instead, explicitly inquiring into the detail of how environmental principles operate (or do not operate) as part of the legal fabric of different legal systems.

---

[32] Boer sees this as part of the globalisation of environmental law, particularly based on common principles: Ben Boer, 'The Rise of Environmental Law in the Asian Region' (1999) 32 *U Rich L Rev* 1503, 1510. See also Robert Carnwath, 'Judicial Protection of the Environment: At Home and Abroad' (2004) 16(3) *JEL* 315; Brian Preston, 'The Role of the Judiciary in Promoting Sustainable Development: The Experience of Asia and the Pacific' (2005) 9(2) *Asia Pac J Envtl L* 109; Lord Carnwath, 'Environmental Law in a Global Society' (2015) 3 *JPEL* 269; Preston, 'The Judicial Development of Ecologically Sustainable Development' (n 24).

[33] eg *Telstra Corporation v Hornsby Shire Council* [2006] NSWLEC 133; (2006) 146 LGERA 10; (2006) 67 NSWLR 256 [156–9] (Preston CJ drew on European cases to elucidate the precautionary principle); *Gray v Minister for Planning* [2006] NSWLEC 720; (2006) 152 LGERA 258 [121] (Pain J refers to *Minors Oposa v Secretary of the Department of Environment and Natural Resources* 33 ILM 174 (1994) (Supreme Court of the Philippines) to 'underscore the importance of [the principle of intergenerational equity]'). See ch 5.

[34] *Nayudu* (n 31) 821 (referring to New Zealand Decision *Ashburton Acclimatisation Society v Federated Farmers of New Zealand* [1998] 1 NZLR 78); *114957 Canada Ltee v Hudson (Town)* [2001] 2 SCR 241 [32] (referring to Indian cases, above n 31).

[35] These include the Asian Judges Network for the Environment (<http://www.asianjudges.org> accessed 28 July 2016), the European Union of Judges for the Environment (<http://www.eufje.org/index.php/en?> accessed 28 July 2016), and UNEP's Judges Programme under the Division of Environmental Law and Conventions (http://www.unep.org/delc/judgesprogramme> accessed 28 July 2016). On the role of judicial networks in globalising law, see Anne-Marie Slaughter, 'Judicial Globalisation' (2000) 40 *Va J Int'l L* 1103.

[36] Carnwath, 'Environmental Law in a Global Society' (n 32) 274.

[37] Doherty, 'Hard Cases' (n 24) 58.

# III. Methodology and Scope

As with scholarship concerning 'global governance' or 'globalisation studies', there has been a 'rush into the global space' in the legal appraisal of environmental principles.[38] Much scholarly writing about environmental principles adopts a universalist perspective, assuming that environmental principles are generally equivalent concepts across jurisdictional boundaries.[39] However, the increasing existence of environmental principles at different jurisdictional levels raises questions, rather than suggesting easy answers, about their normative status and interaction.[40] As indicated above, this presents a significant and methodological challenge in appraising the developing legal roles of environmental principles across jurisdictions.

To meet this challenge, this book localises the focus. Whilst environmental principles reflect global aspirations, their legal manifestations crystallise within discrete legal systems, and the book's main research captures how this crystallisation is occurring within the judicial reasoning of courts that have embraced the use of environmental principles. The full 'global' legal picture of environmental principles can only be captured through multiple refractions from local and regional levels, including through authoritative interpretive communities such as courts. This insight has been recognised by scholars of transnational or global law,[41] and it is the starting point for building the methodology of this book. Localising the focus for analysis however still leaves a range of analytical choices. This is particularly the case for environmental principles, which have no settled meanings and have legal identities that are nascent, fragmented and idiosyncratic across jurisdictions.[42]

The localised analytical framework adopted in this book involves four elements that are designed to catch the variety of ways in which environmental principles are taking on distinctive legal roles within legal systems, including how they are provoking or reflecting new legal developments and modes of legal reasoning, and

---

[38] Peer Zumbansen, 'Transnational Comparisons: Theory and Practice of Comparative Law as a Critique of Global Governance' in Maurice Adams and Jacco Bomhoff (eds), *Practice and Theory in Comparative Law* (CUP 2012) 211.

[39] See ch 2(II).

[40] Law and globalisation scholars have highlighted the complexity of norms that develop across different levels of governance in 'multifaceted ways': Berman, 'From International Law to Law and Globalisation' (n 3) 551 and generally.

[41] Martin Shapiro, 'The Globalisation of Law' [1993] 1 *Global Legal Studies Journal* 37; Peer Zumbansen, 'Defining the Space of Transnational Law: Legal Theory, Global Governance and Legal Pluralism' (2012) 21 *Transnat'l L & Contemp Probs* 305.

[42] This kind of legal uncertainty is again typical of emerging transnational norms: Craig Scott, '"Transnational Law" as Proto-Concept: Three Conceptions' (2009) 10 *German Law Journal* 859. In relation to environmental law, de Sadeleer highlights that environmental norms have become more uncertain due to the 'shattering of traditional legal boundaries', increasing regulatory flexibility, and uncertain scientific information: de Sadeleer (n 11) 255–258.

also forming connections between jurisdictions. Thus the book's method is: (1) localised and focused on jurisdictions and courts as key sites of legal development; (2) comparative in using an 'extended' form of legal culture analysis to determine how environmental principles are adopted by, and transformed through, the discrete legal cultures in which they are employed, including when those processes are partly inspired by instruments or developments in other normative contexts; (3) doctrinal in a broad sense that captures new forms of legal reasoning; and (4) focused on judicial technique in mapping the use of environmental principles to elucidate the fine grain of their evolving roles in legal reasoning.

This methodological foundation avoids assuming legal roles for environmental principles or assuming legal models for their analysis. This is important in light of the legally ambiguous nature of environmental principles, their evolving roles in judicial reasoning (including the evolving bodies of law of which they form part), as well as the extensive and methodologically pluralistic legal scholarship concerning environmental principles, which includes assumptions that environmental principles fit established models of 'legal principles',[43] as well as suggestions that environmental principles are foundational of a new legal order.[44] As will be seen, the doctrinal maps of judicial reasoning generated through this analysis are anything but simple; the complexity of the legal situations in different legal systems in which environmental principles are playing roles requires a careful but open method in order to navigate them.

## A.  Localising the Focus

Environmental principles, particularly with their connection to the international sustainable development agenda, are often viewed as global phenomena that are devised or agreed internationally and which then translate down to regional, national and local levels for implementation.[45] On this view, national courts around the world, in incorporating environmental principles into their reasoning, are doing their bit to contribute to a universal picture of environmental law based on principles.[46] This might seem to fit the pithy aim of international sustainable development instruments to 'think globally, act locally'.[47] However, such an aim

---

[43] See ch 2(II)(D)(i).

[44] See ch 2(II)(E).

[45] See ch 3, nn 43–48 and accompanying text; cf Yang and Percival, 'The Emergence of Global Environmental Law' (n 4) 625–6 who argue that principles of global environmental law are emerging from borrowing both ways between national and international legal systems but also more generally as a 'set of independent and convergent legal principles'. See also Jonathan B Weiner, 'Something Borrowed for Something Blue: Legal Transplants and the Evolution of Global Environmental Law' (2001) 27 *Ecology LQ* 1295 (on the translation of environmental regulatory concepts from national law to international law).

[46] See n 32 and accompanying text. See also Macrory et al, *Principles of European Environmental Law* (n 24) chs 5–12.

[47] This aim derives from the 1972 Stockholm Conference on the Human Environment when this phrase was coined by the chairman of the scientific committee René Dubos, and is reflected by the detailed plan of implementing the subsequent 'Rio principles' in *Agenda 21*: Barbara Ward and René

does not necessarily imply that global thinking about environmental principles simply equates to or translates into equivalent local action in particular jurisdictions;[48] rather it suggests that global policies are distinct from local action and that both are required. Legal phenomena with global dimensions cannot be assumed to be universally equivalent, certainly not without a firm foundation in public international law or jurisprudence.[49] There is no such firm foundation for environmental principles, which are mainly found in soft law instruments in the international legal sphere,[50] and which do not have a robust jurisprudential foundation.[51] With environmental principles, scholars are faced with analysing the evolution of ambiguous, shifting norms within, across and between domestic and international legal spheres. Peer Zumbansen identifies this kind of normative puzzle as a form of 'transnational legal pluralism' and highlights the importance of domestic spheres in constituting transnational norms, arguing that 'domestic experiences … are crucial points of orientation' for law with transnational dimensions.[52] In a similar vein, Martin Shapiro highlights how 'national regimes of law and lawyering will remain self-generating' in the face of globalising forces.[53] In relation to environmental principles, this book finds that the contingent local (and regional) manifestations of environmental principles are indeed self-generating and that they fundamentally orient the legal story and status of environmental principles.

This view is captured by *Agenda 21* (the sustainable development implementation document agreed at the 1992 Earth Summit in Rio de Janeiro), which suggests that the nature of local action on sustainable development is contingent and idiosyncratic:[54]

> The ability of a country to follow sustainable development paths is determined to a large extent by the capacity of its people and its institutions as well as by its ecological

Dubos, *Only One Earth: The Care and Maintenance of a Small Planet* (United Nations Conference on the Human Environment (Penguin 1972)); UNCED Report I (1992) ('*Agenda 21*') eg [2.32]–[2.38], [37.1]–[37.5].

[48] For Zumbansen, recognising transnational processes of norm creation 'defeats our attempts at understanding the relation between the national and the post-national constellation as a linear one': Zumbansen 'Defining the Space of Transnational Law' (n 41) 323.

[49] Local variation can play a constitutive part of even well-established global norms. Thus 'cosmopolitan' understandings of global governance, whilst embracing norms of universal concern, respect legitimate local differences in the implementation of norms: Roger Brownsword, 'Regulatory Cosmopolitanism: Clubs, Commons, and Questions of Coherence' TILT Working Paper No 018/2010. See generally, Kwame Anthony Appiah, *Cosmopolitanism* (Penguin 2006). A similar insight derives from sociological understandings of globalisation, finding that local environments and systems have important roles in constituting global phenomena: Saskia Sassen, 'The State and Globalization', in Rodney Bruce Hall & Thomas J Biersteker (eds), *The Emergence of Private Authority in Global Governance* (CUP 2002).

[50] See ch 3(II)(B).

[51] Some scholars might contest this. See ch 2(II)(E).

[52] Zumbansen, 'Defining the Space of Transnational Law' (n 41) 324.

[53] Martin Shapiro, 'The Globalisation of Law' [1993] 1 *Global Legal Studies Journal* 37, 63.

[54] *Agenda 21* (n 47) [37.1].

and geographical conditions. Specifically, capacity-building encompasses the country's human, scientific, technological, organizational, institutional and resource capabilities.

Such capabilities include legal capabilities, which must be understood on their own terms. On this view, the wide-ranging profile of environmental principles in environmental law instruments internationally in fact invites wide-ranging academic scrutiny of environmental principles in different legal contexts. However, as will be seen in Chapter Two, environmental law scholarship that has investigated the legal status of environmental principles in environmental law has rarely done so with the contextual consciousness suggested by these insights into local 'capabilities'.[55] In delving into localised contexts, this book focuses on the capabilities and experiences of two systems of courts, in two particular jurisdictions—both of those localising choices require justification.

## i. Why Jurisdictions?

This book takes discrete legal jurisdictions as localised units for analysis rather than nation states. Jurisdictions are defined as such according to the governance arrangements of the relevant different nation states—the federation of states in Australia and the formation of the EU respectively in this case.[56] It might still be questioned whether New South Wales and the EU *as jurisdictions* are appropriate legal systems to analyse and compare when analysing the legal roles of environmental principles. Zumbansen suggests that 'jurisdictional reference points are ... becoming less reliable as demarcating lines' for comparative law study,[57] and that a 'transnational legal pluralist lens' reorients study towards regimes that are 'not as entirely detached from national political and legal orders, but as emerging out of and reaching beyond them'.[58] These insights are helpful, in that they remind us that we need to account for the normative interactions that extend beyond and between jurisdictional spaces. However, the force of this methodological argument is limited in relation to environmental principles to the extent that the project of transnationalism focuses on non-state actors and private forms of ordering. Networked and private forms of transnational governance have a high profile in some regulatory spheres, such as corporate governance, and transcend jurisdictional boundaries in profound ways.[59] Environmental principles, by contrast, have been

---

[55] See ch 2(III)(A).

[56] Note that within the NSW and Australian legal system, the NSWLEC occupies a unique jurisdictional space: see ch 5(II)(A). In the EU, EU legal jurisdiction sits above Member State jurisdictions, being defined and bounded by the constitutional EU Treaties, and by the CJEU's exposition of the supreme 'new legal order' within which it operates: Joined Cases 98 & 230/83 *van Gend en Loos v Commission* [1984] ECR 3763.

[57] Peer Zumbansen, 'Transnational Comparisons: Theory and Practice of Comparative Law as a Critique of Global Governance' in Maurice Adams & Jacco Bomhoff (eds), *Practice and Theory in Comparative Law* (CUP 2012) 188–189.

[58] Zumbansen, 'Defining the Space of Transnational Law' (n 41) 330.

[59] ibid.

developing distinct legal profiles, not through their regulatory force, but by their migration from politics and policy into formal legal instruments and institutional legal environments such as courts. This is not to say that there are not interesting examples of transnational private ordering in the environmental sphere,[60] but that significant legal developments involving environmental principles have been occurring in jurisdiction-specific contexts.

Furthermore, the jurisdictions covered in this book represent a study of environmental principles operating at different levels of governance—from the international sphere, to the regional and multilevel governance site of the European Union, to the domestic law of NSW (albeit within the context of a federal political system). This range of legal contexts provides a mixed jurisdictional platform for exploring how environmental principles are operating within these different spheres of governance and their jurisdictional contexts, whilst remaining open to transnational interactions concerning environmental principles between these legal spheres.

Concerns about relying on jurisdictional boundaries have also been raised in the process of identifying different legal cultures, which the next section introduces as a key concept for appraising how environmental principles are assimilated and recognised in particular jurisdictions. Comparing legal cultures is not necessarily equivalent to comparing legal systems according to strict jurisdictional boundaries, since legal cultures may transcend legal boundaries.[61] However, while jurisdictional boundaries might not mark perfect limits to the legal cultures studied in EU law and NSW law,[62] they provide a good starting point for comparing legal culture. As David Nelken points out:[63]

> Given the way [the nation state] often sets boundaries of jurisdiction, politics and language, the nation state will often serve as a relevant starting point for comparing legal culture.

---

[60] This is especially seen in the roles of transnational financial actors and international markets: eg Megan Bowman, *Banking on Climate Change: How Finance Actors and Transnational Regulatory Regimes are Responding* (Kluwer Law International 2015); Steven Bernstein et al, 'A Tale of Two Copenhagens: Carbon Markets and Climate Governance' (2010) 39(1) *Journal of International Studies* 161; Benjamin Richardson, 'Socially Responsible Investing for Sustainability: Overcoming Its Incomplete and Conflicting Rationales' (2013) 2(2) *TEL* 311.

[61] Anne-Marie Slaughter, 'The Real New World Order' (1997) 76(5) *Foreign Affairs* 183.

[62] eg Australia is a federation of states and territories (including NSW), with discrete legal jurisdictions existing at both federal and state levels. However, these jurisdictions overlap, united in legal terms by Australian constitutional law and by the convenient legal doctrine that there is one common law in Australia: *Lange v Australian Broadcasting Corporation* (1997) 189 CLR 520. Similarly, there is legal interaction between EU law and the laws of EU Member States, both in terms of formal doctrine (eg *van Gend* (n 56)), and to a lesser extent informal influences on the development of EU law (eg EU law relating to fundamental rights: Paul Craig and Gráinne de Búrca, *EU Law: Text, Cases and Materials* (6th edn, OUP 2015) 388–390).

[63] David Nelken, 'Defining and Using the Concept of Legal Culture' in Esin Örücü and David Nelken (eds), *Comparative Law: A Handbook* (Hart 2007) 117.

## *ii. Why Courts? Why These Courts?*

Within the two jurisdictions of the EU and NSW, the case law of the EU courts and NSWLEC is an obvious focus for analysis. In the last 15 years, significant bodies of case law concerning environmental principles have developed in both sets of courts. Judicial reasoning in these courts is where environmental principles are being interpreted, used, and embedded within the doctrine of these different legal systems. Beyond this opportunistic platform for research, there are good reasons to focus on courts as authoritative forums for giving legal identities to otherwise amorphous, policy-based environmental principles, and to focus on these two sets of courts in particular.

In comparative law terms, courts, through their case law, are authoritative 'interpretive communities' that shape the legal roles of environmental principles within particular legal cultures.[64] As Klaus Bosselmann states, 'the importance of [environmental] principles is not so much determined by their legal status, but by their interpretation through governments, courts and other decision-makers'.[65] Furthermore, in a transnationalised context, where legal systems are being challenged, 'stimulated',[66] or 'impregnated'[67] by external ideas such as environmental principles, which interact with norms in other jurisdictions or normative spheres, courts have an important role in localising such norms (and also 'relativising the local' in a global context). In so doing, courts might re-establish their functions and positions of power.[68] Thus, the interpretation and application of environmental principles by courts can be a particularly rich source of information about their legal roles.

But why focus on these two sets of courts in particular, the EU courts and NSWLEC? Scholarly writing has paid a lot of attention to the full (or at least a broad) range of courts that have engaged in reasoning concerning environmental principles, often without much discrimination between the relevant courts.[69] Indeed, environmental principles have been developing roles in other courts (and tribunals) in Australia,[70] in other national courts, as well as in international

---

[64]  Roger Cotterrell, 'Is there a Logic of Legal Transplants?' in David Nelken and Johannes Feest (eds), *Adapting Legal Cultures* (Hart 2001) 80–81; Pierre Legrand, 'What are "Legal Transplants"?' in David Nelken and Johannes Feest (eds), *Adapting Legal Cultures* (Hart 2001) 63. See also Alan Watson, *Legal Transplants: An Approach to Comparative Law* (2nd edn, University of Georgia Press 1993).

[65]  Klaus Bosselmann, The Principle of Sustainability: Transforming Law and Governance (Ashgate 2008) 44.

[66]  Teubner (n 10) 298.

[67]  Zumbansen, 'Transnational Comparisons' (n 57) 199.

[68]  See Zumbansen, 'Defining the Space of Transnational Law' (n 41) 334.

[69]  eg de Sadeleer, *Environmental Principles* (n 11) chs 1–3; Lisa Wyman, 'Acceptance of the Precautionary Principle—Australian v International Decision-Makers' (2001) 18 *EPLJ* 395; Preston, 'Role of the Judiciary in Promoting Sustainable Development' (n 33); Carnwath, 'Judicial Protection of the Environment' (n 32) 317.

[70]  See ch 5, n 7. See also Charmain Burton, 'The Status of the Precautionary Principle in Australia: Its Emergence in Legislation and as a Common Law Doctrine' (1998) 22 *Harv Envtl L Rev* 509; Elizabeth Fisher, *Risk Regulation and Administrative Constitutionalism* (Hart 2007) ch 6.

decision-making fora. This scholarly focus on identifying a wide range of judicial reasoning concerning environmental principles has been helpful in highlighting the growing legal importance and status of environmental principles in environmental law transnationally. However, it leaves out of account the different roles that environmental principles are playing within legal systems, and how different legal cultures and environments are reacting to and constituting environmental principles as legal ideas. There are two reasons why these two particular courts are valuable contexts in which to explore such developments, beyond providing a multi-level jurisdictional landscape for exploring transnational dimensions of environmental principles.

First, other bodies of case law (at least across the English-speaking world)[71] have generally not been as prolific, although some courts have been very activist in building environmental principles into their case law,[72] and have been developing important bodies of case law around key environmental principles.[73] It should also be noted that the current judicial landscape concerning environmental principles internationally reflects only the position at one moment in time,[74] and this is a developing area of jurisprudence in many jurisdictions. Second, these two court systems—the EU courts and the NSWLEC—are both relatively recent creations as courts,[75] and in different ways progressive in their reasoning. The EU courts are progressive, partly through necessity, in their articulation of a modern and relatively novel body of law—EU law. This progressive agenda is broader than, and largely independent of, the Court's reasoning concerning environmental

[71] There have been important developments concerning principles in non-English speaking courts, including many civil law jurisdictions within the European Union: see further Macrory et al, *Principles of European Environmental Law* (n 22).

[72] In particular, the Indian cases: see above n 31.

[73] A prominent example is the judicial interpretation of 'sustainable management' as the purpose of the Resource Management Act 1991 in New Zealand: *Environmental Defence Society Inc v The New Zealand King Salmon Co Ltd* [2014] NZSC 38, [2014] 1 NZLR 593. For the case law of the Environment Court of New Zealand concerning sustainable management, see Bosselmann (n 65) 64–66.

[74] eg in UK law, ad hoc consideration of environmental principles in judicial reasoning presents an uncertain legal picture: see *R v Secretary of State for Trade and Industry, ex parte Duddridge, The Times* 26 October 1995 (CA); *R (National Grid Gas plc (formerly Transco plc)) v Environment Agency* [2007] UKHL 30, [2007] 1 WLR 1780; *R (Champion) v North Norfolk City Council and anor* [2015] UKSC 52; cf *R (Ludlam) v First Secretary of State, Derbyshire District Council* [2004] EWHC 99 (QB (Admin)) and the increasing presence of sustainable development in UK legislation: Andrea Ross, 'Why Legislate for Sustainable Development? An Examination of Sustainable Development Provisions in the UK and Scottish Statutes' (2008) 20(1) *JEL* 35.

[75] The present Court of Justice of the European Union (comprising the Court of Justice, the General Court and specialised courts: Treaty on European Union (Lisbon Treaty) ('TEU') art 19) grew out of the Court of Justice originally created in 1952 by the Treaty Establishing the European Coal and Steel Community and was subsequently given jurisdiction over the European Economic Community established by the Treaty of Rome: Convention on certain Institutions Common to the European Communities, 25 March 1957. The Lisbon Treaty modified the jurisdictional structure of the EU courts and revised their names. The LEC was established by the Land and Environment Court Act 1979 (NSW).

principles.[76] By contrast, the NSWLEC is progressive in developing a novel institutional identity within the pre-existing NSW legal system, again through ground-breaking jurisprudence, but in a way that is focused on environmental principles. These two court systems thus provide compelling settings for seeing how environmental principles can co-evolve with legal systems, albeit in different ways.

## B. An 'Extended' Comparative Framework: Environmental Principles Reflected in Legal Cultures

The next important aspect of the book's methodology is its focus on legal culture as a comparative frame for discerning the different ways in which environmental principles are being used, interpreted and constituted in the legal settings of the EU courts and NSWLEC. As a matter of comparative law method, a commonly cited norm is that 'like must be compared with like'.[77] This rule is offended by comparing EU law and NSW law, which are very different legal systems in different governance settings. However, differences between legal systems are not inimical to useful comparative study. Much depends on the purpose of the comparative exercise and the 'existence and availability of data'.[78] The purpose of this book's research is not, as in some comparative law scholarship, to examine the transplantation of a legal concept between jurisdictions (or otherwise comparatively to test common legal concepts).[79] On the contrary, its project is to examine the myriad ways in which environmental principles are developing legal roles within different legal settings,[80] with no assumptions of universality of those principles or equivalence of legal settings.[81] This approach accounts for the open-textured nature of environmental principles and the fact that, 'even when similar concepts are being used across jurisdictions, they may not necessarily play

---

[76] The activism of the CJEU has been widely commented on, particularly in relation to constitutional developments: Grainne de Burca, 'The European Court of Justice and the Evolution of EU Law' in TA Borzel and RA Cichowski (eds), *The State of the European Union: Law, Politics and Society* (OUP 2003). See further ch 4, nn 17–21.

[77] Esin Örücü, 'Developing Comparative Law' in Esin Örücü and David Nelken (eds), *Comparative Law: A Handbook* (Hart 2007) 47–8.

[78] ibid 50.

[79] See eg David Nelken and Johannes Feest (eds), *Adapting Legal Cultures* (Hart 2001).

[80] Other work has previously examined the legal roles of environmental principles across jurisdictions: Macrory et al, *Principles of European Law* (n 22), although the overall aim of the work is to analyse the same environmental principles. See also Sheridan and Lavrysen (eds), *Environmental Law Principles in Practice* (n 23). The importance of comparative analysis in environmental law generally is well recognised by some scholars eg Nicholas A Robinson, 'IUCN as Catalyst for a Law of the Biosphere: Acting Globally and Locally' (2005) 35 Envtl L 249, 278–279; Fisher, *Risk Regulation and Administrative Constitutionalism* (n 70).

[81] '[T]here is no point in comparing what is identical, and little point in comparing what has nothing in common': Gerhard Dannemann, 'Comparative Law: Study of Similarities or Differences?' in Mathias Reimann and Reinhard Zimmermann (eds), *The Oxford Handbook of Comparative Law* (OUP 2006) 384.

the same role in each'.[82] More than that, environmental principles are *given* legal meanings by the jurisdictions in which they are used. Or to put it differently, they cannot be 'significantly detached from the world of meanings that defines a legal culture'.[83] For this reason, comparative analysis that takes into account 'legal culture' is required. Furthermore, the book's project is interested in any intersections across jurisdictions in the use of environmental principles and how these connections are absorbed, reflected or rejected within and by legal cultures. This latter aspect, which reflects a 'transnational turn' in thinking about environmental principles, requires an extended comparative method that not only compares different jurisdictions but also recognises any connections across or beyond legal systems.[84]

In adopting this method, this book adopts legal culture as a thin concept, focusing on 'internal legal culture'.[85] In general, 'legal culture' reflects the amalgam of institutional, historical and power-related forces that find particular expressions in the legal language and traditions of a jurisdiction. It can also include broader social, political and economic forces that affect law's development, relevance and implementation in a particular jurisdiction.[86] Internal elements of a legal culture include written law, scholarly commentary, judicial decisions, attitudes of legal professionals, and the architecture of legal institutions.[87] For the purpose of this book, internal legal culture thus expresses the institutional, jurisdictional, constitutional and localised doctrinal norms and constraints that shape the roles for environmental principles within judicial reasoning. This goes beyond equating law with rules, and takes into account the embedded features of jurisdictions through which their legal decisions are filtered and on which they are dependent. In short, the concept of legal culture takes the analysis of environmental principles beyond the crude 'spotting' of them in a range of legal contexts, to focusing the analysis within a particular jurisdiction, and within a particular institutional setting and interpretive community in that jurisdiction.[88] Legal culture is thus both

---

[82] Christopher McCrudden, 'Judicial Comparativism and Human Rights' in Esin Örücü and David Nelken (eds), *Comparative Law: A Handbook* (Hart 2007) 373.

[83] Legrand, 'What are "Legal Transplants"?' (n 64) 59.

[84] See Scott highlighting that comparative law method is important even on a legally conservative appreciation of transnational law: Scott (n 42).

[85] This reflects a pattern of comparative law scholarship, albeit one subject to criticism: Cotterrell (n 64) 71–79.

[86] There is much literature (and debate) on how to define and use the concept of legal culture: Nelken, 'Defining and Using the Concept of Legal Culture' (n 63) 111–114; David Nelken, 'Thinking about Legal Culture' (2014) 1(2) *Asian JLS* 254. The existence of debate does not mean there is not excellent scholarship using the concept of legal culture to inform methodology: see eg Fisher, *Risk Regulation and Administrative Constitutionalism* (n 70) 35–42; Andrea Boggio, *Compensating Asbestos Victims: Law and the Dark Side of Industrialisation* (Ashgate 2013).

[87] *cf* the 'legally-oriented social behaviour and attitudes' that are 'external' elements of legal culture, including responses of those subject to legal decisions, inclination of citizens to engage with formal legal institutions to resolve disputes, and informal organisation of behaviour within a community: Nelken, 'Defining and Using Legal Culture' (n 63) 112 (citing Lawrence Friedman).

[88] Fisher, 'Precaution, Precaution Everywhere' (n 2) 7–8; Fisher, *Risk Regulation and Administrative Constitutionalism* (n 70) 35–42.

the justification for studying the legal roles of environmental principles in the case law of very different legal systems, and the explanation of differences in doctrinal developments in relation to environmental principles within the two legal systems studied.[89]

Legal culture can also provide the basis for an 'extended' comparative study of environmental principles. It is a concept that can capture change within a legal culture, including how internal approaches to legal reasoning react to, adapt to and embrace or reject external concepts and influences. In relation to environmental principles, this is an important analytical dimension, in light of the suggested connections between similarly-named principles internationally and the practice of some judges to refer to 'foreign' uses of environmental principles in developing their jurisprudence. Zumbansen has noted the need to 'deparochialise the traditional comparative … law focus' on distinct legal cultures, partly in light of the 'phenomenon of "judicial globalisation" and the incorporation of "foreign" norms and principles'.[90] The extended comparative law method in this book thus seeks to capture connections concerning environmental principles across jurisdictions through the prism of internal legal culture, since any change and development of doctrine concerning environmental principles is ultimately filtered through the processes and institutional framework of a relevant 'home' jurisdiction. It does this in two ways. First, Chapter Three investigates how environmental principles have developed a legal presence in three different legal cultures—international law, EU law and NSW law—in order to outline the nature of environmental principles in these different legal contexts and also to test the extent of derivative connections between them. Second, the mapping exercises of judicial reasoning in the EU courts and NSWLEC in Chapters Four and Five analyse, particularly in Chapter Five, how judicial reasoning has dealt with international instruments and foreign jurisprudence relating to environmental principles within their internal legal cultures.

Whilst external influences might impact on how environmental principles, and environmental law concepts generally, develop identities within discrete legal cultures, the concept of legal culture makes clear that it is not safe to assume that there are 'fundamental similarities' between systems of law that relate to environmental problems, even if environmental politics and regulation is a 'communal [global] endeavour' in some respects.[91] Fundamentally, legal systems are culturally and socially embedded, and need to be understood on their own terms.

---

[89] Rather than acting as a device that exposes social phenomena in relation to law that require explanation: Nelken, 'Defining and Using Legal Culture' (n 63) 125.

[90] Zumbansen, 'Transnational Comparisons' (n 57) 195, 199.

[91] See Yang and Percival, 'The Emergence of Global Environmental Law' (n 4) 653 for a contrary argument.

## C. Understanding 'Legal' Roles through Doctrinal Developments

This section outlines the legal focus for analysis in the book's research method. As already indicated, I do not assume established or prescribed legal roles for environmental principles, but the book's analysis must nonetheless adopt a framework for understanding what kind of roles for environmental principles can be identified as relevantly 'legal'. Particularly in a transnational context, questions of what constitutes law are vexed, as norms transcend conventional jurisdictional contexts and can regulate behaviour in non-coercive and non-state centred ways.[92] However, whilst environmental principles have transnational dimensions, the main normative focus of this book is contained within two established and self-bounded legal jurisdictions. Even so, the legally ambiguous and policy-based nature of principles means there are no pre-existing frames for identifying legal roles for environmental principles within these particular legal cultures. Further, what is 'legal' within a particular jurisdiction may be uncertain even according to its own doctrinal traditions and terms of reference. This is particularly the case in the evolving case law of the NSWLEC, due to the Court's unique institutional place in the NSW and Australian legal system,[93] and is also a feature of EU law, where European courts are primed with the task of interpreting and applying a relatively new and partly unwritten 'law'.[94]

The book seeks to expose all legal roles taken on by environmental principles in judicial reasoning in EU and NSW case law by adopting a broad doctrinal analysis. By 'doctrine', this book refers to the reasoning of judges that

> [embraces] all those situations in which some maxim—whether rule, principle, policy, classification or whatever—comprised in a historic legal system is supposed to *justify a decision*.[95]

Doctrine is thus what is accepted, and also developed, as legally relevant by judges when they decide cases in a particular legal system. Doctrine is associated with maxims that are authoritative, historically accepted, binding and definitive, and which thus promote consistency and conceptual clarity in a particular system of law.[96] In relation to environmental principles, however, a doctrinal focus opens up less definitive and less well-established legal spaces in legal systems in light of

---

[92] Thus transnational scholars often define law very broadly: see Gregory Shaffer and Terence C Halliday (eds), *Transnational Legal Orders* (CUP 2015) ('law establishes generalised normative expectations understood and used by actors within a particular context for purposes of constraining and facilitating particular behaviours': 11).

[93] See ch 5(II).

[94] Treaty on European Union ('TEU') art 19.

[95] J W Harris, *Legal Philosophies* (2nd edn, Butterworths 1997) 214.

[96] This idea of doctrine is closely associated with judicial precedent, ie judicial pronouncement of rules, standards or patterns of reasoning that are binding on future judicial decision-making, within the same and/or other related and inferior courts.

novel reasoning involving environmental principles. The comparative research in Chapters Four and Five thus identifies all reasoning involving environmental principles that is doctrinal in EU and NSWLEC judgments, both according to the self-referential identification of what is 'legal' within a particular jurisdiction, as well as on a broader appreciation of such reasoning (including developing paths of doctrinal reasoning), thereby including all the ways in which judges use, or do not use, environmental principles to justify their decisions. This broad doctrinal approach reflects Roger Cotterrell's understanding that closed self-referential understandings of law within a legal system might fail to account for all legal developments, 'especially in contemporary conditions of rapid legal change, policy-driven law and transnational pressures on legal regulation'.[97]

Whilst legal doctrine is the body of material that legal scholars tend to focus on in their research,[98] in the context of studying environmental principles, it has particular methodological virtues. First, such legal analysis is not prescriptive as to what does, or what should, constitute environmental law universally, and it can be employed in both EU and NSW law, taking into account the reasoning techniques and doctrinal traditions of each jurisdiction. It allows for difference in legal cultures, by not assuming that the same doctrine, or even the same understanding of doctrine, applies across these legal systems. The different jurisdictions of these two courts, and their differing roles within their respective systems of governance, indicate that no such equation should be made.

Second, as indicated above, these two legal contexts—EU case law and NSWLEC reasoning—are themselves evolving. Thus examining the judicial treatment of environmental principles involves not simply questioning whether and how the principles are employed doctrinally, but also reveals something of the nature of the legal settings in which they are employed. A doctrinal analysis widens the scope of inquiry to capture and expose applications of environmental principles that are legal in an innovative sense, thereby reflecting the evolving nature of these two judicial, and regulatory, settings in which environmental principles are considered. In the EU context, for example, there is a turning point in the case law relating to the precautionary principle, where the Court of First Instance (now General Court) takes note of a Commission policy document on the precautionary principle,[99] and employs it doctrinally in cases involving the principle.[100] This

---

[97] Cotterrell, 'Is there a Logic of Legal Transplants?' (n 64) 79.

[98] Harris, *Legal Philosophies* (n 95) 170. This is particularly the case in environmental law, where scholars are often eager for case law to analyse as substantive and authoritative legal development: Fisher, 'Precaution, Precaution Everywhere' (n 2) 7–8. A doctrinal method in environmental law has its critics, considering the interdisciplinary nature of environmental law and its socio-legal context: Lisa Heinzerling, 'The Environment' in Peter Cane and Mark Tushnet (eds), *The Oxford Handbook of Legal Studies* (OUP 2003) 702–703; Jane Holder, *Environmental Assessment: The Regulation of Decision Making* (OUP 2004) 10.

[99] Commission of the European Communities, 'Communication from the Commission on the Precautionary Principle' COM (2000) 1.

[100] Case T-13/99 *Pfizer Animal Health SA v Council* [2002] ECR II-3305: see ch 4(V)(B)(ii).

signifies an increasing significance of 'soft law' instruments as a form of regulatory control and consequently as a source of legal authority in EU law.[101] This innovative step in judicial reasoning involves an evolving and controversial understanding of what is relevantly legal in EU law,[102] just as it reflects the legal treatment of an environmental principle in EU law (the precautionary principle).

In a different way, the NSWLEC's decisions also involve contested and evolving legal elements. In particular, the predominance and impact of its merits review decisions have created a body of judicial decisions that is not 'case law' in the Australian common law sense, but which engages with conventionally legal questions (such as administrative law doctrine and statutory interpretation) and itself constitutes a source of legal authority. This is in the sense that merits review decisions in fact control and influence behaviour and are backed up by the enforcement of the Court's own authority.[103] They constitute an innovative body of judicial doctrine. In this complex legal setting, environmental principles have been central concepts employed by the NSWLEC in structuring its decisions—extensively in merits review cases but also in the other traditionally 'legal' aspects of its jurisdiction—to justify findings, to connect legal issues, to promote the relevance of environmental principles in all decisions made by the Court, and to consciously to build a body of authoritative doctrine around environmental principles.

In short, the doctrinal framework of this book in examining the role of environmental principles in EU and NSW case law is one that aims to catch all reasoning where environmental principles are involved in justifying judicial decisions, whatever the legal status or novelty of that reasoning or of any decision.

## D. Mapping Environmental Principles by Judicial Technique

Chapters Four and Five use this 'extended' comparative doctrinal methodology to map the current and evolving legal roles of environmental principles in EU and NSWLEC case law. This section gives a brief overview of how this mapping is done, considering the novelty of the legal settings and doctrinal reasoning involving environmental principles. If doctrine is about how judges reason and justify decisions, then the techniques they use to do this are the relevant guides for an exploratory doctrinal mapping exercise. The mapping method used in this book is thus concerned with judicial technique. It is not necessarily the type of

---

[101] Oana Stefan, *Soft Law in Court—Competition Law, State Aid and the Court of Justice of the European Union* (Kluwer 2012). See also Linda Senden, *Soft Law in European Community Law* (Hart 2004).

[102] See Joanne Scott, 'In Legal Limbo: Post-Legislative Guidance as a Challenge for European Administrative Law' (2011) 48 *CML Rev* 329; Fabien Terpan, 'Soft Law in the European Union—The Changing Nature of EU Law' (2015) 21 *ELJ* 68.

[103] Adapting the definition of 'law' set out in Robin Creyke and John McMillan, 'Soft Law v Hard Law' in Linda Pearson, Carol Harlow and Michael Taggart (eds), *Administrative Law in a Changing State* (Hart 2008) 383.

legal action, or its outcome, which gives a doctrinal account of environmental principles (although these factors may be relevant), since environmental principles have no established doctrinal roles or traditions. Rather, it is the reasoning techniques adopted in relation to such principles that reveal their legal roles, along with the distinctive jurisdictional remits, and sometimes constitutional limits, of the respective courts involved. Through their techniques of reasoning, judges can also reach out and beyond established doctrinal traditions to take account of developments concerning environmental principles in other jurisdictions.

In Chapters Four and Five, the maps of reasoning involving environmental principles are charted by *categories* of reasoning technique. The mapping categories do not match each other across EU and NSWLEC case law, demonstrating the quite different doctrinal reasoning used in both contexts, within the jurisdictional and constitutional constraints of each respective court system. In terms of the kinds of cases that are mapped, a wide range of cases concerns environmental principles in these two legal contexts. However, all are public law cases broadly understood. In EU law, the cases are concerned with public law to the extent that they decide on the legality, under EU law, of public action (at EU and Member State level), or they are concerned with interpreting EU law as it is to be applied by administrative decision-makers and courts in Member States.[104] However, this body of case law concerning environmental principles is also very diverse; it reflects varying areas of legislative competence, as well as diverse legal issues in EU law. It involves, amongst other things, internal market law, waste law, nature conservation law, competition law, law relating to the regulation of public health risks,[105] and includes technical EU law questions of legislative interpretation, as well as competence, proportionality and other evolving tests of legality review. There are many ways to put EU cases concerning environmental principles into legal 'categories'—of subject-matter, jurisdictional basis or legal issue—but none provides a coherent view of how environmental principles are being used in the reasoning of the EU courts. However, by following the different judicial techniques used by the EU courts in reasoning doctrinally with environmental principles (for example, whether environmental principles are used as interpretive aids or to inform legal tests), the roles of environmental principles in EU law, and their effects on EU law, are more readily identifiable. This focus on judicial reasoning technique also reveals interactions between cases, which involve a variety of different legal questions and subject matters, showing how the legal roles of environmental principles influence the evolution of EU law in their own unique way.

In NSW law, a similarly broad sweep of cases is encompassed by a doctrinal appraisal of NSWLEC case law involving environmental principles. In terms of

---

[104] TFEU, arts 263 & 267. Some interpretive and legality cases under these Treaty Articles may also bind actions of individuals, particularly in relation to the validity and interpretation of EU Regulations, Decisions or directly effective Directives, all of which are directly applicable to individuals.

[105] Representing the perennial problem that environmental law has no discernable boundaries: Mark Stallworthy, *Understanding Environmental Law* (Sweet & Maxwell 2008) ch 1.

subject matter, these cases are primarily concerned with planning and environmental management (including the management of protected cultural objects), reflecting the types of statutes that refer jurisdiction to the NSWLEC.[106] The cases span the unique jurisdictional composition of the Court, including judicial review cases (understood in common law terms), merits review cases and criminal cases. The legal issues involved in NSWLEC cases concerning environmental principles match these jurisdictional divisions relatively neatly, again being concerned with public law in an overall sense, but more particularly with administrative law questions (judicial review), substantive 'application' of administrative law doctrines and legislative provisions in quasi-administrative decision-making (merits review), and sentencing decisions (criminal law). In mapping the NSWLEC case law involving environmental principles, the judicial techniques adopted by the Court again cross over the Court's jurisdictional divisions. In broad terms, environmental principles are introduced doctrinally as legally required 'relevant considerations' in all types of cases considered by the Court, thus informing the Court's evolving legal jurisprudence, and fundamentally defining its institutional identity.

To conclude, the comparative doctrinal framework adopted to define the scope and analytical method of this book is a careful way of navigating complicated legal landscapes involving environmental principles. This is because these landscapes include wide-ranging subject matters, jurisdictions and legal issues, and embrace novel legal developments. Comprehensively mapping legal developments relating to environmental principles involves uncharted legal territory in both EU and NSW law. A 'straightforward' doctrinal analysis in each jurisdiction reveals that the legal roles played by environmental principles are complex, contingent and evolving, as are the bodies of (environmental) law of which they form part. This is an intricate picture of environmental principles as legal concepts that captures the detailed evolution of environmental law.

# IV. Conclusion

The main project of this book is to undertake a comparative doctrinal analysis of the case law of the EU courts and NSWLEC involving environmental principles, with a focus on legal culture and with no preconceptions as to how this doctrinal picture does or should look. This might be an unremarkable exercise in other established areas of law, but in environmental law it is significant. This is because central to the legal ambiguity of environmental principles are the novel, idiosyncratic and evolving bodies of law in which the principles are employed, so

---

[106] See ch 5, nn 55–60 and accompanying text.

that detailed doctrinal mapping is required to understand the legal roles taken on by environmental principles in judicial reasoning and how they are co-evolving with legal systems. This mapping should provide a basis for further legal inquiries about environmental principles. For example, many of the EU and NSWLEC cases on environmental principles provide a window into administrative and institutional decision-making based on environmental principles.[107] A deeper understanding of these cases also facilitates informed analysis of the proper role of courts in weighing or advocating particular environmental policy considerations, or of the applicability or development of jurisprudential theories for explaining and scrutinising the roles of environmental principles, or of potential legal arguments based on environmental principles that might be of interest to advocates.

Comparatively mapping the evolving legal roles of environmental principles is also a significant exercise because environmental law has been in an almost perpetual state of 'growing up' for the last 30 years,[108] with environmental principles taking on a prominent role in the quest for its maturity, as well as 'effectiveness', as a body of law. Examining their roles in different bodies of judicial reasoning thus contributes to the state of environmental law and to its self-perception as a body of knowledge. To understand this broader role of environmental principles, Chapter Two examines why environmental principles are so prominent in environmental law scholarship, and how the comparative doctrinal analysis undertaken in this book represents a step out of the methodological minefield that characterises much writing about environmental principles.

---

[107] Since environmental principles represent policy goals, administrative and institutional decision-making is a primary site of their application. The legal review of such application by courts thus gives insight into how environmental principles are, and should be, applied in governance processes and in administration: Joanne Scott and Susan Sturm, 'Courts as Catalysts: Re-Thinking the Judicial Role in New Governance' (2006–7) 13 *Colum J Eur L* 565. This role of environmental principles underlies Fisher's thesis on the precautionary principle and its role in constituting administration: Fisher, *Risk Regulation and Administrative Constitutionalism* (n 70).

[108] Elizabeth Fisher, Bettina Lange, Eloise Scotford & Cinnamon Carlarne, 'Maturity and Methodology: Starting a Debate about Environmental Law Scholarship' (2009) 21(2) *JEL* 213.

# 2

## Environmental Principles and Environmental Law

## I. Introduction

This chapter turns to the broader significance of environmental principles in environmental law and investigates their prominence in environmental law scholarship. It shows that much has been expected of environmental principles, demonstrating their potent symbolism in environmental law, whilst also exacerbating conceptual and methodological confusion in relation to their legal character. Environmental law scholarship discloses a range of purposes that environmental principles might fulfil in environmental law, including solving environmental problems, informing and constituting legal development, and legitimising the subject as a scholarly discipline. This range of purposes is unsurprising, considering that environmental principles are open-textured and novel concepts in environmental law and there are no settled frameworks for their legal development or analysis.[1] It is also unsurprising because of the nature of environmental law as a subject—it transcends legal, jurisdictional and disciplinary boundaries and itself reflects a range of meanings, from those that are deeply ethical and purposive to those that are descriptive and doctrinal.[2] The development of methodological frameworks for concepts like environmental principles is thus part of the evolution and maturing of environmental law as a scholarly enterprise.[3] This book contends that too much hope has been invested in environmental principles to date without a close consideration of the roles that they do—and can—play in environmental law within particular jurisdictions. Environmental principles

---

[1] Elizabeth Fisher, Bettina Lange, Eloise Scotford & Cinnamon Carlarne, 'Maturity and Methodology: Starting a Debate about Environmental Law Scholarship' (2009) 21(2) *Journal of Environmental Law* 213, 231, 236–238.

[2] Elizabeth Fisher, Bettina Lange and Eloise Scotford, *Environmental Law: Text, Cases and Materials* (OUP 2013) ch 1.

[3] It is arguably part of the project of legal scholarship more generally: Roger Cotterrell, 'Why Must Legal Ideas Be Interpreted Sociologically?' (1998) 25(2) *Journal of Law & Society* 171, 178 ('law does not have a "methodology of its own"').

are indeed playing important roles in the evolution of environmental law, most prominently as legal ideas that are transformative within discrete systems of law.

In examining scholarly hopes for environmental principles in environmental law, *environmental law* is defined as that body of law that relates to environmental problems.[4] As Chapter One demonstrated, defining 'law' in relation to environmental principles is no straightforward matter, particularly to the extent that environmental principles have transnational dimensions. Their policy foundations, apparent connections across jurisdictions and catalytic roles within jurisdictions all suggest that environmental principles are ideas that 'contest, deconstruct and relativise the boundaries between law and non-law'.[5] To capture new as well as more familiar normative aspects of environmental principles, 'law' for the purposes of this book is taken to include all forms of authority that influence and control behaviour.[6] Due to the book's focus on the reasoning of courts, this broad functional definition mostly covers 'law as we know it',[7] backed up by State or other institutional authority.[8] Further, its mapping exercises focus on the functions that environmental principles pursue—that is, their doctrinal or justificatory roles in judicial reasoning—in order determine their legal character. Even in this narrower positivistic sense, 'legal' dimensions of environmental principles include novel developments and instruments that are not conventionally legal in other legal subjects: for example, merits review decisions,[9] policy documents,[10] international soft law agreements,[11] and, of course, environmental principles themselves (often found within these more unconventional sources of law). This book examines all aspects of environmental principles that bring them within the scope of 'environmental law' so understood, primarily by means of doctrinal analysis of judicial reasoning, but also with a view to any normative dimensions that extend beyond and across the bounds of state-centred jurisdictions.

In order to explore the significance of environmental principles within this rapidly developing legal field, Part II first examines the reasons for the prominence of environmental principles in environmental law scholarship. In short, there

---

[4] Fisher et al (n 2) 6 and generally.

[5] Peer Zumbansen, 'Defining the Space of Transnational Law: Legal Theory, Global Governance and Legal Pluralism' (2012) 21 *Transnat'l L & Contemp Probs* 305, 318.

[6] This reflects a sociological understanding of law: Niklas Luhmann, *A Sociological Theory of Law* (Routledge & Kegan Paul 1985).

[7] Craig Scott, '"Transnational Law" as Proto-Concept: Three Conceptions' (2009) 10 *German Law Journal* 859, 868. Scott explores how transnational law developments challenge understandings of what is 'legal' and give rise to various conceptions of 'law', the most conservative of which resembles law 'as we currently know and practice it' but adapted to actions or events that transcend national boundaries.

[8] See ch 1, n 103.

[9] See ch 5(II)(C).

[10] eg ch 4(V)(B)(ii). Administrative lawyers are also confronted with the increasing use of policy and soft law in governance and (thus) judicial review actions: Robyn Creyke and John McMillan, 'Soft Law v Hard Law' in Linda Pearson, Carol Harlow and Michael Taggart (eds), *Administrative Law in a Changing State* (Hart 2008).

[11] See ch 3(II).

have been various, often unarticulated, scholarly approaches that have advanced the legal study of environmental principles incrementally and pluralistically. The chapter thus covers a wide range of literature—from international law scholarship to scholarship in other jurisdictions, from extra-judicial writing and policy-focused analysis to deeply theoretical work, including legal philosophy beyond environmental law. The point of looking at all this literature is not to respond directly to positions adopted by all these scholars, but to demonstrate the wide range of legal scholarship relating to environmental principles and how much work environmental principles are expected to do legally by scholars.

The basic reason for the popularity of environmental principles amongst legal scholars comes back to their popularity as policy concepts. Environmental principles are politically convenient, and have populist appeal, as well as ethical force. This policy presence feeds into their prominence in environmental law scholarship, which in turn reflects a number of, sometimes overlapping, purposes for environmental principles. On the one hand, it is suggested that environmental principles can direct legal solutions to *environmental problems*. On the other hand, environmental principles are suggested to solve *legal problems* in environmental law. As already indicated, environmental principles are concepts that have open-textured legal identities and can reflect new and transnational approaches to environmental problems that are not conventionally legal. Thus they can be used as shorthand for legally (and politically) complex developments. Some environmental law scholarship suggests that environmental principles—as recognised legal concepts—can overcome the perceived immaturity of the subject in dealing with such challenging ideas. In this sense, environmental principles are cast as legal principles, giving a recognisable label to new developments in environmental law and thereby legitimising environmental law as a subject of legal scholarship.

This legitimising tendency can be seen in at least three dimensions. First, environmental principles might help to cast environmental law in the model of other, more well-established legal subjects, by emulating 'legal principles' that have defined jurisprudential roles in these legal areas, such as in legal philosophy, public international law or EU law. Building particularly on legal philosophical accounts of legal principles, environmental principles might provide conceptual foundations for environmental law generally and guide judicial reasoning. Second, environmental principles might also solve methodological problems in environmental law, for example by unifying environmental law to deal with its challenging multi-jurisdictional scope or by overcoming problems of interdisciplinarity. Third, there are ambitious scholarly claims that environmental principles might characterise and constitute a new form of law altogether.

This scholarly prominence of environmental principles is important to unravel and understand, for at least two reasons. First, while the prolific development of environmental law scholarship concerning environmental principles has been understandable, it has often been problematic from a methodological perspective. Part III examines these problems, which include unjustified presumptions that environmental principles are universal and equivalent legal concepts; that they are legal concepts along the lines of 'legal principles' in other established areas of law; that they have instrumental force in relation to environmental problems; and that they present neat solutions to problems of legal methodology and the perceived immaturity in environmental law. The comparative doctrinal analysis of environmental principles in this book is a direct response to these methodological limits, particularly in presuming no universal or legally prescribed identity for environmental principles, whilst also recognising that they can represent significant developments in the evolution of environmental law across and between legal systems.

The second, related reason for getting to grips with legal scholarship on environmental principles is that it demonstrates the enormous challenges taken on and faced by environmental law as a subject—in methodological as well as instrumental terms—with which the scholarship concerning environmental principles is fundamentally concerned. These challenges are seen in suggestions that environmental principles might operate to solve the environmental problems to which environmental law relates, or that they might form the basis of a new form of law altogether. These suggestions show that environmental principles reflect methodological and conceptual perplexity in environmental law, being a subject that must traverse jurisdictional, legal and disciplinary boundaries through its focus on environmental problems, against the backdrop of policy and political debates relating to environmental issues. All of these dimensions are bound up in scholarship concerning environmental principles, as they are in environmental law more broadly. The study of environmental principles thus concerns both the study of new legal concepts and the study of a subject, and the arguments and conclusions of this book resonate for environmental law generally. Its central research inquiry—investigating the legal identity and roles of environmental principles though the cultures and complexities of the legal systems in which they operate—makes an argument for environmental law as a subject of study. In short, environmental law scholars need to be attentive and detailed before they are big and bold. It is in this attention and detail that the legitimacy of environmental law as a subject of scholarship fundamentally resides, rather than in the symbolic existence of environmental principles as legal concepts.

## II. Why So Much Principle?

In environmental law, policy and scholarship, 'principles are in the air'.[12] This Part considers why there is such a proliferation of diverse environmental principles in environmental law scholarship. It first examines the historical developments

---

[12] Piet Gilhuis, 'The Consequences of Introducing Environmental Law Principles in National Law' in M Sheridan and L Lavrysen (eds), *Environmental Law Principles in Practice* (Bruylant 2002) 45.

that provoked the legal study of environmental principles. Second, it addresses why environmental principles are attractive and popular concepts in non-legal senses, examining their roles in environmental policy development and politics, supported by their populist and ethical appeal. This policy background informs their legal popularity. Third, the Part considers why environmental principles are legally popular concepts, both as legal solutions to environmental problems and as solutions to legal challenges and problems within environmental law. Fourth, beyond addressing problems with existing environmental law, environmental principles are also suggested by legal scholars to form the basis for a new form of law altogether. In the latter two senses, environmental principles might be seen to legitimise environmental law scholarship, and thus to remedy perceived short-comings in environmental law as a subject.

## A. Foundations for the Legal Study of Environmental Principles: An Historical Collision of Policy, Environmental Regulation and Legal Scholarship

The current state of scholarship on environmental principles is the result of an historical collision of developments in environmental law scholarship, international environmental policy and law, and the rapid expansion of environmental regulation in domestic legal settings. In each of these three dimensions, there was a sense that a new body of law was emerging, quite quickly, and scholars and legislators alike looked for concepts that could encapsulate the direction and central themes of developing legal thinking and regulation.

In relation to the origins of environmental law scholarship, when scholars now impress the importance of environmental principles as foundational concepts in environmental law, this has roots in environmental law scholarship as far back as the 1970s. At this point, there had been little judicial or legislative attention paid to environmental principles as such, whether in Australia, Europe or the United States, with the latter being a pioneering jurisdiction for environmental statutes, cases and decision-making processes.[13] Environmental law was then emerging as a subject and some leading scholars suggested that particular values or an ecological 'ethic' should provide the foundation for environmental law.[14] This was posited as

---

[13] Zygmunt JB Plater, 'From the Beginning, A Fundamental Shift of Paradigms: A Theory and Short History of Environmental Law' (1994) 27 *Loyola of Los Angeles Law Review* 981; Brian Preston, 'Environmental Law 1927–2007: Retrospect and Prospect' (2007) 81 *ALJ* 616, 624–628.

[14] Lawrence Tribe, 'Ways Not To Think About Plastic Trees: New Foundations for Environmental Law' (1974) 83(7) *Yale LJ* 1315; Ben Boer, 'Social Ecology and Environmental Law' (1984) 1 *EPLJ* 233. See more recently, Gail Morgan, 'The Dominion of Nature: Can Law Embody a New Attitude?' (1993) 18(60) *Bulletin of the Australian Society of Legal Philosophy* 43; David Wilkinson, 'Using Environmental Ethics to Create Ecological Law' in Jane Holder and Donald McGillivray (eds), *Locality and Identity: Environmental Issues in Law and Society* (Ashgate 1999).

a preferable alternative to prevailing anthropocentric and economic approaches to decision-making affecting the environment, particularly in light of the 'enormous dislocations' that were facing the world due to environmental problems.[15] Such scholarly suggestions were not jurisdiction-specific and were based in environmental ethics and legal philosophy that prioritised human relations with the natural environment,[16] as well as the integrity of that environment for its own sake.[17] It was argued that an ethical or values-based foundation for environmental law should have broad legal ramifications, including 'sanctifying' values, or principles, of intrinsic significance in the process of environmental decision-making.[18] Such values or principles were not clearly enumerated by this early scholarship,[19] although the law's accommodation of 'fuzzy' values such as intergenerational equity and respect for animal and plant life were central to these philosophical arguments.[20] This foundational thinking introduced a scholarly openness and discourse in relation to environmental principles, as general ethical ideas, being core concepts in environmental law.[21]

Alongside these scholarly developments, developments in international environmental policy and law, particularly from the early 1970s, gave environmental principles—as policy concepts—an increasingly prominent profile, particularly in successive attempts to agree and articulate an international framework for sustainable development.[22] The increasing prevalence of environmental principles in international declarations and agreements—such as in the Stockholm and

---

[15] Murray Bookchin, *The Ecology of Freedom: The Emergence and Dissolution of Hierarchy* (Cheshire Books 1982) 21. More recently, see Mary Christina Wood, *Nature's Trust: Environmental Law for the New Ecological Age* (CUP 2014) and Anna Grear and Evadne Grant (eds), *Thought, Law, Rights and Action in the Age of Environmental Crisis* (Edward Elgar 2015).

[16] Tribe draws on political and legal philosophy *and* environmental ethics to devise his ideal basis of environmental law: Tribe, 'Ways Not To Think About Plastic Trees' (n 14); *cf* Klaus Bosselmann, 'Ecological Justice and Law' in Benjamin J Richardson and Stepan Wood (eds), *Environmental Law for Sustainability: A Reader* (Hart 2006). There is a wide literature on ecological ethics and environmental law, eg Mark Sagoff, 'On Preserving the Natural Environment' (1974) 84 *Yale Law Journal* 205; John Alder and David Wilkinson, *Environmental Law and Ethics* (Palgrave Macmillan 1999).

[17] Boer, 'Social Ecology' (n 14) 246.

[18] Tribe, 'Ways Not To Think About Plastic Trees' (n 14) 1339; Boer, 'Social Ecology' (n 14) 247.

[19] *cf* Tribe, 'Ways Not To Think About Plastic Trees' (n 14) 1339–1341.

[20] eg ibid 1317–1319. Marong highlights that efforts to instil a sustainable development ethic into law can be traced back to Leonardo da Vinci's *Codex Leicester*: Alhaji BM Marong, 'From Rio to Johannesburg: Reflections on the Role of International Legal Norms in Sustainable Development' (2003–4) 16 *Geo Int'l Envtl L Rev* 21 23 (citing James R May). See also Klaus Bosselmann, *The Principle of Sustainability: Transforming Law and Governance* (Ashgate 2008) chs 1, 3.

[21] This vein of scholarship has continued, particularly in the writing of Klaus Bosselmann and other scholars who argue that environmental principles are fundamental to building systems of law that embed ethical imperatives to respect and protect nature: eg Bosselmann, *Principle of Sustainability* (n 20); Nicholas A Robinson, 'Evolved Norms: A Canon for the Anthropocene' in Christina Voigt (ed), *Rule of Law for Nature: New Dimensions and Ideas in Environmental Law* (CUP 2013); Anastasia Telesetsky, 'An Emerging Legal Principle to Restore Large-Scale Ecoscapes' in Christina Voigt (ed), *Rule of Law for Nature: New Dimensions and Ideas in Environmental Law* (CUP 2013).

[22] See ch 3, n 20.

Rio Declarations, which at most amounted to 'soft law'—understandably raised questions about their legal status in international environmental law terms, as discussed in Chapter Three.[23] It also raised questions about their legal relevance within other, particularly national, legal systems.[24] These legal inquiries were without legal precedent and were considered against the backdrop of dramatic and often urgent environmental problems, which had prompted the need for international discussion and negotiation in the first place. As discussed in Section C below, such pressing environmental problems generated (and still generate) a desire for *legal* solutions, including enforceable environmental principles, despite the lack of legal precedent.

Partly in response to this developing international sustainable development agenda, environmental regulation was also becoming increasingly prolific in the 1970s and 1980s in domestic and regional legal settings, as well as in international agreements. Such regulation often involved novel and complex governance regimes and statutory frameworks, regulating particular pollutants or media or environmental management more generally. These regimes reflected in different ways the environmental protection ideas embodied in various environmental principles,[25] and increasingly mentioned environmental principles explicitly—in international treaty articles or preambles,[26] in regional policy agreements[27] and legislative frameworks,[28] or increasingly as objects clauses or core decision-making concepts in national legislation.[29] However, as will be seen in relation to

[23] See ch 3(II)(B).

[24] Ben Boer, 'Institutionalising Ecologically Sustainable Development: The Roles of National, State, and Local Governments in Translating Grand Strategy into Action' (1995) 31 *Willamette L Rev* 307; Susan Smith, 'Ecologically Sustainable Development: Integrating Economics, Ecology, and Law' (1995) 31 *Willamette L Rev* 261, 266 and generally; Brian Preston, 'Judicial Implementation of the Principles of Ecologically Sustainable Development in Australia and Asia' (2006) Regional Presidents Meeting, Law Society of New South Wales (<http://www.lec.justice.nsw.gov.au/Documents/preston_judicial%20 implementation%20of%20the%20principles%20of%20eologically%20sustainable%20development. pdf> accessed 29 June 2016); Gilhuis, 'Consequences of Introducing Environmental Law Principles' (n 12).

[25] eg in early international law, for treaties and declarations embodying sustainable development and intergenerational equity, see Smith, 'Integrating Economic, Ecology, and Law' (n 24); see also ch 3, nn 13–15 and accompanying text. In early EU law, for example, successive directives on waste reflected versions of the preventive principle: Council Directive (EC) 75/442 on waste [1975] OJ L194/39; Council Directive (EC) 91/156 amending Directive 75/442 on waste [1991] OJ L078/32.

[26] eg UN Framework Convention on Climate Change (adopted 9/5/1992, entered into force 21/3/1994) (1992) 31 ILM 849, art 3(3); Jonathan Weiner explains that the precautionary principle now appears in over 50 multilateral agreements, starting with agreements in the 1980s, and that some earlier agreements 'employed the logic, if not the terminology, of precaution': Jonathan B Weiner, 'Precaution' in Dan Bodansky, Jutta Brunee and Ellen Hey (eds), *The Oxford Handbook of International Environmental Law* (OUP 2007) 601.

[27] Programme of Action of the EC on the Environment [1973] OJ C112/1 ('1st EAP').

[28] TFEU, arts 11 & 191(2); TEU, recital 9. See ch 3(III)(A) for the historical development of these Treaty provisions.

[29] eg Protection of the Environment Administration Act 1991 (NSW) ss 6(1)(a) & (2); Environmental Planning and Assessment Act 1979 (NSW) s 5; Resource Management Act 1991 (NZ) s 5(2).

the emergence of environmental principles in the international, EU and NSW legal contexts in Chapter Three, these legal developments were non-linear, often independent, and contextually contingent. The methodological challenges faced by environmental law scholars in analysing rapid and wide-ranging developments (in terms of both jurisdiction and subject matter) have been recognised,[30] and it is not surprising that scholars focused on environmental principles as elements of commonality in analysing such novel and speedy regulatory developments across diverse regulatory systems. In particular, scholars have often assumed that environmental principles devised in international law agreements equate to those with similar names found in regional and national regulation.[31] Thus, not only were environmental principles increasingly there to be analysed, but they also offered an appealing methodological foothold for scholars in dealing with wide-ranging and rapidly evolving environmental law across jurisdictions.

This combination of events—embryonic and identity-seeking environmental law scholarship; an international sustainable development agenda expressed in terms of environmental principles, often with legal connotations; and rapid development of binding environmental regulation that reflected policies embodied in environmental principles and increasingly mentioned such principles explicitly— set the scene for environmental law scholars to embrace environmental principles as universally emerging legal concepts. As shown in the sections that follow, environmental scholars have since embraced environmental principles for a range of purposes, placing great importance on their ability to solve both environmental problems and legal problems in environmental law. A common aspect of this pluralistic and ambitious scholarship relates to the popularity of environmental principles as *non-legal* concepts.

## B. Environmental Principles as Non-legal Responses to Environmental Issues

The historical confluence of events in which environmental principles developed a profile in environmental law was partly driven by the fact that environmental principles are inherently attractive concepts to politicians and policymakers in non-legal senses. Thus, for example, the developing international sustainable development agenda, and associated soft law agreements, was primarily a story of politics and international policymaking. The policymaking value of environmental principles lies primarily in their flexibility.[32] They perform a useful role

---

[30] Fisher and others, 'Maturity and Methodology' (n 1) 228–231.

[31] See ch 3(II)(A).

[32] Stephen Tromans, 'High Talk and Low Cunning: Putting Environmental Principles into Legal Practice' [1995] *JPEL* 779, 780; Geoffrey Palmer, 'New Ways to Make International Environmental Law' (1992) 86(2) *AJIL* 259, 269; A Dan Tarlock, 'Ideas Without Institutions: The Paradox of Sustainable Development' (2001) 9 *Ind J Global Legal Stud* 35, 36–7.

in representing shortcut policy positions in respect of multi-dimensional and scientifically complex environmental problems, and also in allowing political compromise about such positions. Environmental principles also carry a desirable message in their commitment to environment protection and sustainability—they reflect popular sentiments of environmental concern and also have forceful ethical connotations. This section examines these different 'non-legal' dimensions and drivers of environmental principles.

The definitional ambiguity of environmental principles[33] has given environmental principles widespread currency in environmental policy. Environmental principles are prevalent in policy terms because environmental problems traverse jurisdictional boundaries, involve scientific uncertainties and long-term timescales—environmental principles can reflect common policy goals across these jurisdictional, disciplinary and temporal dimensions.[34] In addition, they are easier to agree politically. Political positions on environmental policy are often hard-fought, particularly when there are distributional consequences or conflicts with other well-established policy areas, such as trade and investment, transport or fiscal policy. The ambiguity of environmental principles allows political actors to agree on environmental policy in general terms, while maintaining more detailed (and possibly divergent) individual policy positions.[35] It may even be the case that political actors are not *ad idem* in their policy agreement, since environmental principles are open to different interpretations. However, the ambiguity of the principles is arguably what makes them so 'politically potent'.[36] The political expediency of environmental principles has been particularly commented on in the international arena in relation to non-binding agreements such as the Rio Declaration,[37] which centre on environmental principles; but it is also reflected in the NSW and EU experiences of how environmental principles have developed.[38]

Beyond these convenient roles for environmental principles in policy formation and political negotiation, environmental principles also tap into the populist

---

[33] See further ch 3.

[34] Tromans, 'High Talk' (n 32) 779.

[35] Nicolas de Sadeleer, *Environmental Principles: From Political Slogans to Legal Rules* (OUP 2002) 255, 259.

[36] Andrew Jordan and Timothy O'Riordan, 'The Precautionary Principle in Contemporary Environmental Policy and Politics' in Carolyn Raffensperger and Joel Tickner (eds), *Protecting Public Health and the Environment: Implementing the Precautionary Principle* (Island Press 1999) 15 ('the application of the precautionary principle will remain politically potent so long as it continues to be tantalizingly ill-defined and imperfectly translatable into codes of conduct').

[37] de Sadeleer (n 35) 2; Jonathan Verschuuren, 'Sustainable Development and the Nature of Environmental Legal Principles' (2006) 9(1) *Potchefstroom Electronic Law Journal*; Tim Stephens, *International Courts and Environmental Protection* (CUP 2009) 6. Palmer comments that the Stockholm Declaration is a 'masterpiece of international drafting. It wove the politics and the principles together in a web so tight it would not unravel': Palmer, 'New Ways' (n 32) 266.

[38] In NSW, environmental principles, as 'principles of ecologically sustainable development', originated as political negotiating points between environmental groups, industry, government and other actors in a national process concerning sustainable development: see ch 3(IV)(A). In the EU, environmental principles first appeared in the politically agreed 1st EAP (above n 27), although there are no detailed accounts of the political negotiations involved.

nature of environmental issues. They offer 'sexy soundbites' for the media coverage of such issues,[39] giving principles a high public profile. Less superficially, the language of 'principles' in relation to environmental policy also has an ethical dimension, as discussed in the previous section. Environmental principles have moral weight. James Cameron, Paula Pevato and Juli Abouchar thus talk of the 'moral codes in the language of [environmental] principles'.[40] Maurice Evans argues that sustainability principles have a 'logical and moral force'.[41] Klaus Bosselmann also highlights how the original idea and terminology of sustainable development in international policy was based on the introduction of a 'new ethic ... which will enable human societies to live in harmony with the natural world'.[42]

These non-legal roles and aspects of environmental principles explain their prevalence and significance in policy terms and popular debate. While this does not directly explain their steady legal evolution, it is part of the story.[43] Some scholars have assumed a direct link between the legal roles of environmental principles and the policy goals to which they relate, without much analytical consternation.[44] Others have developed ambitious jurisprudential foundations for making such a link.[45] Environmental principles are thus constructed as legal routes to policy outcomes in various instrumental senses, as examined in the following section. This close connection between, or even elision of, policy and law is not uncommon in environmental law,[46] but it sounds a warning for the doctrinal legal scholar. This is because the distinction between policy and law is an important conceptual distinction in other legal subjects,[47] so that tracing the development of policy ideas such as environmental principles in environmental law involves novel legal analysis.

While the policy and political proliferation of environmental principles has been matched by their extensive legal study, this need not have been the case.

---

[39] Tromans, 'High Talk' (n 32) 779.

[40] James Cameron, Paula M Pevato and Juli Abouchar, 'International Implementation of the Principles' (1994) Fenner Conference on the Environment—Sustainability: Principles to Practice (Department of Environment, Sport and Territories, Australian Commonwealth Government) 112.

[41] Maurice Evans, *Principles of Environmental and Heritage Law* (Prospect Media 2000) 100–101. See also Gilhuis, 'Consequences of Introducing Environmental Law Principles' (n 12) 48; Stephens, *International Courts* (n 37) 6.

[42] Quoting from the 1980 World Conservation Strategy, s 13.1. Bosselmann argues that this ethical ambition has been compromised in the international politics of sustainable development but argues that an ecocentric ethic should be fundamental to the principle of sustainability: Bosselmann, *Principle of Sustainability* (n 20) 1–2 and chs 1, 3.

[43] This is obvious from the title of a leading scholarly work on environmental principles in environmental law: de Sadeleer, *Environmental Principles* (n 35).

[44] cf Emma Lees, *Interpreting Environmental Offences: The Need for Certainty* (Hart 2015) ch 8.

[45] Klaus Bosselmann makes a strong and detailed case for the principle of sustainability as a fundamental guide for global legal and governance frameworks in light of its ecocentric ethical basis: Bosselmann, *Principle of Sustainability* (n 20).

[46] Fisher et al, *Environmental Law* (n 2) ch 11, section 2.

[47] See Allan Beever, 'Policy in Private Law: An Admission of Failure' (2006) *UQLJ* 287 and Section II(D)(i) below.

There are areas of environmental decision-making and regulatory policy in which a practical proliferation of ideas and concepts has not led to a high profile in environmental law scholarship.[48] However, as examined in the following sections, there is a range of reasons why environmental law scholars have been eager to embrace environmental principles, beyond and related to the fact that some courts have taken them up extensively in their reasoning.

## C. Environmental Principles as Legal Solutions to Environmental Problems

As a result of the pressing and existential nature of many environmental issues, there is a desire for action, so that, once agreed on as policy positions in relation to environmental problems, environmental principles have been expected to do considerable work as solutions to environmental problems. Thus, commentators stress that they should not be mere 'motherhood' statements,[49] that action is now required to apply the principles, 'not further strategies',[50] and that this action should be *legal*. The scholarly consternation over the legal status of environmental principles in international law can be explained in these instrumental terms. There is a drive for normativity of environmental principles because of the 'gap between political rhetoric and practical action'.[51] As Cameron, Pevato and Abouchar argue:[52]

> Legal structure is necessary to shape, guide or change behaviour. No advantage is to be gained from treating these principles as being less legal because they are general, or from shifting to market mechanisms to implement them as if law or legal redress for failing to follow the principles can be avoided.

More transformatively, Bosselmann argues that the principle of sustainability 'sets jurisprudence and law-making institutions on a new path'.[53]

At a general level, some scholars conceive of environmental law in instrumental terms, as providing solutions to environmental problems,[54] including through the

---

[48] eg the extensive role of models in environmental decision-making, until recently largely ignored in environmental law scholarship: Elizabeth Fisher, Pasky Pascual and Wendy Wagner, 'Understanding Environmental Models in their Legal and Regulatory Context' (2010) 22(2) *JEL* 251.

[49] David Farrier and Elizabeth Fisher, 'Reconstituting Decision Making Processes and Structures in Light of the Precautionary Principle' (1993, Institute of Environmental Studies, The University of New South Wales) 229.

[50] Ronnie Harding (ed), 'Sustainability: Principles to Practice' (Fenner Conference on the Environment 1994) 5.

[51] Marong, 'From Rio to Johannesburg' (n 20) 49. See also Winfried Lang, 'UN Principles and International Environmental Law' (1999) 3 *Max Planck Yrbk UN L* 171.

[52] Cameron, Pevato and Abouchar (n 40) 112.

[53] Bosselmann, *Principle of Sustainability* (n 20) 7.

[54] This instrumental or purposive view of environmental law extends beyond environmental principles: A Dan Tarlock, 'The Future of Environmental Rule of Law Litigation' (2002) 19 *Pace Envtl L Rev* 575, 576.

application of environmental principles. Thus Ben Boer states that 'environmental law is increasingly recognised as playing an important role in the solution to global, regional, national and local environmental problems, particularly through the concept of sustainable development'.[55] For Boer, innovative legal strategies are needed to generate a paradigm shift of behaviour within society.[56] Providing such legal innovation, environmental principles are posited as the critical and legally necessary link between ideal environmental outcomes and the concrete legal rules and decisions that will deliver them. Jonathan Verschuuren posits that environmental principles are the 'necessary medium for ideals of sustainable development to find their way into concrete rules' applying to activities that may harm the environment.[57] Andrea Ross also argues that 'ecological sustainability' should be accorded the status of a legal principle in order to transform decision-making and governance and promote sustainable outcomes.[58] In a similar vein, in relation to judicial reasoning in the European courts, Michael Doherty focuses on how environmental principles, as legal principles, might guide judicial decision-making in 'hard cases' to bring benefits not just to the European legal system but also to the environment.[59] At the global level, Bosselmann considers how international laws of human rights and state sovereignty must adapt to the principle of sustainability in order to respect ecological limits.[60]

Legalising environmental principles is also seen as instrumentally important since legal structures and institutions can facilitate and promote environmental outcomes. Holly Doremus asserts that 'nature advocates cannot afford to ignore the law's potential to change, or to reinforce, cultural attitudes toward nature'.[61] On this view, environmental principles do their work in promoting environmental outcomes when they are legally implemented.[62] This is because lawyers have special expertise in 'structuring institutions and decision-making processes' to achieve environmental goals embodied in environmental principles.[63] The courts

---

[55] Ben Boer, 'The Rise of Environmental Law in the Asian Region' (1999) 32 *U Rich L Rev* 1503, 1506.

[56] Ben Boer, 'Implementation of International Sustainability Imperatives at a National Level' in K Ginther, E Denters and PJIM de Waart (eds), *Sustainable Development and Good Government* (Martinus Nijhoff Publishers 1995) 117–118. See also Nicholas A Robinson, 'Evolved Norms: A Canon for the Anthropocene' in Christina Voigt (ed), *Rule of Law for Nature: New Dimensions and Ideas in Environmental Law* (CUP 2013).

[57] Verschuuren, 'Sustainable Development' (n 37) 17.

[58] Andrea Ross, *Sustainable Development Law in the UK: From Rhetoric to Reality* (Routeledge 2011).

[59] Michael Doherty, 'Hard Cases and Environmental Principles: An Aid to Interpretation?' (2004) 3 *YEEL* 57, 78 and generally.

[60] Bosselmann, *Principle of Sustainability* (n 20) chs 5 and 6.

[61] Holly Doremus, 'The Rhetoric and Reality of Nature Protection: Toward a New Discourse' (2000) 57 *Wash & Lee L Rev* 11, 15.

[62] As Douglas Fisher asks in relation to the concept of 'ecologically sustainable development' in Australian law, 'is it not likely to depend upon integration within the legal system for its very success?': D E Fisher, *Environmental Law: Text and Materials* (Law Book Co 1994) 440.

[63] Smith, 'Integrating Economic, Ecology, and Law' (n 24) 266, in relation to sustainable development in particular. In this vein, Dovers suggests that incorporating ESD principles in legislation was

in particular are seen to play a key institutional role in achieving environmental outcomes, particularly sustainable development.[64] Thus the Chief Justice of Kenya has stated that:[65]

> In the field of environmental law, sustainable development is only achievable if there is compliance with the environmental law. It is the role of the courts to ensure this compliance and support good governance for the sustainable development for the welfare of our generation and for generations to come.

The UNEP *Global Judges Programme* also highlighted the 'crucial' role of the judiciary in weaving values that support environmental protection 'into the fabric of our societies'.[66] Drawing on this, Justice Brian Preston (Chief Judge of the NSWLEC) argues that individual judges around the world should 'each work towards the common goal of achieving an environmentally sustainable future', particularly through applying principles of sustainable development.[67] James Crawford has also acknowledged a special role for Australian courts in resolving environmental disputes, although in more sceptical terms as to their legitimacy, but in any case as a preferred alternative to political processes that might handle scientific issues poorly or act with doubtful integrity.[68] This perceived special role for courts in achieving environmental outcomes is particularly salient with respect to the case law on environmental principles examined in Chapters Four and Five. On this view, the NSW and European courts have an important instrumental role in achieving environmental outcomes.

Thus environmental principles, formulated for the policy, political and popular reasons set out in the previous section, are cast in legal terms by scholars and judges so as to promote action to achieve good environmental outcomes. This promotion of environmental principles in legal terms helps to explain why environmental principles have a high profile in environmental law, but it does not reveal how environmental principles in fact work legally,[69] as further examined in

a significant step in 'internalising the idea of ESD in the processes of government': Stephen Dovers, 'Instituitionlising ESD: What Happened, What Did Not, Why and What Could Have?' in C Hamilton and D Throsby (eds), *The ESD Process: Evaluating a Policy Experiment* (Academy of Social Sciences, ANU 1998) 16.

[64] Patrick McAuslan, 'The Role of Courts and Other Judicial Type Bodies in Environmental Management' (1991) 3(2) *JEL* 195; Preston, 'Judicial Implementation of the Principles of Ecologically Sustainable Development' (n 24).
[65] Quoted favourably in *Bentley v BGP Properties* [2006] NSWLEC 34; (2006) 145 LGERA 234 [142].
[66] United Nations Environment Programme, *Global Judges Programme* (2005), message of Klaus Toepfer.
[67] Brian Preston, 'The Role of the Judiciary in Promoting Sustainable Development: The Experience of Asia and the Pacific' (2005) 9(2) *Asia Pac J Envtl L* 109, 211.
[68] James Crawford, 'The Constitution' in Tim Bonyhady (ed), *Environmental Protection and Legal Change* (Federation Press 1992) 21.
[69] Although some scholars have suggested what legal changes might be required in according legal status to environmental principles: eg Ross, *Sustainable Development Law in the UK* (n 58) (proposing UK legislative interventions to give sustainable development 'explicit legal backing'). See also Bosselmann, *Principle of Sustainability* (n 20) calling for radical legal changes to human rights, citizenship and notions of sovereignty to institute ecological sustainability in legal terms.

Part III below. However, the instrumental importance placed on environmental principles highlights their perceived importance in environmental law generally, and raises expectations about their legal roles.

## D. Environmental Principles as Solutions to Legal Problems in Environmental Law

Environmental principles also offer a different kind of legal hope for environmental law scholars, adding another dimension to their popularity as legal concepts. Rather than offering legal solutions to *environmental* problems, environmental principles offer legal solutions to *legal* problems in environmental law. In this alternative sense, environmental principles are also conceived as 'legal principles' but in a way that seeks to explain, legitimise and entrench environmental law as a legal discipline. In explaining environmental law, environmental principles can perform an important function in representing new norms that are emerging within and across legal systems. However, scholarly hopes for environmental principles as legal principles have been more ambitious that this, reflecting a wider concern with the nature and worth of environmental law as a scholarly enterprise. This is seen in two main ways.

On the one hand, environmental principles, fashioned as 'legal principles', can make environmental law look like other traditional legal areas, particularly within the common law legal tradition, giving the subject a familiar and established disciplinary footing. On the other hand, environmental principles can unify environmental law not only to cast it in the mould of traditional legal areas in having foundational principles, but also to overcome the unique and significant methodological challenges faced by the subject in asserting its legal identity. Environmental principles might also overcome methodological problems of interdisciplinarity in environmental law due to their connection to, and recognition in, other disciplines.

Environmental law scholars, explicitly and implicitly, suggest that environmental principles can fill one or both of these roles, so as to establish environmental law as a more mature legal discipline. This scholarly imperative can be understood as a response to the perceived infancy of environmental law:[70] that it is a 'relatively new and as yet "uncrystallised" branch of law',[71] which is in danger of marginalisation and extinction.[72] Both of these legal hopes for environmental law are

---

[70] Fisher and others, 'Maturity and Methodology' (n 1) 213–226.

[71] Andreas Philippopoulos-Mihalopoulos, *Absent Environments: Theorising Environmental Law and the City* (Routledge-Cavendish 2007) 25.

[72] A Dan Tarlock, 'Is There a There There in Environmental Law?' (2004) 19 *J Land Use & Envtl L* 213, 228; Philippopoulos-Mihalopoulos, *Absent Environments* (n 71) 32.

legitimacy claims, in which environmental principles, as *universal* legal principles, play a key role. The fact that environmental principles are used by scholars to justify the integrity of environmental law makes a strong case for closely examining what environmental principles are in fact doing in different legal systems. It also shows that legal conclusions about the roles of environmental principles from such contextual examination are conclusions about the nature of environmental law and its scholarship.

### i. *Legitimacy Claim 1: Environmental Law as a Conventional Legal Subject*

In both theoretical and doctrinal terms, environmental principles have been cast in the mould of existing 'legal principles' with a view to explaining their legal character and justifying their importance within environmental law. These approaches locate environmental principles, and environmental law as a subject, within the frames of well-established legal jurisprudence and doctrine. This sub-section focuses mainly on the legal philosophical understandings of legal principles that have been used by scholars in analysing environmental principles, and concludes with some doctrinal analogies. Together, these scholarly approaches show various ways in which environmental principles are being used to explain and legitimise environmental law as a discipline.

In Western legal philosophy, 'legal principles' form a central, even if contested, place in the constitution of a legal system.[73] Environmental law scholars have adopted three key elements of this theoretical discourse to explain and justify the role of environmental principles within environmental law, relating to: (1) the identification of legal principles as such, (2) the role of legal principles in judicial reasoning, and (3) the role of legal principles in rationalising a body of law. In these three ways, environmental principles, framed as legal principles, might constitute fundamental elements of environmental law, as a discrete body of law or as a coherent part of a legal system.

Ronald Dworkin's work, as well as that of Robert Alexy,[74] has been particularly influential for environmental law scholars in their appraisal of how environmental

---

[73] Joseph Raz, 'Legal Principles and the Limits of the Law' [1972] *Yale LJ* 823; Ronald Dworkin, *Taking Rights Seriously* (rev edn, Duckworth 1978) ch 2; *cf* HLA Hart, *The Concept of Law* (2nd edn, Clarendon Press 1994) 259–272; *cf* Neil MacCormick, *Legal Reasoning and Legal Theory* (rev edn, Clarendon Press 1994). For Dworkin, legal principles are propositions describing individual rights which *should* guide judicial decision-making, and they are distinct from rules, as well as policies, which should not inform judicial reasoning: 22–28, 84. For Hart, in response to Dworkin's criticism that he had not adequately considered the role of legal principles in his concept of a legal system, legal principles are distinct from rules in their level of generality and in their desirability (they reflect a desirable goal or value), but their distinction from rules is otherwise not clear-cut, their function being to explain and justify reasoning about rules: 260–1. For MacCormick, principles are 'relatively general norms which are conceived of as "rationalising" rules or sets of rules': 232. Prominent legal philosophers from civil law traditions have also theorised about legal principles as central elements of legal systems: Robert Alexy, *A Theory of Constitutional Rights* (OUP 2002) ch 3.
[74] Alexy, *Constitutional Rights* (n 73).

principles constitute legal principles and how courts do and should reason with them.[75] Dworkin's view is that legal 'principles' are distinct from both 'rules' and 'policies'—only rules and principles relevantly constitute the law, particularly as (it should be) applied by judges, while policies reflect goals that should be pursued by political institutions alone.[76] Rules differ from principles in that rules apply in an 'all-or-nothing fashion',[77] while principles do not require a particular decision or outcome. Alexy recognises a similar distinction between principles and rules, arguing that principles are 'optimisation requirements', which require 'something to be realized to the greatest extent possible given the factual and legal possibilities'.[78] Alexy also distinguishes 'principles' from 'values', where the former are deontological (representing what is obligatory and ought to be), and the latter axiological (representing what is good) and thus not legally enforceable.[79] In both philosophical traditions, principles must be taken into account, if relevant, by 'officials', including judges, as a 'consideration inclining in one direction or another', and are open for balancing when principles intersect.[80] Alexy develops a 'law of competing principles', which relies on analytical logic to determine how relations of precedence are established when principles intersect.[81] Dworkin, by contrast, develops a 'rights thesis', which articulates that judges ought to take into account arguments of principle in hard cases,[82] where principles are standards required by justice or morality, primarily representing individual or group rights.[83] In this way, legal principles are legally persuasive because of their foundation in justice or morality,[84] and they have a dimension of 'weight'. Thus principles can be balanced against each other and judged in terms of their relative importance when they intersect.[85]

---

[75]  eg Nele Dhondt, 'Environmental Law Principles and the Case Law of the Court of Justice' in M Sheridan and L Lavrysen (eds), *Environmental Law Principles in Practice* (Bruylant 2002); Doherty, 'Hard Cases' (n 59); Gerd Winter, 'The Legal Nature of Environmental Principles in International, EC and German Law' in Richard Macrory, Ian Havercroft and Ray Purdy (eds), *Principles of European Environmental Law* (Europa Law Publishing 2004); Bernhard Wegener, 'Principles into Practice— The German Case' in Richard Macrory, Ian Havencroft and Ray Purdy (eds), *Principles of European Environmental Law* (Europa Law Publishing 2004). Other environmental scholars rely on the distinction between principles and rules instinctively, with no appeal to legal philosophy: eg Astrid Epiney, 'Environmental Principles' in Richard Macrory (ed), *Reflections on 30 Years of EU Environmental Law* (Europa Law Publishing 2006).

[76]  Above n 73.

[77]  Dworkin, *Taking Rights Seriously* (n 73) 24.

[78]  Alexy, *Constitutional Rights* (n 73) 47.

[79]  ibid 86–92.

[80]  Dworkin, *Taking Rights Seriously* (n 73) 24–26.

[81]  Alexy, *Constitutional Rights* (n 73) 50–54.

[82]  Dworkin, *Taking Rights Seriously* (n 73) 81.

[83]  ibid 22, 82–90.

[84]  *cf* Alexander & Sherwin who argue that Dworkin's theory of legal principles is compromised in its claim to a moral basis: Larry Alexander & Emily Sherwin, *The Rule of Rules: Morality, Rules and the Dilemmas of Law* (Duke University Press 2001) ch 8.

[85]  Dworkin, *Taking Rights Seriously* (n 73) 26–27.

For environmental scholars, these philosophical distinctions and arguments are useful in two ways in promoting a legitimising narrative for environmental principles.[86] First, even though environmental principles are ambiguous and imprecise, leading to definitional difficulties, such imprecision is not inconsistent with their being relevantly 'legal' and fundamental to a legal system.[87] Such ambiguity is inherent in the fact that principles are reasons that '[argue] in one direction, but [do] not necessitate a particular decision'.[88] Thus, for example, Fisher highlights that the precautionary principle is a legal principle, rather than a rule, in jurisprudential terms.[89] Furthermore, the moral underpinnings of Dworkinian principles can facilitate the legal identification of environmental principles. Bosselmann thus argues, drawing on Dworkin's thesis, that the ethical and moral dimensions of the sustainability principle militate in favour of its legal recognition.[90]

Second, environmental principles conceptually can and should be used to guide judicial reasoning. Environmental law scholars give examples of how environmental principles are used by courts to interpret uncertain rules, including statutory provisions, and to guide judicial reasoning in other ways, reflecting the interpretive role suggested for legal principles by Dworkin.[91] Further, environmental principles *should* guide the interpretation of rules and otherwise fill gaps in the legal system, particularly by refining the purposes of environmental law and employing these to resolve legal issues.[92] They should do so, in particular, by force of their moral justification,[93] again tying in with ethical claims for environmental principles and their significance.

Such legal roles for principles follow both Dworkin and Alexy's models of reasoning with principles, and thus attract legitimacy from foundational legal scholarship.[94] This lends authority to environmental law as a legal discipline. In other words, if judges use environmental principles in their reasoning in the way that they use other legal principles to resolve disputes, then their reasoning might build a corpus of environmental law that has legal legitimacy and longevity. Hence

[86] Alexy's theoretical account of principles also lends itself to these uses with respect to environmental principles: Winter, 'Legal Nature of Environmental Principles' (n 75).

[87] eg Dhondt, 'Environmental Law Principles' (n 75) 153; *cf* the debate concerning the normativity of environmental principles in international environmental law: see ch 3(II)(B).

[88] Dworkin, *Taking Rights Seriously* (n 73) 24. See eg Marong, 'From Rio to Johannesburg' (n 20) 58–64.

[89] Elizabeth Fisher, 'Precaution, Precaution Everywhere: Developing a "Common Understanding" of the Precautionary Principle in the European Community' (2002) 9(1) *MJ* 7, 16.

[90] Bosselmann, *Principle of Sustainability* (n 20) 49. Bosselmann sees the principle of sustainability as being a distinct legal principle, with a fundamental moral weight that means it is not subject to trade-offs with other environmental principles, which are not ethically grounded in the same way: 52, 63.

[91] eg Nele Dhondt, *Integration of Environmental Protection into Other EC Policies: Legal Theory and Practice* (Europa Law Publishing 2003) 154; Doherty, 'Hard Cases' (n 59) 60–67.

[92] Doherty, 'Hard Cases' (n 59) 78; de Sadeleer, *Environmental Principles* (n 35) 264–65.

[93] Bosselmann, *Principle of Sustainability* (n 20) 48–49.

[94] Alexy, *Constitutional Rights* (n 73) 57, 87–88, and ch 3 generally. See also Hart in his response to Dworkin: Hart, *Concept of Law* (n 73) 272–76.

Doherty's reference in the previous section suggests that judicial use of environmental principles to guide reasoning might assist not simply the environment, but also the European legal system.[95] His implication is that such reasoning will entrench environmental principles as legal principles within a conceptually consistent legal system.

Missing from this theoretical account of how judges should reason with environmental principles is what it means for principles to be used to 'fill gaps' within a legal system, beyond interpreting ambiguous statutory provisions and resolving legal 'issues' by broadly giving direction (including being relatively balanced if more than one principle is relevant).[96] Dworkin suggests that legal principles have a wide-ranging interpretive function in this sense—including justifying the adoption and application of new rules, in light of the moral weight of principles.[97] This implies a level of potentially considerable activism on the part of judges when reasoning on the basis of legal principles.[98] If these include environmental principles, Dworkin's thesis not only gives environmental principles legitimacy within a legal system, but also bolsters the legal hopes for environmental principles discussed in the previous section (that a legal role for environmental principles might generate policy action). However, the generality of this theoretical perspective, as embraced by environmental scholars, undermines its prescription for how judges should reason with environmental principles in particular cases. It gives no relevantly detailed account of how legal disputes might be resolved by relying on environmental principles, beyond describing a general role of interpreting ambiguous rules and filling gaps. Almost any judicial use of environmental principles might be justified on this and similar authoritative legal models.

The third way in which environmental principles, as legal principles, might benefit environmental law as a discipline is by giving it coherence overall. Environmental principles might constitute a core set of principles that define, unite and preserve environmental law as legal subject. Again, Anglo-American legal philosophy suggests this role for legal principles in giving a legal system coherence in terms of a set of norms that express 'fundamental or at least important values of the system [that are overriding], so that they tend to be regarded as supplying self-sufficient justifications of decisions'.[99] The nature of traditional legal subjects implicates the necessity of such principles for an area of law. Subjects such as contract, tort and equity have a core set of legal doctrines and principles.[100] In this

[95] Above n 59.
[96] As Dworkin states with considerable generality, principles are to be 'taken into account' if relevant as a consideration inclining in one direction or another: above n 80; *cf* the more detailed prescription for judicial reasoning on the basis of principles in Alexy, *Constitutional Rights* (n 73) ch 3 (in relation to the German constitution).
[97] Dworkin, *Taking Rights Seriously* (n 73) 28.
[98] Dworkin acknowledges that using principles to guide judicial reasoning may be controversial, particularly when attributing relative weight to intersecting principles: ibid 26–7.
[99] Neil MacCormick, *Legal Reasoning and Legal Theory* (Clarendon Press 1978) 180.
[100] A more subtle model of how environmental principles might be viewed as unifying foundations for environmental law is provided by the 'maxims' of equity in common law systems: JD Heydon,

vein, some scholars suggest that environmental principles can rationalise environmental law by codifying the proliferation of detailed, reactive, evolving and multijurisdictional rules and regulatory frameworks that comprise environmental law ('many laws but little law').[101] Further, a 'rational unified municipal legal system' is said to demand an 'underlying logic' in the form of environmental principles.[102] With respect to international law, scholars have made similar claims that environmental principles give international environmental law a framework,[103] or that they are required to fulfil such a function.[104]

The importance of these three potential functions of environmental principles for environmental law as a subject—identifying environmental principles as legal principles, legitimately guiding judicial reasoning, and providing a coherent foundation for environmental law—can be seen in the strict attitude of some scholars to isolating 'true' environmental principles, in the sense of complying with a theoretical model of what a 'legal principle' is, and strictly maintaining the distinction between principles and rules.[105] Similarly, international environmental law scholars draw on Dworkin's distinction between principles and rules to scrutinise environmental principles as 'general principles' of international law.[106]

It is not only jurisprudential theories of legal principles that have been relied on by environmental law scholars to identify and characterise environmental principles as legal principles. A similar legitimising tendency can be seen in the way that scholars draw on established doctrinal approaches to legal principles within discrete legal systems. In particular, scholars have drawn on 'general principles' in public international law and in EU law to explain and justify environmental principles as 'legal principles' within those jurisdictions,[107] thereby legitimising

M Leeming and P Turner, *Meagher, Gummow and Lehane's Equity Doctrines and Remedies* (5th edn, LexisNexis 2014) pt 1(3). These maxims have been distinguished from legal rules or principles as 'summary statement[s] of a broad theme which [underline] equitable concepts and principles': *Corin v Patton* (1990) 169 CLR 540, 557. On this view, legal 'maxims' are not legal concepts in any strict theoretical or doctrinal sense.

[101] de Sadeleer, *Environmental Principles* (n 35) 264–68. See also Gilhuis, 'Consequences of Introducing Environmental Law Principles' (n 12) 50–51.

[102] Evans, *Principles of Environmental and Heritage Law* (n 41) 99.

[103] Stephens, *International Courts* (n 37) 6.

[104] Palmer, 'New Ways' (n 32) 268. He notes efforts to develop a code of principles of international environmental law have failed, including those of the International Law Commission from 1978, and the Experts Group on Environmental Law established by the World Commission on Environment and Development in 1986.

[105] Winter, 'Legal Nature of Environmental Principles' (n 75); Verschuuren, 'Sustainable Development' (n 37); Bosselmann, *Principle of Sustainability* (n 20) 45–57.

[106] Philippe Sands and Jacqueline Peel, *Principles of International Environmental Law* (3rd edn, CUP 2012) 189; Marong, 'From Rio to Johannesburg' (n 20) 57–58; Ulrich Beyerlin, 'Different Types of Norms in International Environmental Law: Policies, Principles and Rules' in Dan Bodansky, Jutta Brunnée and Ellen Hey (eds), *The Oxford Handbook of International Environmental Law* (OUP 2007).

[107] Sands and Peel, *Principles of International Environmental Law* (n 106) (public international law); Paul Craig, *EU Administrative Law* (2nd edn, OUP 2012) (EU law); Maria Weimer, 'Applying Precaution in EU Authorisation of Genetically Modified Products-Challenges and Suggestions for Reform' (2010) 16(5) *ELJ* 624 (EU law). See further Section III(B) below. Hilson also examines the difficult

environmental principles as relevantly legal within the context of those legal systems. The problems with drawing on models of legal principles from these different jurisdictions is examined further in Part III below, but for now it reinforces the tendency to draw on existing legal models of principles to explain the legal nature of environmental principles. However, this tendency is misplaced if such models fail to reflect the reality of environmental principles in environmental law. The method and conclusions drawn by mapping the legal roles of environmental principles in discrete jurisdictions are thus important in appraising whether environmental law needs (and can properly use or adopt) pre-existing legal models to explain environmental principles and, further, to justify itself as a legal discipline.

### ii. Legitimacy Claim 2: Environmental Principles Overcome Methodological Problems in Environmental Law

Environmental principles might unify and legitimise environmental law in another sense altogether, which does not rely on adopting authoritative philosophical theories of how a legal system operates and is constituted, or on other established doctrinal approaches to legal principles. Despite scholarly tendencies to borrow legal ideas from other established areas of law, environmental law is recognised by environmental law scholars as being different from other areas of law. In particular, it is intellectually incoherent in that it is 'not an organic mutation of the common law, or more generally, the Western legal tradition'.[108] Instead, it is a subject beset with methodological challenges for the environmental law scholar, particularly due to the multi-jurisdictional and interdisciplinary nature of many environmental problems and thus the law that applies to them, and the speed and scale of environmental legal developments.[109]

In light of these scholarly challenges, which manifest in the perceived immaturity of environmental law as a subject of scholarship,[110] environmental principles are relied on as a legitimising point of methodological consistency in analysing and justifying environmental law. First, environmental principles might overcome problems of studying multiple jurisdictions by providing a common legal reference point between jurisdictions. Both scholars and judges have adopted this position.[111] Second, environmental principles might provide a common legal track

---

distinction between 'principles' with 'rights' in the EU Charter of Fundamental Rights (European Parliament, Council and Commission, 'Charter of Fundamental Rights of the European Union' [2000] OJ C364/1 ('Charter')) in attempting to ascertain the legal status of both as a matter of EU law, including in relation to EU environmental principles and general principles of EU law: Chris Hilson, 'Rights and Principles in EU Law: A Distinction without Foundation?' (2008) 15(2) *MJ* 193. The Charter contains 'principles' as well as rights, and the legal distinction between the two is unclear, as Hilson forcefully argues: see further ch 4, nn 367, 371.

[108]  Tarlock, 'Is There a There There' (n 72) 217.
[109]  Fisher and others, 'Maturity and Methodology' (n 1) 228–243.
[110]  ibid 218–228.
[111]  See ch 3, text accompanying nn 43–53.

and point of interrelationship between the various strands of law that apply to environmental problems. For Evans, environmental principles represent an 'integrating ethic [that] emphasises the joint over the several individual goals' of different bodies of applicable law.[112] They are a means to overcome the challenge of 'legal interdisciplinarity' in environmental law.[113]

Third, and relatedly, it is argued that environmental principles might overcome problems of dealing with rapid, reactive, detailed and novel legal developments in the environmental field. Environmental principles might 'rationalise' or 'codify' such developments. Verschuuren refers to environmental principles as 'dynamic beacons in a wild ocean of ever changing concrete environmental rules'.[114] Nicolas de Sadeleer explains that environmental principles can function as a 'keystone for the structuring and systemisation intended to remedy deficiencies of a law that developed in a piecemeal manner on the basis of scattered and fragmentary provisions.'[115] Such organising principles thus integrate the subject and constitute tools for the legal scholar to appraise and evaluate legal developments.

Fourth, environmental principles might be tools for incorporating interdisciplinary elements into environmental law. Andreas Philippopoulos-Mihalopoulos suggests that the precautionary principle by its nature involves a 'structural coupling' of environmental law, science, politics and public participation.[116] This is one example of an extensive literature on the precautionary principle as a legal concept and its fraught interaction with science in particular.[117] This wide literature in fact shows there is no clear way in which the precautionary principle overcomes methodological problems of interdisciplinarity in environmental law,[118] although a great weight of expectation is placed upon it in this respect. For Bosselmann, *all* environmental principles are derivatively interdisciplinary—their respective derivation from different disciplines (science, ethics, economics, and so on) thus explains their qualitatively different legal natures, in terms of relevance and enforceability. However, their eventual transformation into legal principles gives them a common identity.[119]

---

[112] Evans, *Principles of Environmental and Heritage Law* (n 41) 99.

[113] Fisher and others, 'Maturity and Methodology' (n 1) 230.

[114] Verschuuren, 'Sustainable Development' (n 37) 39. See also Also Andrew Waite, 'The Quest for Environmental Law Equilibrium' (2005) 7 *Env LR* 34, 35–36.

[115] de Sadeleer, *Environmental Principles* (n 35) 258.

[116] Philippopoulos-Mihalopoulos, *Absent Environments* (n 71) 136.

[117] eg Joel Tickner and David Kriebel, 'The Role of Science and Precaution in Environmental and Public Health Policy' in Elizabeth Fisher, Judith Jones and René von Schomberg (eds), *Implementing the Precautionary Principle: Perspectives and Prospects* (MPG Books 2006); Giandomenico Majone, 'What Price Safety? The Precautionary Principle and its Policy Implications' (2002) 40(1) *Journal of Common Market Studies* 89; Karl-Heinz Ladeur, 'The Introduction of the Precautionary Principle into EU law: A Pyrrhic Victory for Environmental and Public Health Law? Decision-making Under Conditions of Complexity in Multi-level Political Systems' (2003) 40(6) *CMLR* 1455, 1458-1462; Nicolas de Sadeleer, 'The Precautionary Principle in EC Health and Environmental Law' (2006) 12(2) *ELJ* 139, 150–162.

[118] Elizabeth Fisher, *Risk Regulation and Administrative Constitutionalism* (Hart 2007).

[119] Bosselmann, *Principle of Sustainability* (n 20) 43.

In these four senses, environmental principles are suggested to provide stable reference points for the study of environmental law, bolstering the legitimacy of the subject in light of its considerable methodological challenges. Some environmental law scholars go even further than adopting environmental principles as useful methodological tools; rather, environmental principles might constitute or represent a new form of legal order. This moves beyond legitimising existing environmental law as a legal discipline, and addresses its very nature and foundation, as examined in the following section.

## E. Environmental Principles Constitute or Represent Environmental Law as a New Legal Order

Some environmental scholars, and international bodies, place great weight on environmental principles constituting or representing environmental law as a new legal order. Identifying environmental law as a new legal order is an alternative and more radical way to legitimise environmental law as a serious intellectual discipline. Scholars making such an argument would acknowledge the unique and intellectually incoherent nature of environmental law in traditional jurisprudential terms so that positivist, Dworkinian or 'real law' accounts of legal principles have little relevance in ascertaining the legal role of environmental principles.[120] However, their view is that environmental law needs to be redefined in legal terms, either by reference to environmental problems to which environmental law relates, or by adopting a novel theoretical foundation to the subject. On both views, scholars have suggested models for environmental law that have environmental principles at their core, although not necessarily the same environmental principles.

On a pragmatic view of redefining environmental law, environmental law should be shaped by the environmental problems to which it relates. According to Dan Tarlock, the 'extremely complex and evolving moral and scientific nature of environmental problems ensures that ... environmental law will be a law about the *process of decision*, rather than a process of evolving *decision rules*'.[121] For such decision processes, Tarlock outlines a series of 'candidate principles of law' that have emerged in recent decades to act as 'rebuttable presumptions' in decision-making.[122] They can be no more than rebuttable because environmental law is a 'series of hypotheses that must be tested (and often modified) over a long time

---

[120] eg Tarlock, 'Is There a There There' (n 72) 222–237.
[121] ibid 219–220.
[122] These comprise: 'minimise uncertainty before and as you act'; 'environmental degradation should be a last resort after all reasonable, feasible alternatives have been exhausted'; 'risk can be a legitimate interim basis for prohibition of an activity'; 'polluters must continually upgrade waste reduction and processing technology'; 'environmental decision-making should be inclusive rather than exclusive within the limits of rationality': ibid 220.

horizon by rigorous monitoring and experimentation',[123] particularly because of the evolving scientific knowledge about environmental problems.

In contrast to this reflexive view of environmental law, but in line with its pragmatic focus on environmental problems, the 1987 Brundtland Report (the report of an international commission on environment and development, sponsored by the United Nations)[124] suggested that environmental law was deficient in failing to reflect the interdependent nature of the environment and biosphere to which it relates.[125] Environmental law should, accordingly, adopt a more holistic and unified philosophy. This philosophy was expressed in the universal legal principles annexed to the Brundtland Report,[126] and in subsequent efforts to draft legal principles of environmental protection and sustainable development at the international level.[127] In the result, a binding international convention along these lines was not agreed, but the non-binding Rio Declaration eventuated, with its set of environmental principles.[128]

Other environmental scholars have approached the (re)definition of environmental law from an explicitly theoretical point of view, suggesting that environmental principles constitute or represent a new legal foundation for environmental law in two, to some extent overlapping, senses. First, some scholars suggest that environmental law, and particularly the environmental principles at its foundation, represents a new emerging form of legal order. For de Sadeleer, this is 'post-modern law', which is characterised by an increase in discretion, competing norms, multiple jurisdictions and 'openness to extra-legal spheres', including economic, ethical and policy spheres.[129] In this new form of law, of which environmental law is representative, environmental principles have the following critical role as legal principles:[130]

> …'principles' no longer serve merely to rationalize law or to fill gaps in a given legal system… Rather, they are intended to spur public policies, to allow courts to weigh and reconcile highly divergent interests. These principles mark a policy path to be followed, outline the context within which the law-maker must act, and guide the course of his passage. [Environmental principles are] 'directing principles'… As legal systems multiply and intersect, this new generation of principles plays an important role in maintaining the links among weakly structured networks, ensuring the practical effectiveness of the legal system as a whole … They are needed to introduce a degree of rationality in

---

[123] ibid 220.
[124] World Commission on Environment and Development, 'Report of the World Commission on Environment and Development: Our Common Future' (20 March 1987) UN Doc A/42/427 ('Brundtland Report'). See further ch 3(II)(A).
[125] Tarlock, 'Is There a There There' (n 72) 330–334.
[126] Brundtland Report (n 124) annexe 1.
[127] See above n 104.
[128] See ch 3, text following n 20.
[129] de Sadeleer, *Environmental Principles* (n 35).
[130] ibid 250–251.

a world that has become Kafkaesque though the production of an excessive number of rules and a high degree of instability ... They provide order to this new view of the legal system...

Another deeply theoretical viewpoint is that of Philippopoulos-Mihalopoulos, who argues that environmental law can only be understood as an autopoetic system due to its unique features, including the 'irreducible complexity of the environment'.[131] For Philippopoulos-Mihalopoulos, environmental law must be redefined in such a way that 'presupposes less normativity than the average law, more cognitive flexibility, and significantly greater "fuzziness" in decision-making'.[132] Within such a system, environmental principles, in particular the precautionary principle and principle of intergenerational equity, have a theoretically significant role.[133]

Second, other scholars argue not that environmental law in its current state represents a new or developing form of legal order, but that a new form of global environmental law *should* exist based on a jurisprudential concept of justice that places the legal (and ethically imperative) principle of 'sustainability' at its core. The aim of this proposed legal development is to make environmental protection goals legally entrenched and thus enforceable, and to reorient the social goals entrenched in laws and dispute resolution mechanisms accordingly.[134] A practical application of this theoretical viewpoint is seen in an edited collection by Alyson Flournoy and David Driesen, which sets out, as the basis of the next (third) generation of US environmental law, concrete wide-ranging legislative proposals that define and entrench the 'concepts' of sustainability and intergenerational equity in order to mandate these environmental protection goals and thus bind government action.[135]

On these more radical scholarly views, environmental principles are expected to do a lot legally. Thus environmental principles represent environmental law as a new form of law, in a pragmatic or theoretical sense, or they constitute the basis for an ideal form of law, which has ecological justice at its jurisprudential core. This latter idealistic vision links to the instrumental hopes for environmental principles set out in Section C above, positing that the correct legal structure will lead to desired environmental outcomes. Again, these scholarly views highlight that environmental principles carry a lot of weight and hope in environmental law scholarship. The next part of this chapter examines how this weight has often been misplaced, or at least too readily assumed.

---

[131] Philippopoulos-Mihalopoulos, *Absent Environments* (n 71) 30.
[132] ibid 31.
[133] ibid 130–36.
[134] Bosselmann, *Principle of Sustainability* (n 20); Bosselmann, 'Ecological Justice' (n 16).
[135] Alyson C Flournoy and David M Driesen (eds), *Beyond Environmental Law: Policy Proposals for a Better Environmental Future* (CUP 2010). See also many of the contributions to Christina Voigt (ed), *Rule of Law for Nature: New Dimensions and Ideas in Environmental Law* (CUP 2013).

# III.  Limitations in Appraising Environmental Principles Legally

In general, the high legal profile of environmental principles, whilst understandable in acknowledging the strong symbolism and novel legal developments related to environmental principles, has not accounted for the different legal cultures in which environmental principles may (or do) have a role. The focus on legitimising environmental law and solving environmental problems has to an extent diverted scholarly attention from environmental law as it is in fact evolving within particular legal systems, including around environmental principles. This Part sets out three methodological positions that are in fact barriers to understanding the evolving legal nature of environmental principles: assuming that environmental principles are universal and impliedly equivalent concepts across jurisdictional boundaries; borrowing legal concepts and methodologies from other legal subjects in order to discern the nature of environmental principles as 'legal principles'; and taking a strong view that environmental law as a subject is instrumental in its function or coherent in its nature.

A sounder starting point for analysis is to see that environmental principles do not come with any predetermined legal meaning, inherently self-fulfilling logical or moral force, programmed function, doctrinal history, or legal scholarly tradition. Their loose nomenclature as 'principles' at best connotes ideas concerning environmental protection that are general and highly symbolic,[136] albeit that they are ideas for which there is a deep scholarly appetite, for moral, environmentalist and discipline-legitimising reasons. Identifying environmental principles as concepts with an increasing legal presence in fact begs the question of what a 'principle' means in environmental law. The methodological approaches of much literature on environmental principles highlight that there is something legally interesting going on in relation to environmental principles, including across jurisdictions in certain respects, but overlook how the evolving legal nature of environmental principles is being determined by their operation within particular legal contexts. De Sadeleer highlights that environmental law is an 'ephemeral body of law, subject to continuous revision'.[137] The evolution of law relating to environmental principles is no exception and its path is not only unpredictable but also contingent on the cultures of the legal systems in which they are playing roles.

---

[136] de Sadeleer, *Environmental Principles* (n 35) 258.
[137] ibid 257.

## A.  Environmental Principles as Universal Legal Concepts

Many of the scholarly hopes for environmental principles examined in Part II are based on an assumption that environmental principles are universal legal concepts across jurisdictions.[138] This position allows scholars to suggest that environmental principles are solutions to environmental problems globally; that they can fit general theoretical models of 'legal principles'; and that they can unite environmental law as a subject, whether across jurisdictions or as a new form of law altogether. According to this view, environmental principles are characterised as *universal*, *equivalent* and *legal*. As Justice Carnwarth has commented extra-judicially:[139]

> … the principles which should guide our response to that challenge (sustainable development, precautionary principle, public trusteeship) form a shared pool of knowledge and experience, which is now recognised in one form or another by most of the legal systems of the world.

The generality of the formulation of environmental principles allows for such an approach, as does the suggestion that they 'trickle down' from international agreements into all legal systems and contexts, examined further in Chapter Three.

The assumption of universality is central to the argument for a global 'sustainability law' based on environmental principles to address pressing environmental problems that transcend jurisdictional boundaries,[140] as well as critiques that environmental principles are meaningless.[141] It also supports judicial cross-fertilisation of case law concerning environmental principles.[142] Judicial cross-referral to decisions of courts in other jurisdictions involving environmental principles often occurs with little analysis of those legal environments, seeming to assume their universal nature across legal contexts.[143] The international judicial agenda to promote sustainable development principles, by collaboration and exchange of information amongst judges within and across regions, also encourages the view that

---

[138]  eg Stuart Bell, Donald McGillivray and Ole Pedersen, *Environmental Law* (8th edn, OUP 2013) 56–76; de Sadeleer, *Environmental Principles* (n 35); Preston, 'Role of the Judiciary in Promoting Sustainable Development' (n 67); Boer, 'Institutionalising Ecologically Sustainable Development' (n 24); Evans, *Principles of Environmental and Heritage Law* (n 41) 141.

[139]  Robert Carnwath, 'Judicial Protection of the Environment: At Home and Abroad' (2004) 16(3) *JEL* 315, 316.

[140]  Boer, 'Implementation of International Sustainability Imperatives' (n 56) 115–121; Evans, *Principles of Environmental and Heritage Law* (n 41) 85, 96; *cf* Bosselmann, *Principle of Sustainability* (n 20) 43.

[141]  The precautionary principle has been criticised as meaningless because it is used differently across jurisdictions: Christopher D Stone, 'Is There a Precautionary Principle?' (2001) 31(7) *Environmental Law Reporter* 10790; Gary E Marchant and Kenneth L Mossman, *Arbitrary and Capricious: The Precautionary Principle in the European Union Courts* (AEI Press 2004); Cass Sunstein, *Laws of Fear: Beyond the Precautionary Principle* (CUP 2005).

[142]  See ch 1, nn 33–35.

[143]  eg *Gray v Minister for Planning* [2006] NSWLEC 720; (2006) 152 LGERA 258 [121].

similarly named principles are being used as equivalent legal concepts in judicial reasoning across jurisdictions.[144]

There are however three problems with assuming that environmental principles are universal legal concepts. First, it is impossible to isolate a single conceptual identity for environmental principles in environmental law scholarship. Second, history does not support claims that environmental principles are universal—they have varying origins and derivations. Third, comparative law warns that universal legal concepts do not readily exist across legal cultures.

### i. Absence of Universal Legal Identity Conceptually

The conceptual focus on environmental principles in environmental law scholarship is a shifting one, undermining claims of their universal identity. Some conceptual approaches focus on the 'environmental', or 'environmental law', aspect of environmental principles, while others focus on the nature of a 'principle'.[145] Others avoid ascribing a generalised meaning to environmental principles altogether.

As an example of a conceptual approach to environmental principles that focuses on their role in environmental law, Bell, McGillivray & Pedersen, in their leading UK environmental law textbook, state that environmental principles are:[146]

> general concepts ... that can accommodate [various disciplinary perspectives in approaching environmental law or decisions] ... A dynamic relationship exists within these principles—which underpin environmental law at all levels—between the formulation of the law, and its implementation and enforcement.

Waite builds on this theme of principles underpinning environmental law and asserts that environmental principles are a crucial layer in the 'environmental law model'—they develop from the 'environmental imperatives' that in turn arise from the 'laws of nature', and they underlie the framework of legal rules.[147]

Other scholarly works take the nature of a 'principle' as the analytical starting point for understanding an environmental principle conceptually. Dictionary definitions of 'principle' are drawn on to identify environmental principles—a principle is a 'fundamental truth as basis of reasoning' or 'general law as guide to action'[148]—as are contrasts between 'principles' and other concepts such as objectives, ideals, rules and policies. In some cases, such contrasts are set out as

---

[144] UNEP, 'Johannesburg Principles on the Role of Law and Sustainable Development', Global Judges Symposium (Johannesburg, South Africa, 18–20 August 2002) principle 4 and programme of work (c).

[145] Some focus on both aspects eg Tromans, 'High Talk' (n 32) 779–780.

[146] Bell, McGillivray and Pedersen, *Environmental Law* (n 138) 56–7.

[147] Waite, 'Quest for Environmental Law' (n 114) 35.

[148] Tromans, 'High Talk' (n 32) 779.

statements of fact in relation to environmental principles;[149] in others, they are drawn in terms of jurisprudential theory relating to 'legal principles', relying primarily on Dworkin as well as other theoretical scholars, as examined in Part II above. In the latter sense, as an example, Verschuuren concludes that environmental legal principles are different from ideals (such as 'sustainable development') and have the following conceptual identity:[150]

> [Environmental principles] go beyond concrete rules or policy goals; instead they say something about the group of rules or policy goals, they indicate what a collection of rules has in common, or what the common goal is of a collection of rules ... Principles usually contain a higher moral and/or legal value. Principles thus form a first attempt to make ideals more concrete. [However] some principles are more principle than others [sic] ... Individual legal principles can be put on a sliding scale, from very abstract and of a high morality, to very concrete and precise; they cover almost all the space between an ideal, on the one hand, and a rule, on the other.

This explanation runs a fine line between jurisprudential theory and conceptual indeterminacy. Philippe Sands and Jacqueline Peel take a functional as well as jurisprudential approach to identifying environmental principles as legal concepts, focussing on their presence in international environmental law. Whilst international environmental law relating to principles is still evolving, Sands and Peel suggest that environmental principles in public international law have three general characteristics. First, they are themselves general, in the sense that they are potentially applicable to all members of the international community across a range of activities concerning all aspects of environmental protection; second, they are broadly supported, in that they are reflected in state practice; and third, they are distinct from rules in the sense set out in an early international law decision:[151]

> A 'rule' ... is essentially practical and, moreover, binding ... [T]here are rules of art and there are rules of government [while 'principle'] expresses a general truth, which guides our action, serves as a theoretical basis for the various acts of our life, and the application of which to reality produces a given consequence.

While it is incongruous to equate such conceptual references to environmental principles in international law with other scholarly references, albeit expressed in generalised terms, this often occurs in environmental law scholarship that analyses environmental principles as including, or being derived from, those principles in international law sources.[152] This trans-jurisdictional basis for environmental

---

[149] Ronnie Harding, Michael Young and Elizabeth Fisher, 'Interpretation of Principles' (Fenner Conference on the Environment—Sustainability: Principles to Practice 1994) 4.

[150] Verschuuren, 'Sustainable Development' (n 37) 18, 25–6. This leads Verschuuren to conclude that 'each principle must be valued in its own respect': 28.

[151] Sands and Peel, *Principles of International Environmental Law* (n 106) 187–189, citing *Gentini* case (*Italy v Venezuela*) (1903) 10 *RIAA* 551. See also Marong, 'From Rio to Johannesburg' (n 20) 57–73.

[152] eg Winter, 'Legal Nature of Environmental Principles' (n 75); Verschuuren, 'Sustainable Development' (n 37). See further ch 3(II)(A).

principles allows general, or universal, conceptual assertions about environmental principles to be advanced.

At the same time, a large body of scholarly work also focuses conceptual analysis of environmental principles within the realm of international environmental law only, along the lines set out above by Sands and Peel. Even within this legal domain, the conceptual understanding of environmental principles is inconsistent. For some scholars, environmental principles are principles of international environmental law;[153] for others, they are principles of 'sustainable development'.[154] The latter approach focuses the conceptual understanding of principles on their being constitutive of an overarching concept—or sometimes 'principle'—of sustainable development. Some even argue that there has been a paradigmatic shift from international environmental law to international law for sustainable development, with a range of 'legal and normative' principles representing the latter, which have a different substantive emphasis in relation to environmental protection since they are centrally concerned with development.[155]

Then there are scholarly approaches to environmental principles that do not focus on environmental principles conceptually at all.[156] This is a safer approach considering the lack of conceptual clarity around environmental principles just outlined. It also allows for an appreciation of varying legal culture in understanding the legal roles of environmental principles. In short, it is not possible to ascribe a general conceptual meaning to environmental principles in environmental law without a closer examination of their developing roles within particular legal contexts, despite a widespread inclination to identify environmental principles as universal legal concepts, albeit according to different conceptual benchmarks.

## ii. Absence of Universal Legal Identity Historically

The second reason why environmental principles are not readily identifiable as universal legal concepts is that, despite assumptions that environmental principles are commonly derived from international soft law instruments setting out lists of environmental principles, such as the Rio Declaration, their history is not so neat.

---

[153] eg Sands and Peel, *Principles of International Environmental Law* (n 106); Patricia Birnie, Alan Boyle and Catherine Redgwell, *International Law & the Environment* (3rd edn, OUP 2009) 115–204; Tim Stephens, 'Multiple International Courts and the 'Fragmentation' of International Environmental Law' (2006) 25 *Aust YBIL* 227, 236–240.

[154] eg Boer, 'Institutionalising Ecologically Sustainable Development' (n 24); Preston, 'Role of the Judiciary in Promoting Sustainable Development' (n 67); Paul Stein, 'Turning Soft Law into Hard—An Australian Experience with ESD Principles in Practice' (1997) 3(2) *The Judicial Review* 91; Paul Stein and Susan Mahoney, 'Incorporating Sustainability Principles into Legislation' in Paul Leadbeter, Neil Gunningham and Ben Boer (eds), *Environmental Outlook No 3: Law and Policy* (Federation Press 1999); Marong, 'From Rio to Johannesburg' (n 20); Verschuuren, 'Sustainable Development' (n 37).

[155] Mary Pat Williams Silveira, 'International Legal Instruments and Sustainable Development: Principles, Requirements, and Restructuring' (1995) 31 *Willamette L Rev* 239, 241–3 and generally.

[156] eg Doherty does not define environmental principles in general terms but finds that the role and meaning of environmental principles will only be determined by their implementation: Michael Doherty, 'The Judicial Use of the Principles of EC Environmental Policy' (2000) 2(4) *Env LR* 251, 263.

This history is elaborated in more detail in Chapter Three.[157] In short, groupings of environmental principles are not identical across legal contexts, and different environmental principles have emerged in particular legal systems with their own particular histories, some of which have been the subject of international agreements and some of which have not. This variation in groupings of legally interesting environmental principles is reflected in the fact that scholars themselves choose to study or acknowledge different groups of principles as 'environmental principles', particularly within discrete legal systems such as international law or EU law.[158] As a result, that there are many different taxonomies of groups of environmental principles in the literature.[159]

Furthermore, even where environmental principles might be seen to derive in a broad sense from principles that are internationally agreed, they can look quite different once established within a particular legal culture. This can be seen in the historical development of environmental principles in NSW law, examined in Chapter Three,[160] which have followed a contingent and unique legal path in that legal culture. Many scholars acknowledge some kind of contextualisation of environmental principles by highlighting that environmental principles are subject to flexible interpretation,[161] and that their application in specific instances is dependent on the 'facts and circumstances of each case'.[162] However, this contextual appreciation is not merely definitional, it is a fundamental part of the methodological care than is required in analysing environmental principles in legal terms.

### iii. Absence of Universal Legal Identity in Comparative Law Terms

The third reason not to assume that environmental principles are universal legal concepts relates to Chapter One's discussion of the work of comparative law

---

[157] See ch 3(II)(A), (III)(A) and (IV)(A)–(C).

[158] eg Dhondt, 'Environmental Law Principles' (n 75) 146–152 (high level of protection principle, precautionary principle, preventive principle, rectification at source principle, polluter pays principle, integration principle—EU law); cf de Sadeleer, *Environmental Principles* (n 35) (polluter pays principle, preventive principle, precautionary principle—generally); cf Boer, 'Institutionalising Ecologically Sustainable Development' (n 24) 319–323 (principles of intergenerational and intra-generational equity, precautionary principle, conservation of biological diversity, internalisation of environmental costs—international law and generally).

[159] eg International Law Association has found that 'sustainable development' principles comprise seven principles (duty of states to ensure sustainable use of natural resources; equity and eradication of poverty; common but differentiated responsibility; precautionary approach to human health, natural resources and ecosystems; public participation and access to information and justice; good governance; integration and interrelationship, particularly in relation to human rights and social, economic and environmental objectives): International Law Association, New Delhi Declaration on the Principles of International Law Related to Sustainable Development (London, 2002; ILA Resolution 2/2002). Boer sets out only three different principles of sustainability (above n 24); cf Marong, 'From Rio to Johannesburg' (n 20) 59–64.

[160] See ch 3(IV)(C).

[161] Bell, McGillivray and Pedersen, *Environmental Law* (n 138) 57.

[162] Sands and Peel, *Principles of International Environmental Law* (n 106) 188.

scholars who caution against a simplistic view of legal transplantation of norms.[163] This discussion is particularly relevant if environmental principles are perceived to derive from international law or otherwise to transfer across jurisdictions. In comparative law scholarship, the 'implementation' of suggested norms, such as environmental principles, which might be transplanted from an external legal environmental into a different legal culture, is recognised as a complex business.[164] Some scholars go so far as to claim that '[a]t best, what can be displaced from one jurisdiction to another is, literally, a meaningless form of words'.[165] This is not overcome by the fact that 'generally speaking, environmental principles are fairly similar around the world as they are responding to the same subject matter'.[166] This is so even where the evolution of environmental principles within a discrete legal system is influenced by external developments, as with environmental principles in NSW law and their evolution in light of international developments involving environmental principles.[167] These principles still need to find their own form and legal meaning within the legal culture of a discrete jurisdiction. The reasoning of judges who have relied on developments concerning environmental principles in other jurisdictions, as noted above,[168] is another potential basis for assuming that environmental principles translate directly across legal systems. Brian Preston, writing extra-judicially, has supported this view:[169]

> The harmonisation of principles [of ecologically sustainable development] between international and national law, and between the laws of different nations, facilitates a judge drawing guidance across borders and jurisdictions and the cross-fertilisation between laws of different nations and jurisdictions.

However, as indicated in the previous sub-section and demonstrated in Chapter Three, the direct vertical or horizontal transplantation of environmental principles as legal concepts between jurisdictions is not readily established. As Preston also recognised, environmental principles are 'domesticated into national laws'.[170] What such transnational legal developments indicate is that there is a need to identify, analyse and explain any legal connections or interactions between jurisdictions in the form of environmental principles, and to understand how these interactions are welcomed, avoided and accommodated within discrete legal systems. The 'extended' comparative analysis of this book, as set out in Chapter One,

---

[163] See ch 1(III)(B).
[164] Otto Kahn-Freund, 'On Uses and Misuses of Comparative Law' (1974) 37 *MLR* 1; Pierre Legrand, 'European Legal Systems are not Converging' (1996) 45 *Int'l & Comp LQ* 52.
[165] Pierre Legrand, 'What "Legal Transplants?"' in D Nelken and J Feest (eds), *Adapting Legal Cultures* (Hart Publishing 2001) 63.
[166] Bosselmann, *Principle of Sustainability* (n 20) 44.
[167] See ch 3(IV).
[168] See nn 142–143 and accompanying text.
[169] Brian Preston, 'Leadership by the Courts in Achieving Sustainability' (2010) 27 *EPLJ* 321, 322.
[170] ibid.

seeks to capture these kinds of developments without assuming any universal and directly translated legal identities for environmental principles at the outset.

## iv. Conclusion

While some scholars and jurists acknowledge the 'wide variations in culture, legal systems, language and levels of development' between different jurisdictions and countries in relation to environmental principles,[171] this has not halted the drive to consider and analyse environmental principles as universal legal concepts that transcend boundaries of legal jurisdiction and context.[172] This has been enhanced by, and responds to, judicial steps to develop reasoning concerning environmental principles, including by borrowing from judgments on similar-sounding principles in other jurisdictions. Much of the literature on environmental principles is grappling with a picture of legal development that is highly variegated and in a state of evolution, but usually still steers towards a core position of commonality for environmental principles. Thus many academic works analyse a selected group of principles that are 'fundamental',[173] 'worth highlighting',[174] or the 'foremost' principles,[175] which have the 'broadest acceptance around the world'.[176] Other works avoid the problem of choosing which general group of environmental principles to study by focusing on a certain principle. Thus there is a huge body of legal scholarship concerning the precautionary principle,[177] and the principle of sustainable development.[178]

However, in much of this work, there lurks a difficult problem of methodology, with scholars 'picking and mixing' across jurisdictions and legal (and non-legal) contexts to analyse their environmental principle(s) of choice and to draw legal conclusions.[179] Even when scholars focus on a group of environmental principles

[171] Carnwath, 'Judicial Protection of the Environment' (n 139) 316. See also Bosselmann, *Principle of Sustainability* (n 20) 43–4; Richard Macrory, Ian Havercroft and Ray Purdy (eds), *Principles of European Environmental Law* (Europa Law Publishing 2004) 8; Doherty, 'Hard Cases' (n 59) 8.

[172] eg Bosselmann, *Principle of Sustainability* (n 20) 44.

[173] Tromans, 'High Talk' (n 32) 780.

[174] Preston, 'Environmental Law 1927–2007' (n 13) 635.

[175] de Sadeleer, *Environmental Principles* (n 35) 2.

[176] Sharon Beder, *Environmental Principles and Policies: An Interdisciplinary Introduction* (Earthscan 2006) 1.

[177] eg Elizabeth Fisher, 'Is the Precautionary Principle Justiciable?' (2001) 13(3) *JEL* 317; Jaye Ellis, 'Overexploitation of a Valuable Resource? New Literature on the Precautionary Principle' (2006) 17 *EJIL* 445; Ilona Cheyne, 'The Precautionary Principle in EC and WTO Law: Searching for a Common Understanding' (2006) 8(4) *Env LR* 257; Rosemary Lyster and Eric Coonan, 'The Precautionary Principle: A Thrill Ride on the Roller Coaster of Energy and Climate Law' (2009) 18(1) *RECIEL* 38.

[178] eg Bosselmann, *Principle of Sustainability* (n 20); Marc Pallemaerts, 'International Environmental Law in the Age of Sustainable Development: A Critical Assessment of the UNCED Process' (1995–6) 15 *JL & Com* 623; J B Ruhl, 'Sustainable Development: A Five-Dimensional Algorithm for Environmental Law' (2009) 18 *Stan Envtl LJ* 31; Andrea Ross, 'Modern Interpretations of Sustainable Development' (2009) 36(1) *JLS* 32.

[179] Fisher, 'Precaution, Precaution Everywhere' (n 89) 7–8, 13–14.

with legal relevance within one particular jurisdiction, as in Australian law or EU law, this often still assumes that environmental principles are broadly universal through loose terminological and derivative associations.[180] As the extended comparative law approach of this book acknowledges, recognising these associations is getting at something important. However, to the extent there are suggested normative associations between certain environmental principles across jurisdictions, these legal interactions do not establish universal legal identities for environmental principles across legal contexts. Rather, they raise complex normative questions about the type of law that environmental principles are generating or constituting.[181]

## B. Application of Legal Concepts and Methodologies from Other Legal Subjects

As set out in Section D(i) of Part II above, legal scholars analysing or prescribing the legal status of environmental principles draw on at least three sets of non-environmental legal jurisprudence and doctrine concerning legal principles to establish whether and how environmental principles are 'legal principles'.[182] These bodies of law are Western legal philosophy, public international law doctrine, and EU law doctrine, with Dworkin's legal philosophy being a dominant frame of reference. In all three areas of law, there is well-established doctrine or long-standing jurisprudence on the nature and role of a 'legal principle'. Environmental law scholars rely on these contexts singly, or in combination, to give environmental principles, and environmental law scholarship concerning them, mainstream legal authority. Whilst these are appealing routes of legal scholarly inquiry, they are also problematic.[183] At the very least, these bodies of legal thought and doctrine must be justified as appropriate frames of legal reference before they are adopted in appraising environmental principles.

With respect to legal philosophical accounts of principles, and particularly Dworkin's account of legal principles, there are at least two incongruous elements of his theoretical approach for analysing environmental principles. First, in contrast to Dworkin's conception of how legal principles develop and operate within a legal system, in environmental law there has been no incremental development of a body of judicial doctrine from which environmental principles might be

---

[180] eg Evans, *Principles of Environmental and Heritage Law* (n 41); Preston, 'Environmental Law 1927–2007' (n 13) 635–637; Doherty, 'Hard Cases' (n 59) 59.

[181] This is acknowledged by de Sadeleer in identifying environmental principles as 'directing principles' that are a new legal category of principles, representing a new type of 'post-modern' law: de Sadeleer, *Environmental Principles* (n 35) 261 and Part II generally.

[182] 'Non-environmental law' contexts mean bodies of law that have developed in their own jurisprudential and doctrinal terms, not being concerned with environment problems in any general way.

[183] Philippopoulos-Mihalopoulos, *Absent Environments* (n 71) 26.

deduced, and there is no single legal system in which environmental principles might best fit and justify the 'institutional history of [its] settled law'.[184] Not only do environmental principles have some legal roles *across* legal systems, so that Dworkin's thesis is an inappropriate frame of reference for environmental principles in general, but environmental principles have not evolved from one body (or many bodies) of judicial reasoning.[185] Moreover, there is no unique and universal set of environmental principles.

Second, a key purpose of Dworkin's rights thesis is to justify judicial reasoning that promotes individual rights and individual justice, particularly through legal principles that encapsulate these moral concepts. This purpose clashes with legal hopes for environmental principles because Dworkin, in formulating his thesis, explicitly excludes from its ambit of his thesis 'policies', which he defines as 'standard[s] that set out a goal to be reached, generally an improvement in some economic, political or social feature of the community'.[186] For Dworkin, policies are not legal norms that should inform judicial reasoning.[187] The problem in applying Dworkin's thesis to environmental principles is obvious—despite their definitional difficulties, environmental principles represent collective goals of environmental protection and sustainable development, and are thus excluded by Dworkin's thesis as being relevant and appropriate legal norms on his model of law. Some environmental scholars acknowledge this difficulty, but construe environmental principles as conferring subjective rights.[188] Others acknowledge the difficulty but seek to justify the legal nature of environmental principles using Dworkin's ideas,[189] or otherwise use them selectively.[190] Gerd Winter is more forthright in acknowledging the constraints of existing philosophical theories. Whilst making a strong case for identifying environmental principles as 'principles' only when they meet the jurisprudential threshold of what constitutes a legal principle, he ultimately distinguishes his position from both Dworkin and Alexy's work, arguing that principles can represent policy positions and are also dynamic 'based on their somewhat elusive status behind the scene'.[191]

---

[184] Hart, *Concept of Law* (n 73) 263 (Hart on Dworkin). See Dworkin, *Taking Rights Seriously* (n 73) generally.

[185] Alternatively, there is no single constitutional document setting out environmental principles as legal norms. Alexy's thesis on principles is thus also marginalised, as it is developed to analyse and prescribe reasoning about rights deriving from a constitutional instrument: Alexy, *Constitutional Rights* (n 73).

[186] Dworkin, *Taking Rights Seriously* (n 73) 22.

[187] Above n 73; *cf* Alexy, for whom principles can be related both to individual rights and to collective interests: Alexy, *Constitutional Rights* (n 73) 65–66.

[188] eg Hilson, 'Rights and Principles in EU Law', who argues that many environmental principles can act as 'principle' as well as 'policy' in Dworkinian terms, depending on the context: above n 107. See also Richard Macrory, 'Principles into Practice' in Richard Macrory, Ian Havercroft and Ray Purdy (eds), *Principles of European Environmental Law* (Europa Law Publishing 2004) 3–4.

[189] Doherty, 'Hard Cases' (n 59).

[190] eg Bosselmann, *Principle of Sustainability* (n 20) 47–48.

[191] Winter, 'Legal Nature of Environmental Principles' (n 75).

Turning to international environmental law doctrines of 'general principles of law', again this framework of analysis is fraught for analysing environmental principles. This problem has been exposed and much debated by international environmental lawyers themselves, as they struggle to apply international environmental law doctrines to determine the normativity of environmental principles.[192] While some jurists simply override the controversy and make bold claims that environment principles are legal principles in international environmental law because it should be so,[193] other scholars develop new kinds of international legal norms to accommodate environmental principles,[194] while others again turn to Dworkin to justify concluding that environmental principles are general principles of international environmental law.[195] Then there are scholars who assert that most environmental principles are *not* general principles of international environmental law, and leave them as soft law concepts of uncertain, albeit important, legal influence.[196]

Finally, the EU law doctrine of 'general principles of law' has also been a tempting source of legal analysis for appraising environmental principles in EU law.[197] In EU law, general principles of law have developed, through judicial reasoning over time, to fill gaps left by successive EU Treaties in interpreting EU law and in testing the legality of EU actions. The most well-known of these principles are those of proportionality, equality and legitimate expectations,[198] and a significant body of doctrine has developed around these and other general principles.[199] The temptation to class and analyse environmental principles as such general principles of EU law has been encouraged by a particularly bold statement by the European Court of First Instance ('CFI') in *Artegodan v Commission*, describing the precautionary principle as an autonomous 'general principle of Community law'.[200] This description might suggest that the precautionary principle is akin to

---

[192]  See ch 3(II)(B).

[193]  *eg Gabčikovo-Nagymaros Project (Hungary v Slovakia)* [1997] ICJ Rep 7, 90 (separate opinion of Weeramantry J).

[194]  See eg above n 63 and accompanying text.

[195]  See above n 106.

[196]  Birnie, Boyle and Redgwell, *International Law* (n 153) 125–7; Palmer, 'New Ways' (n 32) 266–270; Frank Maes, 'Environmental Law Principles, Their Nature and the Law of the Sea: A Challenge for Legislators' in M Sheridan and L Lavrysen (eds), *Environmental Law Principles in Practice* (Bruylant 2002); Kim Boon Foo, 'The Rio Declaration and its Influence on International Environmental Law' [1992] *Sing JLS* 347.

[197]  As indicated in n 107 above, the Charter's 'rights' and 'principles' might also be a source of legal comparison and analysis for environmental principles in EU law, particularly as art 37 of the Charter contains a version of the integration principle and the linked principle of sustainable development, but as yet EU law doctrine concerning the legal status of the Charter principles in EU law is embryonic: see further, ch 4(VI)(B).

[198]  General principles of EU law either embody rule of law values or underlie the constitutional architecture of the EU: Takis Tridimas, *The General Principles of EU Law* (2nd edn, OUP 2006) 4.

[199]  ibid.

[200]  Joined Cases T-74/00, T-76/00, T-83/00 to T-85/00, T-132/00, T-137/00, T-141/00 *Artegodan v Commission* [2002] ECR II-4945 [184].

other general principles of EU law. However, on reading the reasoning in *Arte-godan* closely, the Court's focus is on the *generality* of the principle: the CFI identi-fies a principle that, while articulated only in Article 191 TFEU, is reflected in a range of Treaty provisions requiring a 'high level of protection' beyond the Treaty's title of environmental competence,[201] and so it mandates related policy objectives across the domains of public health, consumer safety and the environment.[202] The Court is identifying a common policy position, and its assertion that it is one of 'law' reflects its mandatory nature, as dictated by the Treaty, rather than its nature as a 'general principle' of EU law in doctrinal terms.[203] *Artegodan* is thus a curious case in which the precautionary principle looks like a legal principle in EU law terms, but in which there is something more doctrinally complicated going on.

Despite this, later EU cases and some scholars have repeated the statement that the precautionary principle, in particular, is a general principle of EU law.[204] Other scholars have been more careful in their appraisal, recognising that more legal evi-dence is required than a statement of the CFI to prove that the precautionary prin-ciple is a general principle of EU law.[205] The methodological danger here is that general principles in EU law doctrine have carefully developed legal identities and functions,[206] and it is a bold and potentially erroneous step to assume that envi-ronmental principles are legally equivalent and thus fulfil exactly the same func-tions in EU law, and that they should be analysed and evaluated in the same way. As explored in Chapter Four, environmental principles in fact play more nuanced roles in EU law than are prescribed by the doctrine concerning general principles of EU law, particularly in relation to the precautionary principle and its role in legality review. Thus, a more careful appraisal of the legal roles of environmental principles in EU law is required.

In light of these methodological constraints, this book examines the legal roles of environmental principles as they currently stand in the case law of the EU and NSW courts, without any theoretical or doctrinal presumptions of how environmental principles should operate in judicial reasoning, or indeed without presuming that environmental principles are 'legal principles' at all. Whether the roles of environmental principles in these two legal settings match a pre-existing

---

[201] In particular, TFEU, arts 114(3), 168(1), 169(1), 191(2) (ex-art 3(p), 152(1), and 153(1), (2) EC, as well as ex-art 174(2) EC).

[202] *Artegodan* (n 200) [182] –[183].

[203] See also Joanne Scott, 'The Precautionary Principle before the European Courts' in Richard Macrory, Ian Havercroft and Ray Purdy (eds), *Principles of European Environmental Law* (Europa Law Publishing 2004) 54.

[204] eg Case T-392/02 *Solvay Pharmaceuticals BV v Council* [2004] ECR II-4555 [121]; Craig, *EU Administrative Law* (n 107) ch 19; Weimer, 'Precaution in EU Authorisation of Genetically Modified Products' (n 107) 630–633.

[205] Scott, 'The Precautionary Principle before the European Courts' (n 203) 53–56; Hilson, 'Rights and Principles in EU Law' (n 107) 11–19.

[206] In particular, general principles act as interpretive aids, grounds for reviewing the legality of EU acts, and give rise to liability claims if breached: Tridimas, *General Principles* (n 198) 29–35.

theoretical or doctrinal framework, or adopt a sui generis legal path, is a matter for subsequent reflection.

## C. An Instrumental and Coherent View of Environmental Law

As indicated in Sections C and D of Part II above, principles proliferate in environmental law scholarship because they might provide legal answers to both environmental problems and legal problems. In the former respect, law is assumed to have an instrumental role in responding to pressing environmental issues. In the latter respect, the legitimacy of environmental law as a subject is at stake. In both senses, assumptions are made about the nature of environmental law as a subject that are contestable.

Instrumental thinking that legal environmental principles can facilitate solutions to environmental problems often fails to acknowledge the 'complexity of the legal institutions, ideas and processes involved', and the complexity of the environmental problems to which these relate, in casting environmental principles as legal tools.[207] Certainly, law has a role in shaping decision-making processes and dispute resolution in relation to environmental issues, with consequential environmental effects. However, law cannot easily act as a form of targeted prescription medicine to cure environmental problems.[208] The chain of causation between legal instruments, frameworks, doctrines, decisions and real-world effects is far from straightforward,[209] as exemplified by the doctrinal development of environmental principles examined in EU and NSW case law in Chapters Four and Five. With respect to environmental principles, in particular, Douglas Fisher suggests that they represent a new form of outcome-oriented law that is 'adapted to the nature of environmental protection'.[210] However, even if outcome-oriented, there is much work to do in understanding the particular legal frameworks in which environmental principles might operate and what legal roles they might play

---

[207] Fisher and others, 'Maturity and Methodology' (n 1) 234.

[208] Environmental systems are notoriously difficult to understand in terms of cause and effect: James Lovelock, *The Vanishing Face of Gaia: A Final Warning* (Penguin 2010). Accordingly, Dovers identifies sustainability as a policy goal beset by enormous challenges, due to its 'problematic spatial and temporal scales', 'irreversibility and urgency', 'connectivity', 'cumulative effects', 'new moral dimensions' and 'sheer novelty', amongst other things, and that desires for 'instant policy gratification' through the Australian ESD process in this instance, including through its 'ESD principles', were unreasonable: Dovers, 'Instituitionalising ESD' (n 63) 23. For strong views that the law should play an instrumental role in relation to environmental problems (and is failing to the extent that environmental problems remain), see Bosselmann (n 20) and Wood (n 15).

[209] Fisher, *Risk Regulation* (n 118) 14–16. See also Gunther Teubner, 'Autopoesis in Law and Society: A Rejoinder to Blankenburg' (1984) 18(2) *Law and Society Review* 291, 298 (the idea of purposive laws embodies a 'primitive' linear causal model of social reality).

[210] D E Fisher, *Australian Environmental Law: Norms, Principles and Rules* (Thomson Reuters 2014) 125 and ch 5 generally.

within them,[211] as well as the complexity of the environmental problems to which they might apply. As set out in Chapter One, judicial decisions are important elements, and reflections, of these frameworks, and their formulation is contingent on the internal legal culture of a particular jurisdiction. As a result, a cloak of legal enforceability is not sufficient to overcome the basic problem of environmental principles being policy goals, that is, they 'tell us little about how to translate the concepts into practical action'.[212]

In relation to scholarly hopes of what environmental principles might do for environmental *law*, particularly that they might rationalise environmental law and give it coherence, Emma Lees deftly points out that these hopes can be compromised by the very fact that environmental principles represent 'short-cuts to justifications for environmental policy'.[213] Furthermore, there is a fundamental conceptual problem with the idea of rationalising environmental law as a legal discipline. While it is important to identify legal connections within the subject, including across jurisdictions, environmental law is a subject that is 'fragmented and sprawling'.[214] It involves a range of legal subjects (public law, criminal law, tort, property law, EU law, public international law, and so on), a range of jurisdictions, and a range of disciplinary lenses for its study (from doctrinal to socio-legal). In light of this incoherent reality, it is the careful methodological treatment of environmental law issues, rather than the taming of environmental law into coherent universal legal submission, that is a priority for environmental law scholarship.[215]

Thus high legal hopes for environment principles, in relation to both environmental and legal problems, do not provide a stable starting point for analysing environmental principles. This book avoids a prescriptive view of the legal roles of environmental principles and examines bodies of law in which they have had an impact. Environmental principles are impactful and highly symbolic concepts in environmental law at a global level and the book's project is to map how they have been crystallising as legal concepts in legal contexts that have embraced them.

# IV. Conclusion

This chapter has set out a range of limitations and cautionary tales in analysing environmental principles. This is not to deny that legal scholarship to date has

---

[211] As Ross carefully examines in the UK context: Ross, *Sustainable Development Law in the UK* (n 58).

[212] Gerry Bates, 'Legal Perspectives' in Stephen Dovers and Su Wild River (eds), *Managing Australia's Environment* (The Federation Press, 2003) 293. See also Dovers, 'Instituitionalising ESD' (n 63) 23.

[213] Lees focuses on the potential role of principles in promoting legal certainty, particularly by assisting the interpretation of environmental offences, and finds them lacking in this task when they are promoted as proxies for environmental outcomes: Lees (n 44) 172–177.

[214] Fisher and others, 'Maturity and Methodology' (n 1) 231.

[215] ibid 220.

been very thoughtful in identifying interesting legal developments in relation to environmental principles across jurisdictions, and also inspiring in setting out where law might go on the basis of environmental principles.[216] However, the corpus of scholarly work on environmental principles has created a body of legal scholarship, around environmental principles generally and around selected principles, which has taken on a momentum of its own and promoted the legal study of environmental principles as the study of universal legal concepts. Accordingly, much literature has tended to overlook legal culture and context, to borrow uncomfortable legal methodologies and concepts, and to be hopeful as to the instrumental role of environmental principles without close legal analysis. These tendencies all limit how legal analysis of environmental principles might develop. At worst, these limitations misrepresent the nature of environmental principles and the environmental law of which they form part.

The purpose of this chapter's exercise has been to understand the state of legal scholarship on environmental principles and the powerful significance of environmental principles in environmental law as a subject. This understanding has two implications. First, critical reflection on methodology is now required. This was the motivation for the detailed examination of this book's methodology in Chapter One, indicating that an important step in developing legal knowledge about environmental principles is now to analyse the legal evolution of environmental principles in light of concrete legal frameworks and developments, and in a manner that is sensitive to legal culture. Environmental principles have been theorised and prescribed sufficiently.

Second, to the extent that environmental principles are adopted in (often universal) legal terms to justify environmental law as a discipline, an empirical reality check that environmental principles operate differently within different legal systems, as undertaken in Chapters Four and Five, does not imply that environmental law lacks legitimacy. Rather, it demonstrates that doctrinal and legal pluralism is inherent in environmental law that crosses jurisdictional boundaries, and that this reality must be factored into methodologies for examining new legal phenomena such as environmental principles. Legitimacy of scholarship comes from methodological rigour, rather than from environmental principles constituting mirrors of existing bodies of law, short-cuts to methodological complexity, instrumental solutions to environmental problems, or revolutionising existing legal structures to reflect an alternate, environmentally-friendly worldview. Environmental principles are a significant methodological challenge for environmental law, but one that is inevitable in a subject of such complex dimensions. More than that, the study of environmental principles is a vital concern for a subject that is ever evolving and intersecting with urgent socio-political and scientific problems across legal boundaries and cultures.

---

[216] eg Tarlock, 'Is There a There There' (n 72); Bosselmann, *Principle of Sustainability* (n 20); Flournoy and Driesen, *Beyond Environmental Law* (n 135).

# 3

# Legal Contours of Environmental Principles Across Jurisdictions

## I. Introduction

Chapters One and Two outlined the growing legal significance of environmental principles in environmental law and made a case for analysing the legal roles of environmental principles by mapping their legal evolution within discrete legal cultures. Contextual analysis is important for novel legal concepts in environmental law, in light of the methodological challenges involved in studying the subject. It is particularly important in studying environmental principles because there is no long-standing legal history or authoritative legal doctrine relating to them, and they have no clear conceptual identity as 'principles' or definitions in the abstract, despite the fact that they are described in often universal and ambitious legal terms in environmental law scholarship. Legally, environmental principles fall within a 'category of concealed multiple reference',[1] so that something more is required to determine their precise legal meaning and application. That 'something more' is increasingly discernable in different legal systems as environmental principles develop more identifiable legal roles. This can be seen to some degree in public international law—often said to be the source of their universal identity—but is occurring more concretely in at least the two jurisdictions mapped in Chapters Four and Five, EU law and New South Wales law. These different jurisdictions show different ways in which environmental principles are forming legal identities transnationally, within and across levels of governance.

This chapter identifies the groups of environmental principles that have been developing legal roles in each of these three jurisdictions and examines how those roles have evolved, and are continuing to evolve, within these different legal cultures. The chapter takes the term 'environmental principle' at its broadest construction, reflecting the loose terminological and jurisdictional references to such principles that pervade the literature. There are many so-called environmental principles that have a presence in various jurisdictions internationally—from the precautionary principle, the preventive principle and the polluter pays principle, to the principle of intergenerational equity, the principle of integration, and the

---

[1] Julius Stone, *Legal System and Lawyers' Reasonings* (Stanford University Press 1964) 246.

broad principle of sustainable development.[2] The chapter demonstrates that the precise formulations of such principles are inconsistent, their meanings and legal status are unclear or contested, and the groupings of environmental principles vary both within and across the different jurisdictions analysed. This is not to say that environmental principles are not useful and influential concepts in environmental law.[3] Rather, the chapter shows that their usefulness and influence is developing differently across jurisdictions.

This variance is due to the fact that environmental principles are shaped by—and are expressions of—the very different legal cultures in which they have roles. Their particular legal roles depend on the legal, institutional and political peculiarities of each jurisdiction, as well as the evolution of certain environmental principles within each body of law over time. Such evolution is sometimes responsive to legal developments in other jurisdictions, whether at the international, regional or national level, and this chapter examines such interactions when they arise. Overall, it concludes that there is no direct transplantation of a neatly defined set of environmental principles across jurisdictions or automatic transmission of such principles from international law into regional and domestic legal systems. Rather, there is a plurality of contexts in which various environmental principles have been evolving in idiosyncratic and non-linear ways, partly in response to, or alongside, developments in other jurisdictions.

To build this picture of varying environmental principles within different legal cultures, Part II first outlines environmental principles in public international law, examining their grouping, meanings, legal status and evolution within that legal setting, from which 'global' environmental principles are often assumed to proliferate universally. Even within this context, environmental principles have contested meanings and are difficult to isolate as a group. Rather than environmental principles cascading down to domestic legal systems as fully formed concepts from public international law, the normative and definitional ambiguity that characterises environmental principles at the international level might be understood at most as an encouragement and invitation for more concrete legal developments to occur within domestic and regional legal systems. Parts III and IV explore this idea by examining the legal development of environmental principles in EU and NSW law respectively, outlining the different groups of environmental principles that are legally relevant in each jurisdiction, as well as the varying legal frameworks, historical factors and institutional structures that have shaped (and in the case of the courts as legal institutions, have been shaped by)[4] their development. Demonstrating these factors is a relatively lengthy exercise, particularly in NSW law, due to the unique and often convoluted circumstances that have led to the legal development of environmental principles in these different jurisdictions. This detailed background is set out both to test the extent of derivative connections

---

[2] The list could go on: see ch 1, nn 17–18 and accompanying text.
[3] As demonstrated in chs 4 and 5.
[4] Particularly in the case of the NSWLEC: see ch 5.

between environmental principles across these jurisdictional contexts and also to draw the foundational contours for the comparative mapping exercise in Chapters Four and Five. The analysis of this chapter is the first step in determining the legal roles played by environmental principles in EU and NSW case law. The judicial treatment of environmental principles in these two bodies of law can only be understood in light of their historical legal development and the idiosyncratic legal frameworks in each legal culture.

# II. Environmental Principles in Public International Law

Common to many environmental principles is their explicit articulation in a number of key United Nations-sponsored international treaties and declarations and in other international instruments and reports on environmental protection and sustainable development. Such international representation of environmental principles is the main driver of scholarly and judicial assumptions that universal concepts of environmental principles exist in environmental law.[5] This Part examines the legal evolution of environmental principles in public international law in order to examine their groupings, meanings and legal status in this legal setting. It highlights how environmental principles have become prominent concepts in public international law, but also how they are ambiguous, contested or evolving as legal ideas. Whilst this complicates any suggestion that environmental principles are legal concepts that translate from international law directly into regional and national legal systems, it also suggests that there is an interesting, albeit dynamic, story of normative development relating to environmental principles in international law. Fundamentally, environmental principles are deeply malleable concepts in legal terms, including in international law.

## A. The Legal Prominence of Environmental Principles in International Law

Environmental principles have increasingly appeared in various ways in public international law. There is no single binding treaty that sets out requirements or principles of general application in relation to environmental matters, and

> any effort to identify general principles ... of international environmental law must necessarily be based on a considered assessment of state practice, including the adoption and

---

[5] eg Lee Godden and Jacqueline Peel, *Environmental Law: Scientific, Policy and Regulatory Dimensions* (OUP 2010) 239–244; Piet Gilhuis, 'The Consequences of Introducing Environmental Law Principles in National Law' in M Sheridan and L Lavrysen (eds), *Environmental Law Principles in Practice* (Bruylant 2002); Ben Boer, 'Institutionalising Ecologically Sustainably Development: The Roles of National, State, and Local Governments in Translating Grand Strategy into Action' (1995)

implementation of treaties and other international legal acts, as well as … the decisions of international courts and tribunals.[6]

Whilst there is a growing number of treaties as well as some international judicial decisions that explicitly refer to environmental principles, the discourse concerning environmental principles in international law centres on principles that are primarily articulated in soft law instruments. This section considers this international law landscape and highlights the features that make certain international instruments oft-cited sources of environmental principles.

In terms of treaties, there are now many international agreements that commit parties to respecting or applying principles in relation to discrete environmental issues. Commentators have noted that some states prefer 'vague' principles to be included in multilateral agreements for reasons of political expediency,[7] highlighting one reason for the proliferation of environmental principles in international environmental policy generally.[8] Within treaties, environmental principles can appear in myriad ways. Thus, for example, the principle of sustainable development appears in at least the following forms: in the preambles to the WTO Agreement and North American Free Trade Agreement as an overarching objective;[9] in specific provisions of the United Nations Framework Convention on Climate Change as a principle that parties 'have a right to, and should, promote';[10] in the 2015 Paris Agreement on climate change as a contextual factor that qualifies many key provisions;[11] and in other agreements using different formulations of words.[12] In relation to the precautionary principle, Jonathan Wiener notes that there are over 50 international agreements that adopt or rely on some form of the principle, along with 'even earlier international environmental treaties that employed the logic, if not the terminology, of precaution'.[13] Other principles also appear in multilateral

---

31 *Willamette L Rev* 307; Susan Smith, 'Ecologically Sustainable Development: Integrating Economic, Ecology, and Law' (1995) 31 *Willamette L Rev* 261; Brian Preston, 'Leadership by the Courts in Achieving Sustainability' (2010) 27 *EPLJ* 321.

[6] Philippe Sands and Jacqueline Peel, *Principles of International Environmental Law* (3rd edn, CUP 2012) 190.

[7] Ulrich Beyerlin, 'Different Types of Norms in International Environmental Law: Policies, Principles and Rules' in D Bodansky, J Brunee and E Hey (eds), *The Oxford Handbook of International Environmental Law* (OUP 2007) 427; cf Sands and Peel, *Principles of International Environmental Law* (n 6) 189–190.

[8] See ch 2(II)(B).

[9] Marrakesh Agreement Establishing the World Trade Organisation (adopted 15 April 1994, entered into force 1 January 1995) (1994) 33 ILM 15; North American Free Trade Agreement (adopted 1 January 1994, entered into force 1 January 1994) (1994) 32 ILM 612.

[10] United Nations Framework Convention on Climate Change (adopted 9 May 1992, entered into force 21 March 1994) (1992) 31 ILM 851 ('UNFCCC') art 3.

[11] United Nations Paris Agreement, UN Doc FCCC/CP/2015/10/Add.1, arts 2(1), 4(1), 6(8).

[12] eg Sands and Peel, *Principles of International Environmental Law* (n 6) 206–7.

[13] Jonathan B Weiner, 'Precaution' in D Bodansky, J Brunee and E Hey (eds), *The Oxford Handbook of International Environmental Law* (OUP 2007) 601. See eg Montreal Protocol on Substances that Deplete the Ozone Layer (adopted 16/9/1987, entered into force 1/1/1989) (1987) 26 ILM 1541 [6]; UNFCCC (n 10) art 3(3); Cartagena Protocol on Biosafety (adopted 29/1/2000, entered into force 11/9/2003) (2000) 39 ILM 1027 ('Cartagena Protocol') art 10(6).

instruments in varying and ad hoc ways.[14] In addition, some treaties, such as the Convention on Biological Diversity, represent in their entirety an application of an environmental principle (the principle of 'conservation of biological diversity').[15] Overall, it is not possible to isolate a definitive 'group' of environmental principles from instruments of binding treaty law, since they are isolated in issue-specific agreements, and even then not always explicitly framed as principles, often for reasons to minimise direct legal impact or enforceability.[16] At the same time, compromise in international agreements to agree on principles rather than rules 'facilitates the dynamic development of modern international environmental law'.[17]

Environmental principles have a higher profile as a group or collection of norms in international soft law instruments. International soft law has become an increasingly important and contested aspect of public international law.[18] Dinah Shelton identifies various reasons for the developing prominence of soft law, including bureaucratisation of international institutions that generate programmes of action and other policy instruments; unwillingness of states to commit to hard law; and the 'growing strength and maturity of the international system' so that some relations between states can be governed by etiquette, discourse or informal commitments rather than 'law'.[19] These reasons help to explain the development of various instruments containing environmental principles. Such instruments began with the Stockholm Declaration on the Human Environment in 1972 and include: the 1987 Brundtland Report; the 1992 Rio Declaration on Environment and Development; the Johannesburg Declaration on Sustainable Development in 2002; 'The Future We Want' Outcome Document agreed at the Rio+20 conference on sustainable development in 2012; and 'Transforming Our World: the 2030 Agenda for Sustainable Development' declaring new 'sustainable development goals' in 2015.[20] All these instruments contain commitments by signatory states to

---

[14] See Sands and Peel, *Principles of International Environmental Law* (n 6) ch 6 and Beyerlin, 'Policies, Principles and Rules' (n 7).

[15] Convention on Biological Diversity (adopted 5/6/1992, entered into force 29/12/1993) (1992) 31 ILM 818; *cf* other legal instruments in which the 'principle' of conserving biological diversity is listed as a discrete principle: World Commission on Environment and Development, 'Report of the World Commission on Environment and Development: Our Common Future' (20 March 1987) UN Doc A/42/427 ('Brundtland Report') annexe 1, principle 3; Protection of the Environment Administration Act 1991 (NSW) s 6(2)(c).

[16] Commitments are to 'precautionary measures', a 'precautionary approach', or a detailed formulation of the principle, as in Cartagena Protocol (n 13) art 10(6). See Weiner, 'Precaution' (n 13) 601.

[17] Beyerlin, 'Policies, Principles and Rules' (n 7) 427–8.

[18] See generally Dinah Shelton (ed), *Commitment and Compliance: The Role of Non-binding Norms in the International Legal System* (OUP 2000).

[19] Dinah Shelton, 'Law, Non-Law and the Problem of "Soft Law"' in Dinah Shelton (ed), *Commitment and Compliance: The Role of Non-Binding Norms in the International Legal System* (OUP 2000) 12.

[20] United Nations Environment Programme, 'Declaration of the United Nations Conference on the Human Environment' (16 June 1972) UN Doc A/CONF.48/14, 11 ILM 1461 (1972) ('Stockholm Declaration'); Brundtland Report (n 15); United Nations Conference on Environment and Development, 'Rio Declaration on Environment and Development' (14 June 1992) UN Doc A/CONF.151/26 (Vol. I), 31 ILM 874 (1992) ('Rio Declaration'); World Summit on Sustainable Development, 'Johannesburg Declaration on Sustainable Development' (4 September 2002) UN Doc A/CONF.199/20

implement agreed environmental 'principles', which, from the Brundtland Report onwards, are focused on the achievement of 'sustainable development'. The environmental principles in the Rio Declaration ('Rio principles') now have the highest profile in environmental law. They include 27 principles of varying types and formulations, including: versions of the integration principle, precautionary principle and polluter pays principle (principles 4, 15 and 16), as well as more general aspirations, such as commitments to cooperate to eradicate poverty and to eliminate unsustainable patterns of production and consumption (principles 5 and 8). These self-described principles represent a watershed moment for the (ongoing) international sustainable development agenda, particularly in terms of the international consensus that supported them. Commitment to the Rio principles has been reasserted in each of the subsequent sustainable development instruments listed above.

At the same time, the Rio Declaration, and its follow up UN-sponsored instruments, represent failures to agree formal treaties with binding legal commitments relating to sustainable development in international law terms.[21] This has led both to normative uncertainty for the Rio principles (discussed in the following section) and to further efforts to agree action, and more principles, in relation to sustainable development or sustainability. Most notably, the Earth Charter was agreed between thousands of civil society groups between 1992 and 2000[22]—this has no formal legal status in international law, particularly as it is not an agreement between nation states, but it was eventually launched at a UN-sponsored forum,[23] and has been endorsed by UNESCO, the IUCN (International Union for the Conservation of Nature) and a number of states.[24] This agreement is a bold and wide-ranging document, and it sets out aspirational 'interdependent' principles for a sustainable way of life.[25] These principles include versions of environmental principles in the soft law instruments above, but also a range of other principles dealing with global economic and social challenges, and they represent the frustration of civil society groups and NGOs that international institutions

---

('Johannesburg Declaration'); UN Conference on Sustainable Development, 'The Future We Want—Outcome Document' (27 July 2012) A/RES/66/288 [15]; UN Summit for the Adoption of the Post-2015 Development Agenda, 'Transforming our World: the 2030 Agenda for Sustainable Development' (25 September 2015) A/RES/70/1 (although this agreement focused on establishing sustainable development 'goals'). Note also the concept of 'sustainable development' first originated in International Union for the Conservation of Nature and Natural Resources, *World Conservation Strategy: Living Resource Conservation for Sustainable Development* (IUCN 1980). Other soft law instruments containing environmental principles are discussed in Brian Preston, 'The Role of the Judiciary in Promoting Sustainable Development: The Experience of Asia and the Pacific' (2005) 9(2) *Asia Pac J Envtl L* 109, 114–127.

[21] The Brundtland Report had called for a charter to 'prescribe new norms for … state behaviour to maintain livelihoods and life on a shared planet': Brundtland Report (n 15) 332.

[22] Klaus Bosselmann, *The Principle of Sustainability: Transforming Law and Governance* (Ashgate 2008) 2, 35–37.

[23] Earth Charter Commission, 'Earth Charter', The Hague, Netherlands, 2000 ('Earth Charter').

[24] Bosselmann, *The Principle of Sustainability* (n 22) 2.

[25] ibid (arguing that the Charter has 'brought the concept of sustainable development back to its original meaning').

and states have been unable to agree a binding and radical agenda of sustainability. Another consequence of the non-binding legal status of the Rio Declaration was its subsequent endorsement by UN General Assembly resolutions,[26] including Resolution 48/190 that urges all governments to promote widespread dissemination of the Declaration and requires UN organs and bodies to incorporate the Rio principles into their programmes and processes.[27] Thus the Rio principles have led to a range of outcomes and legal effects in international law, albeit in an atypical and pragmatic fashion.

In addition to these UN-sponsored agreements, other prominent international organisations and groups have endorsed various environmental principles, further building and complicating the 'soft law' landscape involving environmental principles in international law. In the 1970s, the Organisation for Economic Cooperation and Development ('OECD') developed recommendations of principles for international environmental policy.[28] In particular, the OECD is considered to have developed the polluter pays principle.[29] There have also been judicial initiatives to collaborate internationally in the development of legal principles designed to promote environmental protection and sustainable development as core aspects of legal systems and judicial reasoning. Two UNEP-sponsored initiatives are of particular note—the *Johannesburg Principles on the Role of Law and Sustainable Development* (developed alongside the Johannesburg Declaration mentioned above),[30] and the *Judicial Handbook on Environmental Law*, developed in 2005 by a group of environmental judges from across the world. The latter aims to 'identify a common core of law and policy most relevant to the world's judiciary',[31] in light of the fact that

> [previous] decades of legal developments have led to the emergence of basic principles of environmental protection that are recognized in international and national law, which have in turn informed the development of environmental law by giving meaning to concepts not yet contained in formal legal instruments.[32]

The principles examined in the Handbook are the principles of prevention, precaution, polluter pays and environmental justice and equity. Other prominent groups of international lawyers and jurists have sought to distil the core set of

---

[26] UNGA Resolution, 'Report of the United Nations Conference on Environment and Development' (22 December 1992) UN Doc A/RES/47/190 (endorsing the Rio Declaration and accompanying documents).

[27] UNGA Resolution, 'Dissemination of the Principles of the Rio Declaration on Environment and Development' (21 December 1993) UN Doc A/RES/48/190.

[28] 1972 Council Recommendation on Guiding Principles concerning International Aspects of Environmental Policies, OECD, C(72) 128 final.

[29] ibid; 1974 Council Recommendation on the Implementation of the Polluter Pays Principle, OECD, C(74) 223 final.

[30] In particular, UNEP, 'Johannesburg Principles on the Role of Law and Sustainable Development', Global Judges Symposium, Johannesburg, South Africa, 18–20 August 2002 ('Johannesburg Principles').

[31] UNEP, *Judicial Handbook on Environmental Law* (UNEP 2005), introduction by Klaus Toepfer, iv.

[32] ibid 19.

environmental principles in international law. Thus an expert group of the UN Commission of Sustainable Development prepared a report identifying principles of international law for sustainable development in 1995;[33] an UNEP expert group undertook to catalogue concepts and principles that are the 'core elements' of international environmental law in 1996;[34] and in 2002 the International Law Association developed a 'New Delhi Declaration of Principles of International Law Relating to Sustainable Development'.[35] These expert reports list varying and overlapping groups of principles, organising them differently and noting that various principles are of uncertain legal status. These efforts highlight both a strong appetite for such principles in international law,[36] and the lawyerly need to corral and organise them as a group.

While these various international instruments and declarations are best described as 'soft law' in an international law sense,[37] they contain a wide range of policy ideas, agendas and normative ambitions. They also have certain characteristics that make them oft-cited sources of environmental principles in environmental law. First, quite simply, they set out *lists of principles* that represent, or seek to codify, the common conviction of states to implement sustainable development globally.[38] 'Principles' are employed as thematic shorthand to represent and guide policy on environmental management and sustainable development.[39] In the case of Annexe 1 to the Brundtland Report, the listed principles for environmental protection and sustainable development are explicitly articulated as being 'legal principles'. This legalising trend is confirmed by the efforts of UNEP judicial and expert groups, including the International Law Association, to identify the key

---

[33] UN Commission on Sustainable Development, *Report of the Expert Meeting on Identification of Principles of International Law for Sustainable Development* (26-28 September 1995) available at <http://www.un.org/documents/ecosoc/cn17/1996/background/ecn171996-bp3.htm> (accessed 5 August 2016).

[34] *Final Report of the Expert Group Workshop on International Environmental Law Aiming at Sustainable Development* (4 October 1996) UN Doc UNEP/IEL/WS/3/2.

[35] Committee on Legal Aspects of Sustainable Development, International Law Association, *Searching for the Contours of International Law in the Field of Sustainable Development: Final Conference Report 7* (New Delhi, April 2002).

[36] The UNEP Governing Council, in commissioning the work of the UNEP expert group, expressed its belief that 'further innovative approaches were required in the field of the progressive development and codification of international environmental law in order to achieve sustainable development': UNEP Governing Council, *Mid-term Report on Implementation of the Programme for the Development and Periodic Review of Environmental Law for the 1990s* (27 March 1997) UN Doc A/S-19/5/Add.1.

[37] See Christine Chinkin, 'The Challenge of Soft Law: Development and Change in International Law' (1989) 38 *Intl & Comp LQ* 850; Geoffrey Palmer, 'New Ways to Make International Environmental Law' (1992) 86(2) *AJIL* 259, 269–270.

[38] Or, subsequent to the Rio Declaration, a commitment to the previous Rio principles: Johannesburg Declaration (n 20); Johannesburg Principles (n 30). The Johannesburg Declaration also manifests its commitment to the Rio principles through a detailed plan for their implementation: WSSD, 'Plan of Implementation of the World Summit on Sustainable Development' (4 September 2002) UN Doc A/CONF.199/20; *cf* Earth Charter (n 23), which does not represent an agreement between states, but indicates the prevalence of 'principles' in international policy discussion on environmental matters.

[39] Often for reasons of political pragmatism: see ch 2(II)(B).

legal principles relevant to sustainable development, established by and since the Rio Declaration.[40]

The second characteristic of these international instruments that makes them attractive sources of principles in environmental law is the *international consensus or authority* they represent. Although these are soft law instruments that do not (yet) slot into orthodox paths for applying international law within national legal systems, they represent commitments by a sizeable section of the international community to achieve agreed goals expressed in the form of principles, or declarations of such commitments by authoritative organisations or groups.[41] This suggests that these principles have some legal force even though they fundamentally express policy ideas and have not been agreed in formal treaty law. It also suggests they have universal meanings and impact, and that they are to be followed and applied internationally.[42] Accordingly, scholars claim that such principles do, or should, 'trickle' or 'cascade' down from the international sphere to action, including legal developments, within regional, national and local spheres.[43] This position is encouraged by UN Resolution 48/190.[44] In this way, Mary Pat Williams Silveira asserts that the Rio Declaration and its accompanying *Agenda 21*[45] are:[46]

> … [the] fundamental legal instruments for sustainable development… that attempt to address the full range of legal principles and political objectives, *at international, regional, and national levels* to reach sustainable development.

Similarly, James Cameron et al have reviewed the implementation of a selection of environmental principles that have 'emerged in the main text of international conventions', looking at legal and policy developments in a range of jurisdictions.[47] Drawing on international soft law instruments as a starting point in this way is

---

[40] See ch 2, n 159.

[41] Palmer, 'New Ways' (n 37) 266–269; Frank Maes, 'Environmental Law Principles, Their Nature and the Law of the Sea: A Challenge for Legislators' in M Sheridan and L Lavrysen (eds), *Environmental Law Principles in Practice* (Bruylant 2002) 73. National and regional governments agree: Ecologically Sustainable Development Steering Committee, 'National Strategy for Ecologically Sustainable Development' (Australian Government Publication Services 1992) ('NSESD') 15; Council of the European Union, Brussels European Council 16/17 June 2005, Presidency Conclusions, 10255/1/05 Rev 1, 2.

[42] Daniel Bodansky, 'Customary (and Not So Customary) International Environmental Law' (1995) 3 *Ind J Global Legal Stud* 105.

[43] eg Maurice Evans, *Principles of Environmental and Heritage Law* (Prospect Media 2000) ch 5 (particularly 138–141); Paul Stein and Susan Mahoney, 'Incorporating Sustainability Principles into Legislation' in Paul Leadbeter, Neil Gunningham and Ben Boer (eds) *Environmental Outlook No 3: Law and Policy* (Federation Press 1999); see above n 5.

[44] See above n 27.

[45] *Agenda 21* accompanied the *Rio Declaration*. While not legally binding, it is a guide to governments in implementing the decisions made at the Rio Conference up until 2000: UNCED, *Agenda 21* (1993) UN Doc A/CONF.151/PC/100/Add.1 ('*Agenda 21*').

[46] Mary Pat Williams Silveira, 'International Legal Instruments and Sustainable Development: Principles, Requirements, and Restructuring' (1995) 31 *Willamette L Rev* 239 241 (emphasis added). See also Alhaji BM Marong, 'From Rio to Johannesburg: Reflections on the Role of International Legal Norms in Sustainable Development' (2003–4) 16 *Geo Int'l Envtl L Rev* 21 56–7.

[47] James Cameron, Paula M Pevato and Juli Abouchar, 'International Implementation of the Principles' (1994) Fenner Conference on the Environment—Sustainability: Principles to Practice (Department of Environment, Sport and Territories, Australian Commonwealth Government).

how many legal scholars approach analysis of environmental principles. Ben Boer explains this in terms of the 'globalisation' and 'internationalisation' of environmental law, with common approaches and principles developed and transferred from one international convention to the next and being absorbed into national law.[48]

The judicial authority of both the Johannesburg Principles and UNEP Judicial Handbook supports this approach. The latter contain a commitment to adhere to the Rio principles through their national 'judicial mandates to implement, develop and enforce the law'.[49] This judicial inclination is seen in national cases that approve scholarly comments on the universal impact of environmental principles in international soft law instruments,[50] or where judicial reasoning in national decisions refers directly to principles in international instruments as a source of legal influence.[51] In these cases, internationally agreed principles are certainly catalysing legal developments within particular jurisdictions. Extra-judicial speeches by prominent environmental judges also reinforce the authority of the idea that environmental principles, or principles of 'ecologically sustainable development',[52] underpin a 'global environmental law' or 'common laws of the environment',[53] and derive from international soft law agreements.

The final characteristic that makes soft law instruments containing environmental principles appealing foundations for asserting the fundamental, global legal importance of environmental principles are the perceived *ethical values they reflect*. Environmental law internationally is thought so far to have failed in its project by those who have a purposive or instrumental view of environmental law.[54] Environmental degradation, climate change and environmental harms proliferate globally and the development of environmental law across Western and other legal systems in the second half of the twentieth century has not halted this. Thus an ambitious reorienting of the subject through underlying norms, such as the principle of sustainability or principle of intergenerational equity, is immensely appealing for some scholars, particularly in light of the ethical case underlying these principles.[55] The Earth Charter is particularly significant in this respect in its call for a 'new ethic' based on 'respect for nature'.[56] Whilst such arguments have a

---

[48] Ben Boer, 'The Rise of Environmental Law in the Asian Region' (1999) 32 *U Rich L Rev* 1503, 1508–9.

[49] Johannesburg Principles (n 30) principle 1.

[50] eg *114957 Canada Ltee v Hudson (Town)* [2001] 2 SCR 241 [32].

[51] eg *Vellore Citizens' Welfare Forum v Union of India* AIR 1996 SC 2715 [11]; *Northcompass Inc v Hornsby Shire Council* [1996] NSWLEC 213; (1996) 130 LGERA 248; *BGP Properties v Lake Macquarie CC* [2004] NSWLEC 399; (2004) 138 LGERA 237 [90]–[91].

[52] Preston, 'Leadership by the Courts' (n 5).

[53] Robert Carnwath, 'Environmental Law in a Global Society' (2015) 3 *JPEL* 269; Lord Carnwath, 'Judges and the Common Laws of the Environment—At Home and Abroad' (2014) 26(2) *JEL* 177.

[54] eg Mary Christina Wood, *Nature's Trust: Environmental Law for the New Ecological Age* (CUP 2014).

[55] eg Bosselmann, *Principle of Sustainability* (n 22) ch 2 (arguing in particular that morality is of foundational and increasing importance to international environmental law).

[56] See further ibid, 37 and ch 1 generally.

carefully considered intellectual basis, they also call for closer scrutiny as matters of philosophical argument.[57]

## B. The Legal Ambiguity of Environmental Principles in International Law

Despite these suggested normative foundations for environmental principles in public international law, there is in fact (as yet) no definitive group of environmental principles derived from international law, which might translate directly into regional and national legal systems, and provide a universally coherent group of environmental principles for legal study. Rather, the group of identifiable international environmental law principles is legally ambiguous and inconsistent. This is unsurprising considering that these principles are often the result of political compromise, and is reinforced by scholarly choices to focus analysis on some principles in these instruments—as key 'environmental principles'—more than others.[58] There are four reasons why environmental principles are legally ambiguous in international environmental law: (1) they are contained in instruments of soft law and so have uncertain normative status; (2) they represent between them very different kinds of ideas about environmental protection; (3) their meanings are unclear or contested; and (4) they constitute a shifting but usually select group of principles out of all 'principles' so-called in these instruments.

First, environmental principles in international law are of ambiguous normative status in international law. This has led some scholars to suggest that they are in a state of legal evolution,[59] or that they represent a modern and different form of international law.[60] Other scholars and jurists disagree over whether relevant

---

[57] For example, Christopher Stone argues that the discourse of sustainable development raises two ethical claims (welfare-transfer constraint and preservationist) but these need to be more carefully distinguished in international environmental law: Christopher D Stone, 'Ethics and International Environmental Law' in Daniel Bodansky et al, *Handbook on International Environmental Law* (OUP 2007).

[58] To confuse matters further, international environmental law scholars group 'environmental principles' in various ways. Thus some group established principles of international environmental law, such as the principle of co-operation and the duty not to cause transboundary damage, along with principles such as the polluter pays principle, precautionary principle and principle of preventive action. The latter represent, at least terminologically, those environmental principles discussed more generally in environmental law scholarship and have a more contested normative status in international law (see nn 59–63 and accompanying text). See eg Sands and Peel, *Principles of International Law* (n 6) ch 6; Patricia Birnie, Alan Boyle and Catherine Redgwell, *International Law & the Environment* (3rd edn, OUP 2009) 106–204; Ellen Hey, *Advanced Introduction to International Environmental Law* (Edward Elgar 2016) 52–86; David M Ong, 'From "International" to "Transnational" Environmental Law? A Legal Assessment of the Contribution of "Equator Principles" to International Environmental Law' (2010) 79 *Nordic Journal of International Law* 35.

[59] Palmer, 'New Ways' (n 37) 269–270; Luis E Rodriguez-Rivera, 'Is the Human Right to Environment Recognised Under International Law? It Depends on the Source' (2001) 12(1) *Colo J Intl Envtl L & Poly* 1, 41–44; Maes, 'Law of the Sea' (n 41) 60–73.

[60] Chinkin, 'The Challenge of Soft Law' (n 37) 866; Bodansky, 'Customary (and Not So Customary) International Environmental Law' (n 42); Winfried Lang, 'UN Principles and International

principles (particularly the precautionary principle and principle of sustainable development) constitute 'general principles' of customary international law,[61] or focus on whether they can translate into more specific rights and duties on states.[62] Ulrich Beyerlin usefully characterises environmental principles as 'twilight norms' of public international law, which are at the 'bottom of the normative hierarchy of modern international environmental law' and reflect patterns of 'relative normativity' in this legal field.[63] To reach this conclusion, Beyerlin undertakes a close analytical exercise, relying on Dworkin's distinction between policies, principles and rules, in order to determine the precise legal status of different environmental principles in international law (coming up with varying conclusions for different principles). Taking a different approach, Alhaji Marong avoids a positivist analysis altogether and finds the distinction between legal and non-legal norms to be 'largely rhetorical' in relation to environmental principles. For Marong, in relation to sustainable development in particular, the usefulness of the concept lies not in its status as a rule of customary international law but as a 'social objective towards the realisation of which law has an important role to play'.[64] Whilst such blurring of law and non-law is normatively controversial in public international law,[65] it is less so for scholars of transnational law.[66]

Second, environmental principles in international law represent a wide range of ideas about environmental protection and sustainability. Some principles represent economic ideas,[67] some procedural ideas,[68] some involve scientific issues,[69] and some are more overarching, such as sustainable development. In fact, different environmental principles reflect different approaches to environmental protection

---

Environmental Law' (1999) 3 *Max Planck Yrbk UN L* 171, 157–72; Vaughan Lowe, 'Sustainable Development and Unsustainable Arguments' in A Boyle and D Freestone (eds), *International Law and Sustainable Development: Past Achievements and Future Challenges* (OUP 1999); Ulrich Beyerlin, 'Different Types of Norms in International Environmental Law: Policies, Principles and Rules' in Daniel Bodansky, Jutta Brunée and Ellen Hey (eds), *The Oxford Handbook of International Environmental Law* (OUP 2007).

[61] In relation to sustainable development: *Vellore* (n 51) [10]; *Gabčikovo-Nagymaros Project (Hungary v Slovakia)* [1997] ICJ Rep 7, 90 (separate opinion of Weeramantry J); Dire Tladi, *Sustainable Development in International Law* (Pretoria University Press 2007) 112; Bosselmann, *Principle of Sustainability* (n 22) 57; cf *Gabčikovo-Nagymaros Project*, 78 (majority opinion); Marong, 'From Rio to Johannesburg' (n 46) 48–49. In relation to the precautionary principle, see Owen McIntyre and Tom Mosedale, 'The Precautionary Principle as a Norm of Customary International Law' (1997) 9 *JEL* 221; Sands and Peel, *Principles of International Law* (n 6) 217–228; cf Birnie, Boyle and Redgwell, *International Law* (n 58) 159–162; Ole Pedersen, 'From Abundance to Indeterminacy: The Precautionary Principle and its Two Camps of Custom' (2014) 3(2) *TEL* 323.

[62] Ong, 'From "International" to "Transnational" Environmental Law?' (n 58) 51–52.

[63] Beyerlin, 'Policies, Principles and Rules' (n 7) 426 (citing Prosper Weil, 'Towards Relative Normativity in International Law?' (1983) 77 *Am J Int'l L* 413).

[64] Marong, 'From Rio to Johannesburg' (n 46) 60–61.

[65] Christine Chinkin, 'Normative Development in the International Legal System' in D Shelton (ed), *Commitment and Compliance: The Role of Non-Binding Norms in the International Legal System* (OUP 2000).

[66] See ch 1, nn 41, 92.

[67] Rio Declaration (n 20) principle 16.

[68] ibid, principle 17.

[69] ibid, principle 15.

altogether (although they can overlap and apply in respect of the same problem). While the precautionary principle is concerned with risk regulation, the polluter pays principle and principle of prevention are primarily concerned with pollution control, and the principle of sustainable development represents quite a different approach to environmental policy again, incorporating notions of environmental justice as well as non-environmental considerations. Such a diverse set of ideas in international instruments of environmental 'principles' reflects the pluralistic state of environmental law as a subject when viewed from a purposive point of view. Thus environmental principles not only fail to constitute a group of settled legal concepts in international law, but they vary substantially as policy ideas.

Third, the precise meanings of these environmental principles in international law are unclear. They are 'verbal entities' that can apply to a range of factual situations in various and potentially conflicting ways.[70] This flexibility might be seen as advantageous—ambiguity allows environmental principles to have 'resonance, power and creativity' and to evolve and apply across contexts.[71] But it also implies indeterminacy and compromise,[72] and opens up potential for bad faith interpretations of environmental principles. This situation has caused consternation for scholars, and some try to assert the definitive definition of particular principles,[73] or express frustration at their vagueness, overuse and multiple meanings.[74] The *principle of sustainable development* is a prominent example of definitional confusion. The Brundtland Report's commonly cited exposition of 'sustainable development' as development that 'meets the needs of the present without compromising the ability of future generations to meet their own needs' is indicative but not definitive of sustainable development as a concept.[75] While there is a general understanding that sustainable development 'implies the acceptance of economic development, environmental protection and social development (or equity) as non-hierarchical objectives',[76] the Brundtland formulation is ambiguous due to its multi-faceted generational objectives, its 'soundbite' nature,[77] and the fact that value judgements are

---

[70] Stone (n 1) 246.

[71] Robert W Kates, Thomas M Parris, Anthony A Leiserowitz, 'What is Sustainable Development? Goals, Indicators, Values and Practice' (2005) 47(3) *Environment: Science and Policy for Sustainable Development* 8, 20.

[72] Stone describes the term sustainable development as 'artfully vague' in light of its origins in North-South compromise: Stone (n 1) 308.

[73] eg Bosselmann, *The Principle of Sustainability* (n 22) (principle of sustainability); John C Dernbach and Federico Cheever, 'Sustainable Development and its Discontents' (2015) 4(2) *TEL* 247 (principle of sustainable development); Wiener, 'Precaution' (n 13) (principle of 'optimal precaution').

[74] eg Heather M Farley and Zachary A Smith, *Sustainability: If It's Everything, Is It Nothing?* (Routledge 2013); Nicola Lugaresi, "The Unbearable Tiredness of Sustainable Development (at Different Levels, Lately)' in Robert V Percival, Jolene Lin and William Piermattei (eds), *Global Environmental Law at a Crossroads* (IUCN, Edward Elgar 2014).

[75] Brundtland Report (n 15) 8. See Kates, Parris & Leiserowitz , 'What is Sustainable Development?' (n 71).

[76] Marong, 'From Rio to Johannesburg' (n 46) 31. This is particularly since the 2002 Johannesburg Declaration (n 20), which declared 'the interdependent and mutually reinforcing pillars of sustainable development—economic development, social development and environmental protection'.

[77] Maria Lee, *EU Environmental Law, Governance and Decision-Making* (2nd edn, Hart 2014) 59.

required in determining which needs should be accorded priority in achieving sustainable development.[78] Hallmark aspects of sustainable development are its focus on future generations and its integration of environmental, social and economic factors in policymaking. Defining the concept is however the subject of sometimes intense disagreement,[79] particularly in light of those who reject its anthropocentric focus,[80] or who are frustrated by its lack of operational clarity.[81] Some environmental law scholars prefer the 'principle of sustainability' instead, due to its more explicitly ecological focus.[82] Maria Lee suggests that '[a] single all-embracing definition of sustainable development is probably not possible or desirable'.[83] She highlights that the concept of sustainable development is not 'self-executing'—it does not itself dictate how actual decisions might take into account the different dimensions of sustainable development.[84] Rather the concept is a political one that, 'at best, provides a consensual space for [public] debate about how we pursue some social objectives without compromising others'.[85] John Dernbach and Federico Cheever are more positive about the concept's inherent potential, arguing that a clear definition of sustainable development is both possible and important for harnessing its power as a decision-making framework to achieve an overall objective of ecologically sustainable human development.[86] For Dernbach and Cheever, sustainable development is fundamentally concerned with integrating environmental principles and considerations of human wellbeing into development decisions and, whilst representing an interdisciplinary normative framework,[87] it is increasingly being 'written into law' in nearly every area of legal practice.[88] There is at least scholarly consensus around the

[78] Olivia Hamlyn, 'Sustainability and the Failure of Ambition in European Pesticides Regulation' (2015) 27(2) *JEL* 1, 10.

[79] Michael Jacobs, 'Sustainable Development as a Contested Concept' in Andrew Dobson (ed), *Fairness and Futurity: Essays on Environmental Sustainability and Social Justice* (OUP 1999).

[80] A Dan Tarlock, 'Ideas Without Institutions: The Paradox of Sustainable Development' (2001) 9 *Ind J Global Legal Stud* 35, 38; Bosselmann, *Principle of Sustainability* (n 22) 29–34.

[81] Günther Handl, 'Sustainable Development: General Rules versus Specific Obligations' in Winifried Lang (ed), *Sustainable Development and International Law* (Graham & Trotman 1995) 36; Smith, 'Integrating Economic, Ecology, and Law' (n 5), 301–3; Tarlock, 'Ideas Without Institutions' (n 80); J B Ruhl, 'Sustainable Development: A Five-Dimensional Algorithm for Environmental Law' (2009) 18 *Stan Envtl LJ* 31 44.

[82] Bosselmann, *Principle of Sustainability* (n 22) chs 1–2; Andrea Ross, *Sustainable Development Law in the UK: From Rhetoric to Reality* (Routledge 2011). For a similar view on the core meaning of sustainable development that informs its legal role, see Christina Voigt, 'Sustainable Development in International Law' in Beate Sjåfjell and Anja Wiesbrock (eds), *The Greening of European Business under EU Law: Taking Article 11 TFEU Seriously* (Routledge 2015) ('the core meaning of sustainable development concerns the conservation of life-sustaining ecological processes') 32.

[83] Maria Lee, *EU Environmental Law: Challenges, Change and Decision-making* (Hart 2005) 27. See also Voigt, 'Sustainable Development in International Law' (n 82) 31 ('sustainable development may never be a "finished product"').

[84] Lee, *EU Environmental Law* (n 77) 60, 80.

[85] ibid 57–58.

[86] Dernbach & Cheever, 'Sustainable Development and its Discontents' (n 73). See also Ross, *Sustainable Development Law in the UK* (n 82).

[87] Duncan French, 'Sustainability' in Malgosia Fitzmaurice et al (eds), *Research Handbook on International Environmental Law* (Edward Elgar 2010).

[88] ibid 251.

fact that there is considerable definitional confusion concerning sustainable development (before even considering whether it is a 'legal principle').[89] Such confusion may be troubling from a policy perspective,[90] but it is legally unremarkable in the absence of a more precise legal context or framework.[91]

This lack of definitional clarity is compounded by the fact that sustainable development is often said to be defined by other environmental principles, as indicated above in soft law agreements on sustainable development that catalogue a range of environmental principles. In particular, certain environmental principles—the integration principle, the principle of intergenerational equity and the principle of intra-generational equity—are suggested (variously) by commentators as the key elements of sustainable development.[92] These constitutive principles are however themselves ambiguous. Thus, the *integration principle* is variously understood as the requirement to integrate environmental protection into the development process;[93] or the requirement to integrate environmental protection, economic development and social equity within international policymaking (opening up various possible ways for doing this);[94] or as a 'methodological instrument that enables decision-makers to make a transition from a sector-based (environment versus development; trade versus environment) to a more holistic approach in development planning';[95] or as the necessity to integrate the principle of intergenerational equity and the acceptance of limits on exploitation and consumption into individual as well as public choices.[96] Marie-Claire Cordonier Segger and Ashfaq Khalfan offer a more legally-oriented definition, explaining that the integration principle, as a core norm of sustainable development law, represents and also challenges the intersection between international environmental law, international economic

[89] Smith, 'Integrating Economic, Ecology, and Law' (n 5) 276 (noting more than 70 definitions for 'sustainable development').

[90] Although its ambiguity gives rise to policymaking advantages as well as risks: Lee, *EU Environmental Law* (n 77) ch 3.

[91] *cf* Hamlyn, 'Sustainability and the Failure of Ambition' (n 78) arguing that there are core dimensions of sustainability against which legal frameworks can be evaluated to determine how fully they embrace the concept of sustainability.

[92] Boer, 'Institutionalising Ecologically Sustainable Development' (n 5) 318 (the integration principle is the bedrock of sustainable development); Smith, 'Integrating Economic, Ecology, and Law' (n 5) 274–7 (intergenerational equity as central to sustainable development); Marong, 'From Rio to Johannesburg' (n 46) 61–62 (both intergenerational equity and intra-generational equity are core principles that give substance to sustainable development); Dernbach and Cheever, 'Sustainable Development and its Discontents' (n 73) 258–261 (equity, including intergenerational equity, provides the context for sustainable development to occur; integrated decision-making is the 'foundational action principle of sustainable development', supported by other principles, including the 'precautionary approach', polluter pays principle, public participation, access to information and access to justice). See also Marie-Claire Cordonier Segger and Ashfaq Khalfan, *Sustainable Development Law: Principles, Practices and Prospects* (OUP 2004) ch 5 and French, 'Sustainability' (n 87) 58–62.

[93] Brundtland Report (n 15) annexe 1, principle 7; Rio Declaration (n 20) principle 4. This can refer to both procedural and substantive integration: Dernbach & Cheever, 'Sustainable Development and its Discontents' (n 73) 259–260.

[94] Ruhl, 'Five-Dimensional Algorithm' (n 81).

[95] Marong, 'From Rio to Johannesburg' (n 46) 62–3.

[96] Tarlock, 'Ideas Without Institutions' (n 80).

law, and international social law (including human rights law). They highlight that this intersection happens in contingent ways in specific legal contexts, and identify a spectrum of different degrees of legal integration.[97]

There are similar abstract definitional debates about other environmental principles in international law, in particular the *precautionary principle*, which is notoriously difficult to define. Elizabeth Fisher paraphrases what she finds to be the most common version of the precautionary principle:[98]

> [W]here there is a threat to human health or environmental protection a lack of full scientific certainty should not be used as a reason to postpone measures that would prevent or minimise such a threat.

However, the principle is 'deeply ambivalent and apparently infinitely malleable',[99] so that an 'authoritative and generally accepted definition is nowhere to be found'.[100] This is for many reasons, including the difficult issues of scientific uncertainty and knowledge it raises,[101] and the politically contentious policy contexts in which the principle is debated and applied.[102] Ole Pedersen notes that the 'principle contains a number of constituent parts all of which are themselves very wide-ranging', relating to risk, political and administrative decision-making and scientific uncertainty, within different environmental and socially constructed contexts.[103] Jonathan Weiner argues that the application of the principle is particularly complicated by the fact that the real world is 'an interconnected web of multiple interdependent risks'.[104] Many critics of the precautionary principle focus on an extreme version of the principle that requires action to exclude or prevent certain risky activities.[105] Gregory Mandel and James Gathii, by contrast, identify three versions of the precautionary principle as strong, moderate and weak versions, arguing that the moderate version—'based more upon risk, dominated by science and cost-sensitive'—is a statement of values that can guide decision-makers and policy discussions in flexible ways.[106] Definitional confusion further

---

[97] Segger and Khalfan, *Sustainable Development Law* (n 92) 103–109.

[98] Elizabeth Fisher, *Risk Regulation and Administrative Constitutionalism* (Hart 2007) 40.

[99] Joanne Scott and Ellen Vos, 'The Juridification of Uncertainty: Observations on the Ambivalence of the Precautionary Principle within the EU and the WTO' in C Joerges and R Dehousse (eds), *Good Governance in Europe's Integrated Market* (OUP 2002) 253.

[100] Giandomenico Majone, 'What Price Safety? The Precautionary Principle and its Policy Implications' (2002) 40(1) *Journal of Common Market Studies* 89, 93; Mike Feintuck, 'Precaution Maybe, but What's the Principle? The Precautionary Principle, the Regulation of Risk, and the Public Domain' (2005) 32(3) *JLS* 371; Pedersen, 'Precaution' (n 61) 470–478.

[101] See ch 2, n 117.

[102] eg Theofanis Christoforou, 'Settlement of Science-Based Trade Disputes in the WTO: A Critical Review of the Developing Case Law in the Face of Scientific Uncertainty' [2000] *NYU Envtl LJ* 622; Majone, 'What Price Safety?' (n 100); Rosemary Lyster and Eric Coonan, 'The Precautionary Principle: A Thrill Ride on the Roller Coaster of Energy and Climate Law' (2009) 18(1) *RECIEL* 38.

[103] Pedersen, 'Precaution' (n 61) 327–9.

[104] Weiner, 'Precaution' (n 13) 609.

[105] eg Cass Sunstein, *Laws of Fear: Beyond the Precautionary Principle* (CUP 2005) 4.

[106] Gregory N Mandel and James Thuo Gathii, 'Cost-Benefit Analysis versus the Precautionary Principle: Beyond Cass Sunstein's *Laws of Fear*' (2006) 5 *U Ill L Rev* 1037, 1072–3. See also Bodansky, who deconstructs the principle according to its three functions (purely negative, facilitative and obliga-

derives from the differing formulations of the precautionary principle in various international treaties and instruments.[107] This ambiguity over meaning highlights again that any 'legal' definition of the precautionary principle depends on the legal contexts and cultures in which it plays a role.[108] Other environmental principles in international law also suffer similar definitional uncertainty due to their general formulation.[109]

The fourth reason why environmental principles in international law form a legally ambiguous and inconsistent grouping is that legal commentary concerning environmental principles has developed around some of these principles more than others. The central 'environmental principles' in environmental law scholarship constitute a seemingly arbitrary selection of those principles listed in international soft law instruments. Thus some principles in international instruments, such as the principle of intergenerational equity and the precautionary principle, have a high profile in environmental law scholarship as 'environmental principles'; whilst other Rio Principles, such as the participation of women and role of peace and poverty alleviation in achieving sustainable development, have not translated into principles with legal currency.[110] Other principles again, such as environmental impact assessment and rights of participation in environmental matters, or to a healthy environment,[111] match up with significant bodies of environmental law, without being commonly referred to as 'environmental principles'.[112] What makes something recognised as one of the 'significant environmental principles' of international environmental law?[113] This recognition arguably corresponds to the

tory): Daniel Bodansky, 'Deconstructing the Precautionary Principle' in David D Caron and Harry N Scheiber, *Bringing New Law to Ocean Waters* (Brill 2004).

[107] Preston, 'Role of the Judiciary in Promoting Sustainable Development' (n 20) 133–139.

[108] Elizabeth Fisher, 'Precaution, Precaution Everywhere: Developing a "Common Understanding" of the Precautionary Principle in the European Community' (2002) 9(1) *MJ* 7, 18–20.

[109] eg the principle of intergenerational equity—that each generation must use and develop its natural and cultural heritage so that it can be passed on to future generations in no worse a condition—has a 'conceptual elegance' that is 'deceptive': (Birnie, Boyle and Redgwell, *International Law* (n 58) 122); the polluter pays principle even goes by a range of names (Matthews Humphreys, 'The Polluter Pays Principle in Transport Policy' (2001) 26(5) *ELR* 451, n 3).

[110] Rio Declaration (n 20) principles 5, 20, 25. According to Foo, some Rio principles are too insubstantial in their content to be legal concepts: Kim Boon Foo, 'The Rio Declaration and its Influence on International Environmental Law' [1992] *Sing JLS* 347, 349.

[111] Rio Declaration (n 20) principles 1, 10, 17.

[112] This may be explained by dividing these environmental principles along substantive and procedural lines, where substantive principles are 'environmental principles' most commonly understood. Examples of substantive principles would be the precautionary principle and polluter pays principle; examples of procedural principles would be environmental impact assessment and participation in environmental decision-making. See Gilhuis, 'Consequences of Introducing Environmental Law Principles' (n 5) 47; *cf* Foo, 'Rio Declaration' (n 110). This distinction does not easily explain the legal prominence of the integration principle, and some commentators do refer to some 'procedural' principles as core environmental principles in international environmental law: eg Ong, 'From "International" to "Transnational" Environmental Law?' (n 58) (including the 'environmental impact assessment principle' and 'public participation principle'). For a different taxonomy of international environmental law principles (as operational principles, due diligence principles and principles that concern relations of interdependence), see Hey, *International Environmental Law* (n 58) ch 4.

[113] Ong, 'From "International" to "Transnational" Environmental Law?' (n 58) 51.

higher public policy profiles of some 'environmental principles', and it also reflects scholarly choice and habit, pursuing an instinct that there is something important to identify and analyse. The methodological danger is that 'popular piece[s] of political and policy jargon'[114] are being readily likened to general principles of international law as a matter of doctrine,[115] and the legal gap in between is being exposed by normative uncertainty and inconsistent selectivity. However, the selection of legally significant 'environmental principles' also reflects the fact that some principles are developing legal profiles in more prominent and different ways than others,[116] again complicating efforts to unite them as a group. Seemingly aware of these analytical dangers, some scholars resist the instinct to link together a definitive group of environmental principles, or deliberately avoid nominating some ideas as principles, referring instead to 'ideals', 'concepts', 'approaches' or 'paradigms'. Sustainable development is a case in point. Its nomination as a 'principle' occurs primarily as a scholarly and judicial response to its significance in international instruments (and some key ICJ cases),[117] but others deliberately cast it as a concept, ideal or paradigm, albeit constituted by other environmental principles,[118] or argue strongly that sustainable development cannot constitute a legal principle at all in environmental law, since it has been too compromised politically in relation to environmental protection goals.[119]

In summary, environmental principles in public international law are prominent and evolving, but far from a clearly identifiable grouping of legal principles. They do not (presently) constitute a clear set of fundamental concepts for environmental law universally. Further, there is no extensive body of case law that elaborates the legal roles of environmental principles in international law.[120] However, the textbook chapters, extensive scholarly writing and soft law prominence of environmental principles indicate that environmental principles are increasingly playing an important role in international law, albeit a complex and probably embryonic one. Rather than seeing their definitional and normative uncertainty as barriers to the legal profile of environmental principles, these attributes of ambiguity open up spaces for legal development. Accordingly, whilst there is no

---

[114] French, 'Sustainability' (n 87) 51.

[115] Bosselmann warns against this blurring of law and non-law in this way, since there are 'political, psychological and conceptual advantages in maintaining the distinction between, for example, moral principles and legal principles': Bosselmann, *The Principle of Sustainability* (n 22) 45.

[116] As Beyerlin demonstrates: Beyerlin, 'Policies, Principles and Rules' (n 7).

[117] eg *Gabcikovo-Nagymaros Project* (n 61) 90; Smith, 'Integrating Economic, Ecology, and Law' (n 5) 263; Marong, 'From Rio to Johannesburg' (n 46) 45–50; *cf* Jonathan Verschuuren, 'Sustainable Development and the Nature of Environmental Legal Principles' (2006) 9(1) *Potchefstroom Electronic Law Journal*; Bosselmann, *Principle of Sustainability* (n 22) 5.

[118] eg Verschuuren, 'Sustainable Development' (n 117) (ideal); Daniel Barstow Magraw & Lisa D Hawke, 'Sustainable Development' in Daniel Bodansky et al, *Handbook on International Environmental Law* (OUP 2007) 614 (paradigm); French, 'Sustainability' (n 87) (concept). See also Marong, 'From Rio to Johannesburg' (n 46) 56–64 (avoiding classifying sustainable development a principle of customary international law and focusing instead on its constitutive legal principles).

[119] Bosselmann, *The Principle of Sustainability* (n 22) 50–57.

[120] Although this might yet develop: see above n 61 and accompanying text.

direct transmission belt of law concerning environmental principles from the international sphere to domestic and regional legal frameworks, international law provides considerable normative encouragement to develop law around environmental principles. This is particularly through international soft law developments that have considerable potential to catalyse developments in other legal fora and systems.

The following two Parts show that how the legal development of environmental principles in EU and NSW law has been occurring. They are quite different legal pictures from the international law landscape involving environmental principles. In both EU and NSW law, the evolution of environmental principles as legal concepts has been incremental and multi-faceted, relating to different groups of environmental principles over different timescales, in response to different events. Each jurisdiction tells a fundamentally different and context-specific legal story about the development of environmental principles.

## III. Environmental Principles in EU Law

In EU law, environmental principles are set out in binding legislative and constitutional form in the Treaty on the Functioning of the European Union ('TFEU'), the Treaty on European Union ('TEU') and the EU Charter of Fundamental Rights.[121] These three instruments are the primary source of environmental principles in EU law. In particular, the TFEU is the main legal source of such principles, setting out across its provisions the six principles on which EU policy must be based in law: the preventive principle, the precautionary principle, the polluter pays principle, the principle of rectification at source, the principle of integration and the principle of sustainable development.[122] The TEU and Charter also contain references to the principles of sustainable development and integration. Since the introduction of each principle into these constitutional instruments, which occurred at various stages of the evolution of the EU and for different reasons, these six environment principles have taken on an increasingly prominent role in EU law, in EU legislative as well as formal policy measures,[123] and in the case law of the European

---

[121] Treaty on the Functioning of the European Union (Lisbon Treaty) ('TFEU'); Treaty on European Union (Lisbon Treaty) ('TEU'); European Parliament, Council and Commission, 'Charter of Fundamental Rights of the European Union' [2000] OJ C364/1 ('Charter'). The Charter has the same legal value as the European Treaties since the Lisbon Treaty was introduced in 2009.
[122] TFEU, arts 11, 191(2).
[123] eg Council & Parliament Regulation (EC) 178/2002 laying down the general principles and requirements of food law [2002] OJ L31/1, recitals 20, 21, arts 6(3), 7; Council & Parliament Directive (EC) 2006/12 on waste [2006] OJ L114/9, art 15 ('Waste Directive 2006'); Council & Parliament Directive (EC) 2006/21 on the management of waste from extractive industries, recital 32 ('Mining Waste Directive'); Council & Parliament Regulation (EC) 2006/1907 concerning the Registration, Evaluation, Authorisation and Restriction of Chemicals (REACH) art 1(3); Council & Parliament Directive (EC) 2008/98 on waste and repealing certain Directives [2008] L312/3 ('Waste Directive 2008') recital

courts,[124] so that they now play a significant role in the 'environmental law' of the European Union.[125] This Part examines the suite of environmental principles that are playing legal roles in EU law, through an historical account of how these roles have developed. It shows that environmental principles have been developed for EU-specific reasons, as well as in response to, or alongside, developments in international law and policy. It also shows that, whilst the core group of environmental principles is now firmly based in hard legal sources, they still raise novel legal questions in this legal context (particularly relating to the interplay of policy and law) and overall represent an evolving legal picture.

## A. Early History of Environmental Principles in EU Law

The early history of environmental principles in EU law shows that, while their development corresponded with the increasing prominence of environmental principles in international instruments in the last few decades, their initial derivation in EU law was independent of international developments. Thus the preventive principle, the principle of rectification at source and the polluter pays principle were first suggested in 1972 by a German proposal to the Council devising the first European Community Environmental Action Programme ('EAP')—a non-binding policy document introduced before the EC had a specific Treaty basis to formulate environmental policy and legislation.[126] This coincided roughly with the 1972 Stockholm Declaration in international environmental law, but the

30, arts 4(2), 14(1); Commission of the European Communities, 'Communication from the Commission on a Partnership for Integration—A Strategy for Integrating the Environment into EU Policies' COM (98) 333 ('Communication on Environmental Integration'); Commission of the European Communities, 'Communication from the Commission on the Precautionary Principle' COM (2000) 1 ('Communication on Precautionary Principle'); European Council, 'Renewed Sustainable Development Strategy' (2006) Document 10917/06 ('Renewed SDS'); Decision 1386/2013/EU on a General Union Environment Action Programme to 2020, 'Living Well, Within the Limits of Our Planet' [2013] OJ L354/171.

[124] See ch 4.

[125] As in international law, there are inconsistent groupings of environmental principles in EU law. Thus Reid identifies a different group of 'fundamental principles' of environmental policy, which she suggests are increasingly drawn together in EU policymaking: sustainability, proportionality, integration and the precautionary principle: Emily Reid, *Balancing Human Rights, Environmental Protection and International Trade* (Hart 2015) 55; *cf* Jans and Vedder who identify a group of 'principles of European environmental policy' similar to those covered in this chapter, which are distinct from 'general principles' of EU law relating to environmental protection (such as subsidiary, proportionality and equal treatment): Jan H Jans and Hans HB Vedder, *European Environmental Law: After Lisbon* (4th edn, Europa Law Publishing 2012) ch 1.

[126] Ludwig Krämer, 'The Genesis of EC Environmental Principles' in Richard Macrory, Ian Havercroft and Ray Purdy (eds), *Principles of European Environmental Law* (Europa Law Publishing 2004) 31. The first EAP was adopted jointly by the EC and the Member State governments in 1973: 'Programme of Action of the EC on the Environment' [1973] OJ C112/1 ('1st EAP'). Community EAPs were successively introduced thereafter, repeating these environmental principles, and including the precautionary principle as a basis of EU environmental policy. EAPs are now legally binding, setting the EU environmental legislative agenda: Council & Parliament Decision (EC) 2002/1600 laying down the Sixth Community Environmental Action Programme [2002] OJ L242/1, art 2(1).

enumerated principles in these two instruments are different, as was the motivation for developing these European principles of environmental policy. In particular, the first EAP fitted within a bigger picture of common trade policy in the European Community, and within a multi-level legal framework. In this governance context, it was not failed treaty making or compromised policy negotiation across geo-political divisions that drove agreement on principles. Rather, environmental principles were a first step towards an overarching EU environmental policy, acknowledging that the European single market had environmental externalities. The motivation to agree and adopt *general* environmental priorities,[127] encouraging their formulation as 'principles', is better seen in the context of the EU having no explicit legal basis to adopt specific environmental measures and being a multi-level system of governance. It was a convenient way to accommodate potential tension between the Community's economic and environmental aims, as well as the overlap with Member State environmental policies.

As the environmental agenda of the Community began to grow, primarily through legislation,[128] these environmental principles played no significant explicit role, until they were introduced into the then EC Treaty by the Single European Act ('SEA') in 1986.[129] That Act introduced Title VII into Part Three of the EC Treaty (now Title XX TFEU)—a chapter on environmental policy—which formalised Community environmental policy and gave Community institutions non-exclusive competence to legislate in the environmental field. The SEA introduced Article 130r(2) EC, the predecessor to Article 191(2) TFEU, which provided that Community 'action' relating to the environment shall be based on the *preventive principle*, the *principle of rectification at source* and the *polluter pays principle*. As Krämer observes, not only were the principles introduced 'without much discussion', but there was 'little scientific, administrative and political preparation of the ground for environmental principles'.[130] The Maastricht Treaty in 1992 amended Article 130r(2), changing its wording so that it referred to Community 'policy' on the environment rather than Community 'action', and it also introduced the *precautionary principle* to Article 130r(2), after a suggestion by Belgium and, again, 'apparently … without much discussion'.[131] This Article is substantially equivalent to Article 191(2) TFEU today, and notably introduced the constitutionally and doctrinally complex notion of substantive environmental policy being required

---

[127] Stephen Tromans, 'High Talk and Low Cunning: Putting Environmental Principles into Legal Practice' [1995] *JPEL* 779, 779; Krämer, 'Genesis of EC Principles' (n 126) 31 (referring to the German delegation's motivation in proposing principles).

[128] eg Council Directive (EC) 75/439 on waste oils [1975] OJ L194/23; Council Directive (EC) 75/442 on waste [1975] OJ L194/39; Council Directive (EC) 79/409 on the conservation of wild birds [1979] OJ L103/1.

[129] EC Treaty (Treaty of Rome, as amended) ('EC Treaty'); Single European Act (1986) [1987] OJ L169/1 ('SEA').

[130] Krämer, 'Genesis of EC Principles' (n 126) 33.

[131] ibid 38. The precautionary principle had been previously introduced into the EC's 4th Environmental Action Programme (Resolution of the Council on the continuation and implementation of a European Community policy and action programme on the environment (1987–1992) [1987] OJ C328/1), to promote environmental policy that was preventive rather than reactive: Albert Weale, *The New Politics of Pollution* (Manchester University Press 1992) 80.

by law. And while the timing of the Maastricht Treaty coincided roughly with the agreement of the Rio Declaration, which introduced a precautionary principle of its own, an earlier incarnation of a precautionary principle in German environmental policy and administrative law[132] is suggested to have influenced the introduction of the precautionary principle in EU law.[133] Even this early German version of the principle—*Vorsorge Prinzip*—has an uncertain meaning, with 11 different versions identified.[134] This highlights the simultaneous and staggered development of (related but not equivalent) environmental principles in different legal systems and institutional settings.

The Single European Act also introduced Article 130r(2.2), which provided that 'environmental protection requirements shall be a component of the Community's other policies'.[135] This provision was revised by the 1992 Maastricht Treaty,[136] before being removed from the environmental title and included at the front of the treaty as a provision of general application in EU law by the Amsterdam Treaty in 1997. After the Lisbon Treaty, the *integration principle* is now to be found in Article 11 TFEU in the following terms:[137]

> Environmental protection requirements must be integrated into the definition and implementation of the Union policies and activities, in particular with a view to promoting sustainable development.

This integration principle is concerned with integrating environmental protection requirements into the European Union's internal market project and across the full range of EU competences,[138] and it has its own legal complexities. Gracia Marín Durán and Elisa Morgera suggest that 'in EU law terms, the very essence of Article 11 TFEU resides in the fact that Treaty provisions other than the environmental legal bases may be used by the EU legislator to adopt measures which (may) negatively affect the environment'.[139] The integration principle thus 'calls

---

[132] Nicolas de Sadeleer, *Environmental Principles: From Political Slogans to Legal Rules* (OUP 2002) 125–130. An early version can also be found in Swedish Law: Gabriel Michanek, 'Sweden' in Nicolas de Sadeleer (ed), *Implementing the Precautionary Principle: Approaches from the Nordic Countries, EU and USA* (Earthscan 2006).

[133] Jans & Vedder, *European Environmental Law* (n 125) 43.

[134] E Rehbinder, *Das Vorsorge Prinzip im internationalen Vergleich* (Nomos 1991), as cited in Majone, 'What Price Safety?' (n 100) 93. Majone points out that the EU formulation of the precautionary principle is more permissive than that found in Principle 15 of the Rio Declaration, which qualifies precautionary action by a requirement of cost-effectiveness: 94.

[135] An earlier version of the integration principle, although framed as an 'action' can be traced further back to the 1st EAP and linked to Principle 13 of the Stockholm Declaration: 1st EAP (n 126) 7. See Nele Dhondt, *Integration of Environmental Protection into Other EC Policies: Legal Theory and Practice* (Europa Law Publishing 2003) 18.

[136] 'Environmental protection requirements must be *integrated* into the definition and implementation of other Community policies' (emphasis added): Treaty on the European Union, Together with the Complete Text of the Treaty Establishing the European Community [1992] OJ C224/1 ('Maastricht').

[137] Note that the Lisbon Treaty also introduced a number of other 'integration' or mainstreaming principles, although none are as strongly worded as art 11: see TFEU, arts 8–13.

[138] Communication on Environmental Integration (n 123).

[139] Gracia Marín Durán and Elisa Morgera, *Environmental Integration in the EU's External Relations* (Hart 2012) 28.

for a permanent, continuous "greening" of all Union policies'.[140] Article 11 might be seen either as a 'necessity of procedure' for EU policy depending 'almost entirely on the political will' of the EU institutions for its operation,[141] or as a 'legal obligation demanding substantive integration of environmental protection requirements, and not solely as a policy guideline or procedural requirement'.[142] Even if construed as a firm legal obligation, its legal scope and enforceability in EU law are the subject of ongoing academic discussion.[143] For some scholars, the integration principle also reflects a principle of 'good governance' in the EU.[144] Whilst the integration principle is thus beset by legal ambiguity—particularly in relation to its legal status as a policy-directing obligation—it gives rise to ambiguity and questions in EU law terms. This contrasts with the kind of uncertainty surrounding the integration principle in international law above,[145] which has no firm legal foundation or more specific legal articulation and is caught between accommodating environmental and non-environmental policies in the process of development, and more environmentalist conceptions of integration. This again shows that similarly named principles can represent different ideas across legal contexts, developing a theme that continues in the following section.

## B. Definitional Ambiguity in the EU Context

As in the international context, an inevitable result of the general formulation of environmental principles in the EU Treaties is their definitional ambiguity. The previous section highlighted how the integration principle, even with its legal formulation in Article 11 TFEU, is ambiguous in its legal effect. This lack of legal clarity is compounded by definitional uncertainty. The 'environmental protection requirements' that the principle requires to be integrated into other EU policies and activities are generally understood to include the wide-ranging environmental objectives in Article 191(1) TFEU, the environmental principles listed in Article 191(2), and possibly the 'factors' to be taken into account in EU environmental policy listed in Article 191(3).[146] This would seem to give the integration principle a firm basis for accommodating a broad range of environmental concerns into other EU policies. However, it has been suggested that the environmental focus of the principle is potentially diluted by the qualifying objective to achieve 'sustainable development' (further discussed in the following section), which might allow economic and social considerations to be balanced against environmental

---

[140]  Ludwig Krämer, *EU Environmental Law* (7th ed, Sweet & Maxwell 2012) 20.

[141]  ibid 21.

[142]  Durán and Morgera, *Environmental Integration* (n 139) 30.

[143]  eg Jans and Vedder, *European Environmental Law* (n 125) 22–29; Lee, *EU Environmental Law* (n 77) 67–69.

[144]  Joanne Scott, 'Law and Environmental Governance in the EU' (2002) 51 *Intl & Comp LQ* 996, 997.

[145]  See above nn 92–97 and accompanying text.

[146]  See eg Jans & Vedder, *European Environmental Law* (n 125) 22–23.

requirements.[147] Its definitional challenges reflect the challenges of its implementation. As Maria Lee points out, the integration principle is 'difficult to institutionalise' and identifying a policy of integration 'on the ground' in EU law is poorly understood, in light of the many actors in the 'EU's fragmented decision-making context'.[148] The principle is difficult to define because it is concerned with fundamentally complex, and possibly at times intractable, policy development processes, which are nonetheless subject to the overarching direction of EU constitutional law.

Definitional confusion also characterises the four principles enumerated in Article 191(2), which are undefined and given no further explanation in all Treaty versions. Thus, for example, the idea underlying the polluter pays principle is that polluters should pay for environmental harm that they generate. However, how to identify the relevant polluter and the appropriate measure of liability are matters on which the principle, expressed in general terms, gives no guidance.[149] Similarly, the preventive principle refers to the idea of preventing environmental pollution and damage rather than trying to undo their damaging effects, but the Treaty's general formulation says nothing of how to prevent environmental damage, or who should do the preventing, or when.[150] The principle is also sometimes confusingly conflated with the precautionary principle in EU law,[151] as if they represent an equivalent idea.[152] While both principles are generally concerned with preventing environmental harm, such conflation undermines any clarity in their scope of legal operation.

The precautionary principle is however in a different position in that it has been subject to more detailed articulation in EU law. Its policy significance led the Commission to give an exposition of its meaning and application in the EU context in its 2000 Communication on the precautionary principle.[153] The Communication gives lengthy guidelines on how the principle should be applied by the Commission, 'when faced with taking decisions relating to the containment of risk'.[154] This policy document was an effort by the Commission to explain and legitimise its decision-making in matters of risk regulation,[155] particularly in light of a controversial international trade dispute between the United States and the European Community over the European import ban on beef treated with hormones.[156] The Communication identifies the precautionary principle as a 'key tenet of its

---

[147] Reid, *Balancing Human Rights* (n 125) 60–61.
[148] Lee, *EU Environmental Law* (n 77) 68.
[149] de Sadeleer, *Environmental Principles* (132) 37–44.
[150] This is not necessarily problematic from a policy perspective (suggesting a direction of travel and giving discretion), but it is unhelpful if legal clarity and precision are sought.
[151] These can be seen as conceptually distinct in that the preventive principle is concerned with preventing *known* causes of environmental harm, whereas the precautionary principle is concerned with *unknown* risks of such harm (ie it concerns decisions about how to regulate risk): de Sadeleer, *Environmental Principles* (n 132) 91.
[152] eg Renewed SDS (n 123) [6]; Waste Directive 2008 (n 123) recital 30.
[153] Communication on Precautionary Principle (n 123).
[154] ibid 9.
[155] Fisher, *Risk Regulation* (n 98) 224–5.
[156] WTO, *European Communities—Measures Concerning Meat and Meat Products (Hormones)* (13 February 1998) WT/DS26/AB/R. See Eloise Scotford, 'Mapping the Article 174(2) Case Law: A First

policy' in the areas of the environment, human, animal and plant health,[157] and prescribes the application of the principle within a tripartite risk decision-making process that embraces risk assessment, risk management and risk communication. While the Communication purports to identify the 'constituent parts' of the precautionary principle,[158] its concern is not to define the principle precisely but to set out a decision-making process, centred on scientific evaluation, within which political decisions based on the principle should be made. It prescribes that maximum scientific objectivity should support precautionary decisions,[159] so as to minimise arbitrariness and any possibility of trade protectionism in relation to decisions made in the face of uncertain risk. At the same time, the Communication also indicates that precautionary measures may be justified where there are 'reasonable [presumably scientifically objective] grounds for concern that the potentially dangerous effects on the environment, human, animal or plant health may be inconsistent with the chosen level of protection',[160] indicating that EU institutions retain discretion in taking risk management decisions.[161]

The Communication provides an insight into the institutional policy process with which the precautionary principle is concerned in the EU, indicating that the principle concerns how discretion is exercised by EU institutions in matters of risk regulation, even if its precise direction in this respect is ambiguous.[162] It thus articulates the policymaking context—decision-making over risk regulation—in which the precautionary principle is to be understood in EU law. As indicated above, this interconnection between the role of the precautionary principle in EU law and its EU policymaking role is prescribed by the Treaty itself in (what is now) Article 191(2). The Communication aimed to clarify Article 191(2)'s policy mandate by means of a non-binding policy document relating to the Commission's decision-making procedures. While the Communication does not, in explicit terms, set out any legal role for the precautionary principle, Chapter Four's mapping of EU case law demonstrates that the judicial treatment of the precautionary principle by the EU courts derives directly from this policy document.[163] This highlights the significance of this institutional and policy context in shaping the role of the precautionary principle in EU law, as well as the distinctive interrelationship between 'law' and 'policy' which environmental principles embody and provoke in the EU context.

Step to Analysing Community Environmental Law Principles' (2008) 8 *YEEL* 1, text accompanying nn 21–26.

[157] Communication on Precautionary Principle (n 123) 3.
[158] ibid 13.
[159] ibid 15.
[160] ibid 10 (emphasis added).
[161] Such wide discretion is also suggested by the wide scope of 'scientific' advice that can be taken into account in providing an objective evidentiary basis for a decision on the basis of the principle: ibid 16.
[162] Majone, 'What Price Safety?' (n 100) 98; Fisher, *Risk Regulation* (n 98) 228.
[163] See ch 4(V)(B)(ii)&(v).

## C. The EU Principle of Sustainable Development: Reconnecting to the International Sphere

Finally, the *principle of sustainable development* was introduced into the TFEU and the TEU by the Treaty of Amsterdam in 1999, amending the predecessor Treaty of Rome and previous Treaty on European Union.[164] Unlike the inclusion of previous environmental principles above, these amendments were a direct response to international developments concerning sustainable development, adopting the lexicon of sustainable development and responding to the political impetus of the Brundtland Report and Rio Declaration in particular.[165] These Treaty amendments were soon followed in 2000 by the inclusion of the principle of sustainable development in Article 37 of the Charter of Fundamental Rights of the European Union.[166] This inclusion of sustainable development in the Treaties and Charter was remarkable in two senses. First, it articulated the concept of sustainable development as a 'principle' in EU law, albeit not consistently,[167] building its profile as an 'environmental principle'. Whilst the 'principle' label appears to be more fortuitous than legally deliberate,[168] some international law scholars highlight European developments as the source of this so-called principle.[169] Second, it included sustainable development both as an objective of the EU integration principle and as an overarching objective of the EU, internally and in its relationship with the wider world. In so doing, it inserted sustainable development as a policy concept that was legally relevant in relation to all aspects of EU activity. In relation to the integration principle, Article 11's integration principle is now stated to apply

---

[164] Treaty of Amsterdam, amending the Treaty on European Union, the Treaties Establishing the European Communities and Related Acts [1997] OJ C340, art 12; now TFEU, art 11; TEU, recital 9, art 3(3), art 3(5), art 21(2)(f). It was also articulated and prioritised, alongside the precautionary principle and principle of preventive action, in the Preamble to the 1992 Agreement on the European Economic Area [1994] OJ L1/3.

[165] Resolution of the Council on a European Community Programme of Policy and Action in Relation to the Environment and Sustainable Development [1993] OJ C138/5 ('5th Environmental Action Programme'), 11–12; Lee, *EU Environmental Law* (n 77) 57.

[166] Charter (n 121).

[167] TEU, recital 9 suggests that references to 'sustainable development' in that Treaty (in arts 3(3), 3(5), 21(2)(f)) are manifestations of this 'principle'; *cf* TFEU, art 11, where sustainable development is referred to without any reference to a principle. Sustainable development is repeated as a 'principle' in art 37 of the Charter, and in subsequent secondary EU legislation eg Mining Waste Directive, art 5(1); Waste Directive 2008, art 4(2) ('principle of sustainability'); Council & Parliament Directive (EC) 2008/50 on ambient air quality and cleaner air for Europe [2008] OJ L152/1, recital 30 (*cf* art 12); *cf* REACH, recital 3 (referring to the 'goal' of sustainable development); and no reference to sustainable development in Directive 2010/75/EU on industrial emissions (integrated pollution prevention and control) [2010] OJ L334/17 unlike in the previous IPPC Directive (Directive 2008/1/EC), recital 10.

[168] Sustainable development in the EU law context is also referred to as a 'concept', 'goal' or 'objective': eg Krämer, *EU Environmental Law* (n 140) 9–11. However, in the context of the EU Charter, the description of sustainable development as a 'principle' has a deliberate function in distinguishing art 37 from a 'right' under the Charter: Charter (n 121) art 52(5); 'Explanations Relating to the Charter of Fundamental Rights' [2007] OJ C303/17, 35.

[169] See Sands and Peel, *Principles of International Environmental Law* (n 6) 206 (noting that the general 'principle of sustainable development' first appeared in the 1992 EEA Agreement).

'with a view to promoting sustainable development', as set out above. A related version is found in Article 37 of the Charter,[170] however this version refers to integrating a high level of environmental protection (not 'environmental protection requirements') into EU policies 'in accordance with the *principle* of sustainable development'. These two legal linkages between the sustainable development and integration principles are mutually reinforcing in terms of the legal obligation they prescribe but they also raise difficulties of legal interpretation due to their different wording. As an overarching EU objective, such as found in Article 3(3) TEU, the sustainable development principle (like the integration principle) is different from the four EU environmental principles that prescribe EU environmental policy in Article 191(2) TFEU in that it is a principle governing all the Union's 'policies and activities'.[171] It cuts across the range of policy areas in which the EU has competence, and has both internal and external dimensions.

This cross-cutting and multi-directed identity is at the root of the definitional and operational complexity of sustainable development in EU law and policy. Maria Lee explains that sustainable development in the EU governance context is a 'fragile' concept (subject to potential dominance by growth or appropriation by economic interests) but also a flexible and dynamic one that allows the case for environmental protection to be made.[172] In addition to this conceptual flexibility, the dual internal and external aspects of sustainable development complicate its identity. It explicitly ties into international policymaking concerning sustainable development, reflecting the EU's actions as global 'green leader',[173] whilst also seeking to influence both EU and Member State action, particularly through EU strategies on sustainable development, further discussed below. Durán and Morgera explain that the EU has 'interpreted the goal of sustainable development flexibly and adapted it to different contexts and new developments',[174] so that there is no singular identity of sustainable development in EU law. This multi-functionality arguably dilutes its policy and legal potential.[175] The divided identity of sustainable development also affects the identity (and definition) of the integration principle in EU law. While the integration principle was introduced as a distinctly European concept concerned with qualifying Community competence in terms of environmental protection, as discussed above, the principle's connection with the internationally-derived concept of sustainable development in its

---

[170] 'A high level of environmental protection and the improvement of the quality of the environment must be integrated into the policies of the Union and ensured in accordance with the principle of sustainable development': Charter (n 121) art 37.

[171] Renewed SDS (n 123) [1].

[172] Lee, *EU Environmental Law* (n 77) 79 ('the strength of sustainable development holds the clue to its weakness').

[173] Norman J Vig and Michael G Faure (eds), *Green Giants? Environmental Policies of the United States and the European Union* (MIT Press 2004).

[174] Durán and Morgera, *Environmental Integration* (n 139) 39.

[175] See eg Ludwig Krämer, 'Sustainable Development in the EC' in Hans Bugge and Christina Voigt (eds), *Sustainable Development in International and National Law* (Europa Law Publishing 2008).

more recent Treaty incarnation suggests a link to the broader idea of integration associated with sustainable development in international law.[176] Christina Voigt indeed argues that the international law concept of sustainable development is an important interpretive tool for construing Article 11's integration principle (and other Treaty references to sustainable development) so as to avoid watering down environmental protection requirements in the EU context.[177] Together, these various dimensions of sustainable development and integration reflect the internal and external law of the European Union itself,[178] and its character as a body of multi-level governance.[179] EU law can be seen as a bridge between domestic and international law, as well as being a sui generis body of law,[180] and the norms of sustainable development and integration are flexibly employed across these different levels of EU action.

The impetus for prioritising sustainable development in EU policy has continued since its explicit introduction by the Treaty of Amsterdam, keeping up with international developments, and the EU now has a Sustainable Development Strategy (SDS),[181] which again has both an internal EU aspect and an external dimension, the latter first adopted in response to the Johannesburg World Summit on Sustainable Development in 2002.[182] The internal dimension highlights the challenging EU-specific elements of the concept of sustainable development, particularly its interaction with other EU policies, such as economic and regulatory reform.[183] It has provoked new approaches to policymaking within the EU, particularly through the use of 'impact assessments' for new legislative measures.[184] One aspect of the EU's SDS is a declaration of 'Policy Guiding Principles' for sustainable development, adding a further layer of interest in identifying European 'environmental principles'.[185] While these principles overlap with the Treaty-based

---

[176] See above nn 92–97 and accompanying text. See Durán and Morgera, *Environmental Integration* (n 139) 34–42.

[177] Voigt, 'Sustainable Development in International Law' (n 82) 46–49.

[178] The EU has competences to regulate policy areas within Member States, and also to determine external relations policy with countries outside the EU: TFEU, pt 5. See Durán and Morgera, *Environmental Integration* (n 139) for the role of integration in the external relations law of the EU, and Dhondt, *Integration of Environmental Protection into Other EC Policies* (n 135) and Beate Sjåfjell and Anja Wiesbrock (eds), *The Greening of European Business under EU Law: Taking Article 11 TFEU Seriously* (Routledge 2015) for the internal role of the integration principle in EU law.

[179] Liesbet Hooghe and Gary Marks, *Multilevel Governance and European Integration* (Rowman and Littlefield Publishers 2001).

[180] Case 6/64 *Costa v ENEL* [1964] ECR 585.

[181] Communication of the European Communities, 'Communication from the Commission on a Sustainable Europe for a Better World: A European Union Strategy for Sustainable Development' COM (2001) 264 final ('SDS'); renewed in 2006 with the Renewed SDS (n 123) and reviewed in 2009, European Council, '2009 Review of the EU Sustainable Development Strategy' (2009) DOC 16818/09.

[182] Commission of the European Communities, 'Communication from the Commission: Towards a Global Partnership for Sustainable Development' COM (2002) 83 final.

[183] Commission Communication, 'Mainstreaming Sustainable Development into EU Policies: 2009 Review of the EU Sustainable Developments' COM (2009) 400 final.

[184] Renewed SDS (n 123) [11].

[185] ibid [6].

principles discussed above,[186] they do not correspond exactly, resembling more the principles found in international soft law instruments on sustainable development.[187] These principles are set out in a policy document (the SDS) and thus do not have the legal foundation of the Treaty-based principles in EU law. However, they indicate how loosely the nomenclature of environmental principles slides between different spheres and sites of governance, both in the EU context and generally, and particularly how the group of legally relevant environmental principles might evolve over time.

Sustainable development continues to play a central and primarily policymaking function in the EU, with the Commission undertaking biennial reviews of the EU's progress on sustainable development and providing frameworks for Member State action on sustainable development in addition to EU policy efforts.[188] The EU is deliberately framing sustainable development as a norm that is to be picked up by different levels of EU governance and state and non-state actors alike. More recently, the concept has been 'mainstreamed' into EU policy by informing key ideas in the Europe 2020 strategy that followed the 2008 financial crisis, seeking to build more resilient economic and social systems, including through environmental initiatives, such as the development of a circular economy.[189] Lee suggests that this policy incarnation of sustainable development reflects a 'shallow approach' to sustainable development's social and environmental dimensions, as Europe 2020 focuses on economic growth as a priority.[190] As with the other environmental principles, the definitional ambiguity of sustainable development leaves it vulnerable to competing interpretations and political winds. However, the policymaking role of the principle of sustainable development sits alongside its prominent legal presence in the EU Treaties, generating difficult questions for legal scholars about its legal function, meaning and scope of operation.[191] Jans and Vedder argue that the inclusion of the principle in the Treaties and Charter has given sustainable development 'legal weight',[192] however the nature and extent of this legal weight is yet to be fully understood.

---

[186] The precautionary principle and polluter pays principle are common.

[187] eg 'solidarity within and between generations' (defined similarly to intra- and intergenerational equity in the Rio Declaration), and the integration principle in terms of integrating economic, social and environmental considerations.

[188] eg PRIME-SD, 'Peer Review Improvement through Mutual Exchange on Sustainable Development: A Guidebook for Peer Reviews of National Sustainable Development Strategies' (February 2006), available at <ec.europa.eu/environment/pdf/nsds.pdf> (accessed 30 June 2016).

[189] European Commission, 'Communication from the Commission on Rio +20: Towards the Green Economy and Better Governance' COM/2011/0363 final.

[190] Lee, *EU Environmental Law* (n 77) 64.

[191] Durán and Morgera, *Environmental Integration* (n 139) 35–36. See eg Reid, *Balancing Human Rights* (n 125) arguing that sustainable development can provide a structure for reconciling economic and non-economic interests in EU law; *cf* Lee arguing that sustainable development is a primarily political concept that is unlikely to impose legal constraints in and of itself: Lee, *EU Environmental Law* (n 77) 66.

[192] Jans and Vedder, *European Environmental Law* (n 125) 22–23.

## D. Conclusion

This survey of EU environmental principles shows that there is a distinct group of environmental principles in EU law, which primarily have legal status by virtue of their Treaty foundations. Even with firm legal foundations, the EU grouping of environmental principles is porous and potentially evolving, with further environmental principles developing at the boundaries of EU law. These include the principles of proximity and self-sufficiency found in waste legislation and policy,[193] and the principle of substitution identified by the Court of Justice as relevant in internal market law.[194] Many of these principles are isolated from the international law sphere, in terms of their derivation and legal foundation. This is reflected in the case law examined in Chapter Four—the European courts generally do not appeal to international environmental law to make sense of and reason about EU environmental principles.[195] However, there are some interconnections between these EU environmental 'principles' and those found in international instruments. This is seen most prominently in relation to the principles of sustainable development and integration, which have cross-cutting identities (across policy areas and levels of governance), representing how environmental principles can act as transnational norms that are flexibly applied in different governance and policy contexts, but which are also vulnerable to change and capture by changing political priorities and interests due to their open-textured formulation. In legal terms, this policy ambiguity highlights that these principles have no clear legal roles without more focused contextual applications. Chapter Four will explore the extent to which these two characteristically 'transnational' norms have settled into legal form in EU law, alongside similar analysis for the other EU environmental principles introduced in this Part. It might be that no firmly settled legal form is possible in relation to the broad policy ideas underpinning certain environmental principles, but there is some sense emerging of the legal contours of all these principles. Overall, Chapter Four demonstrates that the story of environmental principles, in this jurisdiction too, is one of legal evolution, albeit within the context of a unique legal and governance framework.

## IV. Environmental Principles in NSW Law

Environmental principles, or 'principles of ecologically sustainable development' ('ESD principles') as they are described in Australian policy and law, are another

---

[193] Waste Directive 2006 (n 123) art 8, although both principles have been qualified in Waste Directive 2008 with respect to recovery of waste: Waste Directive 2008 (n 123) art 16(3); Council Directive 99/31 (EC) on the landfill of waste [1999] OJ L182/1, recital 9.
[194] Case C-473/98 *Kemikalieinspektionen v Toolex Alpha* [2000] ECR I-5681 [47].
[195] Except in relation to the principle of sustainable development: see ch 4(VI).

legal beast altogether. They appear as a relatively consistent albeit not closed grouping in NSW law, which is distinct again from those groups of environmental principles identifiable in international law and EU law. This legal setting for environmental principles involves a body of domestic law,[196] as opposed to the regional, multi-level jurisdiction of EU law examined in the previous Part. ESD principles in NSW law comprise four core principles—the *precautionary principle, intergenerational equity, conservation of biological diversity and ecological integrity,* and *improved valuation, pricing and incentive mechanisms* (embracing within it the polluter pays principle). These four principles now find themselves in legislative form in NSW law, within individual environmental and planning statutes rather than being included in a foundational constitutional instrument. They were introduced by legislation more recently than the Treaty incorporation of environmental principles in EU law.[197] Their history in NSW policy and law is however more complex than simple statutory incorporation, as examined in this Part. There is also an *integration principle* of sorts, which, while not styled as a 'principle' in legislative form, is articulated as such by the NSWLEC. This reflects a trend by the Court to reinforce and extend the list of 'ESD principles' that guides the Court's reasoning,[198] whilst also highlighting the fluid use of the label 'principle' in NSW law involving ESD principles. The NSW version of the integration principle resembles that in many international instruments, referring to the need to integrate economic and environmental considerations in decision-making, along with social considerations in more recent cases.[199] Thus, at the outset, the list of NSW environmental principles overlaps with those in international law and EU law, at least in descriptive terms, but is not an equivalent grouping.

Environmental principles also have a distinct nomenclature in NSW law, being referred to collectively as *principles of ecologically sustainable development.* This difference is due to politics, in particular relating to the Australia-wide policy process concerning sustainable development undertaken by the federal (national) government in the 1980s—the 'ESD process'—which first introduced ESD principles into policy (and subsequently legal) jargon in Australia, as examined in Section A below. The environmental interest groups involved in this policy process were

---

[196] New South Wales exists as a discrete legal jurisdiction (with its own courts and legislature), but also forms part of the wider national (domestic) jurisdiction in Australia's federal system, so that national 'Commonwealth' legislation applies in NSW, appellate judicial decisions in NSW can be finally appealed to the High Court of Australia (with leave), and there is technically a single common law within Australia: *Lange v Australian Broadcasting Corporation* (1997) 189 CLR 520.

[197] The first legislative formulation of ESD principles is found in Protection of the Environment Administration Act 1991 (NSW) ('POEA Act') s 6(2).

[198] *Bentley v BGP Properties* [2006] NSWLEC 34; (2006) 145 LGERA 234 [67]; *Telstra Corporation v Hornsby Shire Council* [2006] NSWLEC 133; (2006) 146 LGERA 10; (2006) 67 NSWLR 256 [108]; *Bonaccorso v City of Canada Bay Council (No 2)* [2007] NSWLEC 537 [55] ; (2008) 158 LGERA 250; *Hub Action Group Incorporated v Minister for Planning* [2008] NSWLEC 116; (2008) 161 LGERA 136 [1]; *Bulga Milbrodale Progress Association Inc v Minister for Planning and Infrastructure and Warkworth Mining Limited* [2013] NSWLEC 48; 194 LGERA 347.

[199] *Hub* (n 198) [1]; *Gerroa Environment Protection Society Inc v Minister for Planning* [2008] NSWLEC 173 [7].

concerned that the negotiations for developing a sustainable development policy for Australia would be hijacked by non-environmental interests without there being a symbolic emphasis that environmental, or here 'ecological', considerations were at its core.[200] This political influence in the evolution of environmental principles in Australian policy highlights their culturally-specific nature. In fact, the subsequent development of environmental principles in NSW law, beginning with this political ESD process, has been influenced by an idiosyncratic combination of factors: by international instruments focused on sustainable development, which heavily influenced the ESD process, but also by distinctive national features, including the constitutional challenges of environmental policymaking and regulation within Australia, and judicial activism within the NSWLEC. The role of the NSWLEC has been particularly significant since the legal status of ESD principles in NSW law has been primarily generated and developed by the innovative reasoning of the NSWLEC itself.[201]

This composite and unique developmental path, examined in more detail in Sections A to C below, has produced a group of principles that are distinct from environmental principles at both the international and EU level. Despite the fact that ESD principles have more direct international law heritage than EU environmental principles,[202] they do not correlate exactly with those environmental principles found at the international (or EU) level, even when they are similarly named. This can be seen in four ways. First, the precise terminology differs. For example, the polluter pays principle appears in NSW policy and law as but one aspect of the ESD 'principle' or 'programme' of 'improved valuation, pricing and incentive mechanisms', along with encouraging incentive structures, such as economic instruments, to pursue environmental goals, and the pricing of goods and services based on life cycle assessments.[203] This is a different guise for the polluter pays principle from that found in the Rio Declaration,[204] or its simple formulation in the TFEU.[205] As another example, the integration principle in NSW law stands in contrast to that in EU law, due to the competence-focused formulation of the integration principle in EU law.[206]

---

[200] Green groups, fearing their interest would be diluted, threatened non-participation in the process unless this nomenclature were adopted: Stuart Harris and Charles David Throsby, 'The ESD Process: Background, Implementation and Aftermath' in Clive Hamilton and Charles David Throsby (eds), *The ESD Process: Evaluating a Policy Experiment* (Canberra, Academy of Social Sciences, ANU 1998) 17.

[201] See below Section IV(C).

[202] Through both the influence of international developments on the Australian ESD process *and* the NSWLEC's inclination to draw on international soft law concerning sustainable development in its reasoning: see Sections IV(A) & (C) below. NSW ESD principles also have a connection to EU environmental principles since the NSWLEC has cross-referred to EU case law in its developing reasoning with respect to ESD principles: eg *Telstra* (n 198) [108]–[112], [116]. The NSWLEC also refers to case law in other jurisdictions: ibid [134]–[135], [152]–[159].

[203] POEA Act, s 6(2). This entire principle has been articulated by the NSWLEC as an 'ESD principle' in subsequent cases: eg *Bentley v BGP* (n 198) [71].

[204] *cf* Rio Declaration (n 20) principle 16.

[205] See above, text accompanying n 149.

[206] See above, text accompanying nn 137–140.

Second, ESD principles are defined to some degree in their most common NSW legislative formulation.[207] Despite this, their legislative elaborations do not define the legal roles of ESD principles with certainty—ambiguities remain in their legislative explanations,[208] and legal clarity comes only through the application of these principles in particular legal contexts. This leads to the third difference between similarly-named principles across jurisdictions. Whilst the NSWLEC cross-refers to judicial reasoning in EU and other case law transnationally, particularly in relation to the precautionary principle, there are very different legal questions being asked in the foreign decisions drawn on by the NSWLEC. As discussed in Chapter Two, such judicial 'borrowing' raises questions in comparative law terms.[209] It involves not so much the development of equivalent concepts internationally as the drawing of inspiration from foreign doctrine, bolstering the legitimacy of new reasoning with respect to environmental principles that have no long-standing legal or doctrinal tradition in NSW law.

Fourth, the distinct nomenclature of environmental principles as 'ESD principles' in NSW law is significant. Unlike in EU law, there is no stand-alone 'principle of sustainable development' that features in NSW legal or policy contexts; rather there is the group of 'principles of ecologically sustainable development'. Thus, whereas 'sustainable development' has some form of doctrinal role that can be mapped in EU law, even if this is more ambiguous and embryonic than the roles of other EU environmental principles;[210] in NSW law, sustainable development is the core idea that links all ESD principles (that themselves have doctrinal roles). It is expressly used by the NSWLEC to identify environmental principles as a unified group, and also to motivate their widespread application in judicial reasoning, thereby defining the institutional ('ESD') identity of the Court.[211]

Furthermore, the grouping of NSW ESD principles is not closed. Additional miscellaneous principles have been included incrementally in NSWLEC judgments as ESD principles. These are less prominent, and include the principles of sustainable use and intra-generational equity.[212] These extra principles reinforce the porous grouping of environmental principles within this legal setting, as well as its distinct composition. Again, the willing recognition by the NSWLEC of a widening group of ESD principles reflects the Court's determination to recognise such principles.

The following three sections trace the derivation of ESD principles in NSW law in detail, from their inception in the Australia-wide ESD process and their significance in Australian intergovernmental environmental policymaking, to their ready adoption by the NSWLEC in its reasoning and proliferation in NSW

[207] POEA Act, s 6(2).
[208] See below text accompanying nn 240-242, 293.
[209] See ch 2(III)(A)(iii).
[210] See ch 4(VI).
[211] See ch 5(III).
[212] *Hub* (n 198) [1].

legislation. This idiosyncratic interaction of developments, different from the derivation of environmental principles in EU law, reinforces how deeply embedded ESD principles now are within the legal culture of NSW law and the NSWLEC.

## A. ESD Principles as Policymaking Tools in the National ESD Process

There were two national (Australia-wide) domestic factors that propelled and shaped the development of ESD principles in Australia—the political ESD process embarked on partly in response to the international sustainable development agenda, and the challenges of intergovernmentalism that otherwise confront environmental policymaking and regulation in Australia. Due to these two factors, ESD principles developed as tools of policymaking,[213] without having any formal legal status or influence. This section examines the first of these national influences that kick-started the development of ESD principles, whilst Section B that follows examines the intergovernmental context that further promoted the use of these principles.

The ESD process was set up by the Australian Federal government in 1990 to deliver the Australian governmental response to the Brundtland Report, prior to the 1992 Rio Conference and Declaration with its 'principles' of sustainable development and the *Agenda 21* requirement for a similar process to be established.[214] However, the ESD policy process was not simply a response to this international agenda—domestic politics were an 'intrinsic part of the ESD process'.[215] Then Prime Minister Hawke's enthusiasm to respond to the Brundtland Report and to set up the ESD process was provoked by volatile environmental issues domestically that were causing industrial trouble, business uncertainty and political divisions in the 1980s.[216]

The purpose of the process was to figure out how to make sustainable development 'operational' in Australia,[217] and to use this opportunity to deal with national public disquiet over environmental problems. The ESD process adopted a cross-sectoral approach to the task, creating an inclusive and consultative process for addressing a policy problem that confronted a wide range of industries. Sector-specific interests and problems were represented in the process by nine

---

[213] For the definition of 'policy': see ch 1, text accompanying nn 13–14.

[214] Commonwealth of Australia, 'Ecologically Sustainable Development: A Commonwealth Government Discussion Paper' (Australian Government Publication Services 1990). This ESD process was precisely what *Agenda 21* required—the development of a national strategy for sustainable development building upon sectoral issues and policies and wide participation (*Agenda 21*, clause 8.7)—but it was begun well before *Agenda 21* was signed.

[215] Harris and Throsby, 'The ESD Process: Background' (n 200) 10.

[216] Elim Papadakis, 'The ESD Process and Agenda 21' in Clive Hamilton and Charles David Throsby (eds), *The ESD Process: Evaluating a Policy Experiment* (Academy of Social Sciences, ANU, Canberra 1998) 69–70.

[217] Harris and Throsby, 'The ESD Process: Background' (n 200) 16.

Working Groups ranging from mining to fisheries to transport,[218] all tasked with considering sustainable development issues within their areas, and resolving conflicts between themselves to agree on sustainability initiatives. The Working Groups produced individual reports and then, after some political stalling with a change of prime minister in 1991,[219] a National Strategy on Ecologically Sustainable Development (NSESD) was produced at the end of 1992.[220]

'ESD principles' were initially introduced into the Working Group process as a means to structure the negotiations of individual Working Groups. Each Working Group was, inter alia, to assess the compliance of its sector with ESD principles. This was the first appearance of any 'environmental principles' in Australian policy and they do not resemble internationally formulated environmental principles, except very loosely. The six initial 'ESD principles' were: improving material and non-material wellbeing; improving equity between generations; improving equity within the present generation; maintaining ecological integrity and biodiversity; dealing cautiously with risk, uncertainty and irreversibility; and taking account of global ramifications of our actions, including on international trade.[221] Since the approach adopted in the ESD process was a consensus-building one that aimed to unite competing interest groups across different sectors, these 'principles' of ESD were tools for allowing different sector-specific policy issues to be addressed and consensus to be reached concerning sectoral obstacles to sustainable development.[222]

In their final form in the NSESD, ESD principles had changed in terms of their 'definitions', grouping and even formulation. Thus 'ESD' as a policy goal was defined as 'development that improves the total quality of life, both now and in the future, in a way that maintains the ecological processes on which life depends'.[223] Then a set of objectives and principles were set out to guide the ESD strategy, with no relevant distinction between them—'no objective or principle should predominate over the others'[224]—yet a semantic difference between principles and objectives was adopted. Considering two of the objectives looked like environmental 'principles' developed in the Working Group process—'to provide for equity within and between generations' and 'to protect biological diversity'[225]—this points to the imprecise and fortuitous use of the term 'principle' in this context, suggesting that principles were one device used to clarify the ambiguous concept

---

[218] The nine working groups included representatives from government, industry and environmental groups across 9 sectors—agriculture, energy use, energy production, forest use, fisheries, manufacturing, mining, tourism and transport.

[219] Giorel Curran and Robyn Hollander, 'Changing Policy Mindsets: ESD and NCP Compared' (2002) 9(3) *AJEM* 158, 159.

[220] NSESD (n 41).

[221] Ecologically Sustainable Development Working Groups, *Final Reports* (9 volumes) (Australian Government Publication Services 1991).

[222] Harris and Throsby, 'The ESD Process: Background' (n 200) 6.

[223] NSESD (n 41) 8.

[224] ibid 9.

[225] ibid 8; *cf* n 221 and accompanying text.

of sustainable development, or here ecologically sustainable development.[226] In addition, many of these objectives and other NSESD 'principles' resemble environmental principles in international environmental law,[227] although some are defined with different emphasis. For example, the NSESD's 'integration principle' refers to long-term and short-term consequences and integrating 'social' and 'equity' considerations as well as economic and environmental concerns.[228] As in the Rio Declaration, environmental principles in the NSESD also adopt economic goals including economic growth and international competitiveness, which rank alongside environmental considerations, indicating that these particular ESD principles cover more than 'environmental principles'.[229] These changes reflect the influence of the evolving international sustainable development agenda, including the concurrent Rio process; however the NSESD remains independent in its agenda, political context and design.[230] As a result, the NSESD presents a broad and ambitious policy agenda integrating but not prioritising environmental issues, and setting out ESD principles as a loose set of directives to pursue that agenda, defined generally but providing little direction for any legal application of these ideas.[231]

In this way, Australian ESD principles began as concepts, with a conveniently evolving international hook to promote their domestic acceptance and formulation, around which domestic policymaking and political pragmatism could be centred. However, they were unsettled and inconsistent concepts, with no suggested legal identities.

## B. Intergovernmentalism: Supporting the Political Rise of ESD Principles

The second national domestic factor that shaped the subsequent emergence of ESD principles in NSW law was the challenge of intergovernmentalism that is particular to Australia's constitutional governance arrangements. Intergovernmentalism causes problems for the development of coherent environmental policy and regulation in Australia due to the division of policymaking power concerning environmental issues between the two levels of Australian government—federal and state. Because of this challenge, the different layers of Australian government were keen to engage with the international sustainable development agenda for

---

[226] Curran & Hollander point out the 'innumerable definitions and conceptualisations of ESD' in the literature: Curran and Hollander, 'Changing Policy Mindsets' (n 219) 162. See also Productivity Commission 'Implementation of Ecologically Sustainable Development by Commonwealth Departments and Agencies: Report No 5' (Canberra, Ausinfo, 25 May 1999) xxii and generally.

[227] eg Stockholm Declaration (n 20) principles 3, 13; Brundtland Report (n 15) annexe 1, principles 2, 3; Rio Declaration (n 20) principle 3.

[228] NSESD (n 41) 8; *cf* Rio Declaration (n 20) principle 4, and above, text accompanying nn 92–97.

[229] eg Rio Declaration (n 20) principle 12.

[230] NSESD (n 41) 15–16.

[231] Nor does it provide much direction for their translation into policy action: Curran and Hollander, 'Changing Policy Mindsets' (n 219) 161–2.

another ulterior domestic motive: to address 'problems of governance' within Australia.

These governance problems are reflected in ongoing conflicts between federal and state governments over responsibility for the environment as an area of policy, which has consequences for budgetary allocation and policy coordination.[232] These problems are caused by the unclear jurisdictional demarcation of responsibility for environmental matters between layers of Australian government. The environment overlaps with other policy areas, and the federal government's power to legislate with respect to environmental issues is, absent an explicit constitutional power to legislate for the environment, constrained by the need for a connection to other heads of power in the federal Constitution.[233] Indeed it is unlikely that a discrete power to govern in relation to environmental policy issues could be easily framed and assigned to one level of government, since environmental issues are often wide-ranging and cross over into other areas of policy,[234] with the result that federal and state governments in Australia find themselves sharing power to govern environmental issues and having to cooperate.[235] In light of the resultant tension in Australian federal-state governance arrangements, work began on an Intergovernmental Agreement on the Environment ('IGAE') after the Brundtland Report but before, and independently of, the UNCED Convention that led to the Rio Declaration.[236]

By the time the IGAE was signed in 1992, the international sustainable development agenda (as progressed and decided at the Rio conference) was built into the Agreement, particularly through the 'principles of environmental policy' included in Section 3 of the Agreement. These principles, which federal, state and local governments agreed to develop and implement in policies and programmes at all levels of government, were a select group that were inspired by the '*legal* principles for environmental protection and sustainable development' set out in Annexe 1 of the Brundtland Report and the Rio principles. The influence of these international instruments is seen in the familiar wording used in the IGAE to articulate its principles, but the selective grouping of principles and discrepancies in exact wording highlight that there is no literal transplantation of environmental principles from these international agreements.[237] Further, the nature of the IGAE is very different from international soft law instruments on sustainable development, as

---

[232] Papadakis, 'ESD Process and *Agenda 21*' (n 216) 70, 80.

[233] Australian Constitution, s 51. This is so even though the federal heads of power in s 51 (eg interstate trade, external affairs, corporations, taxation) have been construed broadly to enable the passing of legislation such as the Commonwealth *Environmental Protection and Biodiversity Conservation Act 1999* (Cth). A landmark case demonstrating federal-state tension over environmental jurisdiction is the Franklin Dam case: *Commonwealth of Australia v Tasmania* (1983) 158 CLR 1.

[234] Final Report of the Australian Constitutional Commission (Australian Government Publication Services 1988) 7573767.

[235] James Crawford, 'The Constitution and the Environment' (1991) 13 *Syd LR* 11. This echoes environmental protection being a 'shared competence' between the EU and Member States in EU law.

[236] Intergovernmental Agreement on the Environment, adopted 1 May 1992 ('IGAE'); Papadakis, 'ESD Process and *Agenda 21*' (n 216) 70.

[237] eg the IGAE includes a precautionary principle resembling Rio Declaration (n 20) principle 15, but with two additional 'guidelines' as to its application; the agreement's principle of intergenerational

demonstrated by the remainder of the IGAE, which is focused on assigning environmental policymaking responsibilities and roles between the various layers of Australian government.

These IGAE principles of environmental policy are particularly important in tracing the legal evolution of NSW ESD principles since, not only is the IGAE directly referred to in some NSWLEC judgments in developing doctrinal roles for ESD principles,[238] but the IGAE forms a blueprint for ESD principles that have since been enshrined in many NSW statutes, which the NSWLEC must interpret and address in resolving cases. That blueprint comprises the four 'principles' in Clause 3.5 IGAE that constitute an agreed intergovernmental basis of policymaking and programme implementation to further 'ecologically sustainable development' (and 'sustainable economic development')[239] in Australia:[240]

3.5.1 *precautionary principle* —

where there are threats of serious or irreversible environmental damage, lack of full scientific certainty should not be used as a reason for postponing measures to prevent environmental degradation. In the application of the precautionary principle, public and private decisions should be guided by:

i.   careful evaluation to avoid, wherever practicable, serious or irreversible damage to the environment; and
ii.  an assessment of the risk-weighted consequences of various options.

3.5.2 *intergenerational equity* —

the present generation should ensure that the health, diversity and productivity of the environment is maintained or enhanced for the benefit of future generations.

3.5.3 *conservation of biological diversity and ecological integrity* —

conservation of biological diversity and ecological integrity should be a fundamental consideration.

3.5.4 *improved valuation, pricing and incentive mechanisms* —

—  environmental factors should be included in the valuation of assets and services.
—  *polluter pays* i.e. those who generate pollution and waste should bear the cost of containment, avoidance, or abatement
—  the users of goods and services should pay prices based on the full life cycle costs of providing goods and services, including the use of natural resources and assets and the ultimate disposal of any wastes

---

equity reflects Brundtland Report (n 15) annexe 1, principle 2, and Rio Declaration, principle 3, but without the reference to intra-generational equity. Further, many principles in the Brundtland Report and Rio Declaration do not find specific expression in the IGAE.

[238] eg *Bentley v BGP* (n 198) [24]; *Telstra* (n 198) [113], [116]–[119].
[239] Clauses 3.2 and 3.3 differently stress the goal to be achieved by the principles of environmental policy set out in Section 3 IGAE.
[240] IGAE, cl 3.5 (emphasis added).

— environmental goals, having been established, should be pursued in the most cost
effective way, by establishing incentive structures, including market mechanisms,
which enable those best placed to maximise benefits and/or minimise costs to
develop their own solutions and responses to environmental problems.

In addition, Clause 3.2 IGAE contains a version of the 'integration principle', set
out in less prescriptive terms than the principles in Clause 3.5, recognising, that:

sound environmental practices and procedures, as a basis for ecologically sustainable
development ... require the effective *integration* of economic and environmental considerations in decision-making processes.

The generality of this clause undermines its clarity, particularly as to how it might
be implemented, either in policy terms or legally.

As for the four 'environmental principles' listed in Clause 3.5 above, they are
partly defined, or at least further elaborated, by their explanatory paragraphs, in
contrast to the articulation of environmental principles as the basis of EU environmental policy in the TFEU.[241] However, these definitions remain broad and
ambiguous. For example, it is not clear what it means to maintain or enhance
the 'health, diversity and productivity of the environment' for the purposes of
the principle of intergenerational equity, nor what precise liability standard and
obligation is imputed by this version of the polluter pays principle.[242] Clause 3.5
also contains a mixture of mandatory language and discretionary direction and
qualification. In mandatory terms, the present generation 'should ensure' environmental health, diversity and productivity for future generations; those who pollute
'should' bear costs. In discretionary and qualified terms, decision-making based
on the precautionary principle 'should be guided by' evaluation to avoid irreversible harm 'where practicable'. Furthermore, the detail of the mandatory language
included in each principle is not necessarily to be taken literally. A literal reading
would imply, for example, that the precautionary principle would be restricted to
cases in which decision-makers refused to take particular action because of scientific uncertainty, leaving the principle irrelevant in all decision-making cases
involving scientific uncertainty but where no particular measures were refused

---

[241] TFEU, art 191(2).
[242] As a further example, 'conservation of biological diversity and ecological integrity' involves a
number of complex elements, including the elusive goals of 'biodiversity' (see M Kaennel, 'Biodiversity:
A Diversity in Definition' in P Bachmann et al, *Assessment of Biodiversity for Improved Forest Planning*
(Kluwer 1988)) and conservation of ecological integrity, which has a broad, contested and scientifically uncertain scope, covering the 'conservation of the earth's life-support systems', preservation of
'ecosystem services' (see Colin Reid and Walter Nsoh, 'Whose Ecosystem is it Anyway? Private and
Public Rights under New Approaches to Biodiversity Conservation' (2014) 5(2) *JHRE* 112), ideas of
natural and cultural integrity, and raising challenges of scientific measurement as well as potential
conflicts between human and non-human interests, and between present and future generations: eg
John Moffett and Francois Bregha, 'The Role of Law in the Promotion of Sustainable Development'
(1996) 6 *Journal of Environmental Law and Practice* 3, 4–5; Stephen Woodley, James Kay and George
Francis, *Ecological Integrity and the Management of Ecosystems* (St Lucie Press 1993). The formulation
of the precautionary principle, resembling that in international law, is affected by similar definitional
ambiguity: see above, text accompanying nn 98–108.

or postponed.[243] In the result, these IGAE formulations of ESD principles do not prescribe a clearly defined route for the application of these principles by policymakers and administrators, or for doctrinal application of these principles by courts, whether in reviewing administrative action based upon them or otherwise.

Furthermore, unlike the EU Treaties from which the environmental principles in EU law derive, the IGAE itself is generally thought to have no legal effect in Australian or NSW law. Despite its formal structure as a deed of agreement, the constitutional status of the IGAE,[244] and its substance and language, show that the IGAE is a 'political compact' only, setting up a co-operative framework concerning the exercise of public power in relation to environmental matters throughout Australia.[245] Particularly relevant for commentators in reaching this conclusion is the fact that the IGAE is 'replete with policy considerations', including the 'aspirational' principles set out in Clause 3.5.[246] These environmental principles are so broad and general as to be incapable of construction as legally certain agreed terms.[247] Thus, Talbot J, in the NSWLEC, faced with an argument that the precautionary principle was a legal standard that he was obliged to apply, set out the legal limitations of the IGAE in the following way:[248]

> The [IGAE is] not legislation and accordingly [is] no more than an understanding between representatives of the Commonwealth, States and Territories. [It comprises] a series of policies and objectives with broad, general agreement on national strategy. [It] create[s] no binding obligation upon ... this Court. [It is] heavily constrained to accommodate differing regional requirements and budgetary priorities.

The informal constitutional status of the IGAE, the policy-directing nature of the environmental principles there set out, and the breadth and generality of those principles, combined to generate a set of environmental principles that had no legal force or status in Australian law. It is only through subsequent state legislation and case law developments that the agreed environmental principles in the IGAE have taken on legal roles in the reasoning of the NSWLEC and NSW law. This is in contrast to EU law, where the constitutional status of the EU Treaties, and their legal prescription of environmental principles as the basis of environmental policy,

---

[243] *Lend Lease Development v Manly Council* [1998] NSWLEC 136; *cf Gray v Minister for Planning* [2006] NSWLEC 720; (2006) 152 LGERA 258 [128]–[129].

[244] While intergovernmental agreements have no legal authority under the Australian Constitution, Australia's system of government has come to depend on hundreds of such agreements between federal and state authorities, demonstrating the 'co-operative federalism' that has pragmatically developed to characterise Australia's federal governance arrangements. Ash brands this the 'silent spread of a quasi-legislative scheme': David Ash, 'Free the Fourth Arm' *Sydney Morning Herald* (Sydney, 23–24 August 2008) 32.

[245] C D Gilbert, 'Future Directions in Commonwealth Environmental Law' in William Duncan (ed), *Planning and Environmental Law in Queensland* (Federation Press 1993) 73–74.

[246] Alex Gardner, 'Federal Intergovernmental Cooperation on Environmental Management: A Comparison of Developments in Australia and Canada' (1994) 11(2) *EPLJ* 104, 119.

[247] *cf South Australia v Commonwealth* (1962) 108 CLR 130, 141, 150.

[248] *Nicholls v Director-General of National Parks & Wildlife Service* [1994] NSWLEC 155; (1994) 84 LGERA 397, 419. See also Pearlman J in *Greenpeace Australia v Redbank Power* [1994] NSWLEC 178; (1994) 86 LGERA 143, 153; *Planning Workshop Ltd v Pittwater Council* [1996] NSWLEC 211.

has provided a clear legal basis for EU courts to use environmental principles doctrinally in their reasoning.[249] The legal evolution of environmental principles in these two jurisdictions has idiosyncratic origins contingent on the applicable legal culture and political context involved.

## C. Historical Development of ESD Principles in NSW Law: Innovative NSWLEC Reasoning and Legislative Proliferation

The two national factors supporting the emergence of ESD principles so far discussed—the national ESD process and intergovernmentalism—are but part of the history of their development in NSW law. The remainder of that history rests in the singular judicial and legislative response at a *state* level to international and national developments concerning sustainable development. The NSWLEC has thus recognised the legal importance of ESD principles, often through innovative reasoning, and there has been a sizeable legislative response to the national ESD agenda, incorporating ESD principles explicitly in many NSW statutes. This more localised history reinforces how ESD principles are more than a naked transplantation of preformed international concepts, or norms from other regional or national jurisdictions, into this domestic legal setting. Environmental principles have been adopted and moulded in this context according to its own legal and institutional framework.

### i. Judicial Incorporation of ESD Principles in NSW Law

Before the widespread introduction of ESD principles into NSW environmental and planning legislation gave ESD principles a visible legal status in NSW law (as discussed in the following sub-section), the innovative reasoning of NSWLEC judges first confirmed and articulated legal roles for these principles. The initial legal emergence of ESD principles was due to a series of groundbreaking steps taken by the judges of the NSWLEC, establishing initially that the precautionary principle, and then ESD principles generally, were legally relevant considerations in deciding merits appeals. Merits appeals are a unique aspect of the NSWLEC's jurisdiction, in which the Court has a quasi-administrative role, deciding appeals from administrative decisions anew and conclusively on the merits. However, merits appeals are also judicial decisions that form part of the Court's case law, and have led to the creation of a novel body of environmental law doctrine in this jurisdictional setting.[250] This sub-section examines the origins of that body of doctrine as it concerns ESD principles.

In order to establish that ESD principles were legally relevant considerations in early merits appeals cases, the NSWLEC was confronted with an initial problem. It

---

[249] See ch 4.
[250] See further ch 5(II)(C).

was reviewing and remaking administrative decisions within the decision-making frameworks of existing statutes that made no explicit mention of ESD principles.[251] To overcome this, the Court employed a range of reasoning techniques, including drawing inspiration from international environmental law and national ESD policy (but not implying legal obligations from them directly),[252] to find that ESD principles were indeed relevant considerations in environmental and planning decision-making. Thus, for example, in *Northcompass Inc v Hornsby Shire Council*,[253] Stein J took particular account of the Rio Declaration in setting an agenda for the NSWLEC to consider ESD principles in deciding merits appeals.

The particular appeal in *Northcompass* concerned a planning consent application for a green waste bioremediation plant under the Environmental Planning and Assessment Act ('EPA Act')—the central planning statute in NSW law, with which a large proportion of the Court's caseload is concerned.[254] Amongst other things, the EPA Act sets out a list of matters for planning consent bodies to take into account in deciding planning applications, which did not explicitly include ESD principles,[255] and the Act at this time made no reference otherwise to ESD. Having decided that the plant should not be approved because it failed to meet departmental guidelines on site selection for such plants, the Court went on to address the Council's argument, defending its decision to grant development consent, that the proposed plant was an 'excellent example of ecologically sustainable development'.[256] Stein J found that the applicability of ESD principles to a case such as this under the EPA Act, as well as the interrelationship between these principles, had yet to be worked out by the Court, but that such exploration was unnecessary in this case given the result otherwise reached. However, by this acknowledgment, Stein J implied that this was a job for the Court to do, since there are 'many Rio principles which are relevant to environmental decision-making, including a case such as this'.[257] Further, they were principles that could potentially conflict since, while this proposed plant might be seen to be consistent with the principles of 'sustainable use of resources' and intergenerational equity, its uncertain environmental success might infringe the precautionary principle.[258] 'ESD principles' in this case were taken to mean *all* relevant principles that could be drawn from

---

[251] Note that ESD principles *did* appear at this early stage in the POEA Act (n 197) as an object of the NSW Environmental Protection Authority; and in the Environmental Planning and Assessment Regulation 1994 (NSW), which required that an Environmental Impact Statement for a particular development include reasons justifying the development having regard to ESD principles. These statutes were not at issue in these cases.

[252] The Court explicitly shied away from the legal problems involved in applying ESD principles as 'international law' concepts directly (eg *Leatch v Director General of National Parks and Wildlife Service* (1993) 81 LGERA 270, 282) and avoided the potential legal applicability of the IGAE: *cf* above n 238.

[253] *Northcompass* (n 51).

[254] Environmental Planning and Assessment Act 1979 (NSW) ('EPA Act').

[255] EPA Act, ex-section 90.

[256] *Northcompass* (n 51).

[257] ibid.

[258] ibid.

the Rio Declaration, which included the precautionary principle, the principle of intergenerational equity, the 'right to a healthy environment', the principle of prevention of environmental harm, 'environment impact assessment processes', and 'full public participation'.[259] In this case, the NSWLEC declared its intention to work out how ESD principles were to be incorporated into its reasoning processes, particularly in merits review decisions involving planning appeals.[260]

The NSWLEC had in fact already begun this process earlier in the 1990s, through novel reasoning involving the precautionary principle in merits appeals, establishing the principle as a legally relevant consideration in decisions made under two NSW statutes: the EPA Act and the National Parks and Wildlife Act ('NPWA').[261] These cases began with *Leatch v National Parks & Wildlife Service*, a landmark case that kick-started momentum for the precautionary principle constituting a legally relevant consideration in merits appeals.[262] In *Leatch*, Stein J gave a range of reasons to find that the precautionary principle was a relevant and legally required decision-making consideration in cases where uncertainty existed concerning the nature or scope of environmental harm.[263] In such cases, the 'premise' of the precautionary principle was that 'decision makers should be cautious', with a view to preventing serious or irreversible harm to the environment.[264] His Honour found that this was a 'statement of commonsense' that decision-makers had already been applying in appropriate cases.[265] Thus Stein J implied that the legal relevance of the precautionary principle was pre-established: he was merely articulating existing and proper—and now legally sanctioned—decision-making practice, which until then had not been spelled out. In addition, Stein J drew on two statutory provisions to support his endorsement of the precautionary principle as being legally relevant: the Land and Environment Court Act's requirement to take into account the 'public interest' in all NSWLEC merits appeals,[266] and the requirement of the NPWA, directly at issue in this case, that 'any matter considered to be relevant' should be taken into account. Both statutory considerations were broad enough to include a reference to the precautionary principle through the Court's interpretation. It was with this domestic legislative support that Stein J then drew on the widespread use of the precautionary principle in international

---

[259] ibid.

[260] These, of the Court's tasks, are obvious examples of 'environmental decision making'.

[261] National Parks and Wildlife Act 1974 (NSW) ('NPWA').

[262] *Leatch* (n 252). Note that the precautionary principle had first been used by the Court in an earlier case as a relevant factor in refusing a planning consent application, but with limited explanation of this reasoning: *Simpson v Ballina Shire Council* [1994] NSWLEC 43.

[263] This case concerned a licence application, under the NPWA to 'take and kill' endangered frogs in the course of a road project, where there was inadequate scientific understanding of the potential impacts of the planned road on an endangered frog species.

[264] *Leatch* (n 252) 282.

[265] ibid.

[266] Land and Environment Court Act 1979 (NSW). Section 39(4) requires that in making a decision in a relevant 'appeal', the Court 'shall have regard to this or any other relevant Act, any instrument made under any such Act, the circumstances of the case and the public interest'.

agreements, including the Rio Declaration, as well as the IGAE, to conclude that the precautionary principle applied to the decision in this case, which was to decline a fauna-removal licence application under the NPWA.

In two cases that followed, different NSWLEC judges accepted the doctrinal development in *Leatch*, but qualified it in different ways. First, there was some early judicial scepticism about how much doctrinal weight should be given to the precautionary principle, in light of concerns that it might prove unworkable in decision-making due to its ambiguous formulation and application in conditions of uncertainty. Thus, for Talbot J in *Nicholls v National Parks & Wildlife Service*,[267] the precautionary principle might give rise to 'interminable forensic argument[s]' if taken literally and might involve nothing more than a cautious approach to environmental decision-making, in which the Court already engaged.[268] Such an approach reflected the IGAE's definition of the precautionary principle, involving 'careful evaluation to avoid, wherever practicable, serious or irreversible damage to the environment [and] assessment of the risk-weighted consequences of various options', and it was 'axiomatic' that the NSWLEC adopted such an approach in environmental assessment.[269] Thus the precautionary principle was best viewed as a 'political aspiration' rather than a legally binding standard.[270] His Honour later retreated from this sceptical view, finding that the doctrinal role of the precautionary principle as a legally required consideration in environmental decision-making had been firmly established in the Court's case law,[271] but this initial prevarication demonstrates how novel and contentious the Court's initial reasoning was in relation to the principle.

Second, cases following *Leatch* qualified the application of the precautionary principle in decision-making by showing that the principle might be taken into account as a 'relevant consideration' in various ways. This is seen in *Nicholls* and also in *Greenpeace Australia v Redbank Power Company*.[272] In both cases, the task of the Court was to apply the principle to different facts and determine the cases on their merits. In so doing, the Court found in one case that a fauna-removal licence should be allowed under the NPWA, despite expert evidence that more scientific evidence was required as to the potential effects on an endangered species;[273] and, in another case, that the principle was not a decisive factor in determining whether planning approval should be granted for a proposed power station, since there was scientific uncertainty on both sides as to the plant's potential environmental effects.[274] Even on the same set of facts, the Court has acknowledged that a

---

[267] *Nicholls* (n 248).
[268] ibid 419.
[269] ibid.
[270] ibid. See also *Alumino Australia v Minister Administering Environmental Planning and Assessment Act 1979* [1995] NSWLEC 177; (1995) 88 LGERA 388.
[271] *Port Stephens Pearls v Minister for Infrastructure and Planning* [2005] NSWLEC 426 [54].
[272] *Greenpeace* (n 248).
[273] *Nicholls* (n 248); cf *Leatch* (n 252).
[274] *Greenpeace* (n 248) 154.

development consent decision based on the precautionary principle could have been resolved either way: 'whereas the decision reached [in the relevant merits appeal] concerning the precautionary principle was perfectly open to [the Court], a different conclusion on that issue was also realistically open'.[275] Thus, the principle was developing an important doctrinal role in the Court's reasoning, but its application—or its meaning or 'definition'— was highly fact-dependent.

The development of this early case law looks quite ad hoc. However, it also demonstrates the innovation and independent inclination of the Court to build doctrinal jurisprudence in relation to the precautionary principle in deciding merits appeals. As Chapter Five demonstrates, this innovative reasoning evolved to build entrenched patterns of doctrinal reasoning across all aspects of the Court's case law in relation to all ESD principles.

## ii. Legislative Incorporation of ESD Principles in NSW Law

This innovative NSWLEC reasoning was soon matched by a spate of legislative innovation incorporating ESD principles into NSW statutes.[276] In the late 1990s and early 2000s, ESD principles were included in widespread NSW legislation, primarily in the 'objects' clauses of Acts relating to environmental protection and planning[277]—provisions at the beginning of statutes that set out the relevant purpose of an Act.[278] Until that point, the only legislative appearances of ESD principles in planning legislation had been in Regulations under the EPA Act,[279] or in statutory 'environmental planning instruments' ('EPIs'), which the Act incorporated as relevant matters required for consideration in planning decisions.[280] They had also appeared in the early 1990s in pollution control legislation.[281] This subsequent and widespread statutory incorporation gave ESD principles an explicit role in NSW law, and provided legal authority for the NSWLEC to develop its evolving doctrinal reasoning involving ESD principles.

---

[275] *Miltonbrook v Kiama Municipal Council* [1998] NSWLEC 281.

[276] This legislative development was partly in response to scholarly and extra-judicial calls for legislative incorporation of ESD principles: eg Ronnie Harding (ed), 'Sustainability: Principles to Practice' (Fenner Conference on the Environment 1994) 6, 8; Paul Stein, 'Turning Soft Law into Hard—An Australian Experience with ESD Principles in Practice' (1997) 3(2) *The Judicial Review* 91, 95; *cf* Evans, *Principles of Environmental and Heritage Law* (n 43) 179 ('sustainability principles' had manifested earlier *implicitly* in NSW environmental and planning legislation).

[277] They were also included in some substantive legislative provisions, eg EPA Act, s 112E.

[278] There are now more than 39 NSW statutes that explicitly aim to implement ESD or ESD principles through their provisions: Jacqueline Peel, 'Ecologically Sustainable Development: More Than Mere Lip Service?' (2008) 12(1) *Australasian Journal of Natural Resources Law and Policy* 1, appendix 1 (this is now out of date but there is still a wide body of such legislation). This trend for legislative incorporation of ESD principles is not confined to NSW; it has been Australia-wide, reflecting the federal and state response to the ESD agenda to which they committed in the IGAE.

[279] See above n 251.

[280] EPA Act, ex-s 90(1)(a)(i) (now s 79C(1)(a)(i)). See eg Wagga Wagga Rural Local Environmental Plan 1991, cl 2(i) (considered in *Brunsdon v Wagga Wagga CC* [2003] NSWLEC 168 [4]–[5], [95–96], [111], [115]); Randwick Local Environmental Plan 1998 (considered in *Commonwealth of Australia v Randwick CC* [2001] NSWLEC 79 [29]).

[281] See below n 289.

A turning point for the legislative inclusion of ESD principles was the insertion of the object 'to encourage ecologically sustainable development' into the list of objects in section 5(a)(vii) of the EPA Act in 1998.[282] This not only confirmed the approach of NSWLEC reasoning in planning appeals under the Act in incorporating ESD principles as relevant considerations, but also reflected the centrality of ESD in NSW environmental and planning law, and in NSWLEC reasoning, considering the fundamental importance of EPA Act in that regime and to the Court's jurisdiction.[283] However, this statutory amendment did not include a definition of 'ecologically sustainable development', leaving its purposive direction vague. Combined with the varying expositions of ESD principles set out in different EPIs that the NSWLEC was required to consider in deciding EPA Act merits appeals,[284] this built legislative impetus for the consideration of ESD and ESD principles in planning decisions, but also a confusing and incomplete picture as to the meaning of these concepts.[285]

Two developments helped to fill in this picture. First, the NSWLEC reasoned to fill in the gaps. Thus in *BGP Properties v Lake Macquarie City Council*[286]—another landmark decision of the LEC in relation to ESD principles—McClellan CJ confirmed and expanded on the legal relevance of ESD principles in planning consent decisions under the Act. His Honour engaged in a process of statutory construction, seeking to understand Parliament's intention when it included 'ecologically sustainable development' in the Act's objects. His purposive interpretation led to doctrinal roles for ESD principles in a wide range of NSWLEC cases.[287] Second, a rationalisation of NSW environmental and planning legislation followed, which did not simply adopt ESD as a common statutory object, but also defined ESD in terms of commonly elaborated 'ESD principles'. This began with the 1999 amendment to section 6(2) of the Protection of the Environment Administration Act 1991 ('POEA Act'),[288] which updated the statutory 'ESD' object of the Environmental Protection Authority (established by the Act) by elaborating it in terms of 'ESD principles'.[289] It did this by explicitly adopting the group of ESD principles in Clauses 3.2 and 3.5 IGAE (with added emphasis):

> [E]cologically sustainable development requires the *effective integration* of economic and environmental considerations in decision-making processes. Ecologically sustainable

---

[282] Environmental Planning and Assessment Amendment Act 1997.

[283] See ch 5(III)(A)&(B).

[284] See above n 280.

[285] eg both the 'concept' of ESD and 'ESD principles' were mentioned in these legislative settings with no indication of the relationship between them.

[286] *BGP* (n 198).

[287] See ch 5(III)(A).

[288] The POEA Act established the Environment Protection Authority to administer integrated environmental protection in NSW: s 4.

[289] The POEA Act had previously introduced the need to maintain ESD as one of the objectives of the EPA in 1991, defining ESD in terms of ESD principles, but setting them out in more abbreviated terms. The Protection of the Environment Operations Act 1997 (NSW) amended this articulation of ESD principles in s 6(2) to match exactly the IGAE's exposition of ESD, with the amendment taking effect from 1999.

development can be achieved through the implementation of the following principles and programs:

(a)  the *precautionary principle*—namely, that if there are threats of serious or irreversible environmental damage, lack of full scientific certainty should not be used as a reason for postponing measures to prevent environmental degradation. In the application of the precautionary principle, public and private decisions should be guided by:

　　i.　　careful evaluation to avoid, wherever practicable, serious or irreversible damage to the environment, and

　　ii.　　an assessment of the risk-weighted consequences of various options,

(b)  *inter-generational equity*—namely, that the present generation should ensure that the health, diversity and productivity of the environment are maintained or enhanced for the benefit of future generations,

(c)  *conservation of biological diversity and ecological integrity*—namely, that conservation of biological diversity and ecological integrity should be a fundamental consideration,

(d)  improved valuation, pricing and incentive mechanisms—namely, that environmental factors should be included in the valuation of assets and services, such as:

　　i.　　*polluter pays*—that is, those who generate pollution and waste should bear the cost of containment, avoidance or abatement,

　　ii.　　the users of goods and services should pay prices based on the full life cycle of costs of providing goods and services, including the use of natural resources and assets and the ultimate disposal of any waste,

　　iii.　　environmental goals, having been established, should be pursued in the most cost effective way, by establishing incentive structures, including market mechanisms, that enable those best placed to maximise benefits or minimise costs to develop their own solutions and responses to environmental problems.

Other environmental and planning legislation has since defined statutory objects and requirements of ESD and ESD principles by reference back to section 6(2) of the POEA Act, or by similarly incorporating the IGAE exposition of ESD.[290] While the EPA Act itself was not amended to define its ESD object by reference to the POEA Act's description of ESD until 2005,[291] the consolidation of statutory ESD references occurred earlier in other important NSW environmental and planning statutes.[292]

This legislative proliferation and consolidation gave ESD principles a legal footing in NSW law through statutory incorporation, and some definitional

---

[290] eg Local Government Act 1993 (NSW) ss 3, 7(e), as amended by the Local Government Amendment (Ecologically Sustainable Development) Act 1997 (NSW) (effective 1999); Environmental Planning and Assessment Regulation 2000 (NSW) sch 2, s 6.

[291] Environmental Planning and Assessment Amendment (Infrastructure and Other Planning Reform) Act 2005 (NSW).

[292] eg NPWA, s 2A(2) was introduced to provide that (all) the Act's objects 'are to be achieved by applying the principles of ecologically sustainable development', with the principles defined by

elaboration. However, the section 6(2) of the POEA Act description of ESD and its constituent principles does not unambiguously define the principles or state clearly how they must be applied in judicial reasoning. For one thing, section 6(2) inherits these problems of definitional ambiguity from the IGAE, as set out above.[293] For another, it is mainly employed to clarify the objects of other Acts, rather than imposing decision-making obligations directly.[294] It gives some general guidance but also generates uncertainty as to how the principles might constrain decision-making under those statutes or otherwise influence legislative obligations. Some statutes do include ESD principles explicitly as mandatory matters for consideration in decision-making,[295] but even then ambiguities and generalities in the IGAE 'definitions' of the principles remain. Overall, the legislative articulation of ESD principles across core environmental and planning legislation in NSW law suggests an important legal role for ESD principles and gives some detailed direction but leaves the principles generally stated and open to interpretation.

This phase of legislative development and rationalisation in relation to ESD is important because it gave ESD principles traction for explicit legal treatment and analysis in the NSWLEC context, albeit with no precisely defined legal role. This provided an opportunity for the NSWLEC. As Stein J put it, the Court had an opportunity, and in his view an obligation, 'to turn soft law [as he saw the ESD principles, deriving from international environmental law and the IGAE] into hard law' and to flesh out the ESD concept, thus providing a 'lead for the common law world'.[296]

The derivation of ESD principles in NSW law demonstrates that, although ESD principles are related to environmental principles in international sustainable development instruments, they are not universal legal concepts simply transplanted into the Australian and NSW context. Rather, they began as (and remain) tools of policymaking in pursuit of both domestic and international agendas, and their subsequent recognition in NSWLEC decisions and NSW legislation was both inspired by international developments and distinctly innovative. ESD principles are sui generis concepts in the NSW legal context, in a state of independent evolution, and they have an identity that is unique to NSW policy and law. It is in such terms, and within this legal culture, that the judicial treatment of ESD principles by the NSWLEC can be understood.

---

reference to s 6(2) of the POEA Act: National Parks and Wildlife Amendment Act 2001 (NSW) s 5. Also by this time, an object of the Threatened Species Conservation Act 1995 (NSW) ('TSC Act') was the promotion of ESD, defined by reference to the POEA Act, ss 3(a) and 4.

[293] See above text accompanying nn 240–243.
[294] Paul Stein, 'Are Decision-Makers Too Cautious with the Precautionary Principle?' (2000) 17(6) *EPLJ* 3, 3.
[295] eg TSC Act, s 97; EPA Act, s 112E; Local Government Act 1993, s 89.
[296] Stein, 'Are Decision-Makers Too Cautious' (n 294) 3.

# V. Conclusion

This chapter has examined the origin and legal evolution of different groups of environmental principles in three jurisdictions in which environmental principles have a high profile: public international law, EU and NSW law. In each of these jurisdictions, environmental principles are prominent and useful, particularly in accommodating political developments or navigating shared governance frameworks, but they also vary considerably in their select grouping and legal basis, and are beset by definitional and legal ambiguity. The overall impression is of different and evolving legal stories in relation to similarly named principles. At the same time, there are some connections between the environmental principles in these three jurisdictions. Their groupings are responsive and porous so that influences, particularly from the international sustainable development agenda, have an interconnecting impact on their evolution in some respects. Environmental principles are thus developing bespoke and increasingly established legal roles within particular jurisdictional contexts, partly encouraged by policy and soft law developments at the international level.

The chapter has shown that there is no universal set of environmental principles in environmental law, confirming the argument in Chapter Two that environmental law scholars should not build a legal picture of environmental principles, and what they might do in environmental law, on the basis of such an assumption. In particular, there is no direct vertical translation of environmental principles as legal concepts from international soft law instruments to regional and national legal systems. This kind of characterisation misses two key aspects of the normative development of environmental principles within discrete legal systems. First, environmental principles are malleable concepts that conceal a range of potential meanings. Even at the public international law level, there are no settled legal roles, meanings or groupings of environmental principles. The chapter demonstrated that it is impossible universally to define the content of environmental principles across jurisdictions. Whether this is because the policy ideas they encapsulate are too complex to pinpoint, because their meaning is contested, or is due to the nature of their being 'principles', environmental principles do not have universally agreed definitions or definitive substantive content which describe or prescribe their legal identities. Acknowledging that environmental principles are not universal legal ideas across legal systems is in fact inevitable once one recognises that environmental principles do not inherently contain, in their pithy phrasing, a detailed route map for achieving the goals they represent. They simply represent ideas of environmental protection and sustainability policy that are elaborated in a general way, and which are convenient signals and goals for a range of reasons across different political, governance and legal contexts.

Second, as discussed in Chapter One, environmental principles reflect patterns of transnational norm development in their legal evolution at a range of governance levels. They are partly driven and framed by developments in international soft law agreements on policies and principles of sustainable development, but they are also products of their own governance settings, legal frameworks, institutions and local politics. It might be tempting to conclude that connections across jurisdictions in relation to certain environmental principles—as in the case of the external dimension of the principle of sustainable development in EU law—indicate that there is a universal set of norms in development. However, the full picture of environmental principles as developing legal norms within jurisdictional settings is fundamentally context-dependent. This is seen in the variations between environmental principles in the three jurisdictions examined in the chapter. Their history in each context depends on institutional forces and priorities, and the legal developments that occur reflect the possibilities and frameworks of each governance setting. Thus the legal profile of environmental principles in EU law centres on their inclusion in successive Treaties (and secondary legislation), whilst, in NSW law, the reasoning of the NSWLEC, against the background politics of intergovernmental relations in the Australian federal system, is critical to their legal evolution. The different groupings of environmental principles in these jurisdictions are expressions of the different legal cultures in which they have evolved, and continue to evolve. These legal cultures might respond to, or absorb, developments concerning environmental principles at the international level or in other legal contexts, but fundamentally each legal setting frames and dictates the legal roles of environmental principles within it.

In sum, the chapter has demonstrated, through its analysis of environmental principles that have legal roles in public international law, EU and NSW law and their respective paths of legal evolution, that different environmental principles have developing legal roles in fundamentally different legal systems and cultures. Analysing those legal roles requires a methodology that takes into account the idiosyncratic legal institutions, frameworks and doctrines of each legal culture. The mapping exercises in the following two chapters undertake such analysis in EU and NSW law, focusing on bodies of case law in these two jurisdictions as key sites of legal developments concerning environmental principles. Through this analysis, Chapters Four and Five demonstrate how environmental principles are driving, or otherwise implicated in, the evolution of these two different bodies of environmental law within very different legal cultures.

# 4

## Environmental Principles in European Union Case Law

## I. Introduction

This Chapter maps the case law of the Court of Justice of the European Union ('CJEU')—formerly the European Court of Justice ('ECJ') and Court of First Instance ('CFI'), now the Court of Justice and General Court[1]—in which EU environmental principles are involved or relied on in judicial doctrine. This analysis shows that environmental principles—as legal concepts—are playing significant and innovative roles in the developing doctrine of the EU courts. These legal roles are partly determined by the EU legal instruments and frameworks in which EU environmental principles are found, as set out in Chapter Three, but they are also shaped by the institutional features of the EU courts and their evolving doctrinal reasoning. The resulting map is an expression of environmental principles as part of EU legal culture.

The main EU environmental principles mapped in this chapter include six principles of EU environmental policy, as outlined in Chapter Three: the preventive principle, the precautionary principle, the polluter pays principle, the principle of rectification at source, the integration principle and the principle of sustainable development.[2] By analysing how these principles are used in judicial reasoning,

---

[1] The Court of Justice of the European Union ('CJEU') has been known as such since the Lisbon Treaty became effective in 2009, and comprises the Court of Justice, General Court and specialised courts: Treaty on European Union (Lisbon Treaty) ('TEU') art 19. Art 19 renames and expands the EU court structure, which formerly comprised the European Court of Justice and Court of First Instance, with judicial panels set up under the latter in specific areas: EC Treaty of Rome (as amended) ('EC Treaty') art 220. Since many cases discussed in this Chapter were decided prior to the Lisbon Treaty, references will often be to pre-Lisbon courts ('ECJ', or 'CFI'). Where there is no need to distinguish between individual EU courts, whether pre- or post-Lisbon, 'EU courts' generally will be referred to.

[2] They also include a number of environmental principles at the fringe of this group in terms of their legal impact in EU law—the substitution principle, and the principles of proximity, self-sufficiency, substitution, and a high level of protection: these are discussed in the chapter as they arise in cases.

the chapter shows that they are performing a range of doctrinal functions in the EU legal context, influencing the development of EU legal doctrine in ways that reflect their character as benchmarks of EU environmental policy. Thus environmental principles give the courts a broad interpretive discretion in construing EU legislation and the Treaties. They also inform, and even generate, legal tests that are applied by the EU courts in reviewing the lawfulness of EU and Member State action within the scope of EU environmental competence. In this chapter, 'EU environmental competence' is referred to as the area of EU-prescribed policy authority concerning environmental matters[3] within which political institutions—legislative and administrative[4]—can lawfully act. This area of competence is partly defined by environmental principles—particularly those in Article 191(2) TFEU outlining EU environmental policy—and can thus be policed by these principles as constitutionally prescribed boundaries of lawful action. This area of policy authority has also expanded in EU law, particularly under the influence of the integration principle in Article 11 TFEU. The chapter shows that the scope of EU environmental competence acts as a moving indicator of the legal roles of environmental principles, which frame the competence of institutions acting in this shifting field of EU policy.

There are also limits to the legal roles played by environmental principles in the reasoning of the EU courts. For the most part, environmental principles do not have freestanding roles to compel or review generally the exercise of policy discretion by EU institutions, or by Member State institutions acting within the scope of EU law. They are not equivalent to 'general principles of EU law' or fundamental rights in doctrinal terms. In fact, they can be a reason to defer to institutional discretion, where this is seen to reflect the application of certain environmental principles. Environmental principles are also used to justify reasoning only to the extent that EU courts are deciding questions about EU environmental competence that has *already* been exercised by EU and Member State institutions on the basis of environmental principles. This final limit can lead to circularity of reasoning in some cases, since identifying when such EU environmental competence has been exercised is partly defined by judicial interpretations of when environmental principles have been relied on and what they mean, which can be open for argument in light of the ambiguous definitions of environmental principles.

---

[3] What are 'environmental matters' itself raises problems of definition, considering that environmental matters may be narrowly understood as pertaining only to non-human ecological concerns, or broadly understood to cover, for example, the built environment, matters of international trade and questions of public health: Stuart Bell, Donald McGillivray and Ole Pedersen, *Environmental Law* (8th edn, OUP 2013) 7–9. See also ch 1, n 105. In relation to 'EU environmental competence', a broad notion of the environment is here adopted to accommodate the wide-ranging subject matter in relation to which environmental principles are employed in EU case law.

[4] In the EU, such institutions comprise the Council, Commission and European Parliament (TEU, arts 13, 14, 16, 17), hereafter the EU 'institutions'. These political institutions also include Member State governments acting within the scope of EU law.

All these limits reflect the self-perceived constitutional limits of the EU courts.[5] Unsurprisingly, such limits are frequently touched on by the doctrinal use of EU environmental principles, since these principles prescribe matters of socio-economic policy in legal terms (in the TFEU). Identifying the boundaries of these constitutional limits is implicitly part of much judicial reasoning involving EU environmental principles. This exercise is complicated by the fact that competence for environmental matters is shared across EU and Member State institutions,[6] and so EU courts are working out these constitutional limits in a context of multi-level governance in their doctrinal use of principles.

In terms of the meanings of EU environmental principles, marginal definitions of environmental principles are identified throughout the chapter when principles are employed in particular legal contexts. This reinforces the position that definitions of environmental principles are end points—or analytical by-products—rather than starting points in analysing environmental principles across the different legal cultures in which they play a role. The chapter shows that there are no short-cuts to analysing the roles of environmental principles in this legal context—they are implicated doctrinally in cases of wide-ranging subject matter, which has expanded beyond narrowly-defined 'environmental' matters in terms of EU competence, and which involve a variety of different EU legal actions, both procedurally and in terms of the legal questions involved.

To identify the different legal roles of environmental principles, the chapter maps the patterns of doctrinal reasoning involving environmental principles in EU case law by tracking the judicial techniques involved in such reasoning. It reveals a doctrinal picture of environmental principles in EU law in terms of 'treatment categories', which are categories of cases characterised by the particular technique used by the courts in employing environmental principles, or declining to use them, to justify their reasoning. Three treatment categories chart the legal use of environmental principles in this chapter: policy cases (where environmental principles are relegated to the policy sphere and not used doctrinally), interpretive cases (where they are used as interpretive aids) or informing legal test cases (where they are used to inform legal tests relating to the boundaries and exercise of EU environmental competence). These three categories are constructed and examined in Parts III to V, analysing cases falling within each category to exemplify and elaborate the respective roles played by environmental principles. A single case might fit into more than one of the treatment categories, as one case might contain environmental principles playing more than one

---

[5] By 'constitutional' limits, role and so on, this chapter refers to the proper role of the Court as an EU institution in constituting—alongside the Council, Commission and Parliament—a governing body of the EU.

[6] TFEU, art 191.

doctrinal role.[7] Furthermore, the chapter does not provide an exhaustive map of all cases involving environmental principles in EU case law since there are over 390 Court of Justice, General Court, ECJ and CFI judgments, Advocate-General opinions and lodged appeals involving environmental principles (at the time of writing). Rather, it discusses representative cases to demonstrate their doctrinal contours.

Overall, the doctrinal map drawn of environmental principles in EU law shows a highly active legal landscape, with interesting and novel legal developments that are fundamentally contingent on the EU law context, in that they reflect issues and questions of EU law. The map also highlights what environmental principles are *not* doing legally in this context. In particular, the idea that environmental principles might represent simple or comprehensive solutions to environmental problems or solutions to legal problems is negated in the EU context. Environmental principles in EU law cannot be called in aid directly as legal responses to environmental problems; they do not fit existing models of 'legal principles' in this legal context; they do not (yet) render EU environmental law comprehensively coherent; and they do not represent a radical new form of law. The mapping exercise of this chapter reveals a range of interesting developments of EU law, focused on environmental principles, but does not support grander claims for their legal roles universally. It is at once a very intricate but more modest legal landscape.

In terms of transnational legal influences in the reasoning of the EU courts, these are limited in this legal context. Most reasoning about environmental principles is internally focused on the treaties, legislation and doctrine of the EU legal order. Some judicial references to external legal influences are found in cases concerned with the concept or principle of sustainable development. These transnational references are considered briefly in Part VI, which considers the special case of sustainable development in EU judicial reasoning. This special treatment reflects its dual identity as an overarching concept in EU law and policy, which informs EU action internally whilst also connecting to the international sustainable development agenda. Sustainable development also has a particularly ambiguous meaning, and accordingly its doctrinal use is less focused than reasoning relating to other EU environmental principles. These distinctive features of sustainable development as a 'principle' were introduced in Chapter Three: the EU principle of sustainable development, along with the integration principle, developed separately from the four environmental principles in Article 191(2) TFEU,[8] at different

---

[7] eg Case C-236/01 *Monsanto Agricoltura Italia* [2003] ECR I-8105, which appears in both Parts III and IV below.

[8] Treaty on the Functioning of the European Union (Lisbon Treaty) ('TFEU' or the 'Treaty'). References throughout this chapter to the 'Treaty' are either to this current Treaty, or to the predecessor EC Treaty (with articles identified by the suffix 'EC'), whichever was relevantly in force. EU legislation adopted under the EC Treaty is variously described as 'EC' or 'Community' legislation.

times, and has both overarching and externally facing roles in the Treaties. Part VI also considers emerging doctrinal possibilities relating to Article 37 of the EU Charter of Fundamental Rights. Article 37 has not featured strongly in the EU courts' jurisprudence to date but it provides scope for legal developments relating to sustainable development in the EU context, and also for connecting the courts' reasoning to international human rights law. Thus, even within a single legal context, environmental principles are not of the same legal order or status. No map can (currently) neatly capture the legal story of EU environmental principles.

This legal variation is also seen in the case of the integration principle.[9] Whilst this principle has legal roles in EU case law that map onto the three main treatment categories developed in this chapter, this is often in ways that shape and influence the very scope of these categories. This influence is due to the fact the integration principle in Article 11 TFEU is concerned with how 'environmental protection requirements', including those reflected in Article 191(2)'s principles of environmental policy, are integrated into other areas of EU policy.[10] Its legal influence thus gives extra dimensions to these other environmental principles, expanding their legal roles beyond the strict domain of EU environmental policy in Title XX of the TFEU,[11] widening the area of EU environmental policy itself,[12] and suggesting more ambitious legal roles for environmental principles in EU law in the future.[13] The integration principle thereby broadens the map of EU case law involving environmental principles, amplifies their legal roles, and suggests that the legal story of environmental principles in EU law will continue to evolve. This is reinforced by the legal potential of Article 37 of the Charter mentioned above, as this also contains a legal version of the integration principle, albeit without reference to 'environmental protection requirements' that link directly to other EU environmental principles.

In order to draw (and then read and understand) this chapter's doctrinal map of EU case law involving environmental principles, Part II first explores in more detail the legal culture in which environmental principles are employed in EU law. It examines the jurisdiction and institutional identity of the EU courts, considering their constitutional role, their openness to developing judicial doctrine within different aspects of their jurisdiction, and their style of judicial reasoning, relating these features to their treatment of environmental principles. This legal background describes the 'internal' legal culture of EU law in which environmental principles have developing doctrinal roles, building on the picture set out in Chapter Three of how six particular environmental principles have evolved to have prominent roles in EU Treaties, legislation and policy documents.

---

[9] As will be seen, the precautionary principle also has a distinctive legal role in EU case law, partly due to the impact of the integration principle, and also because of the quantity of case law involving the principle.

[10] TFEU, arts 11 & 191(2).

[11] See below, Section IV(B).

[12] See below, Section V(A).

[13] See below, Section III(E).

# II. The Jurisdiction and Institutional Identity of EU Courts: Reasoning with Environmental Principles in EU Legal Culture

The legal roles of environmental principles in EU case law are shaped by EU legal culture, and particularly by the jurisdiction and institutional identity of the EU courts and the law they apply. This section sets out the nature of this identity and jurisdiction, examining the EU courts' progressive constitutional role and their reasoning style and doctrine, considering how the body of case law involving environmental principles fits within this legal picture. This case law is very diverse in EU law terms and it is only by appreciating the nature of EU courts, the legal questions they decide, and how they decide them, that a doctrinal map of the legal roles of environmental principles in EU law can be drawn, and made sense of. The treatment categories into which environmental principles fall in EU law are not abstract doctrinal categories; they involve questions of EU law to be answered by the courts, and specific EU legal tests and patterns of doctrinal reasoning developed to answer them. Further, the constitutional role of the EU courts in deciding the lawfulness of EU action—including all action in relation to environmental matters within the scope of EU law—determines the extent to which environmental principles have legal roles at all. In light of this EU law background, the section concludes by introducing the three mapping categories of the chapter as reflections of this EU legal culture.

## A. The Constitutional Role and Progressive Nature of the CJEU

The CJEU has a central constitutional role in EU law. This role is articulated in Article 19 TEU, which provides that the CJEU 'shall ensure that in the interpretation and application of the Treaties the law is observed'. Since the EU Treaties—the TEU and TFEU—constitute the European Union as a polity, with the consent of its Member States (the Treaty signatories), this role for the CJEU establishes it as a key institution in the EU's constitutional architecture, responsible for maintaining its rule of law.[14] The CJEU has taken on this constitutional role and developed a progressive institutional identity, reflecting the novelty of the EU 'law' that it interprets, applies and articulates. As Tridimas states, EU law is 'not only a new legal order but also a novel one in the sense that it has no historical precedent or indeed contemporary equivalent'.[15] As ultimate arbiter of such law, the EU courts have

---

[14] See above n 5.
[15] Takis Tridimas, *The General Principles of EU Law* (2nd edn, OUP 2006) 18.

(had) great scope for innovative doctrinal reasoning, as well as a need to define their own institutional identity in elaborating EU law.[16] Much commentary has reflected on the ECJ's progressive constitutional steps in asserting the supremacy and direct effect of EU law within Member State legal orders,[17] such that it has created a body of European constitutional case law.[18] Member States and Member State courts,[19] as well as academics,[20] have largely supported the bold assertions of constitutional authority by the EU courts.[21] Carol Harlow also notes that the ECJ was equally 'strong and self-confident' as a 'founding father' of EU administrative law, whilst the European Community was in its infancy.[22]

This progressiveness is possible due to the doctrinal freedom given to the EU courts to shape EU law by the EU's founding Treaties. This freedom is seen at a broad level in Article 19 TEU above, which states simply that the CJEU is to ensure that the 'law' is observed. That law comprises the rules set out in the Treaties, and the secondary EU legislation enacted under them, but is otherwise undefined. The resulting space for legal development has allowed the EU courts to develop a wide-ranging body of judicial doctrine,[23] including using environmental principles creatively within that evolving doctrine.

## B. The CJEU's Jurisdiction

There are three main Treaty provisions that provide for the CJEU's jurisdiction in procedural terms: Article 263 TFEU (actions to review the legality of acts of

---

[16] eg Case 6/64 *Costa v ENEL* [1964] ECR 585; Joined Cases 98 & 230/83 *van Gend en Loos v Commission* [1984] ECR 3763; Joined Cases C-6 & 9/90 *Francovich v Italy* [1991] ECR I-5357.

[17] Some scholars have charged the ECJ with illegitimate activism: Hjalte Rasmussen, *On Law and Policy in the European Court of Justice: A Comparitive Study in Judicial Policymaking* (Martinus Nijhoff Publishers 1986) 62; Trevor Hartley, 'The European Court, Judicial Objectitivity and the Constitution of the European Union' (1996) 112 *LQR* 95; *cf* Mauro Cappelletti, *The Judicial Process in Comparative Perspective* (Clarendon Press 1989) 390–391.

[18] Eric Stein, '"Lawyers", Judges & the Making of a Transnational Constitution?' (1981) 75 *AJIL* 1, 3 *et seq*; Joseph Weiler, 'The Transformation of Europe' (1991) 100 *Yale LJ* 2403.

[19] Nial Fennelly, 'Preserving the Legal Coherence Within the New Treaty' (1988) 5(2) *MJ* 185, 198; Miguel Maduro, *We the Court: the European Court of Justice and the European Economic Constitution: A Critical Reading of Article 30 of the EC Treaty* (Hart Publishing 1998) 30–34.

[20] Joseph Weiler, 'Journey to an Unknown Destination: A Retrospective and Prospective of the European Court of Justice in the Arena of Political Integration' (1993) 31(4) *JCMS* 417, 431–432.

[21] Although Member State courts have occasionally rebelled against the CJEU's assertion of constitutional authority: see Anne-Marie Slaughter et al (eds), *The European Courts and National Courts—Doctrine and Jurisprudence* (Hart Publishing 1998).

[22] Carol Harlow, 'Three Phases in the Evolution of EU Administrative Law' in Paul Craig and Grainne de Burca (eds), *The Evolution of EU Law* (2nd edn, OUP 2011).

[23] Including the transformative internal market tests laid down in Case 120/78 *Rewe Zentral v Bundesmonopolverwaltung für Branntweinn (Cassis de Dijon)* [1979] ECR 649 and Case C-55/94 *Reinhard Gebhard v Consiglio dell'Ordine degli Avvocati e Procuratori di Milano* [1994] ECR I-4165, as well as review tests applicable under art 263 TFEU: see below, nn 28–34 and accompanying text.

the EU institutions); Article 267 TFEU (preliminary references from Member States); and Article 258 TFEU (enforcement actions against Member States). Identifying these different procedural avenues of the CJEU's jurisdiction is significant for understanding reasoning involving environmental principles in two respects. First, like Article 19 TEU, they are drafted openly, giving the courts considerable scope to develop doctrine and review tests within these jurisdictional domains. Second, the same legal issues can arise across these different types of action, with the result that the doctrinal use of environmental principles is not determined by the kind of case that the court is hearing procedurally.

A significant number of cases involving environmental principles are Article 263 cases, where the legality of EU institutional acts is under review. Article 263(2) lays down various grounds for reviewing this legality, including, most relevantly, lack of competence, and infringement of the EU Treaties or 'any rule of law relating to their application'.[24] The ground of lack of competence reflects the fact that the EU comprises a set of legally limited competences conferred on it, or attributed to it, by its Member States,[25] some of which are exclusive to EU institutions (such as EU competition policy),[26] and others, including environment policy, which are shared with Member State governments.[27]

In applying these grounds of review in Article 263(2), which are otherwise undefined, the EU courts have developed a range of tests for reviewing EU institutional acts—a body of EU constitutional and administrative law doctrine.[28] For the ground of 'lack of competence', the main test for determining whether a measure is within the scope of (a particular basis of) EU competence relates to its 'centre of gravity', as determined by its predominant aim and content.[29] When considering 'infringement of the Treaties or of any rule of law relating to their application', the CJEU applies a range of tests, including the pervasive test of proportionality to determine whether EU action strays unlawfully beyond its legitimate Treaty objective,[30] as well as a test of 'manifest error of assessment' for judging any discretionary overreach by EU institutions in matters of complex economic or social policy, or scientific fact evaluation.[31] These administrative law tests also include increasingly fine-grained tests that structure and confine the discretion of EU institutions in their decision-making, as EU administrative law has continued to evolve.[32] These review tests are complemented by the 'general principles of EU

---

[24] TFEU, art 263(2).
[25] TEU, art 5(2).
[26] TFEU, art 3(1).
[27] TFEU, art 4.
[28] On the nature of EU administrative law, see Paul Craig, *EU Administrative Law* (2nd edn, OUP 2012). See also Harlow (n 22) 444–450 on how the ECJ had doctrinal freedom to develop the building blocks of administrative law and pursued this against a moving constitutional backdrop.
[29] Case C-300/89 *Commission v Council (Titanium Dioxide)* [1991] ECR I-2867 [10].
[30] Now enshrined in TEU, art 5(4).
[31] Case T-13/99 *Pfizer Animal Health SA v Council* [2002] ECR II-3305 [311]; Craig, *EU Administrative Law* (n 28) ch 15.
[32] See below, Section V(B)(iii).

law', discussed in Chapter Two,[33] which the CJEU has developed in its case law as standards of legality for EU action (including principles such as those of equal treatment or legitimate expectations).[34] EU environmental principles do not constitute general principles in this EU law sense;[35] rather, as will be seen in Section V below, environmental principles have an influential role on the doctrinal development of other review tests that apply in Article 263 actions.

The doctrinal openness of the 'law' to be applied by EU courts is also seen in the second main area of the CJEU's jurisdiction—preliminary references from Member State courts under Article 267 TFEU. Member State courts can refer to the CJEU questions of interpretation of the Treaties and EU legislation, and of any element of the EU legal order more broadly,[36] as well as questions concerning the validity of EU institutional acts. Preliminary reference judgments are important in EU law in establishing precedents of EU law and building uniformity.[37] In deciding on the validity of EU institutional acts, the preliminary reference procedure provides an indirect form of legality review on the same grounds set out in Article 263(2), with equivalent doctrine applied by the EU courts. When it comes to the interpretive function of preliminary references, the EU courts answer a range of legal questions. They may be called on to interpret ambiguous provisions of the Treaties and EU legislation, and they may also be asked to 'interpret' EU law doctrines that constrain or guide Member States when acting within the scope of EU law. In the latter sense, the EU courts effectively review the lawfulness of Member State action through the preliminary reference procedure, even though they do not decide on the legality of such action in EU law on the facts.[38] The tests that the CJEU relies on to review Member State action in this way include the general principles of EU law,[39] the test of proportionality,[40] as well as more specific tests

---

[33] See ch 2(III)(B).

[34] Tridimas, *General Principles* (n 15).

[35] They are not employed by the courts as a stand-alone tests of review for all EU acts, and environmental principles derive from the Treaties as statements of substantive policy, rather than being creatures of judicial doctrine: ibid 5; *cf* Craig, *EU Administrative Law* (n 28) ch 21. In addition, general principles of EU law are also seen as distinct from, and constraining the legal operation of, environmental principles: eg Case C-293/97 *R v Secretary for the Environment, ex p Standley* [1999] ECR I-2603 [52]–[53]; Case C-254/08 *Futura Immobiliare srl Hotel Futura v Comune di Casoria* [2009] ECR I-06995, Opinion of Advocate-General Kokott (23 April 2009) [32]–[33], [55]. See also ch 2(III)(B).

[36] The extent of this jurisdiction is based on a broad interpretation of the CJEU's jurisdiction to give preliminary rulings concerning the interpretation of the Treaties and of acts of EU institutions and bodies: TFEU, art 267. See Damien Chalmers, Gareth Davies and Giorgio Monti, *European Union Law* (3rd edn, CUP 2014) 179–180.

[37] Joined Cases 28-30/62 *Da Costa en Schaake NV v Netherlands Inland Revenue Administration* [1962] ECR Eng Spec Ed 31.

[38] There is an important constitutional demarcation between interpretation and application of EU law in cases referred by Member State courts under art 267, even if it is blurred in practice: Paul Craig & Gráinne de Búrca, *EU Law: Text, Cases and Materials* (6th edn, OUP 2015) 496–498.

[39] Although the extent of such review is unclear: Editorial, 'The Scope of Application of the General Principles of Union Law: An Ever Expanding Union?' (2010) 47 *CMLRev* 1589.

[40] This is similar to the test of proportionality applied to EU action, although with some structural differences: Tridimas, *General Principles* (n 15) chs 3 and 5. See also Craig, *EU Administrative Law* (n 28) chs 19 and 20.

relating to provisions of the Treaties that are alleged to have been infringed or to be otherwise relevant.[41] Through both Article 263 and 267 actions, therefore, the EU courts have developed legal tests of 'review' in relation to environmental action by both EU and Member States acting within the scope of EU law.[42] In developing doctrine relating to these various review tests across the jurisdiction of the EU courts, environmental principles have had an influential, albeit varying, doctrinal role, as examined in Part V.

In Article 267 cases that involve interpreting EU provisions, the EU courts also have doctrinal latitude, particularly due to the teleological approach taken by the courts. The ECJ,[43] and how the Court of Justice, has tended to examine 'the whole context in which a particular provision is situated, and [to give] the interpretation most likely to further *what the Court considers* the provision sought to achieve'.[44] In deciding these kinds of interpretive questions, the ECJ has built doctrine around specific provisions and areas of substantive EU law, including EU environmental law. In so doing, the EU courts have relied on environmental principles to interpret EU legislation in sometimes radical ways,[45] by attributing meanings to environmental principles in the context of particular provisions, in relation to which the courts have identified environmental principles as being relevant purposes. Through the courts' purposive reasoning and the open-ended nature of environmental principles, interpretive reasoning incorporates particular policy visions of environmental principles into the EU legal order.

The CJEU's third main area of jurisdiction—enforcement actions against Member States under Article 258 TFEU—also involves issues of interpretation of EU law, since the courts must interpret the EU Treaties, secondary legislation and related doctrines, in order to enforce them against allegedly delinquent Member States. Similar doctrinal roles for environmental principles can thus occur in both Article 267 and 258 cases, just as there is overlap between Article 263 and 267 cases in the ways that environmental principles can inform review tests.

This outline of the EU courts' jurisdiction demonstrates two points. First, the EU courts have a wide platform (and need) to develop EU law doctrinally through their case law. Second, the different types of action that might be brought before the EU courts do not clearly demarcate the legal questions with which the courts are concerned. These questions overlap between the Court's jurisdictional classes

---

[41] The specific review tests pertinent to reasoning involving environmental principles include the series of tests developed by the Court to determine whether a Member State has infringed art 34 TFEU, and also the tests laid down in, and developed by the Court in relation to, arts 114(4) and (5) TFEU.

[42] It is in both these senses that the term 'review test' is used in this chapter.

[43] The ECJ (prior to the Lisbon Treaty) had sole jurisdictional responsibility for preliminary references. Since the Lisbon Treaty, there is some shared jurisdiction for preliminary references between the EU courts but the Court of Justice hears the majority of cases.

[44] Craig and de Búrca, *EU Law* (n 38) 64 (emphasis added).

[45] eg Case C-127/02 *Landelijke Vereniging tot Behoud van de Waddenzee and Nederlandse Vereniging tot Bescherming van Vogels* [2004] ECR I-7405, and see Part IV generally.

in procedural terms. This overlap is seen in the CJEU cases involving environmental principles. To an extent, in different forms of action, different types of argument and reasoning apply. For example, arguments challenging the legality of EU legislation have no place in Article 258 enforcement actions, thus preventing any legality arguments involving environmental principles in such cases.[46] However, there are several ways in which there are doctrinal connections between legal issues across different aspects of the CJEU's jurisdiction, as outlined above. The following section examines further the EU law-specific challenges in mapping the diverse body of case law involving environmental principles.

## C. Diversity of EU Case Law Involving Environmental Principles

The previous section showed how the EU case law involving environmental principles is not readily classifiable by the types of action brought in procedural terms. This section highlights two further aspects of the diversity of EU cases involving environmental principles that give rise to challenges in making sense of them. First, cases involving environmental principles involve a range of legal questions and subject matters. Second, the reasoning style involving environmental principles varies across the cases. These challenges reinforce the mapping method of this project, indicating that close scrutiny of the reasoning techniques employed by the EU courts is required to determine the legal roles played by environmental principles. Environmental principles follow no clearly established model in EU law with their doctrinal roles in a state of evolution.

Chapter One explained that all EU cases involving environmental principles are public law cases, broadly understood, in that they decide on the legality of, or otherwise guide, public action. However, they represent many different types of case, depending on how one might choose to categorise them. In terms of the particular questions of EU law decided in this case law, the legal points at issue give rise to some predictable lines of doctrinal reasoning involving environmental principles, as seen in cases where the precautionary principle is used to inform the issue of proportionality of Member State action taken on precautionary grounds which infringes Article 34's guarantee of the free movement of goods.[47] However, the doctrinal reasoning involving the precautionary principle employed in these cases also overlaps with reasoning in relation to other questions of EU law, revealing doctrinal connections between different areas of EU law through reliance on the precautionary principle.[48] This demonstrates the openness and evolving nature of EU law, and how the mapping exercise of this chapter might be used to draw con-

---

[46] Case C-1/00 *Commission v France* [2001] ECR I-9989.
[47] See Section V(B)(v).
[48] See Section V(B)(ii)–(iv).

clusions about the development of EU law itself, as well as drawing conclusions for environmental law and environmental law scholarship.

In terms of subject matter, again the case law is diverse, extending beyond narrowly drawn 'environmental' matters.[49] The case law is in fact skewed by the number of public health cases in which the precautionary principle is discussed—Paul Craig describes this highly contested area as an 'eclectic' area of EU law.[50] However, as discussed below, the role of the integration principle, which has extended the influence of the precautionary principle into public health cases, has also begun to extend the role of other environmental principles into legal disputes involving other areas of EU competence, including competition and transport policy. The current subject matter profile of EU cases involving environmental principles appears to represent a stage in the developing doctrine of environmental principles in EU law, which reflects a developing integration of environmental policy requirements into other areas of EU law.

Another challenge in identifying the role of environmental principles in CJEU reasoning concerns the nature of that reasoning. The Court of Justice, and previously the ECJ, often gives limited reasoning for its decisions. It is difficult to discern the legal roles played by environmental principles when references to them are brief, whether those references are dismissive or integral to the outcome of the case. In other cases, particularly those involving the precautionary principle, very lengthy and complex reasoning is delivered, by the General Court (formerly CFI) in particular. Detailed reasoning gives more clues about the legal role, if any, played by the precautionary principle in these cases, but its helpfulness can also be limited when it involves overlapping threads of reasoning, which are inconsistent from case to case. Furthermore, there is often also no linearity in the judicial discussion of environmental principles, so that, for example, the principles might be mentioned in the Opinion of an Advocate-General or in arguments put to the relevant court, but then not picked up on in the reasoning of the Court of Justice, or vice versa (the courts might address the principles without prompting). A doctrinal focus minimises these difficulties by identifying the patterns of judicial reasoning or technique across the case law, and organising the cases according to these patterns (the 'treatment categories' in this chapter).

In sum, the EU case law involving environmental principles follows no simple patterns. It is a miscellany of cases that involve different types of actions, different subject matter, and different legal issues, with no consistent linearity of judicial discussion, although there are some identifiable patterns of reasoning. The limitations of these classifications are both exposed and cured by a doctrinal analysis of the case law involving environmental principles. This chapter analyses the judicial treatment of environmental principles in EU law with no presumed boundaries

---

[49] See above n 3.
[50] Craig, *EU Administrative Law* (n 28) 473.

in the reasoning of the EU courts concerning environmental principles, so as to capture all their legal roles. The contextual considerations examined in this section are not tools or categories for mapping the case law, but attributes of the cases in EU law terms that help in navigating the resulting map.

## D. Mapping Environmental Principles: Treatment Categories Shaped by EU Legal Culture

In doctrinally mapping the EU case law involving environmental principles, the cases fall into three treatment categories according to the judicial techniques used to engage (or not engage) environmental principles in the reasoning of decisions. These categories—policy cases, interpretive cases, and 'informing legal test' cases—are explained in this section. An important feature of these three categories is that, in different ways, they each reflect the CJEU's position on its proper constitutional role in reasoning with principles. The Court is certainly prepared to reason using environmental principles, taking the lead from the Treaties that dictate environmental principles as the legal basis of the EU's environmental policy. However, the Court's reasoning with these principles is also limited, reflecting the fact that environmental principles are policy ideas, which are employed by the EU institutions in domains of complex social and economic policy. Without always making this explicit, the doctrinal limits adopted in reasoning with environmental principles prevent the Court from straying too far into the sphere of policymaking. The CJEU's self-imposed doctrinal limits have a common link—the Court only employs environmental principles doctrinally in its reasoning when reviewing or interpreting acts of 'EU environmental competence' adopted first by the EU institutions on the basis of environmental principles.[51] The delimiting factor of 'EU environmental competence' is a notion that characterises the boundaries of EU environmental law generally and it is a central aspect of EU legal culture that shapes the roles of environmental principles in EU law.

As set out in the Introduction to the Chapter, 'EU environmental competence' is defined as the area of EU-prescribed policy authority concerning environmental matters within which political institutions can lawfully act.[52] EU environmental competence is set out, first and foremost, in Title XX of the TFEU, which confers competence on EU institutions to act in the area of environmental policy.[53] However EU environmental competence is a wider domain of competence than this for two reasons. First, under the integration principle, as Article 11 TFEU explicitly requires, environmental protection requirements are to be incorporated into

---

[51] A similar limit applies to constrain the legal roles of 'principles' in the EU Charter: Charter of Fundamental Rights of the European Union [2012] OJ C326/391, art 52(5). See further below, n 371.

[52] See above, text accompanying nn 3–4.

[53] TEU, art 5(1).

other EU policy domains. Whilst the legal impact of Article 11 in EU law is not yet fully resolved,[54] the EU case law involving environmental principles shows that the integration principle has widened the area of EU competence within which the CJEU recognises the legal relevance of environmental principles, to include at least public health, agriculture, transport and competition policy.

Second, this area of regulatory competence is shared with Member State governments, with the demarcation of policy authority for environmental matters determined by the principle of subsidiarity.[55] Section V(B)(v) demonstrates that '*Union* policy on the environment' in Article 191(2) TFEU[56] is interpreted by the CJEU to extend beyond the environmental policy of EU institutions to include the environmental policy of Member States when acting *within the scope of EU law*—that is, when Member States implement EU environmental policy but also when Member State environmental regulation encroaches on any area of EU harmonisation or on EU internal market rules in particular. In this expanded sense of EU environmental competence, environmental principles also have doctrinal roles to play, guiding the lawful discretion of Member States within this shared policy domain. These legal roles are triggered when the EU courts have to decide legal questions relating to purported exercises of EU environmental competence, understood in this broad sense.

There are other factors that limit the legal roles of environmental principles in EU legal reasoning—such as the openness of the review test applied by the Court (some Treaty provisions restrict the scope of EU environmental competence so as to generate review tests that leave no room for environmental principles in the Court's doctrine),[57] and the standing restrictions applied with respect to private litigants in bringing direct Article 263 actions[58]—but the boundaries of EU environmental competence limit are critical in this respect. They reflect a jurisdictional limit accepted by the EU courts in considering arguments and developing doctrine by reference to environmental principles. However, this limit is not a straitjacket for the CJEU. As indicated above in relation to the integration principle, the very notion of EU environmental competence can be stretched by the Court's own reasoning. Further, the Court's interpretation of when other institutions have taken action on the basis of environmental principles is sometimes a matter only of the Court's interpretation.[59]

In light of this appreciation of the internal EU legal culture in which environmental principles have legal roles, the chapter identifies that there are three different ways in which the EU courts reason with environmental principles as a matter

---

[54] See ch 3, Section III(A)–(C).
[55] TEU, art 5(1) & 5(3).
[56] Formerly 'Community policy on the environment': ex-174(2) TEC.
[57] See Section III(D).
[58] Case C-263/02 P *Commission v Jego-Quere et Cie SA* [2004] ECR I-3425.
[59] eg *Monsanto* (n 7): see Section IV(B)(i).

of doctrine. That is, there are three treatment categories that map the case law. The first category—*policy cases*—comprises cases in which environmental principles are mentioned or argued about but the EU courts do not use them in any way to resolve the legal issue before them. Rather they treat the principles as policy ideas either that are yet to be applied in legislative or decision-making processes of EU and Member State institutions acting within the scope of EU environmental competence, or that have otherwise been applied in such processes by EU institutions exhaustively. Environmental principles do not act as independent legal standards against which any EU action might be reviewed, or by which any Member State action might be defended. In all these cases, the EU courts are not being asked to interpret or determine the lawfulness of EU or Member State action taken on the basis of environmental principles within the scope of EU environmental competence. Thus they have no proper role to engage with legal arguments involving environmental principles. Principles are adduced in argument beyond the constitutional competence of the courts, or discussed in a way that is extraneous to the decisive reasoning of the case. Thus also included in this category of cases are cases in which environmental principles are mentioned simply as part of the policy background to the case. In all these cases, environmental principles have no doctrinal roles; they do not inform the reasoning of the courts in any decisive way. Rather, they remain policy ideas that are for the non-judicial institutions of the EU to pursue and implement, with no legal compulsion for them to do so.

The second treatment category—*interpretive cases*—comprises those cases in which EU courts use environmental principles to interpret expressions of EU environmental competence. That is, environmental principles are employed doctrinally to interpret EU legislation enacted on the basis of EU environmental competence in Title XX of the TFEU, or to interpret EU Treaty provisions beyond Title XX that fall within the scope of EU environmental competence by virtue of the integration principle. The judicial technique adopted with respect to environmental principles in these cases is teleological interpretation that engages environmental principles as purposes underlying the legislation or Treaty provision at issue. Environmental principles are thus relied on to elaborate the nature and direction of the EU environmental competence exercised, or to be exercised, in a range of discrete regulatory contexts. There are two constitutionally contentious aspects of this interpretive function. First, whilst the EU courts engage in purposive interpretation of EU measures that are determined to be based on environmental principles, the courts also determine when such measures are so based, even when this might not be obvious on the face of a particular Directive or Treaty provision. Through their interpretive function, the EU courts can thus expand the boundaries of EU environmental competence in relation to which environmental principles are found to be legally relevant as interpretive aids. Second, the open-textured formulation of environmental principles gives the courts a broad discretion in such interpretive tasks, so that the courts are effectively defining the competence of EU and Member State institutions acting in this policy domain through their interpretive findings, sometimes in unexpected or significant ways. Furthermore, the principles are themselves being interpreted in these cases and given marginal definitions as they are used to clarify ambiguous EU legislation or Treaty provisions. As indicated in Chapter Three,[60] environmental principles conceal multiple potential meanings, so they must be interpreted and find contingent expression within discrete legal cultures.

The third treatment category—*informing legal test cases*—is the group of cases in which environmental principles are used in reviewing the lawful boundaries and exercise of EU environmental competence. This category includes two types of cases: *legal basis cases* (informing legal tests for reviewing the boundaries within which EU institutions must exercise their Treaty competence in environmental matters), and *exercise of competence cases* (informing tests of administrative review that determine the lawfulness of environmental competence exercised within the scope of EU law). In both types of cases, either EU or Member State institutions have (purportedly) exercised EU environmental competence on the basis of environmental principles, but the validity of this exercise is under review. In both cases, environmental principles are used to inform the relevant legal review tests that are applied. The central issue in both types of these cases is the lawful extent of discretionary power afforded to these institutions to adopt environmental policy on the basis of environmental principles, when acting within the scope of EU law. The issue is not whether these institutions *should* adopt any particular line of policy—the EU courts are not engaged in reviewing the merits of institutional decision-making in these cases.[61] Again, environmental principles are employed legally to define and delimit the nature of EU environmental competence, broadly understood, rather than compelling its exercise in any way.

The second set of cases in this treatment category—cases concerning the proper exercise of EU environmental competence—is the most voluminous and complex. These cases are complex because they include review of both EU and Member State action in environmental matters (including public health matters), and because of the doctrinal openness and ongoing evolution of the review tests that environmental principles are used to inform. These review tests include manifest error of assessment and proportionality, which are commonly applied tests in EU administrative law, along with developing administrative law tests for scrutinising factual decision-making, as well as rules relating to lawful derogations from the free movement of goods guarantee in Article 34 TFEU. Further, with respect to the precautionary principle, a new review test is generated by the principle itself: a test of 'adequate scientific evidence' or 'due diligence'. The precautionary principle, in light of the Commission Communication on the precautionary

---

[60] See ch 3, text accompanying n 1 and generally.

[61] While the courts do not evaluate or remake institutional decisions on the merits, they do scrutinise closely the factual basis of institutional decision-making and will annul decisions where there has been a failure to evaluate factual evidence with sufficient rigour, particularly in relation to scientific decision-making in the context of risk regulation: see Section V(B).

principle ('Communication'),[62] is used to generate this legal review test, which has been applied to review EU and Member State discretion exercised in public health cases. While the courts are using a different reasoning technique with respect to the precautionary principle by *generating* a new legal test, these cases are considered together because a version of this test is usually applied to inform a broader review test in reviewing the exercise of EU environmental competence by either EU or Member State institutions. This makes for somewhat confusing analysis, which reflects the particularly complicated doctrinal role of the precautionary principle in EU law, but this confusion reflects the fact that environmental principles are being used both to define and to police the boundaries of EU environmental competence.

These three treatment categories demonstrate that environmental principles have legal roles in EU law that match three different techniques of judicial reasoning: avoiding their use altogether in developing doctrine; their use as interpretive aids; and their use to inform legal review tests. These treatment categories are not qualitatively equivalent in a taxonomic sense—they involve different types of judicial reasoning *and* different reasons. This includes differing reasons relied on by the courts within treatment categories. Thus policy cases avoid doctrinal reasoning involving environmental principles for several distinct reasons, which are not neatly or logically connected. These three treatment categories are best understood as reflecting key elements of EU legal culture—including the nature of the CJEU's jurisdiction, the central role of competence in EU environmental law (including the Treaties' prescription of environmental principles to inform this), the evolving role of the CJEU in interpreting and policing this competence, and the constitutional limits of the Court's role. The doctrinal roles of environmental principles in EU law are mapped within these categories in the Parts that follow, reflecting and expressing these elements of EU legal culture.

## III. Policy Cases

The first treatment category comprises 'policy cases'—cases in which environmental principles are raised in argument, or mentioned or discussed by the EU courts, but are legally irrelevant in deciding the question at issue in the particular case. Advocate-General Sharpston, in the ECJ appeal of *Land Oberösterreich*, observes why EU courts are often reluctant to engage with environmental principles—in this instance the precautionary principle—to resolve particular legal issues, although this observation is not decisive for the legal question in this case.[63]

---

[62] Commission of the European Communities, 'Communication from the Commission on the Precautionary Principle', COM (2000) 1 ('Communication'). See ch 3, text accompanying nn 153–163.

[63] See below, text accompanying nn 110–113.

The Austrian government had defended its national ban on genetically modified plants and animals, which contravened an applicable EU Directive, arguing that the Commission's refusal to approve the ban did not adequately take into account the precautionary principle. Reflecting the view of the CFI at first instance, Advocate-General Sharpston observed that:[64]

> ... the concerns [raised by the Austrian government in argument] are *policy concerns* which must be dealt with in political fora. It is not for this or any other court to determine proper national or Community environmental policy. And the concerns in question are not in themselves directly relevant to the legal issues raised in this case ...

The idea of separation between legal issues and environmental principles as policy concerns filters through the cases in this treatment category, reflecting the fact that the legal issues in these cases do not involve the review or interpretation of EU environmental competence first exercised by EU or Member State institutions. Further, the EU courts have no business legally compelling EU institutions to take particular policy actions on the basis of environmental principles, and they resist arguments encouraging them to do so. As a result, there is no room for the courts to consider legal arguments based on environmental principles. Rather, environmental principles articulate policy positions to be adopted at the discretion of EU and Member State institutions within the scope of EU environmental competence. As the Court of Justice held in *Fipa Group*:[65]

> Article 191(2) TFEU ... does no more than define the general environmental objectives of the European Union, since Article 192 TFEU confers on the European Parliament and the Council of the European Union ... responsibility for deciding what action is to be taken in order to attain those objectives.

In the cases in this section, this institutional discretion has not been exercised at all, or it has been exercised but is not at issue in the cases, or it has been exercised unlawfully in other EU law terms. In all these cases, environmental principles appear as policy ideas, which inform EU environmental competence generally but have no effect on the legal outcomes of each case.

Four kinds of policy cases are identifiable in this treatment category. First, there are cases in which the principles are observed as part of the policy background to the case, but have no doctrinal role in its resolution.[66] Second, there are cases in

---

[64] Joined Cases C-439/05 P and C-454/05 P *Land Oberösterreich v Commission* [2007] 3 CMLR 52, Opinion of Advocate-General Sharpston (15 May 2007) [145]. In its judgment on appeal, the ECJ upheld the decision of the CFI, but did not comment on Austria's precautionary principle argument specifically: Joined Cases C-439/05 P and C-454/05 P *Land Oberösterreich v Commission* [2007] 3 CMLR 52 (ECJ).

[65] Case C-534/13 *Ministero dell'Ambiente e della Tutela del Territorio e del Mare v Fipa Group SrL* [2015] ECLI:EU:C:2015:140 [39].

[66] Joined Cases C-164/97 & C-165/97 *Parliament v Council (Forest Protection)* [1999] ECR I-1139, Opinion of Advocate-General Jacobs (17 December 1998); Case C-318/98 *Fornasar* [2000] ECR I-4785; Case C-6/03 *Deponiezweckverband Eiterköpfe v Land Rheinland-Pfalz* [2005] ECR I-2753; Case

which the policy discretion conferred by EU environmental principles has *yet to be exercised* in an area of EU environmental competence not yet subject to harmonisation, which exercise the courts have no business to compel.[67] Third, there are cases in which the policy discretion of the EU legislative institutions *has been exercised* to harmonise or otherwise legislate in an area of EU environmental competence, on the basis of environmental principles, but where the exercise of such competence is not the subject of legal inquiry.[68] Arguments challenging related EU action on the basis of environmental principles, or challenging or defending Member State action outside the relevant scheme of EU legislation on similar grounds, are rejected by the Court. Environmental principles do not constitute freestanding legal standards for compelling, interpreting or defending EU and Member State environmental actions generally. Fourth, there are cases in which Member States have purported to exercise EU environmental competence, on the basis of the precautionary principle in particular (derogating from internal market harmonising measures on environmental grounds under Article 114(4) and (5) TFEU), but have done so unlawfully in terms of the Treaty, thus leaving no room for legal arguments based on environmental principles.[69] In this final set of cases, the explicit provisions of the relevant review tests in the TFEU limit the discretion of Member States to exercise EU environment competence and thus limit the legal roles of environmental principles.

Cases in all these four groups are linked by the common theme that, while environmental principles might provide a policy basis for EU environmental competence (within the limits of the Treaty), they are not principles that are directly engaged or relevant in resolving the legal issues before the courts. Rather, the principles are part of EU and Member State institutional decision-making processes—whether legislative or administrative—relevant to these cases, whether in the background or built into the legislative structure under consideration, but not legally at issue or justiciable. Or, they are excluded altogether from the institutional decision-making processes concerned by explicit limits within the Treaties. For all these reasons, environmental principles have no doctrinal roles in these cases.

The following four sections consider representative cases that fall within these four sets of policy cases. The Part concludes by examining a further group of cases that challenge the boundaries of this treatment category, by extending the Court's

---

C-494/01 *Commission v Ireland* [2005] ECR I-3331; Case C-176/03 *Commission v Council (Environmental Crime)* [2005] ECR I-07879, Opinion of Advocate-General Colomer (26 May 2005).

[67] Case C-379/92 *Re Peralta* [1994] ECR I-3453; Case C-445/00 *Austria v Council* [2003] ECR I-8549.

[68] *Standley* (n 35); Case C-6/99 *Association Greenpeace France v Ministère de l'Agriculture et de la Pêche* [2000] ECR I-1651; *Monsanto* (n 7); *Waddenzee* (n 45); Case C-132/03 *Ministero della Salute v Codacons* [2005] ECR I-3465; Case C-221/06 *Stadtgemeinde Frohnleiten v Bundesminister für Land- und Forstwirtschaft* [2007] ECR I-09643.

[69] Case C-3/00 *Denmark v Commission (Sulphites)* [2003] ECR I-2643; Joined Cases T-366/03 and T-235/04 *Land Oberösterreich and Austria v Commission* [2005] ECR II-4005.

role in reviewing EU action on the basis of environmental principles. This devia-tion in the case law reflects a potentially significant change in terms of the legal roles that environmental principles might play in EU law, but one that has yet to be adopted by the EU courts.

## A. Principles as Policy Background

In this first set of EU policy cases, judicial references to environmental principles are passing ones. The EU courts observe the principles as part of the contextual policy background to a case, but they play no direct role in justifying the reasoning of decisions.

One such case is *Deponiezweckverband Eiterköpfe v Land Rheinland-Pfalz*,[70] in which the interpretation of the Landfill Directive and Article 193 TFEU (ex-Article 176 EC) were at issue.[71] The ECJ found that German national landfill meas-ures, which were more stringently protective than those set out in the Directive, were compatible with EU law, primarily because the EU rules did not exhaustively harmonise this area of waste regulation. In finding that the Landfill Directive per-mitted this shared regulation of German landfill waste, the ECJ set out the policy background informing the adoption of the Directive, including the four principles in Article 191(2) TFEU (ex-Article 174(2) EC).[72] The principles of Article 191(2) are often referred to as a group of policy ideas in Court of Justice judgments in this way.

Another policy case, in which the principle of sustainable development is dis-cussed by the Advocate-General with some enthusiasm to set out the policy back-ground of the case,[73] is *Commission v Council (Environmental Crime)*.[74] In this case, Advocate-General Ruiz-Jarabo Colomer considers the nature of sustainable development in the EC Treaty, in light of the overall 'globalisation' of environmen-tal policy concerning sustainable development, in order to '[illustrate] the impor-tance which "ecological consciousness" has acquired in recent decades'.[75] This global policy background provides a platform from which the Advocate-General then develops a radical legal argument—that Community competence to develop environmental policy should go so far as to require criminal sanctions where this is the only 'effective, proportionate and dissuasive' means for its enforcement.[76] While the sustainable development principle is not used doctrinally in this legal

---

[70] *Deponiezweckverband Eiterköpfe* (n 66).
[71] Council Directive (EC) 1999/31 on the landfill of waste [1999] OJ L182/1 ('Landfill Directive').
[72] *Deponiezweckverband Eiterköpfe* (n 66) [28].
[73] Although it is not consistently described as a 'principle', being also described as a 'concept'.
[74] Case C-176/03 *Commission v Council (Environmental Crime)* [2005] ECR I-07879.
[75] *Environmental Crime, Opinion of Advocate-General Colomer* (n 66) [61]–[71].
[76] ibid [72].

conclusion—indeed, it is not mentioned by the ECJ, which nevertheless arrives at the conclusion suggested by the Advocate-General—the principle paints a policy picture that contextualises the legal arguments made to support the Court's ultimate conclusion.[77]

## B. Principles of EU Environmental Competence—Unexercised Discretion

In this second set of policy cases, the EU courts reject arguments based on environmental principles, finding them legally irrelevant since environmental principles are limited to defining policy discretion exercised within the scope of EU environmental competence and do not empower the courts to compel its exercise. It is in this sense that EU environmental policy '*shall* be based' on the four environmental principles set out in Article 191(2). Environmental principles do not justify stand-alone legal arguments for compelling environmental action. Rather, EU courts will wait for institutions to exercise their discretion within this area before employing environmental principles doctrinally to interpret or police the scope of EU environmental competence.

*Re Peralta* is an exemplary case.[78] In this case, the ECJ found that it had no business compelling the exercise of EU environmental policy discretion. It involved an Article 267 TFEU (ex-Article 177 TEC) reference to the ECJ from an Italian court asking, inter alia, whether an Italian law that prohibited national vessels from discharging certain harmful substances into the sea, in contravention of internationally accepted practice, was precluded by the preventive principle.[79] The ECJ found that the preventive principle did not preclude the national legislation because Article 191 TFEU (ex-Article 174 TEC) is 'confined to defining the general [environmental] objectives of the Community'.[80] Moreover it is the responsibility of the Council to determine what action is to be taken in this policy field, and Article 193 TFEU (ex-Article 176 TEC) allows Member States to adopt more stringent environmental protective measures in any case, so long as they are compatible with the Treaty.

This reasoning can be read in one of two ways. First, the appeal to the preventive principle was unsuccessful since Article 191(2) extends only to *EU*

---

[77] Although the integration principle does play a doctrinal role in the Court's reasoning: see below, text accompanying nn 209–210.

[78] *Re Peralta* (n 67). See also *Austria v Council* (n 67).

[79] This argument may seem counter-intuitive. The argument put to the Italian court was that the level of environmental protection required by the preventive principle in the Treaty should match that set out in the MARPOL Convention (*UNTS, vols 1340 and 1341, no 22484*), the relevant provisions of which were not as stringent as those in Italian national law.

[80] *Re Peralta* (n 67) [57].

environmental policy, and does not affect Member State actions,[81] at least to the extent that they are acting outside the scope of EU law.[82] However the ECJ did not explicitly say this—it referred instead to the general nature of Article 191, to the responsibility of the Council to adopt EU environmental policy, and to the latitude afforded to Member States to adopt complementary and more protective measures. The better way to read this case is that the preventive principle argument was unsuccessful because the ECJ was being asked to adopt and compel an environmental policy position, which it felt it is not its job to do. While Member State action was at issue, EU environmental policy and Member State environmental policy (covering common territory) overlap (as acknowledged by Article 193), and, while the EU could take action in this unharmonised area if it wanted to, whether it does so is not an issue for the EU courts. The preventive principle did not have legal force beyond its general policy prescription role.[83]

## C. Principles of EU Environmental Competence—Exercised but Unchallenged Discretion

In this third set of policy cases, environmental principles have been unsuccessfully relied on in argument to either challenge or interpret legislative schemes regulating environmental and public health matters. The EU courts have found, with respect to each legislative scheme examined, that environmental principles were legally relevant only in guiding the policy discretion afforded to EU or Member State institutions in exercising decision-making power under, or in implementing, the elements of these schemes that are based on environmental principles. However, the exercise of such discretion was not at issue in these cases. Rather, legal arguments are made, on the basis of environmental principles, to challenge or defend EU action and Member State action in relation to these schemes more broadly. The outcomes of these cases show that environmental principles do not support such independent legal arguments for challenging or interpreting EU environmental action generally.

In these cases, the ECJ or Court of Justice identifies environmental principles as being legally relevant in guiding institutional policy discretion within EU

---

[81] Nicolas de Sadeleer, 'The Precautionary Principle in EC Health and Environmental Law' (2006) 12(2) *ELJ* 139, 143.

[82] *cf* Section V(B)(v) below.

[83] This position is reinforced by Advocate-General Kokott in Case C-378/08 *Raffinerie Mediterranee (ERG)*, where she rejects a preliminary reference question suggesting art 191 as a legal basis for assessing national rules on environmental liability; rather art 191 'simply sets out the general objectives of [EU] environmental law, which the [EU] legislature must give substance to before they can be binding on the Member States': Case C-378/08 *Raffinerie Mediterranee (ERG) v Ministero dello Sviluppo Economico* ECR I-01919, Opinion of Advocate-General Kokott (22 October 2009) [45]; approved by the ECJ: Case C-378/08 *Raffinerie Mediterranee (ERG) v Ministero dello Sviluppo Economico* [2010] ECR I-01919 [46].

environmental regulatory frameworks, but they have no role in deciding the specific legal questions involved in these cases. This is because, whilst environmental principles underlie and guide the exercise of EU environmental competence in these cases, they do not have independent legal roles that extend beyond this. There are various ways in which environmental principles inform the exercise of EU environmental competence in these cases. They are taken into account by relevant Commission decision-making processes established by or supporting the regulatory scheme under consideration;[84] they guide Member State discretion in opting out of a regulatory scheme through a safeguard clause based on the principles;[85] they guide Member State discretion in implementing EU environmental schemes;[86] and they also define the limits of such EU environmental schemes.[87] However, the legal questions in these cases are not concerned with these legal roles for environmental principles in defining and constraining EU environmental competence. They are concerned with challenging EU and Member State measures in a way that undermines the policymaking discretion of institutions and extends beyond the boundaries of EU environmental competence exercised on the basis of environmental principles.

Several of these cases involve harmonising EU legislation relating to genetically modified organisms (GMOs). In these cases, the precautionary principle has an important role in guiding the policy discretion exercised by EU institutions that are tasked with making decisions under frameworks of harmonised GMO regulation, and that of Member States under safeguard clauses within these EU frameworks. This legal function exhausts any broader legal role for the precautionary principle in challenging elements of these regulatory schemes.

An example is *Ministero della Salute v Codacons*.[88] This was a preliminary reference from an Italian court concerning the interpretation of Article 2(2)(b) of Regulation 1139/98 on the compulsory labelling of certain genetically modified (GM) food.[89] Article 2(2)(b) provided an exception from the Regulation's labelling requirements in the case of foodstuffs where the concentration of GM food was less than 1 per cent and such presence was 'adventitious'. The issue for the ECJ was whether that exception applied to infant food, and the Court found that it did, since there was no indication from the wording, the context or the purpose of Article 2(2)(b) that it should not so apply, and EU measures adopted with respect to the labelling of infant food had not been extended to derogate from this provision.[90] There was no room for calling into question this interpretation 'on the

---

[84] *Monsanto* (n 7); *Codacons* (n 68).

[85] *Greenpeace* (n 68); *Monsanto* (n 7).

[86] *Standley* (n 35); *Stadtgemeinde* (n 68).

[87] *Fipa Group* (n 65).

[88] *Codacons* (n 68).

[89] Council Regulation (EC) 1139/98 concerning the compulsory indication on the labelling of certain foodstuffs produced from genetically modified organisms [1998] OJ L159/4 (as amended) art (2)(b).

[90] *Codacons* (n 68) [54]–[55].

basis of the precautionary principle', which was found to be applicable only as part of the decision-making process involved in putting the relevant GM foods on the market in the first place, which is intended to ensure that the genetically modified organisms (GMOs) are safe for the consumer.[91] Once such a decision had been made, there was no longer any relevant 'uncertainty as to the existence or extent of risks to human health', a 'presupposition' of the precautionary principle.[92] The Court made no attempt to explore this prior decision-making process, since it was not challenged in argument (or because the referred question did not extend that far).[93] In any case, the precautionary principle, whatever it involves, was confined to influencing the decision-making of the Commission under the relevant EU legislation that embodied the precautionary principle and not the particular legal issue of interpretation before the Court.

*Monsanto* is another GM food case in which the precautionary principle was raised in argument, largely unsuccessfully. The *Monsanto* case arose out of the Italian government's abiding concern over the risks involved in releasing GMOs and putting GM products on the market. At issue in the case was the 'simplified procedure' in the previous Regulation 258/97 on novel foods for authorising the introduction of novel GM foods on to the European market, which could be employed when a novel food was produced from, but no longer contained, any GMOs, *and* when it was 'substantially equivalent' to an existing food.[94] This simplified procedure required mere notification to the Commission once substantial equivalence was established (by existing science or in the opinion of a relevant national food authority), and no detailed risk assessment by the Commission, as required by the formal (non-simplified) novel food authorisation process. The Italian government, relying on the safeguard procedure in Article 12 of the Regulation,[95] passed a decree temporarily banning novel foods produced from particular strands of GM maize that still contained small amounts of transgenic protein. This decree was challenged in the Italian national courts by the producers of the GM maize (Monsanto). The Italian court referred several questions to the ECJ, the two most relevant concerning: (a) the interpretation of the safeguard clause in Article 12, particularly in relation to the ability of Member States to take action on the basis of the precautionary principle, and (b) the legality of the 'simplified procedure', in particular whether it breached Articles 169 and 191 TFEU (ex-Articles 153 and 174 EC) and the principles of precaution and proportionality.

Arguments on the basis of the precautionary principle were made on both questions, suggesting that the principle might have a legal role which overlaid the

---

[91] ibid [56], [63].

[92] ibid [61].

[93] cf *Pfizer* (n 31): see Section V(B)(ii).

[94] Regulation 258/97/EC concerning novel foods and novel food ingredients [1997] OJ L43/1, arts 3(4), 5. Note this regulation has been replaced with Regulation 2015/2283/EU on novel foods [2015] OJ 327/1.

[95] ibid, art 12.

scheme of the Regulation, and which could be relied on to guide or contest its operation. The Court gave a limited legal role to the precautionary principle as an aid in interpreting Article 12, discussed in Part IV below.[96] However, the precautionary principle was not found to have a legal role independent of the scheme of the Regulation. The Court found that a Member State could only take action on the basis of the precautionary principle in accordance with Article 12, which is based on and gives legislative expression to the principle in this EU regulatory context. When it came to challenging the lawfulness of the Regulation's simplified procedure, the ECJ gave short shrift to the argument based on the precautionary principle, finding that the principle was already relevantly taken into account in the authorisation and safeguard decision-making procedures set up by the Regulation.[97] The precautionary principle was not a general legal ground for reviewing the legality of the simplified authorisation procedure. Rather, as in *Codacons*, it was to be taken into account in the decision-making processes involved in the normal authorisation and safeguard procedures of the Regulation, undertaken by the Commission.

Three other cases, which relate to a range of EU environmental schemes, also exemplify this set of policy cases. In each of these cases, environmental principles underlie an EU environmental measure but there is a legal challenge to the EU measure or related Member State action, which either undermines the policymaking discretion of the institutions involved or extends beyond the scope of the EU measure in question. The first case, *Standley*, is a premature challenge to EU environmental competence exercised on the basis of environmental principles. This case involved a challenge to the legality of provisions of Directive 91/676 on nitrate pollution from agricultural sources,[98] on the basis of, inter alia, infringement of the principle of rectification at source and the polluter pays principle.[99] In this case, the relevant provisions of the Directive were found to be consistent with these principles, and should be interpreted in accordance with them. The Directive's scheme was based on the environmental title (Title XX TFEU) and its provisions were sufficiently flexible for Member States to implement its measures in accordance with the principle of rectification at source and polluter pays principle.[100] The result of the case was that, until the Directive was interpreted and applied by the Member States in a manner incompatible with those principles, they remain principles of policy that are incorporated into the provisions of the Directive and guide the discretion of Member States in overseeing its implementation into national law.

---

[96] See below Section IV(B)(i).

[97] *Monsanto* (n 7) [133].

[98] Council Directive (EC) 91/676 concerning the protection of waters against pollution caused by nitrates from agricultural sources [1991] OJ L375/1.

[99] *Standley* (n 35).

[100] ibid [51]–[53]. For these reasons, this case could also be seen as a prospective interpretive case involving reasoning with principles (see Part IV).

The second environmental case is *Stadtgemeinde Frohnleiten*,[101] which concerned the shipment of waste from Italy to Austria. In the course of deciding the
legal issue in this case—whether an Austrian tax on contaminated waste breached
Article 110 TFEU[102]—the ECJ considered the extent to which a Member State can
rely on the principles of proximity and self-sufficiency to defend the operation of
a tax that discriminated against imported waste. These environmental principles
are not found in the Treaties but are principles of EU waste policy, which generally provide that waste should be treated (recovered or disposed of) as near to its
source as possible, and that a designated area (region, Member State, or the EU as
a whole) should be self-sufficient in dealing with its own waste.[103] These environmental principles extend the grouping of environmental principles that are legally
relevant in EU law. In this case, there was no scope for a Member State to rely
on these principles to justify a discriminatory tax because they had already been
relied on by the EU institutions in harmonising waste shipment regulation within
this area of EU environmental competence,[104] thereby exhausting their legal roles
and limiting the discretion of Member States to take independent environmental
action.[105] Member States could only rely on these environmental principles, to
object to or to hinder imported waste on environmental grounds, by following the
explicit procedures implementing these principles in the Waste Shipment Regulation. They could not rely on them as independent grounds of legal argument in
this case, which raised a different legal question.

A third case that complements *Stadtgemeinde Frohnleiten* is *Fipa Group*.[106] This
case also questioned the legality of a Member State measure aiming to pursue an
environmental objective, in light of EU environmental principles. However, the
harmonising EU environmental measure in this case—the Environmental Liability Directive[107]—was not so extensive in its regulatory scope. The case was a preliminary reference from the Italian courts, concerning the obligations on owners
of contaminated land in cases where the original polluters could not be found.
Italian legislation provided that owners of such land could only be liable for the
costs of remedial work up to the value of the site, and were not required to take

---

[101] *Stadtgemeinde* (n 68).
[102] Ex-art 90 EC ('No Member State shall impose, directly or indirectly, on the products of other
Member States any internal taxation of any kind in excess of that imposed directly or indirectly on
similar domestic products').
[103] On the ambiguous meaning of these principles that are found in EU waste legislation, see Eloise
Scotford, 'The New Waste Directive—Trying to Do it All … An Early Assessment' (2009) 11(2) *Env LR*
75, 87–88.
[104] Council Regulation (EC) 259/93 on the supervision and control of shipments of waste within,
into and out of the EC [1993] OJ L030/1 ('WSR').
[105] *cf* Case 402/09 *Ioan Tatu v Statul român prin Ministerul Finanțelor și Economiei and others* [2011]
ECR I-02711 (where Romania sought to rely on environmental objectives to defend a national tax that
otherwise breached art 110, unsuccessfully).
[106] *Fipa Group* (n 65).
[107] Council & Parliament Directive (EC) 2004/35 on environmental liability with regard to the prevention and remedying of environmental damage [2004] OJ L143/56 ('ELD').

remedial measures themselves. The Italian courts referred a question to the Court of Justice, asking whether this Italian law was consistent with the environmental principles in the Environmental Liability Directive and in Article 191(2) TFEU. The Court of Justice found that there was no problem with the Italian law as a matter of EU law, since it applied to circumstances outside the scope of the Environmental Liability Directive and thus was not based on the principles in Article 191(2), including the polluter pays principle, and did not need to be guided by them. The Court of Justice emphasised that the principles in Article 191(2) were legally relevant only to measures covered by EU environmental competence that had been exercised:[108]

> [S]ince Article 191(2) TFEU, which establishes the 'polluter pays' principle, is directed at action at EU level, that provision cannot be relied on as such by individuals in order to exclude the application of national legislation—such as that at issue in the main proceedings—in an area covered by environmental policy for which there is no EU legislation adopted on the basis of Article 192 TFEU that specifically covers the situation in question.

All these cases show that environmental principles have been used in legal argument in various ways to question or impugn EU and Member State measures relating to environmental and public health policy. They also show that such arguments have to be carefully targeted in order to be successful. In particular, environmental principles are not legally relevant in relation to measures that are not within the scope of EU environmental competence, which has first been exercised by EU and Member State institutions exercising their policy discretion under the Treaties.

## D.  Purported Exercises of EU Environmental Competence: Member State Derogation under Articles 114(4) and (5) TFEU

This final set of policy cases comprises cases in which Member States purport to exercise EU environmental competence on the basis of environmental principles, but do so unlawfully because their action is outside the permissible bounds of the TFEU, thereby restricting doctrinal roles for environmental principles in subsequent legal challenges. While environmental policy is a shared competence, the scope for unilateral Member State environmental action is restricted by directly applicable Treaty provisions (such as Article 110 TFEU in *Stadtgemeinde Frohnleiten* above) and harmonising measures taken by EU institutions, whether in relation to environmental policy (again exemplified in *Stadtgemeinde Frohnleiten*) or in relation to the internal market. In relation to internal market harmonising measures, Article 114 TFEU explicitly provides restricted grounds for Member

---

[108]  *Fipa Group* (n 65) [40].

States to take unilateral action on environmental protection grounds where this conflicts with a harmonising measure. These limited grounds give rise to Treaty-based 'review' tests for examining the legality of derogating Member State action. In this set of cases, the ECJ rejected arguments of Member States defending such derogation from internal market harmonising measures on the basis of the precautionary principle. Such arguments were rejected since they are not directly relevant to the particular legal inquiries required by Articles 114(4) and (5), which set out precise and limited circumstances in which Member States are permitted to derogate from harmonising measures, leaving no room for consideration of the precautionary principle.[109] The ECJ thus held that the Treaty precludes Member States having any discretion to exercise EU environmental competence on the basis of the precautionary principle in these cases. Arguments based on the precautionary principle are dismissed as considerations that should be addressed in national and EU political arenas.

In *Land Oberösterreich*, mentioned above,[110] the Austrian government had sought to derogate from Directive 2001/18 on the release of GMOs (a harmonising measure) by imposing, in a particular farming area, a general ban on the cultivation of genetically modified plants or seed, and on the breeding and release of transgenic animals.[111] The Commission had refused to allow this derogation, and the CFI and ECJ supported the Commission's position,[112] since Austria had failed to fulfil the conditions in Article 114(5) that permit derogation for internal market measures adopted under Article 114 (in particular, it failed to present 'new scientific evidence' and to identify 'a problem specific to that Member State'). Arguments that the Commission had failed adequately to consider the precautionary principle in assessing the submissions of the Austrian government, in this case where the risks associated with releasing and propagating GMOs were highly contestable, thus failed. These arguments added nothing to the legal conditions imposed by the Treaty. Rather than being a reason to derogate from the Directive, the precautionary principle was found to inform fundamentally its harmonised procedures of GMO authorisation. Each GMO underwent rigorous assessment by the Commission of the potential risks it might pose for environmental and human health, in accordance with the precautionary principle, in order to be approved for release under the procedures laid down in Directive 2001/18. The precautionary

---

[109] ie these review tests are not sufficiently open to allow the EU courts to use environmental principles to inform their application: *cf* Section V(B)(v).

[110] See above, text accompanying n 64.

[111] Council & Parliament Directive (EC) 2001/18 on the deliberate release into the environment of genetically modified organisms [2001] OJ L106/1. This was an internal market measure adopted under ex-art 95 EC (now art 114 TFEU).

[112] *Land Oberösterreich* (CFI) (n 69); *Land Oberösterreich* (ECJ) (n 64). See also Case C-3/00 *Denmark v Commission (Sulphites)* [2003] ECR I-2643, Opinion of Advocate-General Tizzano (30 May 2002) [100] in relation to art 114(4).

principle had no further doctrinal role in relation to the particular tests, mandated by the Treaty conditions in Article 114(5), applied by the ECJ to decide this case.[113]

Again, in these policy cases, environmental principles do not constitute free-standing legal arguments, here for defending Member State action on environmental grounds. Rather, the purported exercise of EU environmental competence by the Member States was unlawful under the internal market provisions of the Treaty, which limit the scope of EU environmental competence exercised by Member States, and thus the doctrinal roles of environmental principles in EU law.

## E. Integration Principle: Breaking Down the Barrier of Policy Cases?

In the policy cases considered so far, EU courts have found that environmental principles have no doctrinal roles to play. In these cases, the legal questions at issue have not directly concerned the exercise, by EU or Member State institutions, of EU environmental competence based on environmental principles. There is however some suggestion in the case law that this competence limit, which demarcates policy cases and constrains the Court's role in developing doctrine with respect to environmental principles, can be stretched or overridden. These cases involve the integration principle (and other environmental principles incidental to, or in combination with, the integration principle) as an independent legal ground for challenging EU action generally. These cases suggest that environmental principles might have an overriding legal role in constraining *all* action within the scope of EU law, which can be challenged by way of review in court, giving the CJEU a robust constitutional role in the domain of environmental policy and undermining the policy discretion of EU institutions (and potentially Member State institutions acting within the scope of EU law).

Early cases militated against such a view, but left room for its development. In *Austria v Parliament*,[114] a case involving a challenge to the legality of an EU Regulation establishing an eco-points system for heavy goods vehicles under the EU's transport policy, the Austrian government argued that the Regulation violated the 'objective of promoting sustainable development laid down in [Article 11 TFEU]' because it resulted in an increase of NOx emissions.[115] Advocate-General Geelhoed responded to this argument by finding that the integration principle in Article 11 does not act with 'simple rigidity' as a binding rule: 'it cannot be

---

[113] *cf* Case C-165/08 *Commission v Poland* [2009] ECR I-06843. In pre-litigation procedure, the Polish government raised a similar precautionary principle argument to defend a measure derogating from Directive 2001/18, but shifted to an (unsuccessful) argument based on ethical principles: see [59] and generally.

[114] Case C-161/04 *Austria v Parliament and Council (Ecopoints)* [2006] ECR I-7183.

[115] Case C-161/04 *Austria v Parliament and Council (Ecopoints)* [2006] ECR I-7183, Opinion of Advocate-General Geelhoed (26 January 2006) [54].

regarded as laying down a standard according to which in defining [EU] policies environmental protection must always be taken to be the prevalent interest'.[116] The Court's role did not extend to 'unacceptably [restricting]' the discretionary powers of the EU institutions in this way. However, the Advocate-General did suggest that where ecological interests 'manifestly have not been taken into account or have been completely disregarded', the integration principle may serve as the standard for reviewing the validity of EU legislation.[117] Advocate-General Jacobs had previously picked up on this suggested legal role for the integration principle in *PreussenElektra*, arguing that it is 'not merely programmatic; it imposes legal obligations'.[118]

In the CFI decision of *Sweden v Commission*, such legal obligations based on the integration principle are demonstrated.[119] This case was a legality challenge to the Commission's decision to include a weedkiller substance—paraquat—in the list of approved plant protection products on the market under Directive 91/414 ('Plant Protection Product Directive').[120] Sweden claimed that the decision breached the integration principle, as well as the precautionary principle and the principle that 'a high level of protection should be ensured'.[121] The CFI accepted these arguments. The reasoning of the Court is quite technical, turning on scientific evidence that demonstrated compelling environmental and health risks associated with paraquat, which informed the Court's finding that these environmental principles were infringed. However, this was a case in which the Commission did *not* purport to act on the basis of any environmental principle (since it had approved the relevant substance) and yet these environmental principles were employed doctrinally to review its action. On one view, this is a case in which the integration principle was used to expand the scope of 'EU environmental competence' (to EU agricultural policy), so as to give other environmental principles (here the precautionary principle and principle of a high level of protection) doctrinal roles

---

[116] ibid [59].

[117] ibid. He also gave another proviso that the totality of measures in a policy area needs to be taken into account. The case was withdrawn by the Austrian government before it was decided by the ECJ.

[118] Case C-379/98 *PreussenElektra v Schhleswag* [2001] ECR I-2099, Opinion of Advocate-General Jacobs (26 October 2000) [231].

[119] Case T-229/04 *Sweden v Commission* [2007] ECR II-02437.

[120] Council Directive (EC) 91/414 concerning the placing of plant protection products on the market [1991] OJ L230/1.

[121] This so-called 'principle' is another EU environmental principle that demonstrates the porous grouping of environmental principles in EU law. It derives from art 191(2) TFEU ('Union policy on the environment shall aim at a high level of protection'), as well as references throughout the Treaty to a 'high level of protection' in various policy areas (see below n 167), but its description as a principle is inconsistent and it can be seen as an overall policy objective that does not set any particular standard, which is mediated by the need to take into account the diversity of situations across the EU: Ludwig Krämer, *EU Environmental Law* (7th edn, Sweet & Maxwell 2012) 11–13; *cf* Jan H Jans and Hans HB Vedder, *EU Environmental Law*, (4th edn, Europa Law Publishing 2012) 41–43. However, its doctrinal treatment as an environmental 'principle' in this case includes it within the group of legally relevant EU environmental principles for the purpose of this mapping exercise.

across a wider range of cases, in terms of subject-matter and policy competence. It thus potentially indicates that such expansion may occur to cover any area, or all areas, of EU policy competence, giving environmental principles wide-ranging legal roles in EU law.

It is also a remarkable case because the integration principle is not simply a linking and expanding principle in this case but, in doctrinal terms, it constitutes an explicit and separate ground for testing the lawfulness of the Commission decision.[122] The detailed reasoning of the CFI in arriving at this conclusion is obscure. Much of the reasoning focuses on the precautionary principle, and the case can also be viewed as an interpretive case, since the precautionary principle is applied to interpret provisions of the relevant Directive to determine a breach of that principle.[123] Its reasoning on the breach of the integration principle appears largely to rely on finding that other environmental principles have been infringed. However, the *independent* doctrinal roles of all three environmental principles are explicitly articulated by the Court—the nature of the legal reasoning is thus different from most EU cases in which environmental principles have doctrinal roles where there is some prior exercise of environmental competence by the EU institutions triggering the legal relevance of environmental principles.[124] More recent cases of the General Court also suggest that the precautionary principle can act as an independent ground of review in cases where EU measures are challenged on public health grounds. As discussed in Part V, these cases reflect that fact that the precautionary principle has been increasingly recognised as generally guiding risk-based decision-making in the area of public health.[125] These cases at least reflect a trend, throughout the case law mapped in this chapter, of the integration principle being relied on to expand the scope of EU law in which environmental principles have ever more influential doctrinal roles. Environmental principles not only have unique legal roles in EU law, but these roles are in a state of evolution.

## F. Conclusion

This Part has demonstrated that there are limits to the doctrinal roles taken on environmental principles in EU law. The scope of EU environmental competence,

---

[122] Environmental principles might also be 'infringed' by Member State measures if they are expressed in sufficiently clear terms in secondary legislation so that they are directly effective in EU law: *Futura, Opinion of Advocate-General Kokott* (n 35) [58]–[59]; *cf ERG* (n 83) [46].

[123] See below, text accompanying nn 181–186.

[124] While this case in some ways resembles the reasoning techniques used in informing legal review test cases examined in Section V(B) where Commission decisions are challenged for breach of the precautionary principle (eg in *Pfizer* (n 31) and Case T-392/02 *Solvay Pharmaceuticals BV v Council* [2004] ECR II-4555), *Sweden v Commission* is distinct in that the Court isolates environmental principles as independent standards that can be breached.

[125] eg Case C-77/09 *Gowan v Ministero della Salute* [2010] ECR I-13533; Case T-31/07 *Du Pont v Commission* [2013] ECLI:EU:T:2013:167; *cf* Case T-475/07 *Dow AgroSciences Ltd v Commission* [2011] ECR II-05937. See further n 297 and accompanying text.

and the proper role of the EU courts in interfering with EU and Member State institutional discretion, constrains legal arguments that might be made on the basis of environmental principles. In particular, the EU courts generally cannot compel the taking of particular environmental action on the basis of environmental principles, where EU institutions have not first acted to exercise their competence.

As a result, environmental principles do not operate as prescriptive legal solutions to environmental problems, in the manner hoped by some scholars and outlined in Chapter Two,[126] in this EU legal context. Further, environmental principles do not have pervasive and independent legal roles across EU law. Thus, rather than cohering EU environmental law, they signify both its competence-bounded reach, as well as its incremental expansion by virtue of the integration principle. Environmental principles also have a prominent role in guiding the policy discretion of EU and Member State institutions, which is often outside the preserve of legal control. Scholarly hopes with respect to environmental principles as legal concepts are thus often incorrectly focused within EU law, considering its developing doctrine, institutional constraints and distinctive legal culture.

## IV. Interpretive Cases

This second treatment category comprises cases in which EU courts interpret the EU Treaties or secondary EU legislation and rely on environmental principles to elucidate the meaning of ambiguous provisions.[127] The Court of Justice (and the ECJ before it) adopts the judicial technique of teleological interpretation in these cases, relying on the principles to inform the purposive inquiry undertaken, thereby introducing a doctrinal role for environmental principles in resolving questions of legal interpretation.

In these cases, the EU institutions have first exercised their EU environmental competence to legislate, or to act under a particular Treaty provision, on the basis of environmental principles and that exercise of competence is then legally constrained by environmental principles through their interpretive influence. In this way, environmental principles define the nature of EU environmental competence exercised by EU institutions.[128] However, because environmental principles are so general in their formulation, such 'definition' of competence also involves the

---

[126] See ch 2(II)(C).

[127] These are primarily referred by Member State courts under art 267 TFEU, but also include art 258 and 263 proceedings in which issues of interpretation arise.

[128] There are also indications that environmental principles can have interpretive roles in relation to EU environmental competence as exercised by Member State institutions. In one case, the polluter pays principle was suggested to have a role in interpreting a UK tax (levied on extracted materials used commercially for aggregates) in a dispute about the nature of the tax. This was a measure that fell within the scope of EU law in that it was designed to incentivise waste recovery, pursuing the aims of EU waste law

marginal definition of environmental principles themselves in each interpretive context—the way in which environmental principles are employed by the courts to elucidate ambiguous provisions gives insight into the meaning of these principles, without constituting universal definitions for them. Their general formulation also gives the courts some latitude in defining the nature and scope of the EU environmental competence exercised on the part of the EU institutions (and Member States acting within the scope of EU law).

The interpretive cases to date fall into two groups. First, there are cases in which the Court of Justice has interpreted ambiguous EU legislation enacted under Title XX of the TFEU. These cases concern institutional acts of EU environmental competence in a narrow sense. Second, this Part considers interpretive cases in which the scope of EU environmental competence is extended beyond Title XX, largely by virtue of the integration principle, giving environmental principles a wider doctrinal role in construing Treaty provisions and EU legislation, concerning public health, agriculture, competition and transport policy. In these cases, the interpretive roles of environmental principles are limited to cases where this expanded EU competence has been exercised on the basis of environmental principles. Even so, they demonstrate how far the scope of EU environmental competence—and concomitantly the legal relevance of environmental principles—has become intertwined with other areas of EU policy and law.

## A. Interpreting EU Environmental Competence in a Narrow Sense: Environmental Principles under Title XX TFEU

The interpretive cases that concern exercises of EU environmental competence under Title XX TFEU involve the construction of a group of EU environmental directives: the Waste Directive,[129] Landfill Directive,[130] Habitats Directive,[131] Urban Waste Water Treatment Directive,[132] Environmental Liability Directive,[133]

---

(see n 129), and it was successfully challenged as a state aid under EU law. The principle was found not to have an interpretive role as all parties agreed that it was not 'apparent' on the wording or operation of the tax that it was based on the polluter pays principle. See Case T-210/02 RENV *British Aggregates Association v European Commission* [2012] ECLI:EU:T:2012:110 [66].

[129] Council & Parliament Directive (EC) 2008/98 on waste [2008] OJ L312/3 ('Waste Directive 2008'), replacing previous Council Directive (EC) 91/156 amending Directive 75/442 on waste [1991] OJ L78/32 ('Old Waste Directive'). See Joined Cases C-175/98 and C-177/98 *Lirussi and Bizzaro* [1999] ECR I-6881.
   [130] Landfill Directive (n 71).
   [131] Council Directive (EC) 92/43 on the conservation of natural habitats and of wild fauna and flora [1992] OJ L206/7 ('Habitats Directive').
   [132] Council Directive (EC) 91/271 concerning urban waste-water treatment [1991] OJ L135/40. See Case C-280/02 *Commission v France* [2004] ECR I-8573; *cf* Case C-119/02 *Commission v Greece* [2004] ECLI:EU:C:2004:385.
   [133] ELD (n 107).

and the Water Framework Directive.[134] All these directives are either based on, or have specific provisions that give concrete expression to, environmental principles. It is notable that these particular directives, as opposed to other EU environmental directives with ambiguous provisions that have come before the courts for interpretation,[135] have been interpreted in light of environmental principles. If environmental principles are hoped to unify environmental law,[136] the selective use of environmental principles as interpretive aids indicates that this hope is either misplaced or yet to be realised in EU environmental law. In the interpretive cases discussed in this section, the TFEU's legal prescription that EU environmental policy 'shall be based' on the four environmental principles in Article 191(2) is reflected in these environmental principles having doctrinal roles as interpretive aids.

A significant number of these interpretive cases concern the definition of 'waste' in the Waste Directive.[137] There has been much litigation about the definition of waste, because it is undefined in the Directive and it is the central concept that triggers regulatory consequences that follow under the Directive.[138] In *ARCO*,[139] the ECJ concluded from the fact that Community policy on the environment, under Article 191(2) (ex-Article 174(2) EC), 'is to aim at a high level of protection and is to be based, in particular, on the precautionary principle and the principle that preventive action should be taken', that the definition of 'waste' in the Directive should not be interpreted restrictively.[140] In reaching this interpretive conclusion, the ECJ relied explicitly on the interpretive influence of the preventive and precautionary principles, giving these principles doctrinal roles. However, it is far from clear that either principle should have led to this interpretive outcome. Both principles have open and not obviously overlapping meanings.[141] And it is not obvious that the idea of either preventing waste, or avoiding uncertain risks that might be associated with it, leads to a broad definition of waste, which may in fact discourage efforts to develop innovative production processes that maximise the use of resources and thereby prevent waste.[142] However, the ECJ's conclusion,

---

[134] Council & Parliament Directive (EC) 2000/60 establishing a framework for Community action in the field of water policy [2000] OJ L327/1 ('Water Framework Directive').

[135] *cf* Council & Parliament Directive (EU) 2011/92 on the assessment of the effects of certain public and private projects on the environment [2012] OJ L26/1, art 2(1). See eg Case C-72/95 *Aannemersbedrijf PK Kraaijeveld BV ea v Gedeputeerde Staten van Zuid-Holland (Dutch Dykes)* [1996] ECR I-05403; Case C-201/02 *R (Wells) v Secretary of State for Transport, Local Government and the Regions* [2004] ECR I-723. However, note an interesting decision of the UK Supreme Court interpreting the EIA Directive in UK law in light of the precautionary principle: *R (Champion) v North Norfolk District Council and anor* [2015] UKSC 52 [51].

[136] See ch 2(II)(D).

[137] Waste Directive 2008 (n 129) art 3(1).

[138] Eloise Scotford, 'Trash or Treasure: Policy Tensions in EC Waste Regulation' (2007) 19(3) *JEL* 367, 374–376.

[139] Joined Cases C-418/97 & C-419/97 *ARCO Chemie Nederland v Minister Van Volkshuisvesting* [2000] ECR I-4475.

[140] ibid [36]–[40].

[141] See ch 3, nn 150–152 and accompanying text.

[142] Scotford, 'Trash or Treasure' (n 138).

despite its lack of explanation, demonstrates what these general environmental principles mean legally *in this particular regulatory context*. In a line of cases following *ARCO*, the ECJ has repeatedly adopted this same interpretive reasoning.[143]

A recent spate of cases has involved the polluter pays principle being used as an interpretive aid. These cases are remarkable in demonstrating the flexibility of this principle. Not only is the principle expressed by different marginal definitions, which are applied to interpret the Waste Directive, Landfill Directive, and Environmental Liability Directive respectively, but its precise manner of implementation as a scheme of cost allocation for pollution under those directives leaves Member States a wide margin of discretion that depends on local conditions.[144] At the same time, the Court also makes general statements about the nature and meaning of the polluter pays principle, which resonate across the different environmental regulatory contexts to which these various directives relate. Thus the ECJ clarifies, over a series of cases, that the polluter pays principle applies only to impose on polluters the burden of remedying pollution to which they have contributed.[145] This kind of general statement about the polluter pays principle gives it doctrinal continuity across the Court's case law and informs its evolving interpretive role, deepening its doctrinal role in EU law over time.

Having said that, how the general element of 'contribution' by a polluter is identified varies across the cases, in light of different legislative expressions of the polluter pays principle, again giving rise to marginal definitions of the principle. Thus in *Commune de Mesquer*,[146] the ECJ used the polluter pays principle to interpret Article 15 of the former Waste Directive, which mentioned this principle explicitly,[147] providing, inter alia, that 'producers' of products that become waste are responsible for bearing the cost of disposing of waste, 'in accordance with the polluter pays principle'. In this case, the interpretive issue for the ECJ was the meaning of a 'producer'. The ECJ found, 'in accordance with the "polluter pays" principle', that a producer will only fall within the Article 15 obligation if 'he has contributed by his conduct to the risk that the pollution caused [by the waste] will occur'.[148]

---

[143] Case C-9/00 *Palin Granit Oy* [2002] ECR I-3533; Case C-114/01 *AvestaPolarit Chrome Oy* [2003] ECR I-8725; Case C-457/02 *Criminal Proceedings against Niselli* [2004] ECR I-10853; Case C-235/02 *Criminal Proceedings against Saetti and Frediani* [2004] ECR I-1005; Case C-1/03 *Criminal Proceedings against Van de Walle* [2004] ECR I-7613; Case C-176/05 *KVZ retec v Republik Österreich* [2007] ECR I-01721.

[144] Case C-254/08 *Futura Immobiliare srl Hotel Futura v Comune di Casoria* [2009] 3 CMLR 45 [48], [55]; *ERG* (n 83) [55]. Such national implementation of the polluter pays principle would be open to potential review under EU law, not as an infringement of the polluter pays principle but as an infringement of the principle of proportionality: *Futura* [56]; see also *Standley* (n 35) [52].

[145] Case C-188/07 *Commune de Mesquer v Total France SA and Total International Ltd* [2008] 3 CMLR 16 [77]; *Futura* (n 144) [45]; *ERG* (n 83) [57], [67].

[146] *Commune de Mesquer* (n 145).

[147] Old Waste Directive (n 129) art 15.

[148] *Commune de Mesquer* (n 145) [82] (emphasis added). In *Futura Immobiliare*, the ECJ interpreted the same provision of the Waste Directive using the polluter pays principle as an interpretive aid in

In this case, such conduct included that of the seller of hydrocarbons chartering a ship to transport the oil, particularly if he failed to take measures to prevent the incident of a shipwreck that would cause pollution of the sea (for example, by choice of ship).[149]

By contrast, in *ERG*,[150] the ECJ was concerned with interpreting a different expression of the polluter pays principle—various articles of the Environmental Liability Directive, which overall itself represents an expression of the principle.[151] In this case, the Court employed the polluter pays principle doctrinally to find that the causal link required under the Directive between a relevant activity and pollution, in order to establish liability, can be presumed if the responsible national authority has 'plausible evidence' capable of justifying the presumption (such as the fact that an installation is located close to pollution and there is a correlation between the substances used and emitted by the installation and the pollution).[152] This is a different aspect of how a polluter might 'contribute' to pollution within the interpretive scope of the polluter pays principle, and it ascribes a different marginal definition to the principle.[153]

Another case on the interpretation of the Environmental Liability Directive, *Fipa Group*,[154] discussed above, demonstrates the limits of the interpretive role of the polluter pays principle in this regulatory context. As seen in *ERG*, the polluter pays principle relates to the Directive's imposition of liability on operators who have caused relevant environmental damage, and the Italian law at issue in *Fipa* related to different circumstances, concerning liability for contaminated land in cases where those operators could not be found. The polluter pays principle thus did not have an interpretive role in this case, as it related to factual circumstances beyond the scope of the Directive.

In another line of interpretive cases, concerning the interpretation of Article 6(3) of the Habitats Directive, the Court of Justice has relied on the precautionary principle as an interpretive aid, revealing some precision about its content in this

---

quite different circumstances—concerning the cost allocation mechanism for the collection of urban waste by national authorities—giving rise to a different marginal definition of the principle: *Futura* (n 144) [50]–[52].

[149] *Futura* (n 144).

[150] *ERG* (n 83).

[151] ELD (n 107) arts 1, 6 & 8(1). The ELD 'seeks to implement the "polluter pays" principle in a certain form': *ERG, Opinion of Advocate-General Kokott* (n 83) [94].

[152] *ERG* (n 83) [57]. Note Advocate-General Kokott goes further than the ECJ in using the polluter pays principle to interpret the *ELD*, examining how Member States might take more stringent measures under the Directive in accordance with the polluter pays principle: *ERG, Opinion of Advocate-General Kokott* (n 83) [96]–[115].

[153] For another regulatory context in which the polluter pays principle is used doctrinally as an interpretive aid, reflecting again differently how polluters must make good the costs of pollution to which they contribute, see Case C-172/08 *Pontina Ambiente Srl v Regione Lazio* [2010] ECR I-01175.

[154] *Fipa Group* (n 65).

different EU legislative context.[155] The Court has established that, with respect to uncertain environmental risks, the precautionary principle dictates that the protective measures of the Directive should apply where environmental risks cannot be excluded. In relation to this particular regulatory scheme, the precautionary principle requires erring on the side of caution, and the Directive is interpreted accordingly. In these interpretive cases, the precise issue that has come repeatedly before the ECJ concerns when a plan or project is 'likely to have a significant effect' on a special area of conservation, thereby triggering the requirement for an 'appropriate assessment' to be carried out in Article 6(3). The Court has concluded:[156]

> In the light … of the precautionary principle, which is one of the foundations of the high level of protection pursued by Community policy on the environment [under Article 191(2) TFEU], and by reference to which the Habitats Directive must be interpreted, such a risk [ie likelihood] exists if it cannot be excluded on the basis of objective information that the plan or project will have significant effects on the site concerned.

This risk of significant effects, so identified by the precautionary principle, is an important trigger in the scheme of the Habitats Directive. This is because, once an appropriate assessment is then carried out, the second sentence of Article 6(3) provides that a Member State consenting authority cannot authorise the project in question if the assessment indicates that there will be an adverse impact on the integrity of the EU protected area in question. The Court of Justice has also relied on the precautionary principle to give this authorisation restriction a strict interpretation. Thus, in *Sweetman*,[157] the Court found that national authorities cannot authorise projects, after an appropriate assessment has been carried out, where there is 'a risk of lasting harm to the ecological characteristics of sites which host priority natural habitat types'.[158] Such a risk exists where there is any reasonable doubt about the absence of such effects. The Court based this interpretation on the fact that the second sentence of Article 6(3) 'integrates the precautionary principle', making it possible to 'prevent in an effective manner adverse effects on the integrity of protected sites'.[159] In the subsequent case of *Briels*, the Court of Justice similarly relied on the precautionary principle to find that the appropriate assessment carried out under Article 6(3) 'cannot have lacunae and must contain complete, precise and definitive findings and conclusions capable of removing all

---

[155] *Waddenzee* (n 45); Case C-6/04 *Commission v UK (Conformity)* [2005] ECR I-9017; Case C-98/03 *Commission v Germany* [2006] ECR I-53; Case C-538/08 *Commission v Belgium* [2011] ECR I-04687. For a different example of how the Habitats Directive might be interpreted by drawing on an environmental principle—the sustainable development principle—see Case C-371/98 *R v Secretary of State for the Environment, Transport and the Regions ex parte First Corporate Shipping* [2000] ECR I-9235, Opinion of Advocate-General Leger (7 March 2000): see further text accompanying n 347.

[156] *Waddenzee* (n 45) [44].

[157] Case C-258/11 *Sweetman v An Bord Pleanála* [2013] ECLI:EU:C:2013:220.

[158] ibid [43].

[159] ibid [41].

reasonable scientific doubt' as to the effects of the proposed works.[160] Overall, these interpretations of Article 6(3), informed by the precautionary principle, lead to a robust interpretation of this important rule of EU nature conservation law. This interpretation is not uncontroversial due to its prescriptive direction as to how national land use decisions should be made.[161]

A more recent case is a reminder that the teleological interpretation of the Court of Justice does not rest on environmental principles alone. Environmental principles are not ends in themselves—they have interpretive roles that are rooted in their legislative and regulatory contexts. By contrast with Article 6(3) of the Habitats Directive, the relevant provision in *Commission v Germany* was Article 9 of the Water Framework Directive, which is a very different kind of provision in a very different kind of Directive. Article 9 requires Member States to take into account the 'principle of recovery of the costs of water services, including environmental and resource costs … in accordance in particular with the polluter pays principle'. It thus requires Member States to introduce water pricing policies by 2020, and to ensure by that time that different water uses (including industry, household and agriculture uses) adequately contribute to the recovery of the costs of water services. This provision is concerned with providing adequate incentives for the efficient use of water resources so as to comply with the environmental objectives of the WFD.[162] In *Commission v Germany*,[163] the interpretive issue was whether Article 9, and the polluter pays principle that supports it, required pricing schemes for all water use activities specified in the Directive, as argued by the Commission.[164] The Court of Justice found that Article 9 did not impose a generalised pricing obligation on all water uses. It reached this conclusion by taking into account the overall scheme of the Directive, which establishes a system of management of river basins based on programmes devised by Member States that are adapted to local and regional conditions, rather than pursuing harmonisation

---

[160] Case C-521/12 *Briels v Minister van Infrastructuur en Milieu* ECLI:EU:C:2014:330 (this meant that an appropriate assessment should take into account protective measures to the extent that they reduce adverse effects on the site, but not measures that are proposed to compensate for damage caused to the site).

[161] Art 6(3) impacts significantly on land use planning of Member States, an area that is otherwise outside the competence of EU action. The requirements of art 6(3) can be contrasted with EU environmental impact assessment processes, which require assessment and consideration of environmental effects of risky developments, but leave final consent decisions to Member State authorities: Directive 2011/92/EU on the assessment of the effects of certain public and private projects on the environment [2012] OJ L26/1, as amended.

[162] These objectives of non-deterioration of water resources and achieving good surface and groundwater status are found in art 4 of the Water Framework Directive (n 134).

[163] Case C-525/12 *Commission v Germany* [2014] ECLI:EU:C:2014:2202.

[164] This argument relied on a particular interpretation of the polluter pays principle—that it required *all* 'polluters' (here those involved in water abstraction) to pay the price for the environmental impacts of their water use. Similar arguments have been made in other cases, ie that the principle requires all actors involved in a particular environmentally harmful activity to pay for the impacts of their activities: eg Case 402/09 *Ioan Tatu v Statul român prin Ministerul Finanţelor şi Economiei and others* [2011] ECLI:EU:C:2011:219 [60].

of water regulation. In this context, the Court of Justice found that water pricing is one instrument available to Member States to manage water quality and its rational use. The polluter pays principle was part of the interpretive picture but not the definitive purpose of Article 9. As the court stated, the 'interpretation of a provision of EU law requires that account be taken not only of its wording and the objectives it pursues, but also its context and the provisions of EU law as a whole'.[165] This case highlights that EU environmental principles can be important interpretive aids when EU institutions rely on them to introduce particular measures and obligations, but it reinforces that their interpretive role and meaning will critically depend on the regulatory context in which they are employed.

## B. Interpreting EU Environmental Competence More Broadly: Environmental Principles Beyond Title XX TFEU

Environmental principles are also used as interpretive aids in cases involving Treaty provisions and EU legislation beyond Title XX of the TFEU. These cases involve legislative or administrative acts by EU institutions in an expanded area of EU environmental competence, which is based on, and thus legally guided by, environmental principles. The Court finds that these acts exercising broader EU environmental competence are based on environmental principles, either by determining (or assuming) this is the case in the context of the relevant measure, or by finding that the integration principle has expanded the policy area in relation to which EU environmental principles apply. However, there are limits to the interpretive roles of environmental principles in relation to EU acts: environmental principles will have no interpretive roles where the Court finds that the relevant provision or measure is not based on environmental principles, as seen in some policy cases above.[166] The interpretive cases involving environmental principles in relation to EU legislation beyond Title XX fall into two sub-groups: those involving the precautionary principle and areas of EU competence guided by a 'high level of protection'; and cases in which the integration principle drives the interpretive role of environmental principles even further into other areas of EU competence.

### i. A 'High Level of Protection' and the Precautionary Principle

First, there are cases in which EU environmental competence extends into other areas of competence in which a 'high level of protection' is required by the Treaty or secondary legislation—these include EU competences relating to public health, the internal market and consumer protection.[167] In these areas, the precautionary

---

[165] *Commission v Germany* (n 163) [43].
[166] See above, Section III(C).
[167] TFEU, arts 114, 168, 169.

principle is employed to resolve interpretive issues in light of the 'high level of protection' required in these areas, just as it is required in relation to environmental
protection in Article 191(2) TFEU. Since the CFI's judgment in *Artegodan*,[168] the
CFI and subsequently the General Court have often asserted that the precautionary
principle is a 'general principle' that applies to guide and inform EU policy across
these areas, expanding the area of competence in which the precautionary principle has a legal role, by virtue of the integration principle in Article 11 TFEU and
the so-called 'principle of a high level of protection'.[169] The interpretive role for the
precautionary principle across these different areas of EU competence highlights
that there is no clear demarcation of 'environmental' issues in EU law.[170] Rather,
environmental protection issues are interconnected with other policy areas, and
the widening doctrinal role of the precautionary principle examined in this sub-
section (as well as of other environmental principles examined in sub-section (ii)
below) demonstrates how these areas of overlapping policy manifest legally.

In *Monsanto*, discussed above,[171] the ECJ deflected most of the arguments based
on the precautionary principle, but observed that the precautionary principle was
given expression in the safeguard clause (Article 12) of the previous novel food
GMO Regulation. This Regulation was an internal market measure based on
Article 114 TFEU (ex-Article 95 EC), which was required to take as its base a 'high
level of protection' in relation to any environmental protection or health issues.[172]
The Court found that 'the conditions for the application of [the safeguard]
clause must be interpreted having due regard to [the precautionary] principle'.[173]
Relying on previous case law, the ECJ asserted that it follows from the precaution-
ary principle that:[174]

> where there is uncertainty as to the existence or extent of risks to human health, protec-
> tive measures may be taken without having to wait until the reality and seriousness of
> those risks become fully apparent.

Accordingly a Member State may take protective measures under Article 12 even if
a full risk assessment cannot be carried out because of inadequate available scientific data. The ECJ identified the relevant content of the precautionary principle,
and used this to influence the interpretive outcome.[175]

---

[168] Joined Cases T-74/00, T-76/00, T-83/00 to T-85/00, T-132/00, T-137/00, T-141/00 *Artegodan
v Commission* [2002] ECR II-4945.

[169] See above n 121.

[170] See above n 3.

[171] *Monsanto* (n 7); see above, text accompanying nn 94–95.

[172] TFEU, art 114(3) (ex-art 95(3) EC).

[173] *Monsanto* (n 7) [110].

[174] ibid [111].

[175] The Court of Justice undertakes a similar interpretive exercise in Joined Cases C-58/10 to
C-68/10 *Monsanto SAS and others v Ministre de l'Agriculture et de la Pêche* [2011] ECR I-07763, albeit
reaching a conclusion that restricts the scope of Member States to take unilateral protective measures
(in relation to the safeguard clause under Regulation 1829/2003/EU on genetically modified food and
feed [2003] OJ 2003 L268/1).

The Court went on to expand on the content of the precautionary principle, asserting that, despite inadequate scientific data, there must be[176]

> specific evidence which ... makes it possible reasonably to conclude on the basis of the most reliable scientific evidence available ... that the implementation of those measures is necessary in order to avoid ... potential risks.

The requirement of reliable scientific evidence in cases of scientific uncertainty is a theme that recurs in other public health cases involving the precautionary principle,[177] and it gives the principle quite a different identity from that isolated in *Waddenzee* above.[178] This difference, or conflict, can again be explained by appreciating that the courts are defining the principles marginally with respect to different legal issues in different EU regulatory contexts. As a result, the overall definitional picture appears confused.[179] Since legal definitions of environmental principles are the end points of their legal analysis in EU case law, they may constitute a variety of end points.

Another definitional end-point of the precautionary principle is seen in *Sweden v Commission*, also discussed above,[180] a case in which the principle is employed by the CFI to interpret an EU legislative framework outside the environmental title of the Treaty. In this case, the relevant legislation was the assessment framework for approving pesticides for use within the EU under the Plant Protection Product Directive, adopted on the basis of the common agricultural policy in ex-Title II of the EC Treaty. While this Title contained no reference to environmental protection or a high level of protection, the Directive does,[181] particularly in its requirement that no pesticides be approved unless they have no harmful effects on human or animal health or groundwater or any unacceptable influence on the environment.[182] In interpreting this requirement, the CFI used the precautionary principle to find that a substance may be refused approval if there is 'solid evidence [which] may reasonably raise doubts as to [its] safety', but not if there are only hypothetical risks.[183] This echoes the ECJ's version of the principle in *Monsanto*,

---

[176] Monsanto (n 7) [113].

[177] For analogous interpretive cases, see Case C-446/08 *Solgar Vitamin's France v Ministre de l'Économie, des Finances et de l'Emploi* (ECJ 29 April 2010) [63]–[70]; *Monsanto SAS and others v Ministre de l'Agriculture et de la Pêche* (n 175) [70]–[77]. For further cases and discussion on the precautionary principle's requirement of adequate scientific evidence, see below: Section V(B)(ii)–(iii), (v).

[178] See above, text accompanying nn 155–156.

[179] Arguably, the key difference lies in the nature of the legal issue; in environmental cases such as *Waddenzee* (n 45), the Court needed to determine when environmental protective measures should apply (ie when they are *required* to apply), whereas, in this case, the concern is when a Member State is allowed to rely on the safeguard clause (ie when it *may* do so).

[180] See above, text accompanying nn 119–123.

[181] Plant Protection Product Directive (n 120) recital 9 ('high standard of protection' in relation to environmental, human and animal health).

[182] Plant Protection Product Directive (n 120) art 5(1).

[183] *Sweden v Commission* (n 119) [161].

which has been further elaborated in more recent cases as requiring review by the courts into whether the evidence relied on is:[184]

> factually accurate, reliable and consistent, whether that evidence contains all the information which must be taken into account in order to assess a complex situation, and whether it is capable of substantiating the conclusions drawn from it.

However, the CFI in *Sweden v Commission* also goes on to find that the possibility of placing restrictions on the use of pesticides under the Directive, as interpreted by the precautionary principle, means that a substance may only be approved if it is established 'beyond a reasonable doubt' that restrictions on use make it possible to 'ensure' that its use will not have harmful health or environmental effects.[185] This is a stricter approach to the precautionary principle, highlighting again its marginal definition in this different regulatory context.[186]

## ii. The Expansive Reach of the Integration Principle

There are other cases in which the integration principle is used to extend the interpretive roles of environmental principles even further, so that they inform the meaning of ambiguous provisions in areas of policy where there is no clear Treaty mandate or legislative direction for a 'high level of protection', only the overarching environmental protection requirements of Article 11 TFEU itself. This is seen particularly in public procurement and state aid cases, where the integration principle is used directly as an interpretive aid, or as a linking device to employ other environmental principles or requirements to interpret provisions within an expanded scope of EU environmental competence.

An example where the integration principle is directly used to interpret an ambiguous provision is found in *Concordia Bus Finland*,[187] concerning Article 36(1)(a) of Directive 92/50,[188] which set out criteria on the basis of which a national contracting authority may award a public service contract. The ECJ held, in light of the integration principle, that Article 36(1)(a) does not exclude the possibility of a contracting authority using other criteria relating to environmental

---

[184] *Dow AgroSciences Ltd v Commission* (n 125) [153].

[185] *Sweden v Commission* (n 119) [170]. For a similar interpretation, see *Du Pont v Commission* (n 125) [153].

[186] For a case in which the precautionary principle has a similar interpretive role, see *Solvay* (n 124) [121], in which the principle informs EC authorisation provisions under Directive 70/524 on additives to feeding stuffs [1970] OJ Eng Spec Ed (III) 840: [122]–[123]. The principle is again defined differently in light of the different regulatory context: ibid [148]–[149].

[187] Case C-513/99 *Concordia Bus Finland Oy Ab v Helsingin Kaupunki and HKL-Bussiliikenne* [2002] ECR I-7213.

[188] Council Directive (EC) 92/50 relating to the co-ordination of procedures for the award of public service contracts [1992] OJ L209/1. This has now been repealed and replaced by Council & Parliament Directive (EC) 2004/18 on the coordination of procedures for the award of public works contracts, public supply contracts and public service contracts [2004] OJ L134/114.

protection when assessing the 'economically most advantageous' tender under the Directive.[189]

An example of a case in which the integration principle has been used as a linking principle is in the Opinion of Advocate-General Jacobs in *GEMO*,[190] which is the first in a group of state aid cases in which environmental principles are employed doctrinally to interpret Article 107 TFEU (ex-Article 87(1) EC) (prohibiting state aids that distort or threaten to distort competition). In this case, Advocate-General Jacobs found that a French law establishing a compulsory and free public service for the collection and disposal of animal slaughterhouse waste constituted a state aid because the waste constituted an economic burden that would normally, in accordance with the polluter pays principle, have to be borne by slaughterhouses. Advocate-General Jacobs justified his use of the polluter pays principle as an 'analytical tool' to resolve this issue of competition law by appealing to the integration principle.[191] Whilst the ECJ did not rely explicitly on environmental principles in its reasoning, it arrived at the same conclusion as the Advocate-General, finding that the financial cost involved in disposing of animal carcasses and slaughterhouse waste, which are harmful to the environment, is an inherent cost of the businesses that generate this waste.

There have since followed other state aid cases in which environmental principles have been adduced in argument and reasoning as interpretive aids in different ways. In some cases, arguments based on environmental principles are dismissed since the measure in question was not based in any way on environmental principles.[192] In other cases, there have been innovative suggestions about the interpretive use of the integration principle that stretches its doctrinal role into the fundamental structure of EU competition law. In two particular cases, the CFI relied on the integration principle to interpret Article 107(1) TFEU (ex-Article 87(1) EC) to conclude that a national environmental tax and an emission trading scheme respectively were not unlawful state aids.[193] The environmental objectives of both schemes altered how the CFI determined that the Commission should interpret and apply the Treaty's state aid rules, so that Member State measures pursuing environmental aims were found not to be unlawful state aids, in light of the integration principle and the importance of including environmental protection requirements in all aspects of EU policy. Whilst the reasoning of the CFI in both cases has been overturned on appeal,[194] the doctrinal role of the integration

---

[189] *Concordia* (n 187) [57].

[190] Case C-126/01 *Ministre de l'Économie, des Finances et de l'Industrie v GEMO* [2003] ECR I-13769, Opinion of Advocate-General Jacobs (30 April 2002).

[191] ibid.

[192] eg Case T-57/11 *Castelnou Energía, SL v Commission* [2014] ECLI:EU:T:2014:1021.

[193] Case T-210/02 *British Aggregates Association v Commission* [2006] ECR II-02789; Case T-233/04 *Netherlands v Commission* [2008] ECR II-00591. See also Case T-295/12 *Germany v Commission* [2014] EU:T:2014:675.

[194] Case C-487/06 P *British Aggregates Association v Commission* [2008] ECR I-10515 [79]–[92]; Case 279/08 P *Commission v Netherlands* [2011] ECR I-07671 [74]–[79].

principle was not dismissed altogether. The reasoning of the ECJ on appeal in *British Aggregates Association v Commission* is particularly interesting in finding that the integration principle can still play a role determining whether measures constitute unlawful state aids. This is because:[195]

> [I]t is for the Commission, when assessing ... a specific measure such as an environmental levy adopted by Member States in a field in which they retain their powers in the absence of harmonisation measures, to take account of the environmental protection requirements referred to in Article 6 EC [now Article 11 TFEU], which provides that those requirements are to be integrated into the definition and implementation of, inter alia, arrangements which ensure that competition is not distorted within the internal market ... [This] cannot justify the exclusion of selective measures, even specific ones such as environmental levies, from the scope of Article 87(1) EC ... as account may in any event usefully be taken of the environmental objectives when the compatibility of the State aid measure with the common market is being assessed pursuant to Article 87(3) EC.

In other words, whilst the CFI had gone too far in interpreting state aid principles in light of environmental objectives to support a selective Member State measure in this case,[196] the Commission could still take into account environmental goals at a different stage of the state aid assessment process, in determining the ultimate compatibility of state aids with the internal market under Article 107(3) TFEU (ex-Article 87(3) EC). The Court of Justice's suggestion here reflects another legal dimension of the integration principle within a widened scope of EU environmental competence. This scope is widened in that these cases are dealing with measures that relate to the internal market—a core economic area of EU competence—and which also relate to Member States exercising their own environmental competence within the scope of EU law. Yet again, this judicial expansion of the scope of EU environmental competence in which environmental principles have doctrinal roles shows that the legal roles of EU environmental principles are continually evolving.[197]

## C. Conclusion

In this Part, environmental principles have been used doctrinally by the EU courts to interpret provisions of EU legislation based on the environmental title of the Treaty, as well as EU legislation and Treaty provisions beyond that discrete area of

---

[195] *British Aggregates Association v Commission* (ECJ) (n 194) [90]–[92].
[196] In particular, the CFI erred by assessing measures by their objectives rather than their effects, improperly excusing their character as state aids by virtue of their environmental objectives: ibid [85]–[88].
[197] For discussion as to the interpretive limits of the integration principle in relation to internal market measures: Case C-246/99 *Commission v Denmark* [2002] ECR I-6943, Opinion of Advocate-General Colomer (13 September 2001).

EU competence. Environmental principles have doctrinal roles in these cases in that they act as reasons that influence the outcomes of legal issues of interpretation, purposively guiding the courts' interpretation. In the second category of cases considered in this Part, the case law of the EU courts reveals how environmental considerations infiltrate areas of EU competence beyond the environmental title, expanding the area of EU environmental competence in which environmental principles have legal roles and showing how environmental principles are linking different policy domains legally through their interpretive roles. This aspect of the doctrinal picture of environmental principles demonstrates, in particular, an important legal dimension of the integration principle in EU law. The interpretive cases in this Part also give rise to marginal definitions for environmental principles in different regulatory contexts. In employing environmental principles doctrinally in these cases, the courts need to substantiate them to some extent. Through such acts of 'definition for interpretation', the courts effectively have discretion to identify and define the competence of the institutions acting on the basis of environmental principles. This is due to the open-textured nature of these principles, which can and do have multiple meanings in different contexts.

In sum, the interpretive cases in this Part display a particular technique of judicial reasoning but they do not create definitive, universal legal meanings for environmental principles. Nor do they compel particular actions by institutions to solve environmental problems, although they do restrict permissible lines of administrative decision-making by EU institutions and Member State institutions acting within the scope of EU law, particularly on the stricter manifestations of the precautionary principle seen in cases such as *Waddenzee* and *Sweden v Commission*. Nor do environmental principles, in their interpretive guise, solve perceived legal problems in environmental law. They do not unify EU environmental law since they are not employed to interpret all EU environmental legislation, although their doctrinal scope is expanding. By contrast, their legal use within an expanded area of EU environmental competence, which overlaps with other policy areas, shows that EU environmental law is not in fact a discrete area of law that requires coherence, but an evolving and wide-ranging legal area.

It might be argued that environmental principles in this treatment category look like Dworkinian 'legal principles', in that they guide judicial reasoning in a particular direction without mandating a particular outcome.[198] On a very general level, this is a fair description of these cases, but it does not account for the fact that the same environmental principles might point in quite different directions, depending on the regulatory context; nor for the more complex role played by the integration principle in these cases; nor for the fact that the EU courts use environmental principles interpretively only when they determine that EU (or Member State) institutions have first acted on the basis of the principles, reinforcing that environmental principles are intertwined with the exercise of

---

[198] See ch 2(II)(D)(i).

institutional competence in the EU context. The legal roles played by environmental principles in this sense are a unique manifestation of EU legal culture, reflecting the teleological reasoning style of the EU courts, the regulatory frameworks which they consider (as well as the Treaty context within which these frameworks are devised), and the particular legal questions being considered by the courts.

## V. Informing Legal Test Cases: Reviewing the Boundaries and Exercise of EU Environmental Competence

In this third treatment category, environmental principles have doctrinal roles in informing tests of legal review that are applied by the EU courts. The cases in this category involve EU and Member State institutions acting on the basis of environmental principles, purportedly within the boundaries of EU environmental competence, to introduce legislative measures or implement administrative regimes, and the legality of this action is then questioned under EU law. The primary issue in these cases is the lawful extent of discretionary power afforded to these institutions to adopt policy and make decisions on the basis of environmental principles—in constitutional or administrative law terms—rather than any particular line of policy that should be adopted by them.

Since environmental principles legally prescribe the limits of policy discretion exercisable by EU (and Member State)[199] institutions under the Treaties, they are employed by the courts to inform review tests in determining whether those institutions have overstepped the bounds of their policy authority. The nature of the legal inquiry in such review is finely balanced in that the courts have a duty to police the legality of exercises of discretion,[200] but they also need to allow policy decisions to be made. This balance is reflected in a careful constitutional path trodden by the EU courts in reviewing the legality of EU and Member State institutional decision-making in many cases considered in this Part. The delicacy of this balancing exercise often translates into doctrinal opacity in the treatment of environmental principles, since they form the basis for the exercise of policy discretion, but also for legally testing its bounds. The courts thus use the principles to inform, and to generate, legal tests applied to review institutional discretion in these cases, but also as the basis for deferring to the policy decisions of the EU institutions (and of the Member States in unharmonised domains) within the limits of permissible policy identified by the courts. This dual role of EU environmental principles, as directing legal outcomes but preserving policy discretion,

---

[199] When Member States institutions are acting within the scope of EU law: see below, Section V(B)(v).

[200] TEU, art 19; TFEU, art 263.

features in several cases in this treatment category, particularly in Section V(B) below.

In using environmental principles to inform various tests of review, the EU courts often give marginal definitions to the principles. Again, the general formulation of environmental principles requires this so that they can inform review tests in a meaningful way. The courts have gone a step further in relation to the precautionary principle, defining and elaborating it to the point of generating a new test of review—a test of adequate scientific evidence—which now (in various guises) appears in much of the EU case law in this treatment category involving the precautionary principle. This review test is used mainly in a supplementary manner, so that its determination is relied on to inform the primary review test being applied by the Court, which is often whether a 'manifest error of assessment' has been committed on the part of the relevant institutional decision-maker. Some cases go so far as to suggest that the precautionary principle acts as a test of review in its own right, along with its self-generated test of adequate scientific evidence.

The cases in this Part fall into two groups: (1) those concerned with the boundaries of EU environmental competence as exercised by EU institutions, and (2) those concerned with the lawful exercise of discretion within the scope of EU environmental competence, by both EU and Member State institutions. In both cases, environmental principles are used to inform review tests that have been developed in the doctrine of the EU courts for the relevant legal question at issue. These review tests are all relatively open in their formulation, leaving scope for environmental principles to inform their application. Some of these review tests have also themselves been evolving, partly through the influence of environmental principles, particularly as the body of EU administrative law has become more sophisticated and penetrating in holding EU decision-makers to account.

## A. Legal Basis Cases

In this group of cases, the ECJ employed environmental principles to inform legal tests in resolving disputes between the EU institutions over the correct legal basis for Community measures before the Lisbon Treaty came into force.[201] These are disputes about the legality of EC measures on the ground of 'lack of competence' in Article 263 TFEU. Arguments about lack of competence are arguments about the proper boundaries of EU (previously EC) law making, where those boundaries are determined by the relevant legal basis for legislating set out in the Treaty. A measure must be properly based on a Treaty provision and title, and introduced in accordance with its prescribed legislative method, for the relevant EU legislative

---

[201] These cases were decided under the pre-Lisbon Treaty structure, which distinguished EC from EU measures by its three discrete pillars of competence. Similar cases are unlikely in the future.

institutions to have acted within their competence. This ground of review—lack of competence—is not further elaborated in the Treaty, and the ECJ developed tests for deciding whether an EU (or EC) measure is properly based, which involve isolating the predominant aim and content of a measure to determine its centre of gravity.[202] In a number of cases, the Court used environmental principles to inform these tests.[203] This was done in two ways.

First, environmental principles have been used to identify when EU environmental competence has been validly exercised under Title XX of the TFEU. In *Commission v Council (Waste Directive)*, the ECJ considered whether the Waste Directive[204] was properly adopted on the basis of Article 192 TFEU (ex-Article 130s EC).[205] In finding that it was properly adopted on that basis, the ECJ looked to the aim and content of the measure,[206] finding that its aim was to implement the principle of rectification at source,[207] and that its content included, inter alia, a 'confirmation' of the polluter pays principle in Article 15.[208] In this way, environmental principles were observed as the legislative policy underlying the contested Directive, and employed to inform the relevant legal test through purposive reasoning.

A contentious case in which the integration principle was used to inform a Title XX legal basis decision is *Commission v Council (Environmental Crime)*.[209] In this case, the ECJ found that the Community had competence to adopt legislative provisions establishing environmental offences, despite the general exclusion of criminal law and procedure from what was then EC competence. This is because environmental protection was a 'fundamental' objective of the Community, as emphasised by the integration principle.[210] Here the integration principle was used to inform the aim and content tests indirectly by giving extra weight to the environmental protection aim and content of the contested measure, thereby

---

[202] See above n 29 and accompanying text. For doctrinal developments in relation to these tests, see Chalmers, Davies and Monti, *European Union Law* (n 36) 110–111.

[203] The jurisprudence of these cases is now out of date in that the legislative procedure under the environmental title (with the exception of legislation passed under art 192(2)) is now equivalent to that under the internal market basis of competence—both areas of competence require the 'ordinary legislative procedure' under the TFEU, previously the 'co-decision' procedure. Thus there is no longer the same competition for institutional influence along this dividing line of legal basis. The abolition of the pillar structure with the Lisbon Treaty also means that there is no longer institutional tension in relation to decision-making across different Treaty pillars. However, questions of legal basis remain relevant under the new Treaty structure, since EU competence remains legally bounded, and the doctrinal use of environmental principles in informing legal competence issues in this general sense remains relevant in EU law.

[204] Old Waste Directive (n 129).

[205] Case C-155/91 *Commission v Council (Waste Directive)* [1993] ECR I-939. See also Case C-187/93 *Parliament v Council (Waste Regulation)* [1994] ECR I-2857 [20].

[206] *Waste Directive case* (n 205) [7].

[207] ibid [13]–[14].

[208] ibid [9]

[209] *Environmental Crime* (n 74).

[210] ibid [42].

justifying the assertion of competence in this case. The integration principle served to expand EC environmental competence under Title XX.

The second type of legal basis case in which environmental principles have played doctrinal roles involves the expansion of EU environmental competence beyond Title XX. There is a line of cases in which the integration principle has been used as a reason why a contested measure is *not* properly based on Article 192 TFEU, because that principle cannot be used to create a bias that a measure has an environmental aim and content whenever it serves environmental protection objectives.[211] On the contrary, the integration principle indicates that environmental objectives may, and should, feature in EU measures enacted on the full range of legal bases in the Treaty (including, in various cases, transport policy, regulation of the internal market, and the common commercial policy). It is only when the environmental protection objective of a measure is predominant that it will be properly based on Title XX.[212] In these cases, the integration principle limits any environmental bias that might inform tests of legal basis. This finding qualifies the conclusion in the *Environmental Crime case*, and indicates that EU environmental competence, beyond Title XX, overlaps with other areas of EU policy, creating blurred competence boundaries. This overlapping and extended competence reflects the trend, seen in some policy and interpretive cases above, of the integration principle expanding, or potentially expanding, the doctrinal roles of environmental principles into various spheres of EU action.[213]

## B. Exercise of EU Environmental Competence Cases

So far, this Part has mapped cases in which environmental principles have been used doctrinally to inform the proper boundaries of EU competence. In this second set of cases, environmental principles are employed to inform legal tests of review in relation to acts taken by EU and Member State institutions on the basis of environmental principles within the scope of EU environmental competence. The question in these cases is not whether the correct institutions adopted an EU measure, by the correct legislative procedure, or whether they had the power to do so. The question is whether the relevant institution exercised its policy discretion validly under EU law.

The grounds for such review include a range of EU 'administrative law' tests, such as proportionality and manifest error of assessment, as well as breach of substantive internal market rules. Notably, the administrative law tests to determine

---

[211] Case C-62/88 *Hellenic Republic v Council (Chernobyl I)* [1990] ECR I-1527 [20]; *Titanium Dioxide* (n 29) [22]; Case C-440/05 *Commission v Council (Ship-Source Pollution)* [2007] I-09097 [60].

[212] Case C-411/06 *Commission v Parliament and Council (Waste Shipment Regulation)* [2009] I-07585, Opinion of Advocate-General Maduro (26 March 2009) [17].

[213] See above, Sections III(E) & IV(B).

whether institutions have properly exercised their discretion have been developing in sophistication and complexity as the case law involving environmental principles has similarly progressed, so that these doctrinal areas have been co-evolving. In all cases in this section, the review tests are broadly formulated, involving doctrine derived from the Court's own case law in light of minimal Treaty guidance,[214] and environmental principles play a role in their determination. The EU courts draw on environmental principles as the basis of the policy discretion exercised by the institutions and then use principles to inform the relevant legal tests. In almost all cases, they do not use environmental principles as freestanding grounds of review for challenging the legality of EU (or Member State) action. Any identified 'infringements' of an environmental principle are generally used to inform a legal test of review.[215] In using environmental principles to inform tests of review, the courts again ascribe marginal meanings to the principles in this body of case law.

The cases examined in Section V(B)(v) below, which concern the legality of unilateral Member State action within EU law, expand the scope of EU environmental competence in which environmental principles have legal roles. In these cases, the Court of Justice applies review tests in relation to alleged breach of internal market rules by Member States acting on public health and environmental grounds, which prima facie infringe the free movement of goods obligation in Article 34 TFEU. In these cases, Member States purport to act on the basis of environmental principles, thereby justifying infringement of Article 34, and the Court employs a number of tests to determine the legality of this action. The Treaty gives some guidance as to the 'law' to be applied in these cases: Article 36 TFEU provides a general description of some market disruptive measures (infringing Article 34) that Member States are entitled to take in the name of public health, and to an extent environmental, protection.[216] However, Article 36 gives few clues as to the nature of or limits to that idea, leaving doctrinal space for the courts to use environmental principles, particularly in relation to the test of proportionality applied by the Court to qualify reliance on Article 36.[217] Further, the Court has developed its own doctrine beyond this to determine when Member States might justify infringement of Article 34—a 'rule of reason'.[218] This doctrine involves a number of stages of reasoning and two legal tests in particular: Member States might justify infringement of Article 34 on the basis of a mandatory or imperative requirement (including environmental or public health protection) when the relevant measure is: (1) indistinctly applicable to domestic and imported goods ('discrimination' test),

---

[214] *cf* TFEU, art 114(4)–(5) policy cases: see above Section III(D).

[215] Although this position may change: see above nn 122–125 and accompanying text.

[216] Art 36 TFEU allows Member States to justify infringements of art 34 on the ground of 'the protection of health and life of humans, animals or plants'.

[217] The open-ended nature of the legal inquiries provoked by arts 34 and 36 are highlighted in academic analysis of art 34 cases: Maduro, *We the Court* (n 19) chs 2, 3.

[218] *Cassis de Dijon* (n 23) [8].

and (2) necessary and proportionate to its objective.[219] Again, these tests provide scope for the Court of Justice to develop doctrine involving environmental principles.

In this section, there is a progression from cases in which principles are employed by EU courts to inform legal tests of review (the rule of reason, proportionality), to cases in which the principles are discussed in greater detail by the courts and used also to generate legal tests (adequate scientific evidence) as well as to inform legal review tests (manifest error, proportionality), to suggestions that the precautionary principle constitutes a ground of review in its own right. The latter developments have occurred in relation to the precautionary principle in public health cases, inspired initially by the policy guidance in the Commission Communication.[220] This progression of cases is examined sequentially in the sub-sections that follow, demonstrating the increasing doctrinal complexity of environmental principles, particularly relating to the precautionary principle, alongside the increasing complexity of EU administrative law and the continuing development of Article 34 TFEU internal market law, which remains one of the most litigated areas of the EU Treaties.

### i. Early Cases of Informing Review Tests: Expanding EU Environmental Competence, Defining Precaution and Embracing More Principles

In these early cases, EU courts used a range of environmental principles to inform legal tests in reviewing EU and Member State discretion exercised in the overlapping areas of environmental, agricultural and public health policy. These cases show a variety of ways in which environmental principles can inform legal tests that review acts of institutions, including Member State institutions acting within the scope of EU law. They also set the scene for more complex legal developments to follow, involving the precautionary principle in particular. Overall, these early cases show that there is no single or obvious mode of reasoning by which environmental principles inform legal review tests, but that they can be flexible and powerful devices in informing EU administrative and substantive legal doctrine.

An early landmark and controversial case was *Walloon Waste*.[221] In this case, the ECJ used the principle of rectification at source to inform the rule of reason under Article 34 TFEU (ex-Article 30 EC at the time), in proceedings brought against Belgium for preventing the import of waste from other Member States. The issue was whether this infringement of Article 34 was justified by 'imperative requirements relating to environmental protection',[222] which could only be relied

---

[219] Case 302/86 *Commission v Denmark (Danish Bottles)* [1988] ECR 4607 [6], [9].
[220] Communication (n 62).
[221] Case C-2/90 *Commission v Belgium (Walloon Waste)* [1992] ECR I-4431; *cf* Case C-209/98 *Sydhavnens Sten & Grus* [2000] ECR I-3743; Case C-320/03 *Commission v Austria* [2005] ECR I-9871.
[222] *Walloon Waste* (n 221) [29], [34].

on if the Belgian measure were indistinctly applicable to waste from Belgium and from other Member States. The ECJ found that the infringement was justified, and that the rule of reason applied. The Court referred to the principle of rectification at source, relied on in argument by Belgium, in resolving this legal question as follows:[223]

> In assessing whether or not the barrier in question is discriminatory, account must be taken of the particular nature of waste. The principle that environmental damage should as a matter of priority be remedied at source, laid down by [Article 191(2)] of the Treaty as a basis for action by the Community relating to the environment, entails that it is for each region ... to take appropriate steps to ensure that its own waste is collected, treated and disposed of; it must accordingly be disposed of as close as possible to the place where it is produced, in order to limit as far as possible the transport of waste ... It follows that having regard to the differences between waste produced in different places and to the connection of the waste with its place of production, the contested measures cannot be regarded as discriminatory.

The principle of rectification at source here informed the test of discrimination that triggers the 'imperative requirements' justification, since it was prescribed in the EC Treaty as founding 'Community' environmental policy.[224] The principle informed the rule of reason in such a way that expanded the scope of EU environmental competence to include Member State action, which was also legally prescribed and delimited by environmental principles. This was not obviously the case, since Article 191(2) TFEU concerns *EU* (previously *Community*)[225] environmental policy, but the ECJ's conclusion in *Walloon Waste* indicated that such policy includes Member State environmental policy when Member States are acting within the scope of EU law. EU environmental policy thus dictated what Member State policy may lawfully be adopted to derogate from the Article 34 free movement guarantee in the name of environmental protection.[226]

This doctrinal use of the principle of rectification at source is somewhat crude. The decision has been criticised on the ground that waste in one Member State is not qualitatively different from waste in another Member State, and so the measures at issue should be seen as discriminatory.[227] This crudeness might be explained

---

[223] ibid [34], [36].

[224] cf Michael Doherty, 'Hard Cases and Environmental Principles: An Aid to Interpretation?' (2004) 3 *YEEL* 57, 60–62; Stephen Weatherill, 'Publication Review: "Free Movement of Goods in the European Community" (Peter Oliver)' (2003) 28(5) *ELR* 756, 758.

[225] Ex-art 130r(2) EC.

[226] See Case C-463/01 *Commission v Germany* [2004] ECR I-11705 [74]. This resembles how EU fundamental rights doctrine has a wide-ranging scope in binding Member State action: Case C-260/89 *Elliniki Radiophonia Tiléorassi v Dimotiki Etairia Pliroforissis* [1991] ECR I-2925.

[227] eg Francis Jacobs, 'The Role of the European Court of Justice in the Protection of the Environment' (2006) 18 *JEL* 185, 189. Note the decision itself is out of date in light of the WSR (n 104), which now applies to *all* waste shipments between Member States, and otherwise is likely overruled: *Stadtgemeinde* (n 68) [59], [62]–[63], *cf* [69].

by the ECJ's inclination to endorse a policy that conformed to the requirements of Article 191(2) TFEU and adjusting its legal reasoning to fit. The doctrinal roles of environmental principles in EU law are thus not obvious or predictable. This is reinforced by the fact that a series of Advocate Generals' opinions have encouraged the Court of Justice to depart from the rule of reason's requirement for discrimination in cases where Member States seek to justify environmental measures that infringe Article 34, on the basis that this departure is supported by the integration principle, 'according to which environmental objectives, the transverse and fundamental nature of which have been noted by the Court, should be taken into account in the definition and implementation of European Union policies'.[228] This suggested legal argument displays another creative potential role for environmental principles in informing this body of EU legal doctrine. From this early case in *Walloon Waste*, despite its doctrinal limitations, environmental principles have come to inform both EU and Member State review tests, and, while they do so in different ways, they perform the same overarching function in these cases: identifying the limits of the policy discretion afforded to EU and Member State institutions when exercising EU environmental competence.

Another fundamental early informing legal test case, *BSE*,[229] involved the precautionary principle in the review of an EU measure. The relevant review test in this case was the test of proportionality, or the proportionality principle. Proportionality—a 'general principle of Community law'[230]—is an independent ground of review,[231] comprised of discrete legal tests, which limits the discretionary power of both EU and Member State institutions as they legislate and make decisions within the scope of EU law. The precise tests comprising, and manner of application of, the proportionality principle differ slightly from case to case, and particularly between review of EU and Member State measures.[232] However, the basic three-pronged test of proportionality appears with some consistency across

---

[228] Joined Cases C-204/12 to C-208/12 *Essent Belgium NV v Vlaamse Reguleringsinstantie voor de Elektriciteits—en Gasmarkt* [2014] ECLI:EU:C:2014:2192, Opinion of Advocate-General Bot (8 May 2013) [96]–[97] (arguing that the requirement that Member State measures be non-discriminatory should be dropped in environmental cases so as to ensure the 'pre-eminence' of environmental protection over other considerations, justifying this on the basis of the integration principle). See also *PreussenElektra*, Opinion of Advocate-General Jacobs (n 118) [230]–[231]; Case C-320/03 *Commission v Austria* [2005] ECR I-9871, Opinion of Advocate-General Geelhoed (14 July 2005) [107]. While the Court has not explicitly adopted this suggested shift in doctrine, it has avoided addressing the discrimination question by focusing its reasoning on the issue of proportionality instead, a trend which has continued in more recent art 34 environmental cases: eg Case C-142/05 *Åklagaren v Mickelsson & Roos* [2009] I-04273; Case C-573/12 *Ålands Vindkraft AB v Energimyndigheten* [2014] ECLI:EU:C:2014:2037.
[229] Case C-180/96 *United Kingdom v Commission* [1998] ECR I-3906 ('*BSE*').
[230] ibid [96].
[231] It is a 'rule of law relating to [the application of the Treaties]' under art 263: see above text accompanying n 30. The principle is now enshrined in TEU, art 5.
[232] Case C-434/04 *Ahokainen & Leppik v Virallinen Syyttäjä* [2006] ECR I-9171, Opinion of Advocate-General Maduro (13 July 2006) [23]–[31].

EU legal contexts, and has been informed in various ways by environmental principles in EU case law. The proportionality principle requires that:[233]

— measures adopted by EU institutions do not exceed the limits of what is *appropriate and necessary* in order to attain the objectives legitimately pursued by the legislation in question ('necessity' or 'suitability' test);
— when there is a choice between several appropriate measures, recourse must be had to the *least onerous or restrictive*;
— the disadvantages caused must not be *disproportionate* to the aims pursued ('proportionality *stricto sensu*', or in a narrow sense).

These three discrete limbs of the proportionality principle are informed differently by environmental principles in different cases.[234]

*BSE* and its accompanying case—*NFU*—were public health cases,[235] which involved legality challenges to an emergency Commission decision banning the export of British beef.[236] The 'precautionary principle', as recognised in later cases and the Commission Communication on the precautionary principle,[237] was first defined (although not mentioned by name) in the following way by the ECJ in these cases:[238]

> Where there is uncertainty as to the existence or extent of risks to human health, the institutions may take protective measures without having to wait until the reality and seriousness of those risks become fully apparent.

This principle was articulated to represent a policy position that the EU legislative institutions could lawfully adopt within this area of EU environmental competence, beyond the environmental title of the Treaty. The ECJ found that this principle derived from ex-Article 130r EC (now Article 191 TFEU),[239] which was equally applicable in this area of agricultural and public health policy, in light of the objective of Community environmental policy to protect human health, and in light of the integration principle.[240] Having acknowledged this expression of the precautionary principle as demarcating the scope of permissible policy discretion

---

[233] Case C-331/88 *Fedesa* [1990] ECR I-4023 [13].

[234] On environmental principles informing the different elements of proportionality, see Nicolas de Sadeleer, *Environmental Principles: From Political Slogans to Legal Rules* (OUP 2002) 291–391; *cf* Joanne Scott, 'The Precautionary Principle before the European Courts' in Richard Macrory, Ian Havercroft and Ray Purdy (eds), *Principles of European Environmental Law* (Europa Law Publishing 2004) 54.

[235] In this expanded area of EU environmental competence, extensive treatment of the precautionary principle in review cases has developed.

[236] *BSE* (n 229); Case C-157/96 *Queen v Ministry of Agriculture, Fisheries and Food, Commissioners of Customs & Excise, ex parte National Farmers' Union* [1998] ECR I-2265 ('*NFU*'). References will be to *BSE* only, since *NFU* is identical in all relevant respects.

[237] eg *Monsanto* (n 7) [111]; Communication (n 62) 24.

[238] *BSE* (n 229) [99].

[239] These equivalent Treaty provisions are similar but not identical in their incorporation of environmental principles: see ch 3(III)(A).

[240] *BSE* (n 229) [100].

in this case, the ECJ used it to inform the first limb of the proportionality test (the suitability test) in reviewing the legality of the contested Commission decision. The ECJ found that, in the context of EC agricultural policy, Community institutions in that domain had considerable discretion; the legality of a measure taken could only be judged inappropriate and unnecessary if 'manifestly inappropriate' in relation to the objective pursued.[241] In this case, where the risks to human health were uncertain, it was not manifestly inappropriate for the institutions to adopt protective measures before the reality of risks became apparent.[242]

Thus, the precautionary principle, as defined by the Court, marked out the permissible area of Community discretion in this policy domain, and informed part of the legal review test applied by the ECJ in reviewing this discretion.[243] This doctrinal treatment of the precautionary principle, informing proportionality review, is a trend that extends throughout the cases in this section. In later cases, environmental principles are also used to inform other parts of the three-part proportionality test.[244] The formulation of the precautionary principle in *BSE* is a classic formulation in EU case law, particularly due to its repetition in later cases.[245] However, it is not the only formulation of the principle used to inform review tests. The definition is further adapted in later cases, giving rise to different versions of the principle associated with evolving tests of administrative law and patterns of doctrinal reasoning in different EU regulatory contexts.[246]

A final early case in which an environmental principle informed a legal review test was *Safety Hi-Tech*, which extended the group of EU environmental principles employed doctrinally in reviewing EU action.[247] In this case, the legality of a Council Regulation banning the use and marketing of certain ozone-depleting substances was indirectly challenged in a preliminary reference action, on the ground that it breached Article 191(2) TFEU (ex-Article 130r(2) EC) for failing to ensure a 'high level of protection',[248] since it did not ban *all* ozone-depleting substances. The relevant review test applied by the ECJ was whether the measure, based on Article 192(1), constituted a 'manifest error of appraisal' by the EU institutions in exercising the policy discretion under Article 191, particularly on

---

[241] ibid [97].

[242] ibid [99], [103].

[243] In *Artegodan*, the CFI acknowledged that the precautionary principle was 'implicitly applied in the review of proportionality' in *BSE: Artegodan* (n 168) [185].

[244] eg *Pfizer* (n 31) [441]–[444] (duty to take less onerous measures), [456], [471] (proportionality in the strict sense); Case C-304/01 *Spain v Council* [2004] I-07655, Opinion of Advocate-General Kokott (18 November 2003) [68] (proportionality in the strict sense); Case T-158/03 *Industrias Químicas del Vallés v Commission* [2005] ECR II-2425 [133], [137] (identification of objectives legitimately pursued); Case T-370/11 *Poland v Commission* [2013] ECLI:EU:T:2013:113 [90] (proportionality in the strict sense).

[245] *Pfizer* (n 31) [139]; Case C-192/01 *Commission v Denmark* [2003] ECR I-9693 [49]; Case C-269/13 P *Acino v Commission* [2014] EU:C:2014:255 [57].

[246] See below Sections V(B)(iii)–(v); *cf* n 326.

[247] Case C-284/95 *Safety Hi-Tech Srl v S&T Srl* [1998] ECR I-4301.

[248] Ex-art 130r(2) EC.

the basis of the 'principle' of a high level of protection.[249] In concluding that the institutions had made no such error, the ECJ reasoned that a high level of protection does not require the highest level of environmental protection technically possible—it is sufficient if such measures 'contribute to the preservation, protection and improvement of the quality of the environment'.[250] In this way, this environmental principle was marginally defined and relied on to inform the legal review test in this case.

In these early cases, environmental principles are used to mark out an area of permissible institutional policy discretion to which the courts defer, and then to inform the legal tests applied by the Community courts in reviewing exercises of such discretion. A similarity with the interpretive cases can also be seen in these cases: where the principles take on doctrinal roles, the courts define them marginally, substantiating them to the extent required to resolve the legal test at issue.

### ii. Pfizer

The subsequent cases in which environmental principles inform legal review tests primarily involve the precautionary principle. This is for various reasons—it is a principle that is particularly controversial in its definition and application, and it is a principle that is implicated in highly contested areas of risk regulation that are characterised by scientific uncertainty. As a result, the case law relating to this principle is the most sophisticated and also the most complicated, co-evolving with developing norms of EU administrative law doctrine.[251] The precautionary principle has also been identified in some cases as a 'general principle of EU law',[252] highlighting the well-established competence of EU institutions to act on the basis of the principle, in areas beyond the environmental title of the treaty, particularly in public health regulation. However, this legal characterisation of the principle requires closer analysis to understand how it defines and delimits the exercise of discretion in this area of EU environmental competence as a matter of law.

The doctrinal role of the precautionary principle in EU case law was initially transformed in two seminal decisions of the CFI reviewing the public health discretion of the (then) Community legislature, *Pfizer* and *Alpharma*.[253] These

---

[249] The review test was so limited in light of the 'need to strike a balance' between art 191 objectives and principles and the 'complexity of the implementation' of those criteria: *Safety Hi-Tech* (n 247) [37]. In other words, the courts will not overstep their proper constitutional role and meddle in the policy decision-making of the EU institutions unnecessarily.

[250] ibid [45], [49].

[251] Thus Craig devotes an entire chapter to the precautionary principle in his book on EU administrative law: Craig (n 28) ch 21.

[252] *Artegodan* (n 168); *Dow AgroSciences Ltd v Commission* (n 126) [144]; Case T-257/07 *France v Commission* [2011] ECR II-05827 [66]. See below nn 302–304 and accompanying text.

[253] *Pfizer* (n 31); Case T-70/99 *Alpharma v Council* [2002] ECR II-3495.

cases mark a significant shift in the case law,[254] with the precautionary principle being used to generate as well as inform tests for reviewing institutional policy discretion in these cases. This shift was prompted by the Communication, which elaborated the Commission's view on applying the precautionary principle in its decision-making,[255] the ideas and language of which resonate through *Pfizer* and later cases. Influenced by the contents of this policy document, the CFI gives the precautionary principle much more attention and doctrinal importance. In *Pfizer* and *Alpharma*, the precautionary principle is used both to generate a test of 'adequate scientific cogency and objectivity' and to inform the legal tests of manifest error of assessment and proportionality. Some unpacking of the treatment of the precautionary principle in these cases is necessary to understand this dual role.[256]

*Pfizer* involved a challenge to Regulation 2821/98,[257] which withdrew Community authorisation for an antibiotic, virginiamycin, used as a growth promoter in animals reared for human consumption.[258] The Regulation was explicitly adopted on the basis of the precautionary principle,[259] in light of the risk that use of virginiamycin as an animal growth promoter might promote antibiotic resistance in humans through animal consumption. Pfizer challenged the Regulation on eight different grounds, including manifest errors of assessment, breach of the principle of proportionality, and breach of the precautionary principle. Argued in this fashion, the precautionary principle looks like a stand-alone ground for challenging the review of EU measures. However, the precautionary principle is not a review test in the way that manifest error or proportionality are; rather it sets out a remit of substantive policy exercisable by Community institutions. In the CFI's reasoning, the limits of this remit are policed by the other two review tests as informed by the precautionary principle, including its test of adequate scientific risk assessment and objectivity deriving from the Commission's Communication.

The reasoning of the decision is lengthy and often difficult to follow; in particular, there are layers of reasoning involving the precautionary principle. The Court found that six of the grounds, including the three particularly relevant here (manifest error of assessment, and breach of proportionality and the precautionary principle), all 'in essence' concern alleged misapplication of the precautionary principle, and so were all considered by analysing the application of that principle, understood as a two-step process of risk assessment and risk management.[260] The CFI addressed alleged errors in risk assessment and risk management in turn,

---

[254] Elizabeth Fisher, *Risk Regulation and Administrative Constitutionalism* (Hart 2007) 229.

[255] See ch 3, text accompanying nn 153–163.

[256] *Pfizer* (n 31) will here be addressed in detail; *Alpharma* (n 253) only where relevantly different.

[257] Council Regulation (EC) 2821/98 amending, as regards withdrawal of the authorisation of certain antibiotics, Directive 70/224/EEC concerning additives in feeding stuffs [1998] OJ L351/4.

[258] *Alpharma* (n 253) involved a similar challenge to EC Council Regulation 2821/98, which also banned the use of antibiotic bacitracin zinc as a fattening agent in animal feed.

[259] Regulation 2821/98 (n 257) recital 29.

[260] *Pfizer* (n 31) [108].

applying the various grounds of review that are legal tests (manifest error of assessment and proportionality) within this structure. With the reasoning so structured around the approach to the precautionary principle laid down in the Commission's Communication, it is complicated to understand precisely what legal tests the CFI applied and, more significantly for this mapping exercise, how it treated the precautionary principle. This is best understood in four steps.

First, the CFI found that, in cases of scientifically uncertain risk to human health, the precautionary principle permits EU institutions to take preventive measures without waiting for the reality or seriousness of those risks to become fully apparent.[261] As in *BSE*, the Court relied on ex-Article 130r EC (now Article 191)[262] to mark out this defined scope of policy discretion in which EU institutions might lawfully act. In particular, the Court relied on this Treaty prescription that Community environmental policy should pursue the objective of protecting human health on the basis of the precautionary principle and the integration principle.[263] The latter principle was important since Regulation 2821/98 was an internal market harmonisation measure, and not based on the environmental title.

Second, and unlike in *BSE*, the CFI examined closely the circumstances in which there exists such a scientifically uncertain risk.[264] At this stage, the CFI generated a new legal test: an adequate scientific risk assessment must be carried out before any preventive measures can be taken in the name of the precautionary principle, to ensure that no arbitrary measures are adopted.[265] While a full scientific risk assessment cannot be carried out, since by definition we are in the territory of imperfect scientific information, the purpose of the risk assessment was 'to assess the degree of probability of a certain product or procedure having adverse effects on human health and the seriousness of any such adverse effects'.[266] This process was scrutinised in *Pfizer*, introducing another dimension of legal inquiry on the basis of the precautionary principle, shaping the test of adequate scientific evidence here developed by the CFI: 'as thorough a scientific risk assessment as possible', founded on the principles of 'excellence, transparency and independence', must be carried out to give the institutions 'sufficiently reliable and cogent information' on which to base their policy decision.[267] This risk assessment requirement was influenced by Community policy, as set out in the Communication and other Commission policy documents.[268] The CFI here generated a legal test, based on EU policy guidance.

---

[261] ibid [140]–[141], [385]–[386].
[262] At this stage the integration principle was still contained in art 130r EC: see ch 3(III)(A).
[263] *Pfizer* (n 31) [114], [140].
[264] This is in response to Pfizer's argument that the Community institutions did not correctly assess the scientific risk in this case, and adopted the Regulation 'for reasons of political expediency without a proper scientific basis': ibid [127].
[265] ibid [155], [162].
[266] ibid [148].
[267] *Pfizer* (n 31) [162], [172].
[268] ibid [158].

Third, the CFI identified two aspects of this risk assessment exercise: determining the level of risk to human health deemed unacceptable for society, and then conducting a scientific assessment of the risks.[269] With respect to the former, which involves deciding political objectives, EU institutions enjoy a broad discretion, and any decision taken can only be vitiated by judicial review on the grounds of manifest error, misuse of powers or clear excess of discretion.[270] Unhelpfully, the CFI did not elaborate these tests, but the result of the case helps to illuminate them, since no such vitiation was found on the facts. In relation to the second aspect of risk assessment, which the Court spent considerably more time examining on the facts, the same limited tests are applicable in judicially reviewing the scientific risk assessment undertaken by the institutions. In this case, since the Community institutions were required to 'evaluate highly complex scientific and technical facts', their discretion is broad and it was not the place of the CFI to substitute its assessment of the facts.[271] Again, the result of the case demonstrates the breadth of the institutions' discretion in drawing conclusions from the scientific material to which they have access. Even when the CFI came close to suggesting that inadequate (scientific) reasons were given by the Community institutions for taking a certain position with respect to the scientific evidence—concerning their refusal to adopt the conclusions drawn by the Scientific Committee on Animal Nutrition (an advisory EU scientific body) that no immediate risk was posed by virginiamycin to human health—the Court deferred to the institutions, finding that they adequately explained their divergent opinion by relying on the precautionary principle![272] No manifest error was committed, since the institutions have the political responsibility and entitlement to adopt measures in the interests of human health protection, notwithstanding scientific uncertainty. In essence, and after much analysis, the CFI found that sufficient reliable and cogent scientific evidence (including international scientific reports and a Danish study on live rats) existed for the institutions to conclude that a risk to human health was posed, albeit an uncertain one, by the use of virginiamycin in animal feed.[273] In the midst of this reasoning, verging on circularity, the precautionary principle, operating on multiple levels, both generated a review test (of scientific adequacy/cogency of the risk assessment carried out by the Community institutions) and informed the manifest error standard applied to meet that test. At the same time, it was also a

---

[269] ibid [149].
[270] ibid [166].
[271] ibid [169], [323].
[272] ibid [204]–[205], [208], [382]–[389].
[273] In *Alpharma*, the CFI similarly held that the Community institutions had sufficiently objective and cogent scientific evidence on which to adopt preventive measures, despite their failure to obtain a SCAN opinion or to wait for a relevant forthcoming scientific report. It was in keeping with the precautionary principle, 'in the context of their broad discretion and their responsibility for defining the public health policy', not to await more detailed scientific research: *Alpharma* (n 253) [317]–[318].

principle that informed the policy discretion of the Community institutions and their discretion in applying this principle had to be respected.

Fourth, in the second section of its reasoning engaging the precautionary principle, the CFI was concerned with the risk management decisions made by the Community institutions. It examined whether imposing a total ban on the use of virginiamycin in animal feed, as a response to the identified uncertain risk, was vitiated by manifest error, again in light of the broad discretion of the institutions in adopting such a scientifically complex political decision. At this point the manifest error and proportionality review tests collided in the Court's reasoning, with the CFI applying a four-pronged proportionality test to determine whether any manifest error was committed by the institutions.[274] The precautionary principle was employed by the Court to inform all four aspects of the proportionality inquiry, expanding its role as identified in *BSE* and reinforcing the role of the precautionary principle in informing legal review tests.[275] As in *BSE*, the suitability test was met since the ban was a preventive measure appropriately adopted on the basis of the precautionary principle.[276] In determining that a less onerous measure need not have been adopted, applying the second limb of proportionality, the CFI found that the ban was consonant with the precautionary principle, which can 'require' a public authority to act before any adverse effects have become apparent.[277] Another dimension to the precautionary principle informed whether the ban was 'disproportionate' in a strict sense, under the third limb of proportionality identified earlier. The CFI concluded that 'the protection of public health … must take precedence over economic considerations' to find that the measure was lawful.[278] This policy assertion by the CFI did not necessarily follow from the elaboration of the precautionary principle so far (in this case or in *BSE*): it is an aspect of the principle that is adopted in some later case law and represents a new marginal definition of the precautionary principle.[279]

In summary, from *Pfizer*, the discretionary latitude afforded to EU institutions to act on the basis of the precautionary principle is triggered by 'adequate' scientific assessment, which gives the institutions a broad discretion to take preventive measures. This trigger is a legal test of adequate scientific objectivity and cogency in the identification of (uncertain) risk, which is *generated* by the precautionary

---

[274] The same three tests of proportionality as identified above (see above, text accompanying n 233) are applied, along with an additional test of whether the disadvantages caused by Regulation 2821/98 are disproportionate to the advantages if no action were taken (on a cost-benefit analysis): *Pfizer* (n 31) [413]. Note that this collision of the tests of manifest error and proportionality does not occur consistently in the case law, eg in *Alpharma*, the CFI undertakes a proportionality inquiry separately from its inquiry into manifest errors of assessment: *Alpharma* (n 253) [320]–[369].

[275] *Pfizer* (n 31) [419], [444], [456], [471].

[276] ibid [417], 419].

[277] ibid [444]; cf Joined Cases C-11/04, C- 12/04, C-194/04 & C-453/03 *ABNA Ltd v Secretary of State for Health* [2005] ECR I-10423.

[278] *Pfizer* (n 31) [456], [471].

[279] *Artegodan* (n 168) [184]; *Solvay* (n 124) [121].

principle. The resultant discretion, also an aspect of the principle, *informs* the judicial review tests of manifest error and proportionality that are applied (here together) to monitor the lawful limits of policy decisions taken by EU institutions. When 'breach of the precautionary principle' was pleaded in argument in *Pfizer*, the legal plea was thus interpreted by the CFI as raising some combination of these tests. The precautionary principle both prompted deference by the Court to the discretion exercised by the Commission, and also operated doctrinally (generating and informing legal tests) to the extent that the Court was charged with reviewing the limits of the principle's application. *Pfizer* represents a landmark turn in the doctrine of the EU courts concerning the precautionary principle and has continued to influence the development of EU legal doctrine concerning the principle. The review cases that follow pick up on the different aspects of the judicial treatment of the principle in *Pfizer* in reviewing EU and Member State action taken on the basis of the principle. While the reasoning in these subsequent cases is often conflated, these doctrinal elements are further developed and refined within an evolving body of EU administrative law doctrine.

### iii.  The Precautionary Principle Post-*Pfizer* in the CFI/General Court: The Evolution of EU Administrative Law

Since *Pfizer*, the CFI has reviewed public health measures adopted by EU institutions on the basis of the precautionary principle on many occasions. This body of case law shows three trends. First, there is further refinement of the definition of the precautionary principle in these cases, developing lengthy paragraphs of reasoning that are like 'boilerplate' definitions of the principle. In the field of public health law at least, it looks as though there is an increasingly common definition of the precautionary principle, although there are still notable variances between cases. Second, the administrative review applied by the Court in determining whether EU institutions have lawfully taken action on the basis of the principle has become increasingly robust. This robustness is seen in the Court developing further tests for reviewing factual assessments made by the EU institutions, and in its increasing willingness to find failures of scientific assessment on the part of the EU institutions. Third, there is some ambiguity about whether the precautionary principle is being applied as a test of review in its own right in these cases. The reasoning in some cases suggests this doctrinal shift has occurred, which is consonant with holding the precautionary principle out as a general principle of EU law. However, other cases make clear that, whilst the precautionary principle is the (sometimes obligatory) basis for the institutional discretion that has been exercised, judicial review of this discretion is limited by more specific tests, which are sensitive to the Court's constitutional role. Overall, the increased scrutiny of EU institutional discretion that comes with the enhanced administrative law review applied in these cases reveals the CFI adopting an increasingly robust constitutional role, through deepening the doctrinal role of the precautionary principle.

This sub-section examines a number of CFI cases to demonstrate these trends. It starts by reviewing another relatively early case in detail—*Artegodan v Commission*[280]—in which the CFI concluded there was a breach of administrative law by the Commission in its application of the precautionary principle. The sub-section then considers more recent cases involving challenges to EU measures adopted on the basis of the precautionary principle in the public health arena, some for being insufficiently precautionary, most for being too precautionary. The reasoning of these cases becomes increasingly confident, building a body of precedent around the precautionary principle that is increasingly predictable.

*Artegodan*, briefly discussed in Chapter Two,[281] is a decision in which the CFI found that there was inadequate objective scientific evidence to justify, on the basis of the precautionary principle, the challenged exercise of Commission discretion. In this case, various pharmaceutical manufacturers challenged Commission decisions withdrawing marketing authorisation for medicinal products containing particular amphetamines used in the treatment of obesity.[282] The legal grounds adduced to challenge the decisions were, as in *Pfizer*, numerous and overlapping, and notably they did not include 'infringement of the precautionary principle'. The CFI introduced the precautionary principle in its reasoning to inform the permissible scope of the Commission's discretion in making decisions to withdraw marketing authorisations under Article 11 of Directive 65/65 relating to medicinal products.[283] The logic of its approach was different from that in *Pfizer*—in particular, it identified the precautionary principle as having been *implicitly* relied on by the Commission and as a 'corollary' of the 'general principle' that the requirements of the protection of public health are to prevail over economic interests.[284] The CFI found that the provisions of Directive 65/65 must be interpreted in accordance with this precautionary principle, which 'requires' (rather than allows) Community institutions to take measures to prevent specific potential risks to public health, safety and the environment.[285] In this way, the CFI defined the precautionary principle (and the policy discretion based on it) slightly differently in this case.[286]

As in *Pfizer*, however, the precautionary principle was identified as deriving from ex-Article 174(2) EC (now Article 191(2) TFEU), applying generally in the

---

[280] *Artegodan* (n 168).

[281] See ch 2, text accompanying nn 200–203.

[282] *Artegodan* (n 168). See also Case T-147/00 *Les Laboratoires Servier v Commission* [2003] ECR II-85.

[283] Authorisation could be withdrawn where it is harmful in its normal use, lacking in therapeutic efficacy, or misleading as to its qualitative and quantitative composition: Council Directive (EC) 65/65 on the approximation of provisions laid down by law, regulation or administrative action relating to medicinal products [1965-6] OJ Spec Ed 20 (as amended) art 11.

[284] *Artegodan* (n 168) [174].

[285] ibid [184]. For a similar approach to the precautionary principle: see *Solvay* (n 123) [121].

[286] Note *Artegodan* (n 168) was decided by a different chamber of the CFI shortly after *Pfizer* (n 31) and *Alpharma* (n 253) were handed down.

public health domain to guide the discretion of the Commission,[287] and on which the Commission implicitly based its decisions in this case.[288] Further, as in *Pfizer*, the precautionary principle generated a (slightly differently formulated) test of adequate scientific evidence: the Commission could only rely on the precautionary principle in exercising its discretion to withdraw authorisation if 'a new potential risk or the lack of efficacy is substantiated by new, objective, scientific [evidence]'.[289] On the facts, the CFI found that there was no such new, objective evidence and the Commission decisions were thereby vitiated. As in *Pfizer*, the CFI set out the manifest error test in framing its inquiry, so that the test of adequate scientific evidence generated by the precautionary principle in turn informed the manifest error test more broadly (although the Court does not put it so neatly).

Unlike in *Pfizer*, however, the CFI did not defer (on the basis of the precautionary principle) to the assessment of complex scientific material made by the Commission, possibly because the Commission in this case relied on the advice of the scientific body that it was bound to consult under Directive 65/65—the Committee for Proprietary Medicinal Products ('CPMP')—rather than forming its own view in light of the available evidence.[290] Instead, the Court strictly applied its test of adequate scientific evidence to the CPMP Opinion, finding that there was an unsatisfactory basis for the Commission's exercise of discretion based on the precautionary principle, since the Opinion disclosed no new scientific evidence but merely a change in clinical practice with respect to the contested medicines. Strictly, the CFI's reasoning based on the precautionary principle was superfluous since the Court had already found that the Commission was not competent to adopt the contested decisions on other grounds.[291] However, *Artegodan* was an important step in the CFI's, and more recently the General Court's, developing case law in reviewing institutional discretion exercised on the basis of the precautionary principle.

A notable feature of the subsequent case law is the increasing clarity around what the precautionary principle means and requires in public health decision-making. *France v Commission* is an exemplary case in which the Court's reasoning includes increasingly standard paragraphs 'defining' the precautionary principle:[292]

Precautionary principle

*Definition*

The precautionary principle is a general principle of European Union law arising from Article 3(p) EC, Article 6 EC, Article 152(1) EC, Article 153(1) and (2) EC and Article 174(1)

---

[287] As a 'general principle of Community law': *Artegodan* (n 168) [184].
[288] ibid [174].
[289] ibid [194]. Although such evidence does not need to '[resolve] the scientific uncertainty': [192].
[290] *cf Pfizer* and *Alpharma*, in which the Commission departed from relevant SCAN opinions: above nn 272–273 and accompanying text.
[291] *Artegodan* (n 168) [155].
[292] *France v Commission* (n 252) [66]–[69] (emphasis added and citations omitted). Similar statements are found in *Dow AgroSciences* (n 125) and *Du Pont* (n 125).

and (2) EC, *requiring* the authorities in question, in the particular context of the exercise of the powers conferred on them by the relevant rules, to take appropriate measures to prevent specific potential risks to public health, safety and the environment, by giving precedence to the requirements related to the protection of those interests over economic …

[W]here there is scientific uncertainty as to the existence or extent of risks to human health, the precautionary principle *allows* the institutions to take protective measures without having to wait until the reality and seriousness of those risks become fully apparent … or until the adverse health effects materialise …

Within the process leading to the adoption by an institution of appropriate measures to prevent specific potential risks to public health, safety and the environment by reason of the precautionary principle, three successive stages can be identified: firstly, identification of the potentially adverse effects arising from a phenomenon; secondly, assessment of the risks to public health, safety and the environment which are related to that phenomenon; thirdly, when the potential risks identified exceed the threshold of what is acceptable for society, risk management by the adoption of appropriate protective measures.

This is a much more comprehensive statement of the principle, building on its early incarnation in *BSE* and decided cases since, which highlights that the precautionary principle affords EU institutions a discretion, and responsibility, to act in cases of scientific uncertainty and that a particular decision-making process is to be followed. As *Pfizer* showed, the Court has a role in defining and policing that process in determining whether institutions act lawfully on the basis of the precautionary principle. Building on the reasoning in *Pfizer*, the Court has also developed a tighter articulation of the processes of risk assessment and risk management involved in applying the precautionary principle, which it elaborates as follows:[293]

Risk assessment

*Introduction*

Assessment of the risks to public health, safety and the environment consists, for the institution required to cope with potentially adverse effects arising from a phenomenon, in scientifically assessing those risks and in determining whether they exceed the level of risk deemed acceptable for society. Thus, in order for the European Union institutions to be able to carry out a risk assessment, it is important for them, firstly, to have a scientific assessment of the risks and, secondly, to determine what level of risk is deemed unacceptable for society …

*Scientific risk assessment*

A scientific risk assessment is a scientific process consisting, in so far as possible, in the identification and characterisation of a hazard, the assessment of exposure to that hazard and the characterisation of the risk.

---

[293] *France v Commission* (n 252) [70]–[83] (emphasis added and citations omitted).

In its communication of 2 February 2000 on the precautionary principle (COM(2000) 1), the Commission defined those four components of a scientific risk assessment as follows (see Annex III):

'Hazard identification means identifying the biological, chemical or physical agents that may have adverse effects ...

Hazard characterisation consists of determining, in quantitative and/or qualitative terms, the nature and severity of the adverse effects associated with the causal agents or activity ...

Appraisal of exposure consists of quantitatively or qualitatively evaluating the probability of exposure to the agent under study ...

Risk characterisation corresponds to the qualitative and/or quantitative estimation, taking account of inherent uncertainties, of the probability, of the frequency and of the severity of the known or potential adverse environmental or health effects liable to occur. It is established on the basis of the three preceding [components] and closely depends on the uncertainties, variations, working hypotheses and conjectures made at each stage of the process.'

As a scientific process, the scientific risk assessment must be entrusted by the institution to scientific experts ...

Moreover, ... the scientific risk assessment is to be based on the available scientific evidence and undertaken in an **independent, objective and transparent manner**. It is important to point out in that regard that the duty imposed on the institutions to ensure a high level of protection of public health, safety and the environment means that they must ensure that their decisions are taken in the light of the best scientific information available and that they are based on the most recent results of international research ...

The scientific risk assessment is not required to provide the institutions with conclusive scientific evidence of the reality of the risk and the seriousness of the potential adverse effects were that risk to become a reality. A situation in which the precautionary principle is applied by definition coincides with a situation in which there is scientific uncertainty ...

[A] preventive measure may be taken only if the risk, although the reality and extent thereof have not been 'fully' demonstrated by conclusive scientific evidence, appears nevertheless to be **adequately backed up by the scientific data available at the time** when the measure was taken ... In such a situation, 'risk' thus corresponds to the degree of probability that the acceptance of certain measures or practices will adversely affect the interests safeguarded by the legal order ...

Finally, it must be noted that it may prove impossible to carry out a full scientific risk assessment because of the inadequate nature of the available scientific data ... It is important, in such a situation, that scientific experts carry out a scientific risk assessment notwithstanding the existing scientific uncertainty, so that the competent public authority has available to it **sufficiently reliable and cogent information** to allow it to understand the ramifications of the scientific question raised and decide upon a policy in full knowledge of the facts ...

*Determination of the level of risk*

The responsibility for determining the level of risk which is deemed unacceptable for society lies, provided that the applicable rules are observed, with the institutions responsible for the political choice of determining an appropriate level of protection for society …

In determining the level of risk deemed unacceptable for society, the institutions are bound by their obligation to ensure a high level of protection of public health, safety and the environment. That high level of protection does not necessarily, in order to be compatible with that provision, have to be the highest that is technically possible … Moreover, those institutions may not take a purely hypothetical approach to risk and may not base their decisions on a 'zero risk' …

The level of risk deemed unacceptable for society will depend on the assessment made by the competent public authority of the particular circumstances of each individual case. In that regard, the authority may take account, inter alia, of the severity of the impact on public health, safety and the environment were the risk to occur, including the extent of possible adverse effects, the persistency or reversibility of those effects and the possibility of delayed effects as well as of the more or less concrete perception of the risk based on available scientific knowledge …

Risk management

Risk management corresponds to the body of actions taken by an institution faced with a risk in order to reduce it to a level deemed acceptable for society having regard to its obligation to ensure a high level of protection of public health, safety and the environment. Where that risk exceeds the level of risk deemed acceptable for society, the **institution is bound, by reason of the precautionary principle, to adopt provisional risk management measures** necessary to ensure a high level of protection.

[T]he provisional measures in question must be **proportionate, non-discriminatory, transparent, and consistent with similar measures** already taken.

Finally, it is for the competent authority to review the provisional measures in question within a reasonable period. It has been held that, when new elements change the perception of a risk or show that that risk can be contained by measures less restrictive than the existing measures, it is for the institutions and in particular the Commission, which has the power of legislative initiative, to bring about an amendment to the rules in the light of the new information …

This is a lengthy extract but it demonstrates the level of detail in which the General Court has now articulated and structured the lawful exercise of discretion based on the precautionary principle.[294] This articulation includes the test of adequate scientific evidence as developed in *Pfizer* and *Artegodan*. It also contains a number of other benchmarks and requirements that define this area of policy discretion

---

[294] Notably there are still variations on how the precautionary principle is defined in some cases, depending on the regulatory context: see eg *Solvay* (n 124).

in EU law by structuring decision-making within it. As Elizabeth Fisher argues, this legal articulation of the principle serves to 'constitute, limit and hold public decision-making to account' in the context of EU risk regulation.[295] The Court is constructing a norm of good administration within EU legal culture through its articulation of the precautionary principle.[296] Thus when there is an argument that the EU institutions have 'breached' or 'infringed' the precautionary principle and produced an unlawful measure or decision, this is referring to a failure to respect one or more of these benchmarks and requirements that define good decision-making in this regulatory context.[297] When the General Court is required to determine whether there has been such a failure, this is a process of administrative review, rather determining the breach of a substantive rule. Furthermore, in undertaking this review, the Court does not simply look for naked breaches of the risk assessment and management processes above; rather, it applies tests of administrative law that limit the scope of its review, in light of its proper constitutional role. These include the tests of manifest error of assessment and proportionality, as applied in *Pfizer* and *Artegodan*, but they also include a now more elaborated group of administrative law tests, as set out by the CFI in *France v Commission*:[298]

> In matters concerning the common agricultural policy, the institutions enjoy a broad discretion regarding definition of the objectives to be pursued and choice of the appropriate means of action … In addition, in the context of their risk assessment, they must carry out complex assessments in order to determine, in the light of the technical and scientific information which is provided to them by experts in the context of the scientific risk assessment, whether the risks to public health, safety and the environment exceed the level of risk deemed acceptable for society.

> That broad discretion and those complex assessments imply a limited power of review on the part of the Courts of the European Union. That discretion and those assessments have the effect that review by the Courts as to the substance is limited to verifying whether the exercise by the institutions of their powers is vitiated by a **manifest error of appraisal**, whether there has been a **misuse of powers**, or whether the institutions have **manifestly exceeded the limits of their discretion** …

> As regards the assessment by the Courts of the European Union as to whether an act of an institution is vitiated by a **manifest error of assessment**, it must be stated that, in

---

[295] Fisher (n 254) 23.

[296] ibid 24. See also ibid ch 6 for Fisher's examination of the precautionary principle through the lens of administrative constitutionalism in the EU courts.

[297] This is how one can understand the reasoning in cases where the General Court considers 'breach of the precautionary principle' as a standalone ground of argument: see text accompanying nn 123–125.

[298] *France v Commission* (n 252) [84]–[89] (emphasis added and citations omitted). This approach is supported by the Court of Justice on appeal, although the CJ succinctly articulates a more overarching list of review tests (manifest error of assessment, misuse of powers and whether the legislature has manifestly exceeded the limits of its discretion): Case C-601/11 P *France v Commission* [2013] ECLI:EU:C:2013:465.

order to establish that that institution committed a manifest error in assessing complex facts such as to justify the annulment of that act, the **evidence adduced by the applicant must be sufficient to make the factual assessments used in the act implausible** … Subject to that review of plausibility, it is not the Court's role to substitute its assessment of complex facts for that made by the institution which adopted the decision …

The abovementioned limits to the review by the Courts of the European Union do not, however, affect their duty to establish **whether the evidence relied on is factually accurate, reliable and consistent, whether that evidence contains all the information which must be taken into account in order to assess a complex situation, and whether it is capable of substantiating the conclusions drawn from it** …

Moreover, it must be recalled that, where an institution has a wide discretion, the review of observance of guarantees conferred by the European Union legal order in administrative procedures is of fundamental importance. The Court of Justice has had occasion to specify that those guarantees include, in particular for the competent institution, the **obligations to examine carefully and impartially all the relevant elements of the individual case and to give an adequate statement of the reasons for its decision** …

Thus, it has already been held that a **scientific risk assessment carried out as thoroughly as possible on the basis of scientific advice founded on the principles of excellence, transparency and independence** is an important procedural guarantee whose purpose is to ensure the scientific objectivity of the measures adopted and preclude any arbitrary measures)…

All these requirements above highlighted in bold now make up the administrative law tests that need to be met in order for the precautionary principle to be lawfully applied as an act of institutional discretion. These tests are partly generated by the principle itself—such as requiring a scientific assessment that is as thorough as possible—and others are part of the developing corpus of EU administrative law more generally. While these tests have been repeated and applied in a series of cases that are building a body of precedent, there are also some variations in the case law. For example, in *Animal Trading Company v Commission*, the General Court framed its inquiry into the adequacy of the scientific evidence underpinning a risk assessment as a 'duty of diligence'.[299] The General Court has not shied away from applying these tests to find that the EU institutions have in some cases unlawfully applied the precautionary principle in their decision-making relating to public health risks.[300] Equally, in some cases, where no infringement of these review tests has been found, the Court has deferred to the institutions exercising their discretion on the basis of the principle.[301]

---

[299] Case T-333/10 *Animal Trading Company (ATC) BV v Commission* [2013] ECLI:EU:T:2013:451 [84]–[94].

[300] *eg* Case T-456/11 *ICdA and others v Commission* [2013] ECLI:EU:T:2013:594; ibid.

[301] *eg Solvay* (n 124); *Gowan* (n 125); *Dow AgroSciences* (n 125); *France v Commission* (n 252) (note this was a case where the Commission was found to have lawfully relaxed preventive health measures on the basis of the precautionary principle); *Du Pont* (n 125); Case T-539/10 *Acino v Commission* ECLI:EU:T:2013:110 (upheld on appeal in Case C-269/13 P); Case T-446/10 *Dow AgroSciences v Commission* [2015] ECLI:EU:T:2015:629.

In light of this analysis, what does it mean for the General Court to say that the precautionary principle has become a 'general principle of EU law'? This characterisation reflects the fact that the principle is an established framework for decision-making in the field of public health risk regulation, which transcends discrete regulatory schemes. Thus, in *Gowan*, the General Court states:[302]

> it must be accepted that ... the precautionary principle is an integral part of the decision-making process leading to the adoption of any measure for the protection of human health.

It also reflects the fact that this framework is subject to close administrative review by the General Court according to an increasingly predictable set of tests. The characterisation as a 'general principle' is however also misleading in EU law terms,[303] since the precautionary principle does not represent a singular substantive norm that universally guides and can be relied on to challenge the lawfulness of all EU action, akin to a fundamental right, the principle of equal treatment, or the proportionality principle in EU law.[304] Rather, it is a principle that demarcates an area of substantive policy discretion, which crosses over areas of EU policy competence, and which is defined by a set of decision-making processes that are subject to administrative review by the courts. Its doctrinal treatment by the General Court demonstrates a process of reasoning by which the principle's policy prescription is defined by the courts, with this definition serving to generate and inform the various administrative review tests that monitor the exercise of this prescribed policy competence.

### iv. *The Precautionary Principle Post-*Pfizer *in the Court of Justice: Less Intensive Review of EU Institutions*

In contrast to the General Court's case law involving the precautionary principle, the Court of Justice has also continued to develop its reasoning involving precautionary principle in reviewing the acts of EU institutions,[305] but with less intensive factual review. This is because different legal questions are asked, and different arguments are made, before both courts, which have differing jurisdictions. In particular, the General Court hears most annulment actions that involve the finding and evaluation of complex facts.[306] The Court of Justice hears appeals from all

---

[302] *Gowan* (n 125) [74].

[303] See ch 2(III)(B).

[304] See Tridimas (n 15) 5. This explains why, in *Solvay*, the CFI found that the applicant's argument that the contested regulation 'infringes' the precautionary principle was incorrectly put in isolation: *Solvay* (n 124) [120].

[305] And, in at least one case, the polluter pays principle: see *Poland v Commission* (n 244).

[306] TFEU, art 256; Protocol (No 3) On The Statute Of The Court Of Justice Of The European Union [2010] OJ C83/210.

General Court judgments, but this is on points of law only,[307] as well as most pre-liminary references and certain annulment actions. In terms of the legal treatment of the precautionary principle, this jurisdictional distinction is demonstrated by the Court of Justice conducting a lighter touch of administrative review in review-ing acts of discretion based on the precautionary principle. In particular, the Court does not get involved in lengthy analysis of the quality of factual evidence supporting decisions or acts based on the precautionary principle.

In this vein, there has been a group of Court of Justice cases since *Pfizer*, in which the precautionary principle has been used doctrinally to inform legal tests in reviewing EU measures, but in which the Court has not tested the adequacy of the scientific evidence relied upon by the EU institutions in adopting measures based on the precautionary principle.[308] The Court acknowledges that actions based on the principle must be based on a 'comprehensive risk assessment' of health risks determined by the most recent and reliable scientific data available,[309] but does not question this information or interrogate its credibility in any detail. In these cases involving the review of EU institutional discretion, the Court of Justice has employed the precautionary principle to inform the test of proportion-ality. Thus the grounds of review pleaded in argument (or framed in the prelimi-nary reference) focus on the issue of proportionality, in relation to the lawfulness of measures in various respects, and most do not directly raise the questions of manifest error of factual assessment or 'infringement' of the precautionary prin-ciple.[310] In reviewing acts based on the precautionary principle through the legal lens of proportionality, the Court of Justice also respects a wide margin of discre-tion in reviewing institutional action. The Court recognises that it is reviewing action taken in areas where the EU institutions have to make 'political, economic and social choices …, and in which it is called upon to undertake complex assess-ments'.[311] Thus the Court will look for 'manifest' errors in the application of the precautionary principle to inform the relevant limb of proportionality at issue.

---

[307] '[T]he General Court has exclusive jurisdiction to establish the facts, except where the substan-tive accuracy of its findings is apparent from the documents submitted to it, and to assess the evidence relied on. The establishment of those facts and the assessment of that evidence do not therefore, save where they are distorted, constitute a point of law which is subject as such to review by the Court of Justice': Case C-358/14 *Poland v Parliament & Council* [2014] ECLI:EU:C:2016:323 [34].

[308] Joined Cases C-154/04 & C-155/04 *Alliance for Natural Health v Secretary of State for Health* [2005] ECR I-6451; Case C-504/04 *Agrarproduktion Staebelow v Landrat des Landkreises Bad Doberan* [2006] ECR I-679; Case C-343/09 *Afton Chemical Ltd v Secretary of State for Transport* [2010] I-07027; Case C-157/14 *Neptune Distribution SNC v Ministre de l'Économie et des Finances* [2015] ECLI:EU:C:2015:823; Case C-477/14 *Pillbox 38 (UK) Ltd v Secretary of State for Health* [2016] ECLI:EU:C:2016:324.

[309] *Afton* (n 308) [60]; cf *Neptune Distribution* and *Pillbox 38* (n 308) in which the Court of Justice does not even mention the need for a thorough risk assessment. In these cases, the identification of a public health risk was sufficient to justify the adoption of precautionary measures.

[310] cf ibid [9].

[311] *Pillbox 38* (n 308) [49].

*Agrarproduktion Staebelow* is a good example of this kind of reasoning.[312] In this case, the ECJ found that Article 13(1)(c) of Regulation 999/01,[313] which required animals at risk of contracting BSE to be slaughtered, was not invalid in light of the proportionality principle. In resolving the proportionality inquiry, the ECJ used the precautionary principle to resolve the first limb 'appropriateness' test, as in *BSE*. The measures adopted by the Community legislature were found to be appropriate to the objective of the protection of human health, in light of the policy discretion afforded to Community institutions to take preventive measures in cases of scientific uncertainty.[314] In the subsequent case of *Afton Chemical*,[315] the ECJ used the precautionary principle to inform the third limb of the proportionality inquiry, finding that there was no lack of proportionality in a narrow sense in a provision of Directive 2009/30,[316] which introduced an upper limit of a particular chemical in fuel. The uncertainty in relation to the environmental and health damage caused by the chemical meant that the limit was not manifestly disproportionate in relation to the economic interests of the producers of the chemical.[317] More recent cases have concerned EU measures that prevent misleading advertising in relation to product claims that were contestable in terms of their scientifically accuracy,[318] and a specific EU regime introduced for electronic cigarettes in light of the potential health risks of 'vaping'.[319] Again, in both these cases, the Court of Justice accepted that a relevant risk to public health existed and justified the adoption of restrictive measures on the basis of the precautionary principle, which in turn justified the proportionality and legality of the relevant measure.

In contrast to General Court case law, the Court of Justice in these cases does not test the current state of knowledge and scientific uncertainty at issue in these cases to determine whether the precautionary principle was justifiably exercised by the Community institutions. Rather, the Court accepts their identification of that uncertainty and the limited scientific assessment so far undertaken in relation to the relevant health risks.[320] By virtue of its jurisdictional remit, the Court of Justice has adopted a different jurisprudence from that of the General Court

---

[312] *Agrarproduktion* (n 308).
[313] Council & Parliament Regulation (EC) 999/2001 laying down rules for the prevention, control and eradication of certain transmissible spongiform encephalopathies [2001] OJ L147/1.
[314] *Agrarproduktion* (n 308) [38]–[43].
[315] *Afton* (n 308).
[316] Council & Parliament Directive (EC) 2009/30 regarding the specification of petrol, diesel and gas-oil and introducing a mechanism to monitor and reduce greenhouse gas emissions [2009] L140/88.
[317] *Afton* (n 308) [68].
[318] *Neptune Distribution* (n 308) (notably the EU consumer protection measures at issue were argued to compromise Charter rights of freedom of expression and information in limiting how producers can describe their products, and the proportionality principle was applied in determining infringement of these Charter rights).
[319] *Pillbox 38* (n 308).
[320] *Afton* (n 308) [58]–[59]; *Agrarproduktion* (n 308) [41]–[42].

with respect to the precautionary principle, involving a doctrinal approach that is more deferential to the discretion of EU institutions. The Court of Justice treats the principle as marking out an area of permissible policy discretion and thus informing the review test of proportionality, rather than as a principle that generates tests of administrative review and intrudes more deeply into decision-making by EU institutions. This reflects a self-conscious constitutional position adopted by the Court of Justice in relation to the powers of other EU institutions. As will be seen from the Article 34 cases discussed in the following sub-section, the Court of Justice has not shied away from treating the precautionary principle as a principle that requires close scrutiny of institutional action in all cases.

### v. *Expanding the Doctrinal Reach of Environmental Principles: Informing the Review of Member State Discretion under Article 34 TFEU*

The Court of Justice has engaged in more robust scrutiny of institutional discretion based on the precautionary principle when it comes to Member States acting within the scope of EU law. This is seen in cases where Article 34 TFEU is prima facie infringed by Member States taking precautionary measures on public health grounds, bringing this action within the scope of EU law. In these cases, the Court of Justice scrutinises the purported exercise of environmental competence by Member State institutions to determine whether there has been any breach of the rules that allow Member States to derogate from Article 34. The judicial techniques involved in this scrutiny involve both generating and informing legal tests on the basis of the precautionary principle.[321] These cases are inspired by the CFI's approach in *Pfizer*, with the ECJ (deciding these cases prior to the Lisbon Treaty) using a test of adequate scientific evidence—again inspired by the Commission's Communication on the precautionary principle and its focus on risk assessment, also enshrined in EU secondary legislation[322]—to inform the legal review test of proportionality. As a matter of EU law, these cases involve review of Member State action through the prism of substantive legality review (determining whether Member States have infringed Article 34) but they are nevertheless public law review cases, reviewing the competence of Member States to take unilateral action in the field of environmental and health policy.

In terms of the substantive law at issue, these cases are similar to the review of Member State discretion (relying on the principle of rectification at source) analysed in *Walloon Waste* above.[323] The difference is that these cases do not involve

---

[321] In Case C-473/98 *Kemikalieinspektionen v Toolex Alpha* [2000] ECR I-5681, the ECJ also relied on the 'substitution principle' to inform the second limb of the proportionality test in assessing a Swedish public health measure that infringed art 34 of the TFEU, expanding the range of 'environmental principles' that are used doctrinally in these cases.

[322] Council & Parliament Regulation (EC) 178/2002 laying down the general principles and requirements of food law [2002] OJ L31/1, arts 6 and 7.

[323] See above, text accompanying nn 221–226.

the 'rule of reason' justification for infringing Article 34, but the public health justification in Article 36 TFEU. In these public health cases, the ECJ has focused on interpreting the Article 36 exception strictly, since it allows deviation from a fundamental rule of the internal market.[324] The Court has employed the proportionality principle to qualify reliance by Member States on Article 36, as informed by the precautionary principle, requiring that a current and detailed scientific assessment of the risk alleged by the Member State must demonstrate a real risk to public health and thus the 'necessity' of the contested measure.[325] The precautionary principle, which generates this test of adequate scientific evidence (in a formulation that focuses on adequate risk assessment),[326] is thus treated as informing the first limb of the proportionality inquiry in these cases. Only by satisfying the review tests so generated and informed can Member State discretion, relying on the precautionary principle, be compatible with Article 36. In these cases, the precautionary principle expresses lawful Member State policy discretion within the prescribed policy framework of the Treaty—expanding the area of EU environmental competence defined by environmental principles to include Member State environmental actions within the scope of EU law—and also informs and generates the legal tests applied by the ECJ to monitor the limits of that discretion.

*Commission v Denmark* is the seminal Article 34 case that involves this doctrinal treatment of the precautionary principle,[327] and its reasoning is followed by later cases.[328] In this Article 258 infringement action brought by the Commission, the Danish government argued that its administrative practice of banning nutrient-enriched foods lawfully marketed or produced in other Member States unless they met a need in the Danish population, which infringed Article 34, was justified on public health grounds. In particular, it argued that this practice was justified since the risks of overexposure to vitamins and minerals were uncertain and so danger to human health could not be excluded.[329] The ECJ had previously dealt with similar cases, in which products lawfully marketed in some Member States were refused marketing authorisation in others ostensibly on public health grounds, in the light of uncertain risks to health. In those cases, the ECJ had consistently held that Member States, while scientific uncertainties persisted, and in the absence of

---

[324] Case C-24/00 *Commission v France* [2004] ECR I-1277 [87].

[325] *Commission v Denmark* (n 245) [45]–[46].

[326] This ECJ reasoning echoes the definition of the precautionary principle now adopted most commonly by the General Court: see above nn 292–293 and accompanying text. Thus in *Commission v France*, the ECJ held that 'a correct application of the precautionary principle presupposes, first, identification of the potentially negative consequences for health ... and, secondly, a comprehensive assessment of the risk to health based on the most reliable scientific data available and the most recent results of international research': *Commission v France* (n 324) [92].

[327] *Commission v Denmark* (n 245).

[328] Case C-95/01 *Criminal Proceedings Against Greenham and Abel* [2004] ECR I 1333; Case C-41/02 *Commission v Netherlands* [2005] ECR I-11375; Case C-219/07 *Nationale Raad van Dierenkwekers en Liefhebbers VZW v Belgische Staat* [2008] ECR I-4475; *Commission v France* (n 324).

[329] *Commission v Denmark* (n 245) [29].

Community harmonisation, had discretion to limit the marketing of such products, so long as they demonstrated that their marketing constituted a serious risk to human health.[330]

In *Commission v Denmark*, the ECJ adopted the same approach, but explicitly on the basis of the precautionary principle. Denmark had raised the precautionary principle in argument, asserting that its measures complied with the principle, as laid down in the Commission Communication.[331] The ECJ responded by finding that the scope of discretion accorded to Member States in these cases reflected the precautionary principle,[332] and went on to consider what constituted a 'proper application of the precautionary principle' for the purposes of testing the limits of Denmark's discretion in this case.[333] Relying on similar reasoning to that in *Pfizer*,[334] the ECJ found that lawfully applying the precautionary principle presupposed a detailed scientific risk assessment based on the most recent international research and the most reliable scientific data available, which showed real likelihood of harm—that is, it generated a test of adequate scientific evidence demonstrating a relevant risk to public health. Once this test was satisfied, Member State institutions enjoyed a wide discretion to adopt restrictive measures in the face of scientific uncertainty.[335]

The ECJ thus engaged in more comprehensive scientific inquiry in *Commission v Denmark*, and in the Article 34 cases that followed.[336] This case law was inspired by the CFI's tests of review based on the precautionary principle, although the ECJ still does not investigate the robustness of scientific evidence to the same degree as the General Court. Even so, in the majority of cases, the ECJ finds that the scientific risk assessments relied on by the Member States to justify their infringing measures are inadequate, demonstrating a greater willingness to hold Member State institutions to account in acting on the basis of the precautionary principle.[337] The inadequacy of risk assessments informs the test of proportionality applied. Thus, in *Commission v Denmark*, the Court found that the contested practice was disproportionate, since it systematically prohibited the marketing of all enriched foods, without distinguishing them according to the particular vitamins and minerals

---

[330] Case 174/82 *Sandoz* [1983] ECR 2445 [22]; Case 227/82 *Van Bennekom* [1983] ECR 3883 [40]; Case 178/84 *Commission v Germany (Beer Purity law)* [1987] ECR 1227 [46]; Case C-228/91 *Commission v Italy* [1993] ECR I-2701 [27].

[331] Case C-192/01 *Commission v Denmark* [2003] ECR I-9693, Opinion of Advocate-General Mischo (12 December 2002) [16].

[332] *Commission v Denmark* (n 245) [49].

[333] ibid [51].

[334] *Commission v Denmark, Opinion of Advocate-General Mischo* (n 331) [96].

[335] *Commission v Denmark* (n 245) [49] (drawing on the reasoning in *NFU* (n 236)).

[336] *Commission v France* (n 324); *Commission v Netherlands* (n 328); cf *Greenham and Abel* (n 328), in which the ECJ did not analyse the detail of the scientific assessment relied on, leaving the issue to be resolved by the French referring court.

[337] Exceptions are the findings in *Sandoz* (n 330) and concerning one of the contested measures in *Commission v France* (n 324).

added or according to the level of public risk that their addition might pose.[338] The Danish practice was an unlawful application of the precautionary principle, since no adequate risk assessment was carried out, and this failure informed the proportionality inquiry, vitiating the Dutch government's reliance on Article 36. It could not be said that the practice was 'necessary' for the purpose of protecting public health.

These Article 36 cases contribute to a body of EU law in which the judicial treatment of the precautionary principle is increasingly connected, with resonances across different types of action, different legal questions, and across the reasoning of the CFI and ECJ. However, despite the connections, it is not a unified body of doctrine. In particular, there is a schism in the case law of the Court of Justice in that it reviews EU and Member State precautionary measures with different levels of intensity.[339] This can be explained by the fact that Article 34 cases are derogations from one of the fundamental rules of the EU internal market, prompting the Court to be more rigorous in its scrutiny of Member State measures. Through the application of a substantive rule of EU law, this difference in approach again reflects a constitutional position adopted by the EU courts. They show less deference to Member State institutions on points of substantive EU law, in relation to which the Court's rulings are supreme;[340] whereas they are more deferential in reviewing EU precautionary action, reflecting a different and delicate balance of power between the CJEU and other EU institutions. Overall, these constitutional nuances are fundamental features of EU legal culture that are driving the legal role of the precautionary principle in the reasoning of the Court of Justice.

## C. Conclusion

This Part has examined how environmental principles are employed by the EU courts doctrinally to inform legal tests of review. Through this body of case law, the scope of EU environmental competence in which EU and Member State institutions might act on the basis of environmental principles, thereby triggering such doctrinal roles, has been expanded in two ways. First, and reflecting legal

---

[338] *Commission v Denmark* (n 245) [55].

[339] Case C-41/02 *Commission v Netherlands* [2005] ECR I-11375, Opinion of Advocate-General Maduro (14 September 2004) [30]: different consequences flow from 'recourse to the precautionary principle' depending on whether it is invoked by EU institutions or the Member States.

[340] The primacy of EU law (*Costa v ENEL* (n 16)) is not uncontroversial in the EU multilevel constitutional order, particularly in how Member State legal orders receive and accept this doctrine (Bruno de Witte, 'Direct Effect, Primacy and the Nature of the Legal Order' in Paul Craig and Grainne de Burca (eds), *The Evolution of EU Law* (2nd edn, OUP 2011)). Furthermore, the primacy of EU law has been constitutionally transformative through the Court's role in promoting the penetration of internal market rules across wide areas of regulatory control in Member State legal orders: Maduro, *We the Court* (n 19).

developments in Parts III and IV above, the integration principle expands this area of competence both within the Treaty's environmental title (to include, for example, criminal matters) and beyond it to include agricultural and public health matters, the internal market and the EU's common commercial policy. In the latter sense, the use of the precautionary principle, in particular, in informing and generating legal tests within the area of public health is now a matter of routine for the EU courts. Some case law suggests that it could extend and take a foothold in the reasoning of the courts in areas of policy even further removed from environmental concerns.[341] Second, through the Court of Justice's Article 34 case law, EU environmental competence has expanded to include unilateral Member State action, when implementing national environmental measures within the scope of EU law, so that environmental principles inform legal tests applied to review the legality of such Member State action. Overall, there is an ever-increasing area of EU competence, and thus EU law, in which environmental principles have legal roles in prescribing and delimiting lawful acts of decision-making and exercises of policy discretion.

In sum, environmental principles—particularly the precautionary principle—have generated a complex and detailed body of legal reasoning in this treatment category, which is dependent and focused on the competence of EU and Member State institutions to adopt environmental measures, broadly understood, in EU law. This reasoning also reflects the courts' perception of their proper constitutional role in reviewing institutional action. In early informing legal test cases, such as *Walloon Waste* and *BSE*, the ECJ employed environmental principles to mark out an area of policy discretion in which EU and Member State institutions could properly act (defining environmental principles marginally in doing so), thus to inform the relevant legal review test applied. In later cases, particularly post-*Pfizer*, the EU courts have become more penetrating in their scrutiny of EU and Member State institutional discretion exercised on the basis of environmental principles, although the Court of Justice remains more deferential to EU institutions in carrying out such scrutiny. This reflects a bolder constitutional role for the courts, and a more complex doctrinal role for environmental principles that is co-evolving along with bodies of EU law doctrine.

As a result, the doctrinal roles for environmental principles in this Part are highly contingent on EU legal culture, and particularly on the scope of EU environmental competence, the openness of its existing legal doctrine to influence by environmental principles, and the proper constitutional role of the EU courts in reviewing the discretion of EU and Member State institutions respectively. Environmental principles, in EU law, thus do not neatly meet the high scholarly

---

[341] Case C-348/12 *Council v Manufacturing Support & Procurement Kala Naft* [2013] ECLI:EU:C:2013:470, Opinion of AG Bot (suggesting an extension of precautionary principle to inform the judicial review of EU asset freezing measures under the Common Foreign and Security policy, since the case involved restrictive measures of a preventive nature).

hopes of resolving legal and environmental problems set out in Chapter Two. It is difficult to say that environmental principles might unify EU environmental law. While they might be said to influence the extent of EU environmental law, due to their doctrinal connection to the scope of EU environmental competence, this connection also demonstrates that EU environmental law overlaps with other areas of EU law, particularly by virtue of the integration principle. Environmental principles also do not look like Dworkinian legal principles in this treatment category, nor are they are embraced by the EU courts as guiding a new body of substantive law akin to the law relating to EU fundamental rights. In terms of solving environmental problems, environmental principles do not provide freestanding legal grounds for challenging, or compelling, environmental action (to be) taken by EU or Member State institutions under EU law. Rather, they inform and generate legal tests for reviewing environmental action first taken by those institutions, and also preserve an area of discretion within which the institutions may lawfully act on the basis of the principles without judicial interference or legal compulsion to act in any particular way.

# VI.  Principle of Sustainable Development

This Part is a much shorter one, highlighting that the legal treatment of one environmental principle—the principle of sustainable development—by the EU courts is not constrained within the doctrinal patterns identified so far in the chapter. Sustainable development is an even more amorphous legal concept than other EU environmental principles, and has significant transnational dimensions, complicating any exercise to isolate its legal identity in the EU legal context. As explained in Chapter Three, sustainable development has a dual character in EU law, with both internal and external aspects.[342] In particular, its links to the international sustainable development agenda mark it out as a principle or concept of a different order from the other environmental principles in Article 191(2) TFEU. It is both broader and more ambiguous as a concept, and its 'identity' as a principle with some legal character in EU law is quite tenuous in light of the extensive EU policy agenda implementing sustainable development.[343] Sustainable development is a concept that frames a policy domain, or a policy paradigm shift, rather than establishing or informing any bright-line legal rules. Even as a policy idea, sustainable development is a complex concept in light of its heavily contested meaning. A legal inquiry about sustainable development in EU law is however a valid one, in light of the prominent place of sustainable development in

---

[342]  See ch 3, text accompanying nn 169–180.
[343]  See ch 3, text accompanying nn 181–190.

the EU Treaties, and its articulation as a 'principle' in Article 37 of the Charter of Fundamental Rights. The limited case law concerning the principle to date shows that the sustainable development principle is different from other EU environmental principles in terms of its legal treatment.[344] This is seen in two respects. First, its breadth and definitional ambiguity undermines any clear or consistent doctrinal influence the concept might have. In particular, while it is similar to the integration principle in being overarching in EU law, embracing other environmental principles and crossing different areas of EU policy competence, its doctrinal role is more uncertain, in light of its extension to policy areas beyond even an expanded notion of EU environmental competence.[345] Second, its links to international norms mean that sustainable development incorporates, or has the potential to incorporate, transnational norms into the reasoning of the Court, although this potential has not been realised to any significant extent.

## A. Sustainable Development: Definitional and Doctrinal Uncertainty in EU Law

When relied on in CJEU cases, sustainable development is often mentioned in ambitious terms, particularly in Advocate General opinions, or in argument by parties, representing a forceful position that assumes a certain definition for sustainable development and pursues a particular legal outcome. The definitions of sustainable development adopted are however not consistent, and the legal implications of these suggested definitions are diverse. For example, in *First Corporate Shipping*, Advocate General Leger suggested that sustainable development is a 'fundamental concept of environmental law', deriving from the international sustainable development agenda, which finds specific expression in the Article 11 TFEU integration principle.[346] He drew on the Brundtland Report to find that sustainable development 'means that the conduct of [EU] policies must, at the very least, not endanger the natural systems which give us life, the atmosphere, water, earth and living creatures'.[347] He then defined the concept as requiring development and environmental protection to 'evolve in a coordinated fashion', thus concluding that the Commission's procedure for selecting Sites of Community Interest under the Habitats Directive should involve assessing whether human activities can be reconciled with environmental protection objectives. By contrast, in a case involving the interpretation of the EU waste shipment regime, Advocate General Leger presented

---

[344] This is not to say that other EU environmental principles have equivalent doctrinal roles to one another. The integration principle and precautionary principle, in particular, have distinctive roles in the reasoning of the EU courts: see Parts IV–V.

[345] As in Case C-91/05 *Commission v Council (Small Weapons)* [2008] ECR I-03651, discussed further below in this Part.

[346] *First Corporate Shipping*, Opinion of Advocate-General Leger (n 155) [56].

[347] ibid.

sustainable development as an approach that prioritises environmental protection. In *EU-Wood-Trading*, sustainable development was an 'objective' of the EU of such importance (including sustainable development of 'Europe, and even of the Earth') that the other EU principles 'framing environmental law' were suggested to take on ever-increasing importance in the future of EU law, and in interpreting the EU waste shipment regime in this case.[348]

Other cases further highlight how the legal role of the sustainable development principle is complicated by its definitional ambiguity. In *Spain v Council*, Advocate-General Leger suggested that the 'objective' of sustainable development inherent in EU environmental policy must be understood in light of the 'rule that natural resources must be used in a rational manner' that defines EU environmental competence in Article 191(1) TFEU.[349] The case concerned the scope of environmental decision-making competence under Article 192(1) and whether the correct decision-making procedure was used to support the Convention on cooperation for the protection and sustainable use of the river Danube, adopted by the EU Council.[350] Sustainable development, or sustainable use, was seen to be a fundamental objective of the Convention and thus relevant in determining its proper legal basis. In understanding this objective, the Advocate General indicated that the notion of sustainable development in this context was constrained by the EU's articulated environmental competence in the TFEU, rather than being informed by international norms of sustainable development. The ECJ, whilst reaching the same legal outcome as the Advocate General (that the Convention was properly adopted by the EU institutions), relied on the principle of sustainable development differently, finding that the sustainable development objective of the Convention was informed by its international character in the context of treaties relating to water resources, but that it was a secondary objective of the Convention and could thus be discounted as defining its essential EU competence. This reasoning was necessary because the international water conventions relating to sustainable development, which are characterised by 'an attempt to reconcile the interests of protecting water and the interests of users', concern water management, which would require a different decision-making procedure under the TFEU.[351] This case again shows that lack of definitional clarity compounds the uncertain legal role of sustainable development.[352]

---

[348] Case C-277/02 *EU-Wood-Trading v Sonderabfall-Management-Gesellschaft Rheinland-Pfalz* [2004] ECR I-11957, Opinion of Advocate-General Leger (23 September 2004) [9].

[349] Drawn from TFEU, art 191(1) (ex-art 174(1) EC): Case C-36/98 *Spain v Council* [2001] ECR I-779, Opinion of Advocate-General Leger (16 May 2000) [77].

[350] If the convention was primarily concerned with the 'management of water resources', then it would need to be adopted on the basis of unanimous voting in Council: TFEU, art 192(2) (ex-art 130s(2) EC).

[351] Case C-36/98 *Spain v Council* [2001] ECR I-779 [34]–[35].

[352] This is different from cases in the treatment categories considered in Parts IV and V above, in which environmental principles are given varying marginal definitions across cases, but consistent and doctrinal patterns are discernible.

The normative ambiguity of sustainable development in EU law is further reflected in a range of other legal arguments and forms of reasoning concerning the principle. In *Poland v Commission*, the Polish government (unsuccessfully) argued that the Commission's 'benchmarking' decision for the third phase of the EU emissions trading scheme was unlawful for 'breach of the principle of sustainable development'.[353] This was essentially an argument that the decision failed to recognise the state of the Polish economy and how it could reasonably adapt to environmental incentives to reduce reliance on coal-based energy sources. This argument prioritised the economic aspect of sustainable development, which must be ensured along with environmental concerns. By contrast, through its most recent legal incarnation in Article 37 of the Charter, the principle of sustainable development has been presented in a quite different conceptual sense, with Advocate Generals suggesting that it raises the importance of environmental protection to the 'status of a European target',[354] and reflects 'a recent process of constitutional recognition in respect of protection of the environment'.[355] In the *Environmental Crime case*, Advocate-General Ruiz-Jarabo Colomer described sustainable development differently again, as a 'legal interest the protection of which inspires other [EU] policies, a protective activity which may be clarified, furthermore, as an essential objective of the [EU] system'.[356] What these various statements indicate about the legal nature of sustainable development in terms of EU law doctrine is uncertain on the current state of the law, but they all indicate that the overarching and highly contestable nature of sustainable development gives this 'principle' a different complexion in EU law.

This legal distinctiveness can be seen even where the doctrinal treatment mirrors one of the techniques already discussed in this chapter. An example of this is seen in *Commission v Council (Small Weapons)*,[357] in which sustainable development informs a legal basis test. As in other cases where environmental principles inform legal review tests in Part V above, the case involves action first taken by EU institutions on the basis, inter alia, of sustainable development, which then takes on a doctrinal role in determining the legality of that action under EU law. However, this case does not involve the boundaries of EU environmental competence; it concerns the boundaries of what was then Community competence more generally.[358] The contested EU measures in this case were aimed at reducing the accumulation and spread of small arms and light weapons in West African States, and the question for the ECJ was whether these measures should have been based on Article 209 TFEU (ex-Article 179 EC), within the Community's Development

---

[353] *Poland v Commission* (n 244) [108].
[354] Case C-195/12 *IBV v Région Wallone* [2013] ECLI:EU:C:2013:293, Opinion of Advocate General Bot (8 May 2013) [82].
[355] Case C-120/10 *European Air Transport SA v Collège d'Environnement de la Région de Bruxelles-Capitale* [2011] ECR I-07865, Opinion of Advocate General Cruz Villalón (17 February 2011) [74].
[356] *Environmental Crime, Opinion of Advocate-General Colomer* (n 66) [59].
[357] *Small Weapons* (n 345).
[358] And is, to that extent, out-of-date, as in *Environmental Crime* (n 74) above.

Cooperation Policy ('DCP'), or were properly introduced outside the scope of Community competence under the former Common Foreign and Security Policy pillar.[359] The ECJ found that the aim and content of the contested measures were intimately connected with, inter alia, sustainable development, a central objective of the Community's DCP, and so were properly within the scope of Community competence. Notably, however, the Advocate-General, following a similar line of reasoning, reached the opposite conclusion, attributing a narrower meaning to sustainable development, thereby limiting its doctrinal influence. By adopting a broad definition of sustainable development—so that the aim to reduce small arms and light weapons was found to be concerned with promoting peace and security and the prospect for sustainable development[360]—the ECJ expanded the scope of Community competence. Advocate General Mengozzi, by contrast, adopted a narrower definition of sustainable development, finding that it was relevantly concerned with improving living conditions and/or social and economic conditions, which in this case was a remote objective or indirect consequence of preserving regional security in West African States.[361]

*Small Weapons* shows how different marginal definitions of environmental principles determine their doctrinal influence, and demonstrates particularly the ambiguous nature of sustainable development. It also shows how sustainable development is distinct from other environmental principles in that it can inherently concern matters beyond environmental protection. This case is not one of the broad scope of EU environmental competence, but of the competence of EU institutions generally, as informed by the principle of sustainable development.

## B. The Transnational Influence of Sustainable Development in EU Law: Legal Complexity and Potential

The lack of settled normativity for sustainable development is not only a product of its definitional ambiguity. It is also a result of its link to other realms of law. As Chapter Three outlined, sustainable development has a strong presence in international law, albeit with a normatively unsettled character in that legal sphere as well. The connection to international environmental law does not bring any legal clarity in terms of its role in EU law, but it helps also to explain its uncertain doctrinal status in the case law of the EU courts. The previous section showed a number of ways in which Advocate Generals have referenced sustainable development in an international context. Advocate General Leger, in *First Corporate Shipping*,

---

[359] Ex-TEU, Title V.
[360] *Small Weapons Case* (n 345) [93].
[361] Case C-91/05 *Commission v Council (Small Weapons)* [2008] ECR I-03651, Opinion of Advocate-General Mengozzi (19 September 2007) [206].

referred to sustainable development as a fundamental concept of environmental law in an international sense. In *Commission v Council (Environmental Crime)*,[362] Advocate General Ruiz-Jarabo Colomer considered the nature of sustainable development in the previous EC Treaty, in light of the overall 'globalisation' of environmental policy concerning sustainable development, in order to '[illustrate] the importance which "ecological consciousness" has acquired in recent decades'. These references suggest that the normative role of sustainable development, in driving both international environmental law and policy, adds weight to the legal importance of the concept in EU law.

Whilst the case law to date does not clarify what this legal importance looks like doctrinally (and arguably clarity might not be attainable for such an amorphous concept as sustainable development),[363] this normative connection to the international legal order is a particular feature of this 'principle' of EU environmental law. This kind of transnational connection sparks suggestions that a global legal order of environmental law is developing,[364] but this Part—and this Chapter—show that any such connections still need to settle within the EU legal order for them to have an identifiable legal impact as a matter of EU law. The normative openness of the EU legal order to transnational influences in relation to sustainable development is however an interesting area of potential legal development. An example of this can be seen in relation to Article 37 of the Charter, which brings the principle of sustainable development into the EU legal order as part of a 'principle' of integrating a high level of environmental protection and improving the quality of the environment into all EU policies.[365] Article 37 has not yet taken on any significant legal roles in the case law of the EU courts[366]—it is often referred to in the same grand, overarching way as references to sustainable development discussed in the previous section,[367] or to support other arguments.[368] However, there has been at least one interesting suggestion that Article 37 could be a vehicle for incorporating legal developments and guarantees from the European Court of Human Rights into EU law. This is because the Charter specifies that the meaning and scope of its 'rights' are to be the same as those provided for in the European Convention

---

[362] *Environmental Crime, Opinion of Advocate General Ruiz-Jarabo Colomer* (n 66).

[363] *cf* Klaus Bosselmann, *The Principle of Sustainability: Transforming Law and Governance* (Ashgate 2008).

[364] See ch 3, text accompanying nn 42–53.

[365] These requirements are to be 'ensured in accordance with the principle of sustainable development': Charter (n 51) art 37.

[366] This is partly because art 52(5) of the Charter limits its justiciability. See further Sanja Bogojević, 'EU Human Rights Law and Environmental Protection: The Beginning of a Beautiful Friendship?' in Sionaidh Douglas-Scott and Nicholas Hatzis (eds), *Research Handbook on EU Human Rights Law* (Edward Elgar 2016); Eloise Scotford, 'Environmental Rights and Principles in the European Context' in Sanja Bogojević and Rosemary Rayfuse, *Environmental Rights—in Europe and Beyond* (Hart 2017, forthcoming).

[367] See eg nn 355–356 and accompanying text.

[368] Eg Case C-28/09 *Commission v Austria* [2011] ECR I-13525 [121].

of Human Rights. Advocate General Cruz Villalon suggested in *European Air Transport* that this legal connection could allow for ECHR case law to influence how Article 37 is used to interpret EU legislation.[369] This suggestion shows that the normative links between ideas of sustainable development across legal orders can be crystallised doctrinally. Time will tell whether we see more of this kind of transnational norm development spurring doctrinal change within the EU legal order in relation to the concept of sustainable development or other principles of environmental protection.

# VII. Conclusion

This chapter has mapped the judicial treatment of EU environmental principles to identify the roles played by environmental principles in EU law. Three main treatment categories were identified: policy cases, interpretive cases, and informing legal test cases. This mapping categorisation is not meant to be definitive, especially since the same case may fall within more than one category, and the categories are themselves not qualitatively equivalent in generating a taxonomy of judicial reasoning. Rather, it demonstrates that the principles perform particular legal functions in EU law, which are shaped and constrained by influences of EU legal culture. In policy cases, environmental principles have no role in influencing the legal outcome of the cases, showing there are limits to the doctrinal roles of environmental principles, and to the role of the EU courts in accepting arguments based on environmental principles. Environmental principles do not act as freestanding legal principles on which the courts might draw to resolve all or any of the legal issues before them. EU (or Member State) institutions must first act on the basis of the principles within the scope of EU environmental competence, and this action may then be called into question legally, either in terms of its interpretation or in reviewing its legality. In both these legal senses, environmental principles are employed by the EU courts doctrinally, constituting the two main treatment categories—interpretive cases and informing legal test cases—in which environmental principles have legal roles.

There are other EU law contextual influences that affect the mapping of this case law. First, environmental principles will only have doctrinal roles where the applicable EU law doctrine is open-textured enough to allow this. Thus arguments based on environmental principles, in defending unilateral Member State actions on environmental grounds, are rejected in Article 114(4) and (5) cases but accepted in Article 34 cases. Second, the constitutional role or limits of the EU courts fundamentally define the case law. In particular, the courts generally

---

[369] *European Air Transport* (n 355) [78]–[81].

require prior action by EU or Member State institutions before the courts will employ environmental principles doctrinally. This is because environmental principles represent policy positions that are for political institutions to adopt, with the courts having a role to interpret or police the permissible boundaries of this policy discretion once exercised.[370] At the same time, the courts must allow decisions to be made, and so they employ principles both to scrutinise such policy discretion closely for its meaning and legality (giving marginal definitions to environmental principles to do so), and also to defer to policy decisions made within the legally identified ambit of discretion. The European courts are thus involved in a delicate exercise of constitutional balancing in reviewing and defining environmental principles, and this balancing is carefully, and differently, calibrated in relation to EU and Member State institutions acting within the scope of EU environmental competence. Within a framework of multilevel governance, constitutional norms are being articulated and acting as constraints in the CJEU's case law concerning environmental principles. Thus, as the case law has evolved post-*Pfizer*, the courts have strengthened their constitutional authority through their more developed doctrinal use of the precautionary principle. This is seen both in the jurisdiction of the General Court, which now has a highly developed body of administrative law based on the principle for reviewing EU institutional action, and in the Court of Justice in reviewing derogations from internal market rules by Member States acting on precautionary environmental and health grounds.

Third, the size of the EU law map in which environmental principles have legal roles has been extended as the case law has progressed, particularly by virtue of the integration principle expanding the scope of EU environmental competence, and by the inclusion of Member State action within this area of competence. At the same time, doctrine has developed around some environmental principles more than others, in certain regulatory areas, whether it is the extensive body of public health cases involving the precautionary principle, or involving the polluter pays principle in relation to schemes of environmental regulation. Furthermore, the grouping of environmental principles that have doctrinal roles has been extended in some cases, particularly involving the principle of a 'high level of protection' and other principles of environmental policy beyond those included in the EU Treaties.

---

[370] Note this limit reflects that prescribed for 'principles' of the Charter: art 52(5) provides that '[t]he provisions of this Charter which contain principles may be implemented by legislative and executive acts taken by institutions, bodies, offices and agencies of the Union, and by acts of Member States when they are implementing Union law, in the exercise of their respective powers. They shall be judicially cognisable only in the interpretation of such acts and in the ruling on their legality'. Academics disagree on whether this provision should have a narrow or broad interpretation (see eg Koen Lenaerts, 'Exploring the Limits of the EU Charter of Fundamental Rights' (2012) 8(3) *ECL Rev* 375), but the doctrinal mapping in this chapter supports the so-called narrow reading in the context of EU environmental principles. See further Scotford, "Environmental Rights and Principles' (n 366).

Finally, there are some anomalous cases in this doctrinal map, which demonstrate that the chapter's legal analysis is but one way of viewing the case law, and that the case law is in a state of evolution. In particular, case law involving the sustainable development 'principle' is doctrinally ambiguous and opens channels for transnational legal influence in the development of EU doctrine. There are also some outlying cases in which the doctrinal uses of the precautionary principle extend well beyond the scope of EU environmental competence, or in which environmental principles appear to constitute freestanding grounds of review. These anomalies suggest how EU case law might develop, but also indicate the basic point that environmental principles take on a variety of roles in the case law.

This is a conclusion for environmental law scholarship more broadly—it is not possible to state definitively and generally how environmental principles should and do operate legally across legal systems. Not only are the legal roles of environmental principles contingent on EU legal culture in this chapter, but those roles within this legal context are not doctrinally fixed, although trends in reasoning can be observed. This variance in the legal roles of EU environmental principles can also be seen in the range of marginal definitions given to environmental principles in the case law, which arise as an aspect and consequence of their particular doctrinal treatment[371]—a result possible because of the open and imprecise definitional nature of environmental principles generally.

This variance in the legal treatment and definition of environmental principles in EU law undermines one of the key hopes for environmental principles in solving legal problems in environmental law—that they might unify environmental law. While environmental principles have a high profile in EU environmental law, the doctrinal picture presented in this map of the case law suggests something much more legally complex than coherence. Similarly, a Dworkinian notion of legal principles fails to account for the diversity of doctrinal roles for environmental principles in EU law mapped in this chapter. Neither does the chapter's doctrinal map indicate that environmental principles are promoting a new body of EU law centred on an environmental ethical philosophy. This is because there is a complex constitutional and administrative law framework that is co-evolving with the policy norms expressed in legal applications of EU environmental principles. And while the integration principle pushes doctrinal boundaries in EU environmental law so that environmental law requirements are stretched into a range of EU policy areas, it is EU law doctrines, the jurisdictional and constitutional limits of the EU courts, and the central concepts of attributed and shared competence in EU law, which fundamentally shape EU environmental law, and the roles

---

[371] In the case of the precautionary principle, its 'definition' has developed beyond a discrete substantive definition in a body of case law where it now generates and informs legal review tests, as seen in Part V(B). It is cast as a guide to exercising policy discretion, embodying legally required procedures of decision-making as well as policy ideas.

of environmental principles within this, rather than any unifying environmental philosophy.

In terms of the potential of environmental principles to solve environmental problems in EU law, this is undermined by the constitutional limits on the EU courts to hear freestanding actions based on environmental principles, and in second-guessing institutional discretion by relying on environmental principles. Environmental principles are at base policy ideas, and not legal concepts, which are for EU and Member State institutions to implement within a wide discretion. This is reinforced by the ambiguous case law concerning sustainable development principle, which shows the awkwardness of ascribing grand 'legal' identities to environmental principles, no matter how important they are in policy terms. Environmental principles cannot simply be imbued with legal force to solve environmental problems, no matter how important the policy idea they represent. In short, any legal roles for environmental principles can only be determined by a close contextual analysis of legal developments within, and on the terms of, a particular legal culture, as done in this chapter with respect to EU case law developments.

# 5

# Principles of Ecologically Sustainable Development in the New South Wales Land and Environment Court

## I. Introduction

Environmental principles—or principles of 'ecologically sustainable development' ('ESD principles') as they are known in NSW law—play an important role in the evolving environmental law doctrine of the NSW Land and Environment Court ('NSWLEC'). As in the European context, these environmental principles are general, imperfectly defined and malleable; however they are a different group of environmental principles. ESD principles comprise the precautionary principle, the principle of intergenerational equity, the principle of conservation of biological diversity and ecological integrity, the principle of internalisation of costs (embracing within it the polluter pays principle), and a different version of the integration principle.[1] These environmental principles also play fundamentally different legal roles in NSW law from those in the EU context. This is because the ambiguity of ESD principles is met by the unique legal culture of the NSWLEC, and particularly the unique institutional identity of this judicial setting. The NSWLEC is a specialist environmental court, which has a novel institutional place in the NSW legal system, and an evolving body of distinctive legal reasoning. The meeting of this 'open' judicial setting with open-ended environmental principles has resulted in case law that is legally ground-breaking in NSW law, with the Court giving considerable attention to ESD principles in its reasoning in the last two decades. This period has tracked a turn in the Court's case law, reflecting an increasing confidence on the part of the Court as an institution, and an activist drive to pursue an agenda of sustainability. This chapter maps this ESD case law to understand how environmental principles operate doctrinally in this different legal context, and then how that doctrinal picture matches scholarly hopes for environmental principles.

---

[1] See ch 3(IV). As in EU law, they also comprise an expanding group of environmental principles in NSW law, including the 'sustainable use of natural resources', 'principle of intra-generational equity', and 'principle of good governance': *Hub Action Group Incorporated v Minister for Planning* [2008] NSWLEC 116; (2008) 161 LGERA 136 [1], [69].

From this analysis, environmental principles are again seen as concepts that have a distinct legal identity and construction, which is intimately related to the legal culture in which they are employed. Notably, ESD principles are not only dependent on the legal culture of the NSWLEC, but increasingly they define it. This is very different from the treatment of environmental principles in the European courts, in which the principles largely fit into, and are shaped by, developing legal doctrines and actions within the wider context of EU law. In the NSWLEC, however, the Court takes advantage of the generality and symbolism of environmental principles to set a doctrinal agenda that infiltrates all aspects of its jurisdiction, and thus to make a statement about the nature of law it applies and the identity of the NSWLEC as an institution. ESD principles are doctrinal centrepieces in the law applied and developed by the NSWLEC; whereas they are employed more selectively and less comprehensively in doctrinal spaces within EU law, through discrete instances of reasoning by the EU courts that are building a diverse doctrine relating to environmental principles over time. The NSWLEC uses ESD principles to push doctrinal boundaries in NSW law, in a conscious bid to aid what it recognises as a broader project of developing a 'global jurisprudence' in relation to environmental principles.[2] The Court uses this appeal to international law to give authority to its novel reasoning, drawing on transnational influences to develop its jurisprudence on ESD principles. This outward-looking attitude to environmental law globally is part of the NSWLEC legal culture that shapes its ESD doctrine, along with a range of jurisdictional and doctrinal factors that are particular to the NSW legal system.

The difference in judicial approaches to environmental principles in EU and NSW law means that mapping the doctrinal roles of environmental principles in judicial reasoning produces a different doctrinal landscape in NSWLEC case law. As in the European context, this mapping exercise tracks the techniques of judicial treatment adopted with respect to environmental principles. However, in the NSWLEC context, this judicial treatment breaks down differently. This is because the NSWLEC has a different type of jurisdiction—one referred to it by a range of environmental and planning statutes empowering it to determine legal and administrative questions in relation to environmental matters (broadly understood). For one thing, this means there are different and less significant constitutional constraints on its doctrinal use of environmental principles, compared with the position in the EU courts. Thus there is no distinct group of 'policy cases' involving ESD principles in NSWLEC case law.

Rather, there is a range of factors that facilitate widespread doctrinal engagement with ESD principles in the Court's case law, including the particular statutory jurisdiction of the Court, its creation as a specialist environmental court, its progressive attitude in relation to environmental protection and sustainability, and its interpretation of Australian common law doctrine (especially administrative

---

[2] Peter Biscoe, 'Ecologically Sustainable Development in New South Wales' (5th Worldwide Colloquium of the IUCN Academy of Environmental Law, Brazil, 2 June 2007) [76]. See also Brian Preston, 'Leadership by the Courts in Achieving Sustainability' (2010) 27 EPLJ 321, 322 and generally.

law doctrine) that it must apply. Essentially, the Court incorporates ESD principles into its legal reasoning through a fundamental doctrinal step: determining ESD principles to be legally required 'relevant considerations' in relation to the legal questions put to the Court across all elements of its jurisdiction. This chapter identifies five categories of judicial technique by which ESD principles are determined to be legally relevant considerations in various ways. These mapping categories do not so much reflect historical progression, although this plays some part, as much as they reflect the different techniques used by the Court progressively to infuse its doctrine with ESD principles. Thus the Court interprets relevant provisions of the central NSW planning statute that occupies most of its time—the Environmental Planning and Assessment Act ('EPA Act')[3]—to require consideration of ESD principles as mandatory relevant considerations in many aspects of the statute's application. It also broadens this reasoning to all statutes that have ESD objects, and then to all environmental decision-making undertaken or reviewed by the Court where ESD principles are 'relevant'. Finally, it employs ESD principles doctrinally as relevant considerations across the full range of its jurisdiction.

Through this breakdown of mapping categories, the map of NSWLEC ESD case law focuses on different aspects of judicial reasoning from those that defined Chapter Four's map of environmental principles in the reasoning of the EU courts. This difference is guided by the deeper jurisdictional reach of the NSWLEC into environmental matters and the more extensive doctrinal development of ESD principles in its reasoning. Whereas the doctrinal roles of environmental principles in EU judicial reasoning were confined to interpretive and informing legal test cases—reflecting the jurisdictional mandate of the EU courts to interpret EU law and review the legality of action within appropriate constitutional limits—the legal task of the NSWLEC is more complex, particularly due to its merits review jurisdiction and the extensive fact-finding this involves. While the Court's doctrinal use of ESD principles does involve steps of reasoning in which the principles guide interpretation of legislative provisions or inform legal tests, mapping the case law into such categories would overlook the more complicated and sophisticated doctrinal picture in NSWLEC ESD case law.[4] This is because the Court employs many reasoning techniques at its disposal to find that ESD principles are legally relevant considerations in various senses, to the point that ESD principles are now implicitly part of the Court's reasoning processes in deciding all types of actions that come before it. ESD principles thereby characterise the evolving nature of environmental law in the NSWLEC, and also define the institutional identity of the Court.

As a result of the mapping exercise in this chapter, it is also possible to draw conclusions about the roles of environmental principles in environmental law

---

[3] Environmental Planning and Assessment Act 1979 (NSW) ('EPA Act').

[4] The reasoning techniques focused on in this chapter are not the only way of mapping the case law, but they demonstrate how the entire jurisdiction of the Court has become infused with doctrine involving ESD principles.

scholarship more broadly. The NSWLEC's inclination to embed ESD in the Court's doctrine and its institutional identity brings to mind those theoretical approaches to environmental principles that advocate their founding a new form of law, or at least uniting environmental law, as well as scholarly hopes that legal (particularly judicial) use of environmental principles might assist in solving environmental problems. These scholarly approaches and hopes are relevant but still limited in explaining NSWLEC ESD case law. In short, the map set out in this chapter reinforces the conclusion that environmental principles do not have universal legal identities, or legal roles that prescribe legal solutions or environmental outcomes in the abstract, although ESD principles do frame decision-making to achieve environmentally focused outcomes in some cases.[5]

To reach such conclusions, this chapter proceeds in two stages. First, Part II outlines the nature of the NSWLEC, building on the NSW legal developments set out in Chapter Three to demonstrate the legal culture in which ESD principles have legal roles. It draws on the Court's history, its unique statutory jurisdiction and powers as a planning and environmental court, and the distinctive nature of the law it applies, to demonstrate that the Court is a novel form of judicial institution. It is both constrained by doctrinal and institutional connections to the broader NSW and Australian legal system, but also in a remarkably free position to move forward and create a different kind of environmental doctrine through its case law. Both aspects of the Court's identity can be seen in its treatment of ESD principles. The doctrinal openness of the Court is particularly due to its power to hear merits review appeals, which involve the Court hearing appeals from administrative decisions made under environmental and planning legislation and deciding them anew. This jurisdiction places the Court, as a common law judicial institution, in unique and also controversial territory,[6] but it is central to its identity as a legal institution, occupying a large part of its time and attention. It is in this open and novel legal landscape that ESD principles take on roles in the doctrinal reasoning of the Court. It should be noted that there are other courts and tribunals in Australia in which ESD principles play important legal roles, including through their merits appeal jurisdiction.[7] The NSWLEC borrows and exchanges ideas with these courts

---

[5] *cf* Brian Preston, 'The Judicial Development of Ecologically Sustainable Development' in Douglas Fisher (ed), *Research Handbook on Fundamental Concepts of Environmental Law* (Edward Elgar 2016) ('ESD is at its core the substantive outcome of ecological sustainability' and courts have a role in supporting that outcome through 'instilling ESD and its principles with legal rigour').

[6] Liz Fisher describes how tribunals and courts with merits review jurisdictions represent 'legal pluralism' in the Australian administrative law landscape (being institutions with both adjudicative and administrative functions that have 'been adapted to address the nature of the disputes before them'). This sits awkwardly within a doctrinal and scholarly tradition otherwise dominated by legal formalism, and the co-existence of these ideas of law and administration reflects 'a deeper set of ambiguities that pervade all administrative law systems concerning the nature of law': Elizabeth Fisher, '"Jurisdictional" Facts and "Hot" Facts' (2015) 38 *MULR* 968, 974–5. See also Ceri Warnock, 'Reconceptualising Specialist Environmental Courts and Tribunals' (2017) *Legal Studies* (forthcoming).

[7] In particular, the South Australian Environment, Resources and Development (ERD) Court, the Victorian Civil and Administrative Tribunal, the Victorian Supreme Court, the Queensland Planning and Environmental Court, and the Federal Court of Australia have decided important cases

in some of its reasoning,[8] but predominantly relies on its own decided cases, and those of courts that it is bound to respect as binding precedent, in its developing ESD case law. This chapter focuses on the NSWLEC alone partly for this reason— that its judgments are legally confined within the court system in Australia by the doctrine of precedent—and in order to highlight how the legal culture of a particular court can be powerful in shaping the legal roles of environmental principles, being particularly sensitive the features that are unique to this jurisdictional setting.

Part III then maps NSWLEC reasoning involving ESD principles, setting out five progressive steps in the Court's ESD reasoning as mapping categories, as described above. These categories present a legal picture of ESD principles in NSWLEC case law that covers all aspects of its jurisdiction. The chapter concludes by reflecting on the implications of this mapping exercise for environmental law scholarship.

As in Chapter Four's map of EU cases, the survey of NSWLEC cases in this chapter is representative rather than comprehensive. Again, this is due to the sheer volume of cases—there are more than 300 NSWLEC decisions involving ESD principles. Also similarly, this chapter's doctrinal analysis of ESD principles in NSWLEC case law is not the last word—these legal decisions constitute an evolving body of law.[9]

# II.  The NSW Land and Environment Court: A Unique and Doctrinally Novel Legal Setting

The legal roles of ESD principles in NSWLEC case law are shaped by the legal culture, not of NSW law generally, but of the Land and Environment Court and the law it applies. This is because the NSWLEC is unique as a legal institution within the NSW and Australian legal systems. It is a purpose-built specialist environmental court, which sits within the hierarchy of courts in NSW, but is unlike any other court in that jurisdiction, or in Australia for that matter.[10] The Court is distinctive in terms of its history, composition, procedure, jurisdiction and its evolving doctrine. It occupies an uncharted constitutional place within the NSW system of government. This Part sets out this unique institutional identity, examining four features of its

involving ESD principles. See further Preston, 'The Judicial Development of Ecologically Sustainable Development' (n 5).

[8]  eg *Conservation Council of South Australia v Development Assessment Committee and Tuna Boat Owners Association (No 2)* [1999] SAERDC 86 and *Connell Wagner Pty Ltd v City of Port Phillip* [1998] VCAT 606, on which the court relied in *Telstra Corporation Ltd v Hornsby Shire Council* ([2006] NSWLEC 133; (2006) 146 LGERA 10; (2006) 67 NSWLR 256) to develop its reasoning relating to the precautionary principle.

[9]  This is particularly so due to reforms to the EPA Act in 2011, which have altered the jurisdiction of the court in planning matters concerning major projects: see below nn 199, 235.

[10]  While it is related to a breed of environmental courts established in other Australian states, these are each constructed in slightly different ways in terms of their jurisdiction and powers: see below n 24 and accompanying text.

legal culture, which generate a doctrinal openness and willingness on the part of the Court to embrace ESD principles in its reasoning: the history of the Court's creation as a 'one-stop shop' for environmental and planning disputes in NSW; the Court's idiosyncratic statutory jurisdiction; its progressive ESD agenda; and the ambiguous administrative law doctrine applied and developed by the Court.

These factors are not unrelated and they have provided the Court the opportunity to be bold and innovative in its reasoning, particularly in developing environmental law as a body of doctrine. However, this innovation is not without limit. The Court's decisions on particular issues of 'law' are subject to the supervisory jurisdiction of the NSW Court of Appeal ('NSWCA'), its criminal sentencing decisions subject to the review of the NSW Court of Criminal Appeal, and its administrative decisions operate subject to Australian common law doctrines of administrative law. The 'environmental law' of the NSWLEC is not quarantined from the legal influences of common law courts to which it is connected in the NSW and Australian court system. In this way, the NSWLEC's progressive doctrine is different from that seen in EU courts, which develop innovative doctrine where there are gaps in EU law. By contrast, the NSWLEC is supervised by other courts and sits within a jurisdiction (of NSW and Australian law) that has a long and much analysed legal history. The innovation of NSWLEC reasoning is thus due to the way it adapts within, and challenges, doctrines of this background Australian legal history and framework, as well as being a product of the Court's novel jurisdiction. ESD principles have a high profile in this innovative reasoning, which provides fertile ground for examining the legal roles of environmental principles in a context where they are central to a body of legal doctrine.

As in Chapter Four's map of environmental principles in EU law, this chapter's map of ESD principles in NSWLEC case law can only be understood in light of the elements of NSWLEC legal culture outlined in this Part. In particular, the appreciation of what constitutes legal 'doctrine' in this setting is quite different, since different types of legal decisions are made by the Court, often by way of more detailed and fact-based reasoning than in the EU courts, and the law it applies is doctrinally open in different ways. As set out in Chapter One, a doctrinal analysis of judicial reasoning allows a comparative legal study between such different legal systems and courts, but, in moving from EU to NSW law, it also requires an adjustment of analytical frame in light of the different doctrinal foundations in each jurisdiction.[11] Also in contrast to Chapter Four, the Court's strong inclination to incorporate ESD principles into its case law is itself a significant element in defining the legal culture of the Court and its identity as a judicial institution. This reflexive relationship between the ESD case law of the Court and its legal culture is demonstrated in Part III, while this Part sets the scene for this judicial contribution to the Court's culture and identity.

---

[11] The elements of NSWLEC judicial decisions that articulate and reflect its law, in adopting a maxim (in particular, an ESD principle) to justify a decision, are of a different order from those found in EU law.

## A. History of the Court: A One-stop Shop for NSW Environmental Law

Three features of the history of the NSWLEC demonstrate its uniqueness as a legal institution, with the capacity and opportunity to develop novel legal doctrine: its deliberate but unlikely construction as a court; its amalgamated functions from a range of prior judicial and non-judicial institutions; and its mandate to develop a body of 'environmental law' for NSW.

### i. The Unlikely Construction of a Land and Environment Court

The Court was established at a time when administrative tribunals were being set up across Australia. This was for pragmatic reasons to fill perceived gaps in the system of administrative review of public action. Significantly, the Court was constructed as a judicial (rather than administrative or executive) institution. Since the 1970s, a wave of generalist and specialist tribunals have been created throughout Australia to fulfil dispute resolution requirements in respect of administrative decision-making that could not be accommodated in the court system.[12] In particular, tribunals hear review of administrative decisions on the merits, which the 1971 Kerr Committee Report signally identified as a gap in Australian administrative law review, restricted as it was by common law doctrine to 'errors of law'.[13] Merits appeals are an enigmatic phenomenon—they involve quasi-administrative decision-making but are distinct from administration (as a form of review holding administration to account),[14] and increasingly they have become judicialised.[15] They can be described in the following way:[16]

> [In a merits appeal, a tribunal] sits in the place of the original administrative decision-maker and re-exercises the administrative decision-making functions. The decision of the [tribunal] is final and binding and becomes that of the original decision-maker.

[12] The creation and operation of tribunals is one of the hallmarks of Australian administrative law, albeit that it occupies an uneasy place within this body of law: Peter Cane, 'The Making of Australian Administrative Law' in Peter Cane (ed), *Centenary Essays for the High Court of Australia* (LexisNexis Butterworths 2004) 323, 331; Elizabeth Fisher, *Risk Regulation and Administrative Constitutionalism* (Hart 2007) 133–4; Fisher, '"Jurisdictional" Facts and "Hot" Facts' (n 6).
[13] Commonwealth of Australia, *Commonwealth Administrative Review: Committee Report*, Parl Paper No 144 (1971) 3, 91.
[14] Administrative Review Council, *Better Decisions: Review of Commonwealth Merits Review Tribunals*, Report No 39 (1995) 11; Fisher, *Risk Regulation* (n 12) 134–5; Robin Creyke, John McMillan and Mark Smyth, *Control of Government Action: Text, Cases and Commentary* (4th edn, LexisNexis Butterworths 2015) 186–187.
[15] Merits review tribunals in Australia have 'struggled long and hard to turn themselves into courts': H Whitmore, 'Commentary' (1981) *FL Rev* 117, 118. See also Peter Cane, 'Understanding Administrative Adjudication' in Linda Pearson, Carol Harlow and Michael Taggart (eds), *Administrative Law in a Changing State* (Hart 2008).
[16] NSWLEC, *Land and Environment Court of NSW Annual Review 2014*, 15.

While it is often said that a tribunal 'stands in the shoes' of the original decision-maker, its function in a merits appeal is distinct from the original decision-making process, since it is reviewing administrative decision-making in a different institutional setting with different procedural and jurisdictional powers and is subject to different institutional pressures.[17] Tribunals were deliberately designed to constitute such institutional environments for hearing these appeals. They were established to review and remake administrative decisions with affordable and informal procedures, and often with the expertise of lay members specialising in relevant subject areas, so as to create an efficient and effective avenue of challenging administrative decisions.[18] As institutions, tribunals are thus idiosyncratic—they were ad hoc bodies set up by legislation to serve particular adjudicative needs of the time[19]—and they are constitutionally awkward, occupying an unusual place between the administrative and judicial arms of government.[20] As Ceri Warnock states in relation to specialist environmental courts and tribunals:[21]

> [They] are hugely innovative bodies, creatively responding to the demands of environmental conflict resolution and illustrative of new, dynamic forms of adjudication. One could perceive of these bodes as disaggregated sites of power in the constitutional matrix.

The NSWLEC was set up in the late 1970s in this era of tribunal creation in Australian administrative law, with similar pragmatic motivations and with similar features of informal procedures, specialist members, and jurisdiction to hear merits appeals.[22] However, it was established as a court rather than as a tribunal, thus inherently judicialising its administrative functions through its institutional

---

[17] The Hon FG Brennan, 'Comment: The Anatomy of an Administrative Decision' (1980) 9(1) *Syd LR* 4–5; Elizabeth Fisher, 'Administrative Law, Pluralism and the Legal Construction of Merits Review in Australian Environmental Law' in Linda Pearson, Carol Harlow and Michael Taggart (eds), *Administrative Law in a Changing State* (Hart 2008) 135–6; Peter Cane, *Administrative Tribunals and Adjudication* (Hart 2010) 182–3.

[18] Peter Cane and Leighton McDonald, *Principles of Administrative Law: Legal Regulation of Governance* (OUP 2008) 220–224.

[19] Creyke, McMillan and Smyth, *Control of Government Action* (n 14) 155–186; Gabriel Fleming, 'Administrative Review and the "Normative" Goal—Is Anybody Out There?' (2000) 28 *FL Rev* 61, 65.

[20] This is particularly at the Federal level in the Australian political system, where tribunals are firmly part of the executive branch of government, due to the constitutionally entrenched separation of powers, which prevents questions of law being decided by non-judicial bodies and remaking of administrative decisions being undertaken by courts: *R v Kirby; ex p Boilermakers' Society of Australia* (1956) 94 CLR 254; Peter Cane, 'Merits Review and Judicial Review—The AAT as a Trojan Horse' (2000) 28 *FL Rev* 213. See also Creyke, McMillan and Smyth, *Control of Government Action* (n 14) 161–163.

[21] Warnock (n 6).

[22] Land and Environment Court Act 1979 (NSW) ('LEC Act') ss 12, 17–19, 38. See Patricia Ryan, 'Court of Hope and False Expectations: Land and Environment Court 21 Years On' (2002) 14(3) *JEL* 301, 302. The current Chief Judge has noted that 'the court operates as a form of administrative tribunal' in exercising its merits review jurisdiction: Brian Preston, 'Operating an Environment Court: The Experience of the Land and Environment Court of New South Wales' (2008) 25(6) *EPLJ* 385, 387.

form. Being constituted as a judicial body directly raised questions about its constitutional nature, but its establishment in a state jurisdiction meant that the federal constitutional problems caused by judicial institutions undertaking merits review did not arise.[23] Specialist environmental bodies were also established in other Australian jurisdictions, some as tribunals and some as courts,[24] but the NSWLEC was the only one established as a superior court of record.[25] In the NSW court system, the Court has equivalent status to the Supreme Court of New South Wales.[26] It is composed of Judges, who have the same rank, title, status, precedence, remuneration and other rights as ordinary Judges of the NSW Supreme Court,[27] as well as specialist Commissioners, appointed to the Court for their particular expertise in a range of areas relating to environmental protection, planning, urban design, architecture, and land management.[28] As indicated above, the significance of the Court's judicial status is that it imbues the Court with legal authority and a legal identity. It might be unconventional, particularly in light of the 'non-judicial' task of merits review with which it is charged, amongst other things, but its status as a court means something significant legally. Thus former Chief Judge Pearlman commented that:[29]

> [o]ne of the most important features of the Land and Environment Court is that it is a court. It is part of the administration of justice and its role is to carry out functions which courts conventionally undertake in the adjudication and resolution of disputes and in the prosecution of offenders ... It acts, as all courts do, independently and according to law. The most obvious function of the Court is therefore to apply the law ...

However, considering the unorthodox legal functions and processes of the Court, and its unique status as a judicial institution in NSW, it is not obvious what 'law' the Court must apply, leaving space for original doctrinal (and procedural) development by the Court. As the then Minister for Planning and Environment,

---

[23] *cf* n 20; Fisher, 'Legal Construction of Merits Review' (n 17) 330. The Court was pragmatically 'engineered to meet the specifications of its domestic jurisdiction': Mahla Pearlman, 'The Land and Environment Court of New South Wales a Model for Environmental Protection' (2000) 123 *Water, Air and Soil Pollution* 395, 396.

[24] For more detail on the environmental courts set up in different Australian stares and territories, see Fisher, *Risk Regulation* (n 12) 134–5.

[25] LEC Act, s 5(1). As a superior court of record, the NSWLEC sits at the top of the hierarchy of trial courts in NSW and has inherent jurisdiction, albeit limited by statute in terms of subject-matter, so that it has power, inter alia, to control its own procedures and to prevent abuse of its processes. It has powers of judicial review, appellate review (of summary criminal judgments and questions of law in merits review decisions), and the power to grant equitable remedies, such as injunctions and declarations, in civil enforcement cases, although these only go as far as the LEC Act dictates.

[26] The NSW Supreme Court is the highest court in NSW, a superior court of record which has unlimited 'general' civil jurisdiction and handles serious criminal matters. The Supreme Court sits at the top of the NSW court system, hearing the most important civil and criminal cases, appeals from lower state courts, and exercising federal judicial power where that has been conferred on it by Commonwealth legislation.

[27] LEC Act, ss 7–9.

[28] LEC Act, s 12.

[29] *cf* Paul Stein, 'Specialist Environmental Courts: the Land and Environment Court of New South Wales, Australia' (2002) 4 *Env LR* 5, 7; Preston, 'Operating an Environment Court' (n 22) 406.

Minister Landa, explained in introducing the Land and Environment Court Bill in 1979:[30]

> The court is an entirely innovative concept bringing together in one body the best attributes of a traditional court system and a lay tribunal system. [It] will be able to function with the benefits of procedural reform and lack of legal technicalities … The court will establish its own body of precedents on major planning issues, precedents sorely sought by councils but [currently] totally lacking …

## ii. A Court of Amalgamated Jurisdiction

The second historical feature that resulted in the Court's unique institutional nature was its creation as a body to rationalise the previously fragmented NSW planning and land use system.[31] This system had been procedurally cumbersome, particularly as it involved litigation inefficiencies between different courts,[32] and also between tribunals (or boards) and 'supervising' courts,[33] where the latter alone were responsible for resolving issues of 'law', whereas the former decided land use disputes on the merits. This structural reservation of questions of 'law' for judges reflected constitutional assumptions built into the NSW legal system about what was the proper and protected role of the judicial branch of government. However, the distinction between legal and non-legal issues in the prior labyrinthine land use system was found to be counter-productive and unworkable, and was cast aside in the construction of the Court. This set the scene for a court that was constitutionally unique in having responsibility for deciding all aspects of land use appeals.[34] The Court was a 'one-stop shop' for deciding disputes in relation to land use and planning,[35] as well as disputes arising under newly enacted legislation concerned

---

[30] David Paul Landa, New South Wales Legislative Council, *Parliamentary Debates (Hansard)*, 21 November 1979, at 3355, as quoted in Andrew Edgar, *Managing Non-Compliance: The Land and Environment Court and the Flexible Rules of Development Assessment* (PhD Thesis, University of Sydney 2003) 22.

[31] This system included appeals from land valuation, building and subdivision controls and development assessment. The creation of the Court was part of a package of reforms to rationalise this system, which included introduction of comprehensive new planning legislation—the EPA Act. For accounts of the complexity of the environmental and planning legislation before 1979 and the system of Courts, Boards and Tribunals that the NSWLEC replaced, see Ryan, 'Court of Hope and False Expectations' (n 22) 302–5; Zada Lipman, 'The NSW Land and Environment Court: Reforms to the Merit Review Process' (2004) 21 *EPLJ* 415, 415.

[32] For example, the complicated interaction between the NSW Supreme Court and former Land and Valuation Court when a valuation appeal also involved a question of legal title to property: Ryan, 'Court of Hope and False Expectations' (n 22) 306.

[33] ibid 305–8.

[34] Some criticised the development of a court that could decide issues beyond those that were strictly 'legal' in the Diceyan tradition: see Lipman, 'The NSW Land and Environment Court' (n 31) 416. See also Cane, *Administrative Tribunals and Adjudication* (n 17) 32.

[35] However, note that reforms to the EPA Act have undermined the court's exclusive control over planning appeals, introducing new reviewing bodies to provide 'non-legislative' review options and undermining this historical purpose of the court: Environmental Planning and Assessment Amendment Act 2008 (NSW); Linda Pearson and Peter Williams, 'The New South Wales Planning Reforms: Undermining External Merits Review of Land-Use Decision-Making?' (2009) 26 *EPLJ* 19, 23.

with environmental protection.[36] While the Court has strong roots as a planning court, its creation and evolution corresponded with an increased focus on environmental protection in NSW legislation, giving a broader dimension to its identity as an 'environmental court'. The Court was designed to play a vital role in judicially interpreting this new legislation and its operation.[37] It was designed with an important judicial function of interpreting and applying a new body of NSW law.

### iii. A Mandate to Develop Environmental Law

The Court was seen to have a mandate to develop a body of NSW environmental law. This body of law was 'environmental' in the jurisdiction-specific sense of including a strong focus on planning and land use issues, but the creation of the Court marked an opportunity to develop 'its own body of precedents', as described by Minister Landa above,[38] and to develop 'coherent and consistent principles' in the 'administration of environmental law'. Before the founding of the NSWLEC, there 'was no environmental law as we now know it' in NSW law.[39] Now the activities and judgments of the NSWLEC are the primary mechanism for, and evidence of, the development of this 'special jurisprudence'.[40] Thus, as the first specialist environment court established as a superior court of record in the world,[41] it provides an 'instructive case study' for how environmental law can develop in such a setting.[42]

## B.  The NSWLEC's Fragmented Jurisdiction, Powers and Progressive ESD Agenda: A Sum Greater than Its Parts

The NSWLEC's opportunity to develop innovative judicial doctrine is explained not only by historical factors, but also by the idiosyncratic nature of its jurisdiction, its distinctive procedural powers, and its progressive ESD agenda. These elements of the Court's legal culture combine to define the legal context in which the Court's environmental law doctrine, based on ESD principles, has developed.

The Court's jurisdiction is statutory and exclusive.[43] It is the only judicial forum in NSW for hearing a wide range of disputes that relate to environmental and

---

[36] The Court's creation corresponded with a growing body of specialised legislation in the area of environmental protection as well as planning, which confer jurisdiction on the Court eg National Parks and Wildlife Act 1974 (NSW) ('NPWA'); Protection of the Environment Administration Act 1991 (NSW) ('POEA Act'); Threatened Species Conservation Act 1995 (NSW) ('TSC Act').

[37] Minister Landa (n 30).

[38] See above n 30 and accompanying text.

[39] Preston, 'Operating an Environment Court' (n 22) 387.

[40] Dennis Cowdroy, 'The Land and Environment Court of New South Wales—A Model for the United Kingdom?' [2002] *JPEL* 59, 78.

[41] There are now a host of specialist environmental courts and tribunals around the world: see Warnock (n 6).

[42] Preston, 'Operating an Environment Court' (n 22) 387.

[43] LEC Act, s 16. Proceedings wrongly started in other courts are transferred to the Court: LEC Act, s 72; Civil Procedure Act 2005, s 149B.

planning issues,[44] giving it the platform to control the evolution of environmental law in NSW. The jurisdiction is statutory in that the Court was established by the Land and Environment Court Act 1979 (NSW) ('LEC Act'), and the scope of its jurisdiction is there specified, by breaking down its workload into different classes. These include merits appeals from a range of environmental and planning decisions (Classes 1, 2 and 3),[45] judicial review actions and civil enforcement of planning provisions and environmental offences (Class 4),[46] and criminal matters (Classes 5, 6 and 7).[47] These different classes include the Court sitting as an appellate court in some cases,[48] and they are governed by specific rules as to the composition of the Court and its procedure. Thus matters in some Classes are reserved for the Judges of the Court alone, including undertaking Class 4 judicial review and civil enforcement actions,[49] presiding over criminal trials and appeals in relation to environmental offences,[50] and hearing 'questions of law' that arise during merits appeals.[51] Merits appeals, however, can be heard by specialist Commissioners as well as Judges.[52]

Merits appeals, as well as Class 4 judicial review actions, make up most of the Court's ESD case law. The nature of a merits appeal is again based in statute. The Court's power to undertake such appeals is prescribed by section 39 LEC Act, demonstrating the extensive discretion afforded to the Court in hearing such appeals:

(2) In addition to any other functions and discretions that the Court has apart from this subsection, the Court shall, for the purposes of hearing and disposing of an appeal, have all the functions and discretions which the person or body whose decision is the subject of the appeal had in respect of the matter the subject of the appeal.

(3) An appeal in respect of such a decision shall be by way of rehearing, and fresh evidence or evidence in addition to, or in substitution for, the evidence given on the making of the decision may be given on the appeal.

(4) In making its decision in respect of an appeal, the Court shall have regard to this or any other relevant Act, any instrument made under any such Act, the circumstances of the case and the public interest.

---

[44] Non-judicial forums exist for planning matters, from internal review by consent authorities under s 82A of the EPA Act, to review by more recently created planning arbitrators, a Planning Assessment Commission (exercising delegated Ministerial powers for state significant development) and other specialist panels: see above n 35. These bodies either add layers to the appeal process, or remove jurisdiction for appeals to the NSWLEC on some matters altogether: Pearson and Williams, 'NSW Planning Reforms' (n 35) 20–25.

[45] LEC Act, ss 17–19.

[46] LEC Act, s 20. 'Civil enforcement suits' are brought on the basis of open standing provisions in environmental legislation, eg EPA Act, s 123.

[47] LEC Act, ss 21–21B. There are also Class 8 proceedings, which are disputes under the Mining Act 1992 and the Petroleum (Onshore) Act 1991.

[48] eg in Classes 4 and 6.

[49] LEC Act, s 33(2).

[50] ibid.

[51] LEC Act, s 56A. See also Land and Environment Court Rules 2007, pt 3, r 3.10, restricting the procedural directions that a Commissioner of the Court can make.

[52] LEC Act, s 33(1).

(5) The decision of the Court upon an appeal shall, for the purposes of this or any other Act or instrument, be deemed, where appropriate, to be the final decision of the person or body whose decision is the subject of the appeal and shall be given effect to accordingly.

This provision also indicates why the NSWLEC case law is so different from that of the EU courts: in merits appeals, the NSWLEC decides cases finally, with extensive fact-finding powers, and in the place of administrative decision-makers. It thus applies legal doctrine and statutory frameworks, rather than only interpreting them, or testing the legality of action by other institutions. The NSWLEC determines the law and applies it to the facts in merits appeals.

A different provision of the LEC Act empowers the Court to hear judicial review actions, connecting them to the administrative law jurisdiction of the NSW Supreme Court, but defining this jurisdiction differently, by reference to the environmental and planning remit of the Court:[53]

(2) The Court has the same civil jurisdiction as the Supreme Court would, but for section 71 [which prevents the proceedings here listed from otherwise being brought in the Supreme Court], have to hear and dispose of proceedings:

...

(b) to review, or command, the exercise of a function conferred or imposed by a planning or environmental law...

In terms of procedure, while the Court has deliberately informal rules (including rules relating to evidence) governing merits appeals,[54] statutory and common law rules of procedure and evidence apply in the Court's judicial review jurisdiction, as they do in NSW courts generally.

This composite jurisdiction of the Court is further fragmented by the 73 environmental and planning statutes that confer particular jurisdiction on the Court within its various jurisdictional classes,[55] and they do so in different ways. Some statutes may provide avenues of appeal to the Court by way of judicial review but not merits review.[56] While there were initially perceived to be arbitrary environmental 'gaps' in the subject matter covered by these jurisdiction-conferring statutes,[57] their coverage of 'environmental' issues is now relatively comprehensive,[58] particularly since they are increasingly concerned with environmental protection

---

[53] LEC Act, s 20(2).

[54] So as to deal with them efficiently and adduce expert assistance as necessary: LEC Act, s 38.

[55] These statutes range from the Aboriginal Land Rights Act 1983 (NSW) to the Encroachment of Buildings Act 1922 (NSW) to the EPA Act and TSC Act. A full list can be found at < http://www.lec.justice.nsw.gov.au/Pages/practice_procedure/legislation/actsthatconferjurisdiction.aspx > accessed 21 June 2016.

[56] eg decisions under NPWA, s 90 (concerning consent to destroy Aboriginal objects); Minister's water management plans under the Water Management Act 2000 (NSW) s 50; and planning consent decisions for major infrastructure projects under the former Part 3A of the EPA Act where they are either 'critical infrastructure projects' proposed by a public authority and/or have been reviewed by the Planning Assessment Commission: ss 75K and 75L.

[57] Ryan, 'Court of Hope and False Expectations' (n 22) 303.

[58] To the extent it is possible to define what 'environmental' issues are: see ch 4, n 3.

as well as planning.[59] The Court is charged with hearing matters that relate to pollution, waste, national parks, habitats and threatened species, fisheries, water management, mining, cultural as well as built heritage, in addition to the natural environmental aspects involved in planning for the built environment. Further, this legislation is now linked by a common purpose of promoting 'ecologically sustainable development', which is found in objects clauses of many of these Acts.[60]

This linking of the Court's fragmented statutory jurisdiction can also be seen in other ways. In particular, the procedural and evidential rules of the Court in its different Classes are not as distinct as the LEC Act appears to prescribe. In its merits review jurisdiction, the Court has found that, while it may adopt a flexible approach to evidence-taking, the 'underlying principles' of the law of evidence remain relevant, so that the court is bound by the rules of natural justice and may not make arbitrary decisions.[61] Similarly, the NSWLEC has adopted highly prescribed and uniform rules of procedure to promote efficient and fair case management,[62] formalising the Court's processes.[63] At the same time, the rules of procedure across all judicial proceedings in NSW (including both judicial and merits review in the NSWLEC) are now also governed by the Civil Procedure Act 2005, which is designed to facilitate the 'just, quick and cheap resolution of the real issues in the proceedings',[64] so that the procedural approach to merits appeals is not that different from other NSWLEC (or even NSW) civil proceedings.

These purposive and procedural connections across the Court's jurisdiction set the scene for the NSWLEC to make connections across its case law and to build a body of doctrine involving ESD principles. Furthermore, particularly in relation to merits review and judicial review cases, the Court has doctrinal flexibility in working out how to implement the statutory provisions setting out these two aspects of its jurisdiction.[65] This flexibility is discussed in the following section.

There are two further features of the Court that lay the foundation for doctrinal innovation involving ESD principles across the Court's jurisdiction. First, the distinct Classes of its jurisdiction are not as disparate as they might appear. This is because, by caseload volume, the majority of the Court's cases are merits

---

[59] See above n 36 and accompanying text.
[60] 'Ecologically sustainable development' is also defined by reference to a common 'definition' in POEA Act, s 6(2): see ch 3, text accompanying nn 288–292.
[61] *Minister for Immigration and Ethnic Affairs v Pochi* (1980) 44 FLR 41, 67; *Tim Unity Holdings v Randwick CC* [1998] NSWLEC 96.
[62] Land and Environment Court Rules 2007; range of Notes and Directions in the Court's Practice Collection: < http://www.lec.justice.nsw.gov.au/Pages/practice_procedure/directions.aspx > accessed 21 June 2016.
[63] This formalising of rules of procedure and evidence reflects the judicialisation of administrative tribunals: see above n 15.
[64] Civil Procedure Act 2005 (NSW) ('CPA') s 56(1). The NSWLEC has subscribed to the CPA, and its Uniform Civil Procedure Rules 2005 (NSW), which now binds all NSW courts. The Land and Environment Court Rules do however prevail over the uniform rules: Uniform Rules, r 1.7, sch 2.
[65] See above nn 52–53 and accompanying text.

appeals,[66] or arise out of the EPA Act,[67] giving some consistency to the Court's case law in practice. It is also because the various actions heard by the Court across its jurisdictional classes are public law actions in a broad sense (including criminal cases and merits appeals), which have an interconnected subject matter. This connection, and the opportunity this provides for developing environmental law doctrine, has not been lost on commentators and judges of the Court. Thus a former Judge has reflected:[68]

> The administration of environmental law, whether based on statute or common law, is a matter of enormous consequence to the future well-being of our planet, as well as of crucial significance domestically. To the extent that much of it comprises public law and results in litigation (often between a citizen or group and the Crown, a Government instrumentality or corporation), it is important that the courts are able to respond with the development of coherent and consistent principles, as well as efficient and effective case management. My thesis is that a well qualified specialist court, with exclusive jurisdiction in all matters environmental, has the best chance of succeeding.

This quotation demonstrates a second feature of the Court that gives it a foundation for developing connected and innovative legal doctrine: a progressive environmentalist agenda. This agenda can be seen in the Court's history—the NSWLEC was created as a 'bold answer to calls for the protection of our built and natural environment'.[69] And it has matured with the Court's evolution. The current Chief Judge of the Court, Preston CJ, has commented that a 'unifying ethos and mission' has developed over the Court's 30-year history:[70]

> Court personnel (judges, commissioners, registrars and court staff) all believe they are engaged in an important and worthwhile endeavour [ie the protection of the environment for the public in general]; the court and its work matter and are making a difference. They view themselves as part of a team; not as individuals working independently. There is an "esprit de corps".

This environmentalist agenda is particularly pursued, through the developing doctrine of the Court, in terms of 'ecologically sustainable development' and ESD principles. Preston CJ has observed that the Court's institutional attributes—its specialism, comprehensive jurisdiction and 'interdisciplinary' decision-making—make it 'best placed' to develop innovative and holistic remedies and solutions

---

[66] Merits appeals and other civil proceedings in Classes 1–3 of the Court's jurisdiction (appeals from environmental and planning decision-making, tree disputes, and land tenure, valuation and compensation claims) take up approximately 85% of the Court's finalised caseload: NSWLEC, *Land and Environment Court of NSW Annual Review 2014*, 24.

[67] Such appeals are generally brought by disappointed planning applicants against local government authorities in relation to development consent decisions: EPA Act, s 97. This includes applicants disappointed by 'deemed' refusals of planning consent under s 82(1), ie cases where a consent authority has not determined a development application within the required period prescribed by the Act's regulations.

[68] As quoted in Malcolm Grant, Department of the Environment, Transport & Regions (UK), *Environment Court Project Final Report* (2000) ('Grant Report') 424.

[69] Cowdroy, 'Land and Environment Court of New South Wales' (n 40) 59.

[70] Preston, 'Operating an Environment Court' (n 22) 408.

to environmental problems through its jurisprudence, and thus to play a role in achieving ESD.[71] As Part III shows, ESD principles in NSWLEC case law are very much used as vehicles for this environmentalist spirit of the Court.

In sum, the statutory construction of the Court—with its exclusive and novel jurisdiction establishing a one-stop shop for disputes involving environmental and planning matters in NSW—along with its environmentalist agenda, combine to create a unique judicial institution with a distinct legal culture, which has the opportunity and inclination to create new legal doctrine involving environmental principles. This opportunity is one that the Court is conscious of, as Preston CJ states:[72]

> The court has shown that an environmental court of the requisite status has more specialised knowledge, has an increased number of cases and hence more opportunity to, and is more likely to, develop environmental jurisprudence... Large, established courts can be conservative and have inertia; change is slow and resisted. The fact that this court is a separate court has enabled flexibility and innovation.

## C. Open and Novel Administrative Law Doctrine

The third aspect of the NSWLEC's legal culture that provides the Court with an opportunity to develop innovative doctrine involving ESD principles is the nature of the administrative law doctrine it applies. While the Court sits within the Australian legal system, so that it is bound to apply common law doctrines, including of administrative law (particularly judicial review doctrine), it is also a court whose jurisdiction is uniquely constructed by statute, as seen in the previous section. Any applicable common law doctrine must be accommodated within this jurisdictional framework. There are two particular features of the administrative law doctrine applied by the Court that provide scope for the Court's doctrinal innovation: the openness of common law judicial review tests applied by the Court, and the novel space for doctrinal development provided by merits appeals. Whilst common law grounds of judicial review are the subject of much case law and scholarship in Australian administrative law,[73] the practice of merits review is less familiar legal territory.[74] However, both make up the distinctive 'administrative law' of the Court.[75] This chapter analyses this combined body of administrative law of the

---

[71] ibid 385–6.

[72] ibid 407–9.

[73] eg WB Lane and Simon Young, *Administrative Law in Australia* (Thomson Lawbook Co 2007) ch 1; Mark Aronson and Matthew Groves, *Judicial Review of Administrative Action* (5th edn, Thomson Reuters 2013) ch 1; Peter Cane and Leighton McDonald, *Principles of Administrative Law* (2nd ed, OUP 2013) ch 5.

[74] Although merits review is increasingly attracting scholarly attention in administrative law terms: Fisher, 'Legal Construction of Merits Review' (n 17); Andrew Edgar, 'Institutions and Sustainability: Merits Review Tribunals and the Precautionary Principle' (2013) 16(1) *Australasia Journal of Natural Resources Law and Policy* 61 (see n 22 and generally).

[75] Merits appeals can be included within the body of administrative law both on a legal formalist account of administrative law (they involve appeals from, and remaking of, administrative decisions

NSWLEC, which contains the key doctrinal developments involving ESD principles in NSWLEC reasoning.

In terms of the judicial review doctrines applied by the Court, section 20(2) of the LEC Act extracted above directs that the Court has the same jurisdiction as the NSW Supreme Court in reviewing or commanding the exercise of a function conferred by an environmental or planning law (that refers such jurisdiction to the Court), and, as a NSW court, the NSWLEC is bound to apply common law doctrines of administrative law in undertaking such review. These include judicial review grounds of Wednesbury unreasonableness, procedural unfairness, failure to take into account relevant considerations, acting with improper purpose, and so on.[76] These various grounds of review are all argued and considered in the Court's Class 4 jurisdiction,[77] but it is the common law test of failure to take into account mandatory relevant considerations that is of primary significance in the doctrinal use of ESD principles in NSWLEC cases.

This judicial review doctrine constitutes a relatively open doctrinal space for implicating ESD principles as legally required 'relevant considerations' in NSWLEC law, and so justifying NSWLEC decisions.[78] This is because the authoritative High Court statement of this common law doctrine provides that relevant considerations, which a decision-maker is obliged to take into account, are to be determined by the particular statutory context in which challenged administrative decisions are made, so that if relevant considerations are not set out explicitly in such legislation, they are to be implied from its 'subject-matter, scope and purpose'.[79] Determining what constitute mandatory relevant considerations for the purposes of judicial review is thus a matter of statutory construction and purposive inquiry, giving the court scope to interpret the regulatory context at issue. In the case of the NSWLEC and its particular jurisdictional remit, this interpretive discretion is shaped by the statutes that confer jurisdiction on the Court, including their ESD objects, as well as the progressive ESD agenda pursued by the Court in interpreting their provisions and subject-matter, scope and purpose. At the same time, the established doctrinal traditions of judicial review in Australian administrative law constrain the Court's powers, particularly in reviewing *how* primary decision-makers might take ESD principles into account as

---

by a court) and on a legal pluralist account of administrative law ('merits review powers … are understood to be the way to ensure good public administration because reviewing all aspects of a decision is the way to ensure legitimacy': Fisher, '"Jurisdictional" Facts and "Hot" Facts' (n 6) 976–7).

[76] Creyke, McMillan and Smyth, *Control of Government Action* (n 14) pt C.

[77] eg *Murrumbidgee Ground-Water Preservation Association v Minister for Natural Resources* [2004] NSWLEC 122; *Anderson v Director-General, Department of Environment and Conservation* [2006] NSWLEC 12; (2006) 144 LGERA 43.

[78] For the general manipulability of Australian judicial review doctrines, see Michael Taggart, '"Australian Exceptionalism" in Judicial Review' (2008) 36(1) *FL Rev* 1, 27–29; *cf* Andrew Edgar, 'Between Rules and Discretion: Legislative Principles and the Relevant Considerations Ground of Review' (2013) 20 *AJ Admin Law* 132 (highlighting the normative constraints of the relevant considerations ground, and that is a frequently litigated ground of judicial review).

[79] *Minister for Aboriginal Affairs v Peko-Wallsend* (1986) 162 CLR 24, 39–40.

relevant considerations.[80] At common law, it is dogma that courts, in undertaking judicial review, must never stray into evaluating or deciding the merits of a decision.[81] This bright line between the law and merits can be a difficult distinction for a court to draw in determining whether a decision-maker has failed to take relevant considerations into account.[82] The common law compromise is that a judicially reviewing court must consider whether the relevant administrator gave 'proper, genuine and realistic consideration' to the relevant matter,[83] with the qualification that this formulation does not allow a court to assess the adequacy of that consideration.[84] In the context of NSWLEC judicial review decisions, these constraints need to be respected in determining whether ESD principles have been taken into account where they are found to be relevant considerations, which can be challenging in interpreting and reviewing the 'consideration' of these open-textured principles. Judicial review doctrine, as applied in NSWLEC cases where ESD principles are established as relevant considerations, is adapted to reflect the legal culture of the Court, against the backdrop of binding Australian common law principles.[85]

This body of judicial review doctrine has pivotal significance in NSWLEC ESD case law for two reasons. First, while its application strictly depends on the particular statutory framework in which an impugned administrative decision is made, the NSWLEC has developed a variety of progressive judicial techniques for finding ESD principles to be legally required relevant considerations in its case law, building on and beyond these judicial review principles, so that ESD principles are found to be relevant considerations justifying the Court's reasoning across the jurisdiction of the Court generally. Despite an attempt by the NSWCA, in its supervisory role hearing appeals on questions of law (including judicial review decisions) from the NSWLEC, to overrule this enthusiasm of the Court to impute ESD principles as mandatory relevant considerations in reviewing primary decision-making,[86] Hodgson JA has conceded that:[87]

> … the principles of ESD are likely to come to be seen as so plainly an element of the
> public interest, in relation to most if not all decisions, that failure to consider them will

[80] ibid 40–42 (courts should not review the weight given to relevant considerations by primary decision-makers unless the statutory context indicates otherwise, and allowance should be given to decision-makers taking into account policy matters). See Edgar, 'Between Rules and Discretion' (n 78).

[81] *Attorney-General (NSW) v Quin* (1990) 170 CLR 1, 38; *Peko-Wallsend* (n 79) 41.

[82] One might ask how a court is to decide whether a relevant matter was taken into consideration without investigating the merits of the decision. See Taggart, 'Australian Exceptionalism' (n 78) 27–8.

[83] *Weal v Bathurst CC* [2000] NSWCA 88; (2000) 111 LGERA 181 [9].

[84] *Kindimindi Investments Pty Ltd v Lane Cove Council* [2006] NSWCA 23; (2006) 143 LGERA 277 [79].

[85] eg *Carstens v Pittwater Council* [1999] NSWLEC 249; (1999) 111 LGERA 1; *Gray v Minister for Planning* [2006] NSWLEC 720; (2006) 152 LGERA 258; *Walker v Minister for Planning* [2007] NSWLEC 741; (2007) 157 LGERA 124; *South East Forest Rescue Inc v Bega Valley Shire Council* [2011] NSWLEC 250; (2011) 211 LGERA 1; *Upper Mooki Landcare Inc v Shenhua Watermark Coal Pty Ltd* [2016] NSWLEC 6.

[86] Finding that ESD principles must be 'relevant' on the facts of a particular impugned decision, which is a judgment for the relevant administrator to make, not a judicially reviewing court, albeit that a mistaken judgment as to relevance 'would seem contrary to the supposed mandatory legislative requirement': *Minister for Planning v Walker* [2008] NSWCA 224; (2008) 161 LGERA 423 [54]–[55].

[87] ibid.

become strong evidence of failure to consider the public interest and/or to act bona fide in the exercise of powers granted to the Minister, and thus become capable of avoiding decisions.

This suggestion came in a very awkward passage of reasoning in which Hodgson JA found that it was not mandatory for the Minister to consider ESD principles in approving a concept plan for a major development under the EPA Act,[88] particularly since this would risk reviewing the merits of the Minister's judgment as to relevance (thus overturning a decision of the NSWLEC below that ESD principles did constitute mandatory considerations in this case that were not adequately considered).[89] However, he also found that the Minister had not in fact adequately considered the 'substance' of ESD in approving the plan and that the Minister *should* 'conscientiously address the principles of ESD' in deciding any final development application for the project, or otherwise face a subsequent judicial review claim for failing to take into account the public interest. This case shows how the supervisory court of the NSWLEC—the NSWCA—struggles with reconciling the tradition of its judicial review doctrine, the nature of the ESD objects under the EPA Act, and the evolving culture and law of the NSWLEC. Hodgson JA's warning to the decision-maker to improve its decision-making in line with ESD principles was a way through this struggle, which was possible in light of the multi-stage nature of the development application. However, the simultaneous acknowledgement of the increasing legal relevance of ESD principles, quoted above, also shows how the common law doctrinal constraints imposed on the NSWLEC by appellate courts can also be influenced by the Court's ESD reasoning in working out its own context-specific judicial review doctrine. Since *Walker*, the NSWLEC has continued to find that ESD principles are mandatory relevant considerations for planning decisions under the EPA Act, including in relation to major projects.[90] The Court of Appeal has supported of this direction of travel, subsequently interpreting Hodgson JA's reasoning in *Walker* as 'authority for the proposition that where it is necessary to consider the environmental impact of a project, the public interest [embraces ESD]'.[91] The statutory context in which *Walker* was decided has also been amended, facilitating the conclusion that ESD principles are mandatory relevant considerations in planning consent decision under the Act.[92] At the same time, tensions remain in the case law between formalist accounts of judicial review doctrine that emphasise its limits, and the legal influence of ESD principles, which tend to widen scrutiny of decision-making by way of judicial review.

The second way in which the doctrine of mandatory relevant considerations has been central to NSWLEC doctrine involving ESD principles is through its

---

[88] For the facts and reasoning in the NSWLEC case below, see below text accompanying nn 224–227.

[89] See text accompanying n 228.

[90] See Section III(B)(iii) below.

[91] *Warkworth Mining Limited v Bulga Milbrodale Progress Association Inc* [2014] NSWCA 105; (2014) 200 LGERA 375; (2014) 86 NSWLR 527 [296].

[92] See below n 235.

crossover application in merits appeals. While common law doctrine agonises over the often hair-splitting distinction between judicial review and merits review in relation to the administrative law ground of relevant considerations,[93] the jurisdiction of the NSWLEC creates a judicial setting whereby the Court is not only allowed, but required, to undertake merits review. This leads to an overlap in doctrine between its merits review and judicial review cases,[94] particularly in relation to the doctrine of mandatory relevant considerations. This is because, in both types of action, the Court needs to determine which considerations— in particular, which ESD principles—are legally required and relevant, either to review whether they have been properly taken into account (judicial review) or to apply them directly (merits review). Understood in this way, merits review is not just about 'resolving disputes, but … in doing so it [defines] categories and the boundaries of action'.[95] Administrative law doctrine is shaped by the unique legal jurisdiction and culture of the Court, representing a particular form of environmental law in the NSWLEC,[96] in which merits appeals play an important role.[97]

The mapping exercise in this chapter thus includes the Court's merits appeals within the scope of its doctrinal analysis. These cases are judicial decisions, in which the NSWLEC relies on maxims (including ESD principles as mandatory relevant considerations) to justify its decisions, albeit that these decisions go further than judicial review in terms of making a decision on the facts.[98] It is now

---

[93] *Minister for Planning v Walker* (n 86) [54]. See also Murray Gleeson, 'Judicial Legitimacy' (2000) 20 *AustBarRev* 4, 11.

[94] This is particularly in cases where a judicial review action is brought to challenge a decision when no merits appeal is available: eg *Gray* (n 85); *Walker v Minister for Planning* (n 85).

[95] Fisher, '"Jurisdictional" Facts and "Hot" Facts' (n 6) 982 (merits appeals are thus a form of administrative law in that they are 'part of the day-to-day operation of the accountability of environmental decision making').

[96] This is to the point that some commentators describe the Court's judicial review and merits review decisions as its 'judicial review work': J Cripps, 'Administrative Law' in Tim Bonyhady (ed), *Environmental Protection and Legal Change* (Federation Press 1992) 29. Other examples of novel administrative law evolving in NSWLEC doctrine, in light of the Court's unique legal culture (including its specialist expertise) are seen in relation to the 'jurisdictional fact' doctrine (*Timbarra Protection Coalition Inc v Ross Mining* [1999] NSWCA 8; (1999) 102 LGERA 52): see below Section III(B)(ii).

[97] Australian environmental law scholars have known this for some time, treating merits appeals as part of 'environmental law': Jacqueline Peel, 'Ecologically Sustainable Development: More Than Mere Lip Service?' (2008) 12(1) *Australasian Journal of Natural Resources Law and Policy* 1, 12, 27; Warwick Gullett, 'The Threshold Test of the Precautionary Principle in Australian Courts and Tribunals: Lessons for Judicial Review' in Elizabeth Fisher, Judith Jones and René von Schomberg (eds), *Implementing the Precautionary Principle: Perspectives and Prospects* (Edward Elgar 2006); Mark Smyth, 'Inquisitorial Adjudication: the Duty to Inquire in Merits Review Tribunals' (2010) 34(1) *MULR* 230. Fisher points out that this scholarly tendency is supported by widespread publication of merits review decisions by legal publishers: Fisher, 'Legal Construction of Merits Review' (n 17) 330–1. The NSWLEC has also published decisions of both commissioners and judges on the Internet since 2003, with increasingly lengthy reasoning. The legal conceptualisation of merits review is however still relatively embryonic: Peter Bayne, 'The Proposed Administrative Review Tribunal—Is There a Silver Lining in the Dark Cloud?' (2000) 7 *Australian Journal of Administrative Law* 86, 89; Fleming, 'Administrative Review and the "Normative" Goal' (n 19); Cane, *Administrative Tribunals and Adjudication* (n 17) 182–188.

[98] Merits appeals thus satisfy the definition of judicial doctrine: see ch 1, text accompanying nn 95–96.

recognised that they have a 'normative effect',[99] and that courts undertaking merits review 'can also provide leadership by formulating and applying principles'.[100] Merits appeals are relied on by the Court itself as precedents, justifying subsequent decisions of both judicial and merits review. The decision in *Leatch*, discussed in Chapter Three,[101] in which the Court engaged in innovative reasoning to find the precautionary principle to be a relevant consideration in a planning consent decision, has been relied on in many subsequent NSWLEC decisions to conclude that the precautionary principle is legally relevant to the decision-making under review.[102] Further, the precedent-setting quality of merits appeals is an express aim of the Court.[103] To promote consistency in its decision-making, the Court has built up a bank of merits appeals, characterised as 'planning principles', to function as important contributions to the Court's doctrine.[104] In these cases, the Court formulates extensive reasoning in merits appeals that offer the opportunity to develop general decision-making guidelines,[105] with the decided cases then operating as blueprints for future decision-making.[106] Soon after their initial development, Senior Commissioner Roseth described such planning principles as 'general assumption[s] or belief[s] forming the basis of a chain of reasoning',[107] again highlighting their doctrinal character. With respect to ESD principles, there are two key planning principle cases that apply to guide decision-making under the EPA Act—*BGP Properties Pty Limited v Lake Macquarie City Council* in relation to 'ESD principles' generally and *Telstra Corporation Limited v Hornsby Shire Council* in relation to 'ESD and the precautionary principle'.[108] Both cases are central in the doctrinal development of ESD principles in NSWLEC case law, as examined further below,[109] highlighting the deliberate development of doctrine by the Court in its merits review jurisdiction.[110] This again demonstrates that the

---

[99] Edgar, 'Institutions and Sustainability' (n 74) 74–75.

[100] Preston, 'Leadership by the Courts' (n 2) 328.

[101] See ch 3, text accompanying nn 262–266.

[102] eg *Brunsdon v Wagga Wagga CC* [2003] NSWLEC 168 [116]; *BGP Properties v Lake Macquarie CC* [2004] NSWLEC 399; (2004) 138 LGERA 237 [108].

[103] *cf* Australian tribunals in which there is also a goal to generate consistent decision-making in merits appeals, despite the fact that, as tribunals, they are not bound by a common law doctrine of precedent: *Re Ganchov and Comcare* (1990) 11 AAR 468; (1990) 19 ALD 541, 542.

[104] It has done this since 2003. See Practice Direction No. 17: NSWLEC, *Land and Environment Court of NSW Annual Review 2004*, 4–5.

[105] <http://www.lec.justice.nsw.gov.au/Pages/practice_procedure/principles/planning_principles. aspx> accessed 22 June 2016.

[106] Williams classifies these as either 'process-oriented' or 'outcome-oriented' principles: Peter Williams, 'The Land and Environment Court's Planning Principles: Relationship with Planning Theory and Practice' (2005) 22(6) *EPLJ* 401, 404–405.

[107] Again meeting the definition of 'doctrine' in ch 1: John Roseth 'Planning Principles and Consistency of Decisions' (2005) Talk delivered to the Law Society's Local Government and Planning Law Seminar, 15 February 2005 < http://www.lec.justice.nsw.gov.au/Documents/speech_15feb05_roseth. pdf> accessed 23 June 2016.

[108] *BGP* (n 102); *Telstra* (n 8).

[109] See Sections III(A) & (B) below.

[110] The Court remains conscious that such cases do not constitute binding precedent at common law—*Balgownie v Shoalhaven CC* (1980) 46 LGRA 198)—and argues that it does not engage in

'environmental law' developed and applied by the NSWLEC involves a novel and evolving doctrinal space of administrative law.

## D. Conclusion

The novelty of this evolving environmental law in the NSWLEC, possible due to the unique institutional construction and jurisdiction of the Court and its consciously progressive agenda to build a body of environmental law doctrine, is a key reason to analyse its development by means of a doctrinal analysis, along the lines set out in Chapter One.[111] There is no established scholarly methodology or tradition in NSW or Australian law for examining the case law of the NSWLEC in its entirety, and yet it is a rich legal resource. This is particularly the case in terms of its ESD case law, which is extensive across all aspects of its jurisdiction.

The idiosyncratic institutional identity of the NSWLEC within the NSW and Australian legal system, along with the Court's agenda to promote ESD and develop environmental law as a core goal, means that the ESD case law of the Court itself significantly influences the institutional identity of the Court, in a way that is not seen in EU law. EU law doctrine may be shaped by developments involving environmental principles, but not the entire culture of the Court—the relationship between legal culture and doctrine is only one way, and is thus more limited, in the EU context. Another difference between the respective legal cultures of the EU courts and the NSWLEC, which highlights the distinctive task of doctrinally mapping NSWLEC case law involving environmental principles, is the style of reasoning adopted by the two Courts. Whereas there were challenges in analysing some EU cases due to the courts' variable (sometimes unhelpfully succinct or sometimes convoluted) reasoning involving environmental principles, NSWLEC reasoning in merits appeals involving ESD principles is challenging to analyse for at least three different reasons.

First, since merits appeals involve remaking administrative decisions, their reasoning involves extensive fact-finding, so that the doctrine involved can be difficult to isolate. Second, this reasoning can be specific to the legislative decision-making scheme from which the appeal arises, so that there are distinct legal constraints

---

generalised 'rule-making' that is the proper preserve of the legislature in its merits review jurisdiction: Brian Preston, 'The Role of Courts in relation to Adaptation to Climate Change' in Tim Bonyhady, Jan McDonald and Andrew Macintosh (eds), *Adapting to Climate Change: Australian Law and Policy* (Federation Press 2010) 33–4. However, planning principles and merits appeals *do* have consequences for decision-makers, developers and citizens within the scope of the Court's environmental and planning jurisdiction, generating obligations with respect to those parties, which can be enforced and challenged in court. Some commentators acknowledge the challenge of creating planning principles that promote consistency that are not 'binding precedents' (Pearson and Williams, 'NSW Planning Reforms' (n 35) 30) and also question the legitimacy of the Court engaging in 'policy formulation' in developing these principles: Williams, 'Land and Environment Court's Planning Principles' (n 106) 406–8.

[111] See ch 1(III)(C).

on the Court in undertaking merits review.[112] And third, the procedures by which merits appeals are heard can vary considerably. In particular, merits appeals in some planning disputes can be conducted on-site, where parties agree or where there is no significant impact on neighbouring properties or on the public interest.[113] In such cases, judgments are given orally on site and, while recorded, they contain shorter and less considered reasons than the written judgments of the Court. As a result, it is a select (although extensive) body of merits review decisions, primarily given by the Judges of the Court (or a Judge sitting with Commissioners) rather than Commissioners sitting alone, which are mapped for their doctrinal reasoning in Part III. This is not surprising. The more 'judicially' reasoned decisions of the Court, particularly those designed to carry precedential weight as planning principles, are where doctrinal reasoning involving ESD principles is most obviously found.

In summary, despite its mixed jurisdiction and the doctrinal complexity and novelty of merits appeals, as well as the range of statutes granting it jurisdiction, the NSWLEC has a significant opportunity to develop doctrinal reasoning involving ESD principles. In fact, the Court has 'a unique opportunity ... for a new style of administration of public law',[114] and for a new style of environmental law. This is a consequence of the Court's unique legal culture, in particular its exclusive jurisdiction and specialism, the common ESD object of the statutes that confer jurisdiction on it, its extensive merits review case law, and its agenda both to develop environmental law precedents and to pursue environmental goals. As is seen in the following Part, to date the Court has seized this opportunity to generate progressive and connected reasoning involving ESD principles, turning its complex jigsaw of statutory jurisdiction into a platform for the development of a distinctive body of environmental law.

# III. Mapping the ESD Case Law

This Part maps NSWLEC case law involving ESD principles. Despite the explicit articulation of the four core ESD principles—the precautionary principle, intergenerational equity, conservation of biological diversity and ecological integrity, and internalisation of environmental costs—in the Intergovernmental Agreement on the Environment and subsequently in NSW legislation,[115] these environmental

---

[112] *Thaina Town v City of Sydney Council* [2007] NSWCA 300; (2007) 156 LGERA 150 [6]; *Re Coldham; ex parte Brideson (No 2)* (1990) 170 CLR 267, 230.

[113] LEC Act, ss 34A–34B.

[114] Stein, 'Specialist Environmental Courts' (n 29) 6.

[115] See ch 3(IV), explaining the history of ESD principles in intergovernmental politics and how they have come to be legislatively elaborated in the objects clauses of statutes, usually with a version of the integration principle ('ESD requires effective integration of economic and environmental considerations in decision-making processes': POEA Act, s 6(2)).

principles remained open-textured and legally ambiguous. In theorising the role of courts in interpreting and applying ESD principles, Preston CJ considers that legal rules always contain a 'core of certainty and a penumbra of doubt' and will incorporate 'extra legal norms into the law' when very general standards are used.[116] ESD principles, in legislative form, certainly reflect these attributes of indeterminacy and incorporation of non-legal content. In this Part's analysis, these open principles meet the unique legal culture of the Court to create a novel body of environmental law doctrine.

Both before and after ESD principles were recognised in NSW statutes, the Court has engaged in innovative reasoning involving ESD principles to build a doctrinally progressive body of ESD case law across all aspects of its jurisdiction. In fact, the last 20 years has produced so many NSWLEC ESD decisions, which treat ESD principles in a range of ways, that it is tempting to question whether 'any recognisable application of the principles of ecologically sustainable development' can be isolated.[117] While no consistent and predictable application of ESD principles to particular facts might be identified, there are certainly identifiable doctrinal trends in the ESD case law. These trends have been explicitly crafted by the Court, by referring to its previous decisions involving ESD principles to justify further progressive doctrinal steps, thereby building over time a body of connected doctrine in which ESD principles are now identified as central elements of its reasoning in general.

Analysing the judicial treatment of ESD principles in NSWLEC cases involves isolating steps of doctrinal development, as well as the discrete reasoning techniques used by the Court with respect to ESD principles in individual cases. The resulting doctrinal map shows not simply categories of judicial reasoning, but also a progression or extension of doctrinal ESD reasoning across the Court's case law and jurisdiction. Accordingly, this Part maps the treatment of ESD principles in NSWLEC reasoning, not by reference to discrete reasoning techniques, as in Chapter Four for EU law, but according to the progressive doctrinal steps adopted by the Court in expanding the legal influence of ESD principles in its reasoning. These stages of legal development constitute the five mapping categories of this Part, and they show how the Court has used most available reasoning techniques at its disposal (including using ESD principles to interpret ambiguous legislation and to generate legal tests, as well as implying their legal relevance within various decision-making processes), to find that ESD principles are legally required 'relevant considerations' in relation to the full range of cases before the Court, building a comprehensive and entrenched body of doctrine involving ESD principles across its case law.

In the first mapping category, the Court finds ESD principles to be mandatory considerations in relation to planning consent decisions under the Environmental Planning and Assessment Act 1979—the statute most frequently considered by the

---

[116] Preston, 'Leadership by the Courts' (n 2).
[117] *Corowa v Geographe Point* [2007] NSWLEC 121; (2007) 154 LGERA 117 [81].

Court—by employing ESD principles to interpret key statutory provisions. These planning decisions are both made by the Court (in merits appeals) and legally reviewed by it (in judicial review actions). The doctrinal role of ESD principles in both types of actions before the Court is the same, since merits review cases apply the decision-making requirements of administrative law doctrine that are reviewed in judicial review cases. In the second category, the Court finds that ESD principles both inform and generate more particular legal steps in the different processes of planning consent decision-making under the EPA Act, so that they are relevant considerations across different types and at multiple stages of planning decision-making under the Act.

In the third mapping category, the Court employs ESD principles as mandatory considerations in relation to decisions under a wide range of statutes that refer jurisdiction to the Court and which also have ESD objects, progressing the doctrinal role of ESD principles beyond the scope of the EPA Act. In the fourth category, the doctrinal use of ESD principles in NSWLEC cases evolves further so that the Court adopts the principles implicitly as legally required relevant considerations in its reasoning, irrespective of the legislative frameworks involved, confirming the widespread doctrinal roles of ESD principles in NSWLEC reasoning. Fifth, the Court's progressive doctrinal reasoning in relation to ESD principles is confirmed by the use of ESD principles in all aspects of its jurisdiction, from judicial review and merits review actions, to costs decisions to sentencing decisions in environmental crime cases. Statements by the Court confirm that it sees such doctrinal infusion of ESD principles as part of its institutional duty as an environmental court.[118] In sum, these five mapping categories depict a comprehensive body of ESD doctrine in NSWLEC case law, developed through judicial reasoning that has extended its reach in multiple ways.

In contrast to EU cases involving environmental principles, these mapping categories do not involve any 'policy cases'.[119] While there were some early NSWLEC cases suggesting that the precautionary principle was a 'political aspiration' that had no doctrinal role to play in the Court's reasoning,[120] this suggestion was overturned,[121] and overtaken by the tide of progressive doctrinal reasoning involving ESD principles outlined above. There are also cases in which ESD principles are referred to by way of background but are not employed to justify the Court's reasoning in any way.[122] These are left out of the mapping exercise.

The fact that there is no significant group of 'policy cases' in the NSWLEC's ESD case law highlights the doctrinal openness of the Court to ESD principles, and its inclination to capitalise on this. To the extent that the NSWLEC feels need for restraint in its reasoning involving ESD principles, this arises in judicial review decisions in which it highlights that it must not investigate the merits of a decision

---

[118] eg *Hub* (n 1) [2].
[119] As defined in ch 4(III).
[120] eg *Nicholls v Director-General of National Parks & Wildlife Service* (1994) 84 LGERA 397, 419.
[121] *Port Stephens Pearls v Minister for Infrastructure and Planning* [2005] NSWLEC 426 [54].
[122] eg *Blackington v Tweed Shire Council* [2006] NSWLEC 158; (2006) 145 LGERA 160 [16].

in determining whether an ESD principle, as a mandatory relevant consideration, has been properly considered.[123] The Court must attribute an appropriate amount of discretion to the decision-maker whose decision is under review. At the same time, in order to determine whether ESD principles have been relevantly considered, a judicially reviewing court must articulate their meaning on the facts in order to determine their relevance and the extent of their (lack of) consideration, giving marginal meanings to ESD principles. As indicated above, this makes the line between considering the merits and applying relevant legal doctrine very fine in some judicial review cases.[124]

This common law limitation of administrative law does not however curtail the general doctrinal development of ESD principles as relevant considerations, in the way that EU law constitutional limits do in EU cases involving environmental principles. This is particularly because of the extensive number of merits appeals in which ESD principles are legally relevant considerations and thus 'operationalised' on the facts of the case.[125] Again, in these cases, the relevant principles are given (marginal) meanings on the facts in order for the Court to 'consider' the principle and arrive at a decision on the merits. These 'marginal' meanings for ESD principles tend to be much lengthier than those in EU decisions involving environmental principles, since they involve full application of relevant principles to the facts, whereas the EU courts' penetration into factual issues is often limited, either because Member State courts are left to apply the relevant legal conclusion to the facts (in Article 267 TFEU preliminary references), or by their restrained role in reviewing the legality of actions of other EU institutions.[126]

As mentioned in the conclusion to Part II above, a further methodological complication arises due to the extensive fact-finding involved in merits appeals: isolating doctrinal developments can be difficult. This is particularly so in the case of the precautionary principle. Where relevant in merits appeals, consideration of the principle results in definitions of the principle that are marginal in that they are fact-dependent, but in some cases also explicitly doctrinal in that they involve decision-making steps that are intended to constitute precedent for the principle's future application. Isolating doctrinal elements in such decisions can be challenging as they involve complicated factual scenarios where scientific uncertainty is prevalent, within statutory frameworks that involve multiple decision-making steps and which give the Court (as decision-maker) wide discretion, in relation to a principle that is general and ambiguous in meaning. To accommodate this difficulty, this Part's map stays focused on the primary mapping tool of this

---

[123] eg *Drake-Brockman v Minister for Planning* [2007] NSWLEC 490; (2007) 158 LGERA 349 [123]–[124]. See Edgar, 'Between Rules and Discretion' (n 78).

[124] This mirrors the position in EU law that any doctrinal role for a generally stated environmental principle involves attributing to it a marginal meaning: see generally ch 4.

[125] Edgar, 'Institutions and Sustainability' (n 74) 132–133.

[126] Although judicial review of EU institutions is not restrained in all cases, as seen in decisions of the CFI and General Court eg Case T-13/99 *Pfizer Animal Health SA v Council* [2002] ECR II-3305: see ch 4(V)(B)(ii) and (iii).

book—identifying the techniques of reasoning used by the Court in employing environmental principles to justify its decisions—thus demonstrating that these merits appeals involve more than a 'wilderness' of decisions that turned on their own facts.[127] However, the jurisdictional nature of the cases involved in merits appeals gives a different complexion to this map from that in Chapter Four. The judicial treatment of environmental principles is necessarily different in this legal context.

## A. ESD Principles as Legally Relevant Considerations in Determining Planning Consent Decisions under Section 79C EPA Act

The initial, and now most prolific, set of cases in which ESD principles have been used to justify the reasoning of the NSWLEC concern determinations of general planning (or 'development') consent under Part 4 of the EPA Act.[128] In these cases, the primary decision-maker is often a local council as the relevant planning consent authority, even for environmentally sensitive, or so-called 'designated', developments, and most cases are merits appeals.[129] In these cases, the Court predominantly adopts the precautionary principle as a mandatory relevant consideration in deciding planning applications, in merits appeals and also in judicial review actions. Early cases involving this kind of reasoning were outlined in Chapter Three, as they were vehicles for the original derivation of ESD principles in NSW law.[130]

As Australian administrative law doctrine dictates, the relevant considerations that a decision-maker is obliged to take into account are to be determined by the explicit or implicit requirements of the statutory framework governing the relevant decision-making process. In the NSW planning regime, explicit requirements for determining development applications are set out in section 79C(1) EPA Act, which prescribes a list of matters to be taken into account, where relevant, by a consent authority when considering applications for development consent under the Act.[131] The enumerated matters are general and open in their terms, leaving scope for considerable discretion, having evolved from a longer and more particularised list of matters in ex-section 90(1) EPA Act.[132] They include: any relevant

---

[127] Linda Pearson, Carol Harlow and Michael Taggart, *Administrative Law in a Changing State* (Hart 2008) 7.

[128] These are planning applications decided under Part 4 of the EPA Act; *cf* planning applications for major infrastructure developments under the EPA Act (see below section III(B)(iii)).

[129] In relation to designated developments, objectors as well as development proposal applicants have standing to bring merits appeals, albeit within shorter time periods (EPA Act, s 98). Applicants have general rights to bring merits appeals: EPA Act, s 97.

[130] See ch 3(IV)(C)(i).

[131] The NSWLEC is equally constrained to consider these matters in a merits appeal arising from such a decision.

[132] Ex-s 90(1) EPA Act included more detailed matters for consideration in assessing development applications, such as 'the effect of that development on the landscape or scenic quality of the locality'

environmental planning instruments ('EPIs'), the likely impacts of the proposed development (including environmental impacts), the suitability of the site for the development, and the 'public interest'. They do not include ESD principles,[133] and, while they are not exhaustive,[134] their generality leaves scope for the Court to draw on ESD principles to inform its consent decisions, either by informing the listed statutory matters to be considered, or as an additional relevant consideration implied by the statutory framework overall.

From the earliest case law involving ESD principles, and the precautionary principle in particular, the NSWLEC did just this. As set out in Chapter Three, in the early ground-breaking decision *Leatch*,[135] Stein J found that the precautionary principle was a required consideration under a different statutory framework—the National Parks and Wildlife Act 1974 (NSW) ('NPWA')—which required 'any matter considered to be relevant' to be taken into account in decision-making regarding fauna destruction licence applications. Additionally, the LEC Act itself provides that, in all merits appeals, the 'public interest' should be taken into account. On the basis of both these open statutory requirements, Stein J concluded that the precautionary principle was required to be considered on the facts of the case, relying on international agreements and the IGAE to interpret these statutory provisions as including reference to the principle.

In *K A Cox Constructions v Concord Council*[136]—another merits appeal—Bignold J drew on Stein J's reasoning in *Leatch* to find that the 'public interest' consideration in section 79C EPA Act was to be interpreted to include ESD principles. This interpretive step led to a settled path of doctrinal reasoning implicating ESD principles as relevant considerations in subsequent cases, finding that the 'public interest' consideration under the EPA Act includes ecologically sustainable development and the principles that characterise it.[137]

After an increasing number of cases in which the Court adopted the precautionary principle as a relevant consideration in planning consent decisions,[138] the doctrinal role for ESD principles outlined in *Cox Constructions* was confirmed in two authoritative NSWLEC decisions that interpreted the 'public interest'

---

and 'the character, location, siting, bulk, scale, shape, size, height, density, design or external appearance of that development'. This list was rationalised and amended into its present form in s 79C by the Environmental Planning & Assessment Amendment Act 1997 (date of commencement 1/7/1998).

[133] Note Bignold J's surprise, as far back as 1995, that these listed matters have never included ESD principles: *KA Cox Constructions v Concord Council* [1995] NSWLEC 24.

[134] *Carstens* (n 85) [74].

[135] *Leatch v Director General of National Parks and Wildlife Service* (1993) 81 LGERA 270, 282.

[136] *Cox Constructions* (n 133).

[137] Although in some merits appeals, ESD principles were found to be required matters for consideration through other provisions of s 79C(1), with the principles being included in a relevant EPI or other policy instrument which the decision-maker was bound to consider, under s 79C(1)(a)(i) or (iv): eg *Brunsdon* (n 102); *Commonwealth of Australia v Randwick CC* [2001] NSWLEC 79; *Davfast v Ballina Shire Council* [2000] NSWLEC 128; *NSW Glass and Ceramic Silica Sand Users Association Ltd v Port Stephens Council* [2000] NSWLEC 149.

[138] eg *Greenpeace Australia v Redbank Power* [1994] NSWLEC 178; (1994) 86 LGERA 143; *Fitzpatrick Investments v Blacktown CC* [1999] NSWLEC 290.

consideration in section 79C(1) to include ESD principles. These were cases that came after 'ecologically sustainable development' had been included as an object of the EPA Act,[139] but before this ESD object was defined by reference to its IGAE-like articulation in section 6(2) of the Protection of the Environment Administration Act 1991 ('POEA Act'), highlighting again the innovation of the Court's reasoning in interpreting the legal significance of this new statutory object.

The first decision was *Carstens v Pittwater Council*,[140] a judicial review action brought in the Court's Class 4 jurisdiction, appealing a merits review decision by Commissioner Watts below on the question of whether ESD principles must be a factor in assessing a development application under section 79C. In brief reasoning, Lloyd J held that it was not an 'irrelevant consideration' (in the administrative law sense) for a decision-maker to take into account a matter—ESD principles—relating to the objects of the EPA Act. Further, a decision-maker must take into account the 'public interest' in section 79C(1)(e), which included giving effect to ESD as an object of the Act.[141] This judicial review decision confirmed the position in the merits appeal below that ESD principles must be considered a factor in appraising the environmental impact of the relevant development application.[142]

This conclusion was confirmed and expanded in *BGP Properties v Lake Macquarie City Council*.[143] This was a merits review decision, and it is an authoritative articulation of NSWLEC doctrine because it is a 'planning principle'—the first such decision in relation to ESD principles, demonstrating their increasing significance in the law applied by the Court. In this case, McClellan CJ drew on *Carstens* but engaged in more extensive reasoning to find that the ESD principles set out in the IGAE were 'mandatory considerations' for deciding development consent applications.[144] His Honour took into account a range of factors in seeking 'to understand the intention of the Parliament' when including ESD as object of the Act.[145] These included the increasingly large number of NSW statutes that use the 'description' of ESD, finding that these had a common object in ameliorating the impact of private and government action on the environment.[146] McClellan CJ also drew on the Rio Declaration and previous international developments (from

[139] EPA Act, s 5.

[140] *Carstens* (n 85).

[141] ibid [74].

[142] Brian Preston, as he then was, was counsel for the respondent council in this case. He has since become Chief Judge of the NSWLEC and continued the innovative doctrinal reasoning he argued for in *Carstens* in later cases. The arguments he adduced in *Carstens* included that ESD was now an explicit object of the Act; ESD principles are relevant to many of the 'generic' s 79C categories; the 'desirability of an administrative decision-maker exercising discretionary statutory powers in a way which promotes the objects of the Act'; the facts, which concerned a threatened ecological community; and the acceptance of the relevance of ESD principles to environmental decision-making internationally, nationally and in NSW previously: ibid [73].

[143] *BGP* (n 102).

[144] ibid [113].

[145] ibid [85].

[146] ibid [87].

which ESD principles 'derived'),[147] the IGAE (which, whilst not legally binding on local government authorities, 'reflects the policy which should be applied unless there are cogent reasons to depart from it'),[148] and the NSWLEC's previous case law adopting the precautionary principle as a relevant consideration in determining development consent applications.[149]

These legal influences, in combination, led McClellan CJ to find that the 'public interest' consideration in section 79C(1)(e) EPA Act:[150]

> obliges the decision-maker to have regard to the principles of ecologically sustainable development in cases where issues relevant to those principles arise. This will have the consequence that, amongst other matters, consideration must be given to matters of inter-generational equity, conservation of biological diversity and ecological integrity. Furthermore, where there is a lack of scientific certainty, the precautionary principle must be utilised. As Stein J said in *Leatch*, this will mean that the decision-maker must approach the matter with caution but will also require the decision-maker to avoid, where practicable, serious or irreversible damage to the environment.

Thus McClellan CJ interpreted section 79C(1)(e) to find that the ESD principles contained in the IGAE were mandatory in considering development consent applications under the EPA Act. In doing so, he relied on international and national influences, as well as NSW legal developments. This reasoning does not however demonstrate a simple application of environmental principles derived from international environmental law; rather, it demonstrates that the Court was appealing to a range of relevant sources to lend authority to its innovative doctrinal reasoning. It is the legal innovation of the Court's reasoning that is so remarkable, linking to transnational norms concerning environmental principles but nevertheless remaining embedded in the particular inquiry and statutory framework that arose in this case. The openness of the Court to transnational legal influences is an important feature of the Court's culture, allowing it to draw inspiration and authority from international sources to support and inform localised legal developments.

Another significant aspect of how ESD principles are implicated doctrinally in *BGP* is McClellan CJ's indication that the NSWLEC would give general ESD principles their own meanings. He elaborates the meaning of the precautionary principle by relying on the previous NSWLEC decision in *Leatch*, supplementing this with an obligation that decision-makers should avoid serious environmental damage. This results in a version of the precautionary principle that is reminiscent of the IGAE formulation but different in emphasis, since it includes a positive

---

[147] ibid [90]–[91].
[148] ibid [92], citing *Re Drake and Minister for Immigration and Ethnic Affairs (No 2)* (1979) 2 ALD 634 at 641, 645. See ch 3, text accompanying nn 244–248.
[149] *BGP* (n 102) [100]–[112]. McClellan CJ also here referred to the landmark case of the South Australian Supreme Court (on appeal from the Environmental Resources and Development Court in that State) in *Tuna Boat Owners Association (No 2)* (n 8), in which the precautionary principle was considered in detail and applied.
[150] *BGP* (n 102) [113].

obligation to take preventive action. Further than this, however, McClellan CJ does not give a precise definition of the precautionary principle, or of any other principle, since its application in any planning consent decision will depend on the facts, and thus give rise to marginal definitions, or applications, of the relevant principle. The precautionary principle indeed gave rise to an array of definitions in early NSWLEC planning consent decisions.[151]

By focusing on reasoning techniques rather than definitions of environmental principles, this first mapping category has demonstrated the first stage of doctrinal innovation of the NSWLEC in relation to ESD principles: finding them to be mandatory considerations in determining planning consent decisions under Part 4 of the EPA Act.[152] This innovation was influenced by international and national and policy developments relating to sustainable development, as well as NSW legislative developments, and the precedential force of the Court's own case law. This latter influence confirms that the NSWLEC engages in doctrinal reasoning in its merits review jurisdiction, and that the case law in that jurisdiction acts as a form of precedent. Furthermore, the doctrinal crossover in determining the legal relevance of ESD principles in both judicial review and merits review cases confirms the respective contributions of these two types of case to the Court's evolving body of 'environmental law' doctrine.

## B. ESD Principles as Legally Relevant Considerations Informing Decision-making Processes under the EPA Act

The second mapping category tracks a progression in NSWLEC ESD reasoning: the use of ESD principles to inform and structure decision-making under the EPA Act more comprehensively. This section considers three ways in which this reasoning develops, deepening the doctrinal relevance of ESD principles in NSWLEC case law as markers that define processes of lawful administrative decision-making in the planning context. Each constitutes a body of doctrinal development relating to decision-making steps or processes that are required under the EPA Act. First, the precautionary principle, where a relevant consideration under section 79C(1), itself generates decision-making steps that structure the decision-making process for development consent. This function of the precautionary principle is established in the second 'planning principle' case involving ESD principles—*Telstra Corp Ltd v Hornsby Shire Council*. This case

---

[151] These definitions concern both *when* the principle was relevant on particular facts—ie when there is relevant 'scientific uncertainty' (*Leatch* (n 135); *Nicholls* (n 120); *cf Vertical Telecoms v Hornsby Shire Council* [2000] NSWLEC 172; *NTL Australia Ltd v Willoughby Council* [2000] NSWLEC 244; *cf Brunsdon* (n 102))—and *how* it was to be be applied to determine the development application under consideration (*Leatch* (n 135); *cf Terrace Tower Holdings v Sutherland Shire Council [No2]* [2002] NSWLEC 150; (2002) 122 LGERA 288; *cf Greenpeace* (n 138)).

[152] For a more recent case where a planning consent decision was annulled for failure to take into account ESD principles, see *South East Forest Rescue* (n 85) [158]–[163].

marks a turning point in the NSWLEC's ESD case law, acting as a foundation for a range of doctrinal developments relating to the precautionary principle that follow. Second, the precautionary principle is used to inform the process of screening for impact assessments, defining another aspect of the decision-making process in planning applications. In particular, the issue of whether a development application requires a species impact statement (SIS) is construed as a 'jurisdictional fact'—that is, a legal question—which is informed by application of the precautionary principle. Third, ESD principles inform special consent procedures for major projects, highlighting a real tension between the legal relevance of ESD principles in planning decisions and the proper role of the Court in reviewing major projects. In these three ways, ESD principles have become ingrained in the planning decision-making processes required under the EPA Act through the Court's progressive reasoning.

### i. Structuring Precautionary Decision-making: Telstra Corporation Ltd v Hornsby Shire Council

A prime example of how ESD principles are used to inform intermediary decision-making steps in EPA Act planning consent decisions is seen in the landmark ESD case, *Telstra Corporation Ltd v Hornsby Shire Council*.[153] This second 'planning principle' case focuses on the precautionary principle and its application by decision-makers in the planning context. In this case, the Court continued its innovative path for identifying legally relevant ESD principles, building on NSW legislative developments, but embracing an ESD agenda of its own, inspired by extensive international, national and academic sources to move its case law on. In order to justify *Telstra*'s path-breaking reasoning, Preston CJ considered different (legal and interdisciplinary) scholarly accounts of the precautionary principle, differing applications of the principle in other jurisdictions (including in EU law), and different formulations of the principles in various policy contexts, including drawing on the international sustainable development agenda.[154] However, rather than directly applying all these sources of authority (which would have been impossible since they pointed in many different directions in relation to the principles' meaning and application),[155] Preston CJ drew on them to give authority to his reasoning.[156] Further, his reliance on international developments reveals how Preston CJ sees this judgment as an important step in applying ESD principles internationally, through which might be realised a 'paradigm shift [to a world] where a culture of sustainability extends

---

[153] *Telstra* (n 8).
[154] ibid eg [108]–[112]; [130]–[138]; [144]–[149].
[155] Not to mention the problems of comparative law methodology this raises: Fisher, *Risk Regulation* (n 12) 158. See ch 2(III)(A)(iii).
[156] Edgar highlights how this is unusual as a mode of reasoning in the Australian common law context: Edgar, 'Institutions and Sustainability' (n 74) 72–73.

to institutions, private development interests, communities and individuals'.[157] In this way, ESD principles embody a sustainability agenda that motivates the Court's legal reasoning.

In *Telstra*, the Court aimed to rationalise its growing body of case law involving the precautionary principle in development consent decisions under the EPA Act to set a precedent for consistent decision-making applying the principle. In so doing, the Court did not simply find that the precautionary principle was a mandatory relevant consideration under section 79C of the Act, but that the principle generated tests and decision-making steps that must be met, or undertaken, in properly considering and applying the principle in development consent decisions.[158] This progressive doctrinal development in the Court's reasoning is particular to the precautionary principle, which is cryptic in its meaning and a popular site of controversy and argument in environmental planning disputes, due to the scientific uncertainty involved in so many environmental disputes,[159] and the often interminable arguments the precautionary principle invites in its various ambiguous formulations. The decision in *Telstra* also moves beyond the common law question of what relevant considerations need to be taken into account in decision-making (and whether this has happened) to examine *how* that taking into account should happen with respect to the generally-stated precautionary principle. The Court's merits review jurisdiction makes this deeper doctrinal inquiry possible, and necessary. The legal interpretation of the precautionary principle is 'forged in the fire' of this merits appeal.[160]

The case itself was a merits appeal from Hornsby Shire Council's refusal to approve, under section 79C EPA Act, Telstra's planning application to erect a mobile phone tower in a residential area where there was significant community opposition to its construction, on the basis of suggested harm to human health and the precautionary principle in particular. Having first found that ESD principles were required matters for consideration under section 79C's 'public interest' provision, Preston CJ went on to consider the application of the precautionary principle, which had been the basis of objecting to the proposed development. In doing so, his Honour identified two intermediary decision-making steps required by the principle, which led to a shifting of the burden of proof in the decision-making process and a need to take appropriate preventive measures where the principle is 'activated'. The initial decision-making steps are separate but cumulative threshold tests that must be satisfied before the precautionary principle applies as a mandatory relevant consideration in planning consent decisions. First, a relevant threat of serious or irreversible environmental harm must be established, and second, there must be scientific uncertainty as to the environmental

---

157 *Telstra* (n 8) [120].
158 As a planning principle, it might be categorised as a 'process-oriented' principle: see above n 106.
159 *Tuna Boat Owners (No 2)* (n 8) [22].
160 Edgar, 'Institutions and Sustainability' (n 74) 74.

damage.[161] His Honour structured these as separate decision-making steps generated by the principle.[162]

Drawing on previous NSWLEC decisions concerning the potential effects of electromagnetic radiation (EMR) on residential dwellings,[163] Preston CJ explained several aspects of the first threshold test: it required the establishment of both a threat and its seriousness or irreversibility. Threats included direct, indirect, cumulative, and long-term threats. Assessing seriousness or irreversibility of threatened damage is a complex fact-dependent business that required considering a range of factors, including interdisciplinary and stakeholder assessment, and it also required a scientific basis that is 'adequate'.[164] It was this final element of the decision-making step or test required by the principle—the existence of an adequate scientific basis for the purported threat—that was decisive on the facts of this case. Since the proposed mobile phone tower complied with an 'authoritative and scientifically credible' EMR standard that it was inappropriate 'to set aside or disregard',[165] no threat of serious harm was made out, and the precautionary principle did not apply in this case. This is the doctrinal heart of this decision and it involved the generation of a legal test of 'adequate scientific evidence', reminiscent of that in EU law, for the proper application of the precautionary principle as a mandatory relevant consideration in NSWLEC decisions, and the planning consent decisions that it oversees under the EPA Act. Preston CJ's reasoning adapted 'principles of proper administrative decision-making' in NSW administrative law to unpack the doctrinal implications of the precautionary principle in this merits review decision—common law principles require that a decision-maker should not act without 'probative evidence' in exercising discretion. Such evidence existed in this case, sufficient to dismiss public fear about EMR as 'irrational'.[166]

As for the second threshold test—scientific uncertainty—this related to the nature and scope of the threatened environmental harm.[167] However, aside from stating this decision-making step as required, Preston CJ did not elaborate a precise test for its legal application. His Honour discussed a number of different types of scientific uncertainty,[168] including insufficiency of evidence, methodological and technical uncertainty,[169] and otherwise left this aspect of the precautionary principle to its marginal application in particular cases on their facts. In cases following *Telstra*, the Court has had to deal with a range of fact-finding possibilities

---

[161] *Telstra* (n 8) [128].
[162] See Peel for a criticism of this approach: Jacqueline Peel, 'When (Scientific) Rationality Rules: (Mis)Application of the Precautionary Principle in Australian Mobile Phone Tower Cases' (2007) 19 *JEL* 103.
[163] *Telstra* (n 8) [185].
[164] ibid [134].
[165] ibid [98].
[166] ibid [200]–[207].
[167] ibid [140].
[168] From one that operates in a relationship of inverse proportionality with the level of threat, to one of 'considerable scientific uncertainty', to one of 'reasonable scientific plausibility': ibid [146]–[148].
[169] ibid [141].

in determining whether requisite scientific uncertainty existed. For example, in *Hamilton v Sutherland Shire Council*,[170] Commissioner Fakes focused on the insufficiency of evidence concerning whether the removal of a tree would result in the loss of current habitat for an unknown number of species, having found that there was a threat of serious environmental harm on the facts.[171] In this case, there was simply no data collected on the species that might be affected, just 'incidental sightings of birds and a perhaps a possum'.[172] Accordingly, there was requisite scientific uncertainty and the precautionary principle was activated. By contrast, in *SHCAG Pty Ltd v Minister for Planning and Infrastructure and Boral Cement Limited*,[173] methodological certainty was at issue since studies concerning the impact of mining operations on groundwater hydrology were based on modelling and assumptions and inadequately backed up by actual monitoring data. Again, the Court found that there was relevant scientific uncertainty and that the precautionary principle was activated. These cases are fleshing out the normative direction set in *Telstra* concerning when the precautionary principle properly applies.

In the 'planning principle' reasoning of *Telstra*, Preston CJ went on to set out what happens next in planning decision-making if the precautionary principle is activated (even though it was not activated in this case). He held that there are two consequences for decision-making based on the principle: first, the burden of proof shifts for the decision-maker, and second, the decision-maker must determine what appropriate precautionary action should be taken. Preston CJ explained how the precautionary principle 'shifts' the burden of proof:[174]

> The function of the precautionary principle is, therefore, to require the decision-maker to assume that there is, or will be, a serious or irreversible threat of environmental damage and to take this into account, notwithstanding that there is a degree of scientific uncertainty about whether the threat really exists... [T]he shifting of the evidentiary burden of proof operates in relation to only one input of the decision-making process— the question of environmental damage. If a proponent of a plan, programme or project fails to discharge the burden to prove that there is no threat of serious or irreversible environmental damage, this does not necessarily mean that the plan, programme or project must be refused.

This led into the Court's guidance on what measures should be taken when the precautionary principle is activated. Drawing on EU law,[175] amongst other international legal and academic sources, the Court found that measures adopted

---

[170] *Hamilton v Sutherland Shire Council* [2012] NSWLEC 1015.

[171] See also *Darkinjung Local Aboriginal Land Council v Minister for Planning and Infrastructure & Anor* [2015] NSWLEC 1465.

[172] *Hamilton v Sutherland Shire Council* (n 170) 71.

[173] *SHCAG Pty Ltd v Minister for Planning and Infrastructure and Boral Cement Limited* [2013] NSWLEC 1032.

[174] *Telstra* (n 8) [152].

[175] In particular, Preston CJ drew on the Commission Communication on the precautionary principle, the requirement for 'proportionality' in the context of the precautionary principle, and the overall discretion granted by the principle to take precautionary measures (drawing on *Pfizer* and other EU cases): ibid [156], [158]–[159], [168], [170].

should be proportionate (taking into account the costs of the project and other ESD principles); they should not aim at a 'zero risk precautionary standard'; and that the precaution principle does not necessarily prohibit development.[176] The central guide is that 'the type and level of precautionary measures that will be appropriate will depend on the combined effect of the degree of seriousness and irreversibility of the threat and the degree of uncertainty'.[177] Preston CJ also recommended that a 'margin for error should be retained until all the consequences of the decision to proceed with the development plan, programme or project are known'.[178] He suggested that one such approach is 'a step-wise or adaptive management approach'.[179] This reasoning is all remarkable for the level of detail in which it prescribes how decision-makers should apply the precautionary principle. It shows how the Court is not only prescribing a decision-making process but is also having 'an important role in the development of sustainability principles and making them operational' in a substantive sense.[180] The power of this reasoning in setting a precedent for the application of the precautionary principle has been seen in subsequent cases, where these guidelines for applying the precautionary principle have been followed closely.[181] This is in both merits review and judicial review cases, although the determination of appropriate preventive measures by the Court is only carried out in merits appeals.[182]

The reasoning in *Telstra* is a prime example of the novel doctrine being developed by the Court in NSW law—expanding the role of ESD principles as mandatory relevant considerations that inform and generate decision-making steps in Part 4 EPA Act planning consent decisions—as well as being an explicit statement of the ESD agenda pursued by the Court. While many of the decision-making steps generated by the precautionary principle were visible in previous NSWLEC decisions, and the decision itself focuses on planning consent decisions under section 79C EPA Act, the legal nature of *Telstra*'s reasoning is of a different order. As a precedent-setting planning principle in the Court's merits review jurisdiction, it was intended to resonate as doctrine more broadly in NSW law, marking a turn in the Court's reasoning with respect to ESD principles. This is demonstrated by its extensive citation in subsequent NSWLEC decisions—across classes of its jurisdiction,

---

[176] ibid [156]–[178].
[177] ibid [161].
[178] ibid [162].
[179] ibid [163].
[180] Edgar, 'Between Rules and Discretion' (n 78) 133.
[181] eg *Barrington—Gloucester—Stroud Preservation Alliance Inc v Minister for Planning and Infrastructure* [2012] NSWLEC 197; (2012) 194 LGERA 113; *Darkinjung Local Aboriginal Land Council* (n 171); *Friends of Tumblebee Incorporated v ATB Morton Pty Limited (No 2)* [2016] NSWLEC 16; (2016) 215 LGERA 157.
[182] eg *SHCAG* (n 173) (finding that the proposed water management plan could not be categorised as an appropriate adaptive management plan that would satisfy the precautionary principle); *Newcastle and Hunter Valley Speleological Society Inc v Upper Hunter Shire Council and anor* [2010] NSWLEC 48; (2010) 210 LGERA 126 (applying an adaptive management approach through consent conditions requiring monitoring).

as the following sections demonstrate—and in decisions of the NSWCA,[183] as the NSWLEC's supervisory Court. After *Telstra*, the Court was emboldened to find ESD principles to be required relevant considerations in an even wider range of legal contexts, with decreasing need to justify itself in doing so.

## ii. ESD Principles and Impact Assessment Screening: Informing Jurisdictional Facts

Another way in which the Court has used ESD principles to structure steps in planning decision-making processes—even before the Court's decision in *Telstra*—is in informing the issue of whether a species impact statement (SIS) is legally required for determining a development application under the EPA Act. Sections 78A(8)(b) and 112(1B) of the Act explicitly set out the test for when an SIS is required in relation to proposed 'developments' and 'activities' respectively: whether a development is 'likely to significantly affect threatened species, populations or ecological communities, or their habitats'. In a series of NSWLEC 'SIS screening' cases, involving conflicting expert evidence as to the existence of threatened species or their habitats, or about the impact of a proposed development and activities on such species, the precautionary principle has been used to interpret and inform this openly stated test.[184] These cases involve a range of actions in which this screening issue has been raised, including judicial review actions, merits review actions, and actions preliminary to merits appeals. Again ESD principles, and particularly the precautionary principle, are employed to build NSWLEC doctrine around this issue, acting as legally relevant considerations in a different sense—informing whether the intermediary step of producing a SIS is required in the lawful determination of consent applications under the EPA Act.

The reasoning technique used by the Court to extend its use of ESD principles to inform the section 78A(8)(b) test involved moving beyond interpreting the 'public interest' consideration in section 79C to a broader analysis under the Act. Thus, in *BT Goldsmith*, Pain J found that the EPA Act was an Act that adopted the precautionary principle (and all ESD principles) through its objects clause,[185] with the consequence that:[186]

> the application of the precautionary principle is not merely confined to the final decision as to whether development consent, a licence or approval ought be granted. Rather,

---

[183] *Minister for Planning v Walker* (n 86); *Warkworth v Bulga* (n 91).

[184] *Cooper v Wollondilly Shire Council* [2004] NSWLEC 145; *BT Goldsmith Planning Services v Blacktown CC* [2005] NSWLEC 210; *Gales Holdings v Tweed Shire Council* [2006] NSWLEC 85; (2006) 146 LGERA 236 (see also [2006] NSWLEC 212); *Corowa* (n 117); *Providence Projects v Gosford CC* [2006] NSWLEC 52; (2007) 147 LGERA 274); *Parks and Playgrounds Movement Inc v Newcastle City Council* [2010] NSWLEC 231; (2010) 179 LGERA 346; *Friends of Tumblebee* (n 181). A similar approach has been taken in screening for environmental impact assessment, which is required where a proposed activity is 'likely to significantly affect the environment': *SHCAG Pty Ltd v Hume Coal Pty Ltd* [2015] NSWLEC 122 [208]–[212].

[185] *BT Goldsmith* (n 184) [57].

[186] ibid [72].

decision-makers must consider the precautionary principle whenever decisions are being made under an Act that adopts the precautionary principle as is the case here.

Similarly Bignold J, in *Providence Projects*, found that there is 'legitimacy' in applying the precautionary principle to the various decision-making duties imposed by the EPA Act, beyond simply determining the final result of development applications.[187] This is a progressive extension in Court's reasoning, which is further developed in later mapping categories to give ESD principles doctrinal force in their own right in NSWLEC decisions.[188]

In an ongoing body of case law, the Court uses the precautionary principle to inform the test of whether a proposed development is 'likely to significantly affect' a threatened species or habitat, in order to justify its resolution on the particular facts involved. In doing so, marginal meanings are given to the principle, which are highly fact-dependent. In some cases, the principle informs the test by requiring an SIS where there is conflicting evidence about the existence of a threatened species,[189] or about the impact of a proposed development on a threatened habitat.[190] In other cases again, the principle requires an SIS where there is scientific uncertainty about a development plan to rehabilitate a threatened species,[191] or the principle might only require an SIS where the evidence of potential impact on a threatened species was 'significant' or sufficiently 'weighty'.[192] In *Friends of Tumblebee Incorporated v ATB Morton Pty Limited (No 2)*,[193] the Court identified 10 different kinds of scientific uncertainty relating to the environmental harm or damage that might be caused to a critically endangered species of bird (the Regent Honeyeaters) by the proposed construction of a steel fabrication workshop and distribution facility in this case. The Court identified these types of uncertainty—to show that the threshold test of the precautionary principle was satisfied and thus applicable in this case—by engaging in a lengthy appraisal of the expert factual evidence heard by the Court in this judicial review claim. In judicial review doctrine, this factual assessment was permissible since the valid exercise of power under review turned on the determination of a 'jurisdictional fact'.

This fact-dependency in the application of the precautionary principle—in both judicial review and merits review actions—also reflects the institutional identity of the Court which, as a specialist environmental court, routinely resolves technical factual issues on the merits. This does not detract from the doctrinal significance of this case law in applying the precautionary principle to inform the section 78A(8)(b) test; in fact, it constitutes a novel legal development in the Court's environmental law, as has been highlighted by the Court itself. When confronted with the question of whether NSWLEC SIS screening actions were akin to

[187] *Providence Projects* (n 184) [69], [76].
[188] See below Sections III(D) & (E).
[189] eg *Gales Holdings* (n 184).
[190] eg *Providence Projects* (n 184).
[191] eg *Gales Holdings* (n 184).
[192] eg *Corowa* (n 117) [81].
[193] *Friends of Tumblebee* (n 181).

'ordinary litigation' rather than merits review (so that a different costs rule should apply), Talbot J found that these cases were more like merits review but struggled to characterise them legally:[194]

> [It] is not a black and white situation. There are issues of fact and degree, judgement, discretion and balance required to determine whether a species impact statement is required. Ultimately if doubt remains then the precautionary principle applies so that the Court errs on the side of caution. These are not matters that are capable of clear and precise [legal] definition and characterisation.

The NSWCA has similarly struggled to characterise the legal nature of these SIS screening actions, finding them to involve 'questions of law' for the purposes of administrative law oversight at common law, but adapting the administrative law doctrine of 'jurisdictional fact' to the unique nature of the Court (particularly with its expertise in resolving scientific questions in its merits review jurisdiction) to reach this conclusion.[195] Elizabeth Fisher describes how these species impact assessment screening decisions occupy a twilight legal area of administrative law, where the legal pluralism of the Court meets the legal formalism of common law doctrine. Reviewing such decisions is conceptually challenging since there is a need 'to reconcile the discretionary nature of these decisions with the fundamental role they play in determining when, and how, the power of a decision-maker will be exercised'.[196] Again, common law doctrines of administrative law need to be applied within in the legal context of the NSWLEC, where determining legal issues often requires the consideration of complex factual scenarios. It is in this idiosyncratic legal landscape that the precautionary principle has a doctrinal role. That role is significant not simply in that it extends the roles of ESD principles into more intricate legal steps in administrative decision-making under the EPA Act, but also because it exposes the evolving and novel nature of the 'environmental law' in the NSWLEC.

It should also be noted that, in these jurisdictional fact cases, the reasoning involving the precautionary principle draws on *Telstra* in framing how the precautionary principle informs the relevant screening tests, linking together the reasoning on these different questions of planning law 'in the context of the EPA Act which includes the precautionary principle as part of [its] objects of that Act'.[197] *Telstra* also set the scene for the next set of cases in which ESD principles inform lawful decision-making in the NSW planning system.

### iii. Planning Decision-making for Major Projects and ESD Principles

This set of ESD cases concerns a different type of decision-making under the EPA Act. They are appeals from planning consent decisions for major project and

---

[194] *Gales Holdings Pty Limited v Tweed Shire Council* [2006] NSWLEC 591 [12].
[195] *Timbarra* (n 96) [88]–[90]. See also *Segal v Waverley Council* [2005] NSWCA 310; (2005) 64 NSWLR 177.
[196] Fisher, '"Jurisdictional" Facts and "Hot" Facts' (n 6) 985 and generally.
[197] *SHCAG Pty Ltd v Hume Coal* (n 184) [209]–[212]. See also *Parks and Playgrounds Movement Inc* (n 184) [152].

infrastructure developments, on both questions of law (judicial review) and on the merits (merits review). This legal context was legislatively designed for minimal judicial oversight so that the legal application of ESD principles by the Court is particularly controversial. Between 2005 and 2011,[198] large-scale and sensitive development in NSW was approved not through the Part 4 consent procedure, but through a more streamlined Ministerial procedure under Part 3A of the EPA Act. Before its repeal in 2011,[199] Part 3A set out a complex statutory procedure for approving such development, outlining a highly specific legal context for these cases, with apparently limited opportunities for considering ESD principles. This statutory context proved controversial:[200]

> Some of the main criticisms levelled at Part 3A revolve around the lack of local government autonomy, the lack of appeal rights, the reduction in community consultation and a decreasing emphasis on environmental considerations.

In this legal setting, the doctrinal progressiveness of the Court's ESD reasoning was remarkable. Whilst Part 3A has now been repealed, the Court's reasoning in Part 3A appeals[201] starkly demonstrated the developing jurisprudence of the Court around ESD principles, reflecting its ESD agenda and the Court's evolving legal culture, as well as the tension between this developing doctrine and the 'proper' role Court in judicial review cases.

In contrast to the EPA Act's Part 4 consent procedure, Part 3A did not set out an open-ended list of factors that the planning Minister was required to take into account in approving 'critical infrastructure projects' (so designated by the Minister, including for environmental reasons).[202] In particular, there was no statutory requirement to consider the 'public interest', which might be interpreted by reference to ESD principles. Part 3A also provided less opportunity for appeal by unsuccessful applicants or objectors since there were only limited avenues of merits appeal to the Court available, with none available for 'critical infrastructure projects' or projects that had been through a public inquiry.[203] Part 3A was designed to give the Minister as much discretion as possible, which in turn limited the Court's role in controlling his or her decision-making.

However, the Minister was required to take into account some matters in evaluating critical infrastructure projects, in particular a report of the Director-General of the Planning Department,[204] which was required to include a number of items including: any advice from public authorities in relation to the project, a copy of the proponent's (applicant's) environmental assessment (EA), and 'a statement

---

[198] Environmental Planning and Assessment Amendment (Infrastructure and Other Planning Reform) Act 2005 (NSW).

[199] Environmental Planning and Assessment Amendment (Part 3A Repeal) Act 2011.

[200] Kristian Ruming, 'Cutting Red Tape or Cutting Local Capacity? Responses by Local Government Planners to NSW Planning Changes' (2011) 48(1) *Australian Planner* 46, 47.

[201] Including transitional appeals since 2011.

[202] EPA Act, s 75C(1).

[203] EPA Act, ss 75K, 75L.

[204] EPA Act, s 75J.

relating to compliance with the environmental assessment requirements' with respect to the proposed project.[205] These environmental assessment requirements (EARs) were determined by the Director-General and tailored to the particular project, in accordance with any guidelines that had been published by the Minister and taking into account key issues raised by relevant public authorities.[206] The project proponent was separately required to prepare an environmental assessment—this was not explicitly required to meet the EARs but the Director-General could require the proponent to submit a revised assessment if it did not do so and he or she must 'accept' the EA before making it publicly available.[207] After this EA process, which involved elements of public consultation, the Minister had a final report to consider in making his approval decision, with little recourse for challenge as to his decision.

A further complexity in this Part 3A process is that a major infrastructure project could first be designed as a 'concept plan' for which Ministerial approval was sought as a preliminary stage in the planning process.[208] The purpose of this procedure was for developers to determine whether the significant investment involved in getting a large-scale project off the ground was worth it. In the case of a concept plan approval, the Minister was also required to consider a Director-General report, prepared in the same way described above, and he could also find that no further EA of the project was required or, conversely, that a further EA was required at a future stage.[209] Not only were merits appeals also restricted in the case of concept plan approvals, not being available for critical infrastructure projects at all,[210] but any objector appeals in respect of final Part 3A project approvals were disallowed if there has been a concept plan approval.[211]

The result of this procedure was that challenges to plans for major developments often needed to be made early, or by way of judicial review. This is seen in the case law. Judicial review actions are more common and, even in these cases, the Court's ESD reasoning is remarkable for way in which ESD principles still play significant legal roles despite the constrained statutory context into which they must fit. These cases also display a real tension between accepting ESD principles—which prescribe policy ideas—as legally relevant considerations, and the nature of the judicial review task, which should not impermissibly stray into the merits of decision-making.

The first prominent judicial review case was *Gray v Minister for Planning*, in which Pain J used ESD principles to conclude that the Part 3A process in relation to a planning application for a coal mine project had been flawed.[212] At the time

[205] EPA Act, s 75I.
[206] EPA Act, s 75F.
[207] EPA Act, s 75H.
[208] EPA Act, pt 3A, div 2.
[209] EPA Act, ss 75N–75P.
[210] EPA Act, s 75Q.
[211] EPA Act, s 75L.
[212] *Gray* (n 85).

of this case, the Minister had not yet made a decision on whether to approve the mine. Rather, the Director-General had published EARs, which included 'air quality—including a detailed greenhouse gas assessment', and the applicant had provided an EA that included a limited assessment of greenhouse gases (GHGs). The assessment was limited in that it considered energy consumption and GHG emissions from the mine project itself, but not potential emissions from the burning of coal sold on to third parties (known as 'Scope 3 emissions').[213] Pain J found that the Part 3A process had not been properly followed because these Scope 3 omissions were omitted from the applicant's EA, in breach of the principle of intergenerational equity and the precautionary principle (that is, two ESD principles). The doctrinal reasoning involved in reaching this conclusion was complicated. Initially, Pain J struggled to find any requirements with respect to the content of an EA at all in Part 3A, particularly since there was no explicit requirement that an EA should comply with the Director-General's EARs, leaving maximum discretion in the process for the Director-General as well as the Minister. This also meant that there was no obviously justiciable decision to challenge in a judicial review action. However, Pain J construed the Director-General's duty to 'accept' the EA before publishing it as requiring him to find that it complied with the relevant EARs.[214] This allowed Pain J to explore whether the Director-General had made that finding lawfully, according to administrative law doctrine.

Pain J then examined whether the Director-General had failed to consider mandatory relevant considerations in appraising the EA's compliance with the EARs. Her Honour looked to the 'substantial judicial pronouncement' of *Telstra*, and the (by now) considerable NSWLEC case law confirming the importance of ESD principles for decision-makers under Acts that adopt the principles,[215] and concluded that 'all decisions under the EPA Act require that ESD principles be considered in any event'.[216] Thus the broad discretion of the Director-General was to be exercised in accordance with ESD principles.[217]

Having made this finding that ESD principles generally are mandatory relevant considerations to be taken into account, Pain J then determined whether they were in fact relevant on the facts of this case, and, if so, whether they were taken into account. This aspect of her reasoning required her to engage with questions of fact, overlapping with the 'merits' of the case, thereby giving marginal meanings to the two ESD principles involved.

In the context of Part 3A's EA requirement, the principle of intergenerational equity was applicable in this case because a critical part of implementing the principle was assessing 'cumulative impacts' on the environment, which included the major component of GHG emissions that results from the use of coal caused by

---

[213] 'Scope 3 emissions' is the terminology used in an internationally accepted methodology for assessing GHGs adopted by the applicant in its EA.

[214] *Gray* (n 85) [105].

[215] See Section III(C) below.

[216] *Gray* (n 85) [114].

[217] ibid [115].

Scope 3 emissions. Thus there had been a failure of the 'legal requirement' to consider the principle of intergenerational equity by the Director-General's acceptance of the applicant's EA with no reference to Scope 3 emissions. With respect to the precautionary principle, Pain J engaged in awkward reasoning to find that it was applicable, since the Director-General's decision was not concerned with the final approval of the project to which the application of the precautionary principle would be relevant, if the two thresholds in *Telstra* were met. Suspecting that it would be applicable at that stage, Pain J found that the precautionary principle also had relevance in relation to the EA and its GHG assessment. This was because 'inherent' in the precautionary principle was 'an assessment of the risk-weighted consequences for various options' to allow for 'careful evaluation to avoid serious or irreversible damage', in accordance with the section 6(2) POEA Act definition of the principle.[218] Since the role of environmental impact assessment is crucial as a 'precautionary enabling device', providing sufficient information concerning scientific uncertainty in relation to the serious, irreversible threat of climate change, and to assess risk-weighted consequences of options in relation to the coal mine project, the applicant's EA had failed to satisfy the precautionary principle by leaving out Scope 3 emissions. This was a 'failure to comply with a legal requirement',[219] by leaving out the consideration of the precautionary principle, as defined on the facts, which was a mandatory consideration.

After the bold doctrinal implication of ESD principles as mandatory relevant considerations in decisions under Part 3A in *Gray*, Jagot J delivered a more restrained judgment in *Drake-Brockman*.[220] This case was a challenge to Ministerial approval of a concept plan for the commercial and residential development of a large former industrial site in inner-city Sydney. The project proponent's EA had considered ESD concerns by adopting industry and government standards for energy and water use, which took into account consequential impacts such as GHG emissions. The Director-General's report had subsequently considered the proposal, including the EA, and found the proposal 'consistent with ESD principles'.[221] The applicant, in Class 4 judicial review proceedings, challenged the Minister's consequent approval of the plan, arguing that the Minister had insufficient evidence before him to give 'proper, genuine and realistic consideration' to ESD principles and had merely paid lip service to them, considering that GHG emissions from the project would be substantial. In particular, the Minister had not considered a quantitative assessment of GHG emissions with respect to the site. Jagot J rejected this argument, on the basis that it invited an impermissible intrusion into the merits of the decision. Her Honour could do this by rejecting

---

[218] ibid [131]. This did not in fact invalidate the EA process undertaken under Part 3A in this case, as the applicant subsequently submitted a report assessing the impact of Scope 3 emissions from the project.
[219] ibid 135].
[220] *Drake-Brockman* (n 123).
[221] ibid [116].

any suggestion that ESD principles have inherent meanings or give rise to specific requirements:[222]

> The definition of 'ecologically sustainable development'… nominates the precautionary principle, inter-generational equity, conservation of biological diversity and ecological integrity, and improved valuation, pricing and incentive mechanisms (each as explained in the statutory definition) as 'principles and programs' [that] are not confined to any specific subject matter such as greenhouse gases or climate change. They also do not mandate any particular method of analysis of a potentially relevant subject matter or outcome in any case.

Jagot J thus distinguished *Gray* finding that it did not represent a 'general proposition' that Part 3A required any particular form of GHG assessment for all projects to which it applies; such an understanding would be 'inconsistent with the statutory provisions and established principles of judicial review'.[223] *Drake-Brockman* technically maintained the doctrine that ESD principles were legally required considerations under the Part 3A procedure, whilst emphasising that the application of generally stated ESD principles is marginal and highly fact-dependent. Jagot J's retreat to conventional administrative law reasoning demonstrates that NSWLEC reasoning does not operate in an institutional vacuum—its reasoning is influenced and constrained by legal doctrine in NSW more broadly. It also demonstrates that the Court's reasoning in implying ESD principles as mandatory relevant considerations under Part 3A was quite radical, so that this evolution of NSWLEC doctrine required both careful adjustment of administrative law principles at common law and a settling of judicial attitudes within the NSWLEC itself.

Such a process of adjustment subsequently unfolded through a series of Part 3A cases in which the Court has struggled with the nature of the judicial review task in determining whether ESD cases have been properly taken into account as relevant considerations. In *Walker v Minister for Planning*,[224] Biscoe J conducted a judicial review of, and quashed, a decision of the Minister for Planning to approve a 'concept plan' for a major infrastructure project (a large residential subdivision and retirement development near the coastline) under Part 3A. Biscoe J found that the Minister had failed to take into account a relevant consideration he was bound to take into account—'ESD principles'—which in this case required consideration of the potential impact on the proposed development of increased flood risk due to climate change. To justify the reasoning in this case, Biscoe J focused on a reference to the 'public interest', which the Minister was required to take into account in approving a concept plan, according to secondary legislation,[225] and he also relied on the reasoning in *Gray*.[226] The 'public interest' must be interpreted in light of the

[222] ibid [132].
[223] ibid [131].
[224] *Walker v Minister for Planning* (n 85).
[225] Environmental Planning and Assessment Regulation 2000 (NSW) cl 8B.
[226] *Walker v Minister for Planning* (n 85).

ESD object of the Act,[227] echoing the reasoning in *Telstra* and other section 79C cases. On appeal, however, Biscoe J's reasoning was overturned, with Hodgson JA holding that the requirement to take into account the public interest 'operates at a very high level of generality, and does not of itself require that regard be had to any particular aspect of the public interest'.[228] He thus overruled Biscoe J's finding on this point as well as Pain J's conclusion in *Gray* that a decision-maker under Part 3A is obliged to consider ESD principles. Hodgson JA was concerned that judicial review of whether more specific relevant considerations were taken into account would stray impermissibly into the merits of the decision. At the same time, Hodgson JA indicated that ESD principles were likely to become an aspect of the public interest in 'most if not all decisions', as explained above,[229] reflecting a struggle in reconciling the legal relevance of ESD principles with the formal application of judicial review doctrine.

In light of this uncertain conclusion as to the legal relevance of ESD principles in Part 3A, the case law unsurprisingly did not stop there. What followed is something of a dance in the Court's case law between increasing confidence by the Court to state that ESD principles are in fact legally relevant considerations in Part 3A decision-making,[230] and deferring to the discretion of the primary decision-maker in applying them, for fear of straying into the merits of decisions by inquiring whether particular ESD principles have been properly applied. Judicial review challenges have thus been unsuccessful on the basis that:[231]

> The ESD principles operate a high level of generality. They are not confined to a specific subject matter. They neither mandate a particular method of analysis nor the outcome of that analysis. Also, as long as the substance of the principles is addressed, no specific reference needs to be made to the principles in name.

This indicates a retreat on the part of the Court in figuring out whether ESD principles have been properly applied 'in substance' by primary decision-makers. Even in reviewing the proper consideration of the precautionary principle, the Court has accepted that the decision-making process set out in *Telstra* must be followed but indicated that it is for the decision-maker to decide 'whether or not the two

---

[227] ibid [163].

[228] *Minister for Planning v Walker* (n 86) [41].

[229] See above n 87 and accompanying text.

[230] *Kennedy v NSW Minister for Planning* [2010] NSWLEC 240 [77]–[78] ('the time has come in my view (as foreshadowed in [*Walker*]) when it requires consideration of those principles at the concept plan stage'); *Australians for Sustainable Development Inc v Minister for Planning* [2011] NSWLEC 33; (2011) 182 LGERA 370 [239]–[244]; *cf Haughton v Minister for Planning and Macquarie Generation; Haughton v Minister for Planning and TRUenergy Pty Ltd* [2011] NSWLEC 217; (2011) 185 LGERA 373 ('It is not readily apparent to me that [the provisions relating to concept plant applications] would have the consequence of mandating consideration of the principles of ESD' but 'to the extent to which they are applicable, the principles of ESD were considered': [148], [168]); *cf Barrington-Gloucester-Stroud Preservation Alliance Inc v Minister for Planning and Infrastructure* [2012] NSWLEC 197; (2012) 194 LGERA 113 ('the time has come that "the principles of ESD" can now "be seen as so plainly an element of the public interest"': [170]).

[231] *Haughton* (n 230) [165].

preconditions to the application of the precautionary principle exist, and if so, the extent of the risk, the level of scientific uncertainty and what proportionate response, if any, should be made'.[232] Reviewing whether those elements were properly applied would be to examine matters of merit. This indicates that judicial review cases are limited avenues for operationalising ESD principles in NSW law,[233] but the point is also more nuanced. These cases show the difficulty faced by the Court in taking ESD principles into account as legal considerations when they involve highly fact-specific assessments in their application to particular cases. As Fisher describes this conceptual dilemma, this is the legal pluralism of the Court's ESD agenda meeting the legal formalist of the Court's administrative law doctrine.[234] The Court still has a task to perform in determining whether ESD principles are properly taken into account in judicial review claims and it will be interesting to see whether a case might arise in which the Count finds that decision-makers have failed to consider these relevant considerations as a matter of law.[235]

The merits review jurisdiction of the Court overcomes this legal tension, supporting the development of ESD doctrine in Part 3A cases. There have been merits appeal decisions with notable applications of ESD principles in such cases, fleshing out their meanings by applying them as relevant considerations. An early merits appeal was *Gerroa Environment Protection Society Inc v Minister for Planning*.[236] This case was an appeal from a Ministerial decision to extend a sand quarry within the area of an endangered ecological community ('EEC'). Preston CJ approved the application to extend the quarry on the merits, and his reasoning was notable for two reasons. First, he employed ESD principles (here the integration principle and principle of conservation of biological diversity) to justify his decision on this Part 3A development application, following the doctrinal path established in the Part 3A cases above. Second, he defined these principles, and weighed them against each other, in such a way as to allow the environmentally sensitive development to proceed. Thus he defined the integration principle as requiring the 'effective integration of economic, social and environmental considerations in the decision-making process' so that a consideration of the 'value' of the rich sand mining resource in this case was important.[237] Equally, conservation of biological diversity refers to 'genetic, species and ecosystem diversity',[238] and the conservation of

[232] *Barrington* (n 230) [179].
[233] Edgar, 'Between Rules and Discretion' (n 78).
[234] See Fisher, '"Jurisdictional" Facts and "Hot" Facts' (n 6).
[235] This will continue to be an important task for major projects decided under the post-2011 EPA rules introduced after the repeal of Part 3A. New provisions of the Act—relating to approval processes for 'state significant development' (SSD) and 'state significant infrastructure'—clarify that ESD principles are mandatory relevant considerations, at least for major projects qualifying as SSD, by returning to the section 79C factors (including the 'public interest' informed by ESD principles) as relevant in determining an application: EPA Act, s 89H. See *Upper Mooki Landcare Inc v Shenhua Watermark Coal Pty Ltd* [2016] NSWLEC 6 [178].
[236] *Gerroa Environment Protection Society Inc v Minister for Planning* [2008] NSWLEC 173.
[237] ibid [7].
[238] ibid [65].

vegetation that promotes such diversity (including the EEC in this case) needed to be a 'fundamental consideration' in determining a development application that involves removing such vegetation. In the result, this fundamental consideration could be accommodated in conditions attaching to the planning consent,[239] and the definition and interaction of these two ESD principles in this case demonstrates another fact-specific example of their application. A similar application of the integration principle can be seen in *Hunter Environment Lobby Inc v Minister for Planning*, although this appeal was not as environmentally progressive in its substantiation of ESD principles on the facts.[240]

A more recent Part 3A merits appeal, which is a tour de force of reasoning based on ESD principles,[241] is *Bulga Milbrodale Progress Association Inc v Minister for Planning and Infrastructure and Warkworth Mining Limited*.[242] Both parties in the case accepted the legal relevance of ESD principles in determining the project application, showing how ESD principles have become legally relevant considerations through the force of the Court's case law.[243] The case involved important applications of the principle of conservation of biological diversity and ecological integrity and the principle of intergenerational equity in concluding that an application for approval of a large, open cut coal mine should be refused. In relation to conservation of biological diversity and ecological integrity, the proposed mine was found to have significant and unacceptable impacts on endangered ecological communities, which the proposed offset measures would not adequately compensate. Preston CJ drew this conclusion by defining this principle as having the following operational content:[244]

> The strategies for managing the adverse impacts of a project on biological diversity are, in order of priority of action, avoidance, mitigation and offsets. Avoidance and mitigation measures should be the primary strategies for managing the potential adverse impacts of a project. Avoidance and mitigation measures directly reduce the scale and intensity of the potential impacts of a project. Offsets are then used to address the impacts that remain after avoidance and mitigation measures have been put in place.

---

[239] ibid [135].

[240] *Hunter Environment Lobby Inc v Minister for Planning* [2011] NSWLEC 221 (Pain J approving the expansion of a coal mine project but prioritising the economic interests of the mine through the integration principle).

[241] The judgment reads as a potential candidate as a 'planning principle' for the principles of intergenerational equity and the conservation of biological diversity and ecological integrity.

[242] *Bulga Milbrodale Progress Association Inc v Minister for Planning and Infrastructure and Warkworth Mining Limited* [2013] NSWLEC 48.

[243] Preston CJ relies on the ESD objects of the act and the duty of the Minister to consider the public interest ('Although that requirement is not explicitly stated in the Act, it is so central to the task of a Minister fulfilling functions under the Act that it goes without saying'): ibid [56]. Note that Preston CJ does not find that ESD principles are mandatory relevant considerations, since it was sufficient to conclude that 'as an aspect of the public interest they may be taken into account in cases where issues relevant to the principles of ESD arise': [59].

[244] ibid [147].

In relation to intergenerational equity, Preston CJ was similarly thoughtful in defining the substance of this principle and applying it to the case. He did this alongside the principle of intra-generational equity, which, whilst not included in the section 6(2) POEA Act definition of ESD, was included as a relevant ESD principle that equally defines 'environmental justice' in this context:

> In an assessment of the equity or fairness of the Project's distribution of benefits and burdens, assistance can be gained by consideration of two distinct principles of ecologically sustainable development, inter-generational equity and intra-generational equity. The principle of inter-generational equity provides that the present generation should ensure that the health, diversity and productivity of the environment are maintained or advanced for the future generations (see s 6(2)(b) [POEA Act]). The principle of intra-generational equity involves people within the present generation having equal rights to benefit from the exploitation of resources as well as from the enjoyment of a clean and healthy environment [...] A decision maker should conscientiously address the principles of ESD in dealing with any application for a project.

Drawing on this explanation of these equity-based ESD principles, Preston CJ again found that the proposed mine fell short of taking into account relevant considerations, particularly in the way that the economic cost-benefit analyses justifying the project had failed to take into account impacts on local villagers (intra-generational justice) and on future generations by not considering the value of maintaining or enhancing the health, diversity and productivity of the local environment at Bulga for their benefit (intergenerational justice). *Bulga* was challenged in the Court of Appeal, particularly for taking into account ESD principles as an aspect of the 'public interest'. The Court of Appeal rejected this argument, finding that the public interest embraced ESD principles and that Preston CJ had considered local, regional and national aspects of the public interest and balanced them properly in an overall assessment of relevant matters.[245]

The Part 3A EPA Act cases in this sub-section have shown the centrality of ESD principles in the Court's evolving doctrine. The Court's ESD agenda has flourished across its merits and judicial review jurisdictions, creating an unlikely body of law in this statutory context, whilst also being constrained by the proper role of common law courts in conducting judicial review. This is a legal context in which the legal culture of the court and its ESD principles were co-evolving. The increasing doctrinal penetration of ESD principles under the EPA Act links to the next mapping category involving ESD principles in the reasoning of the Court. In *Telstra*, Preston CJ emphasised that ESD principles are applicable whenever a statute adopts the principles,[246] with the implication that the decision's blueprint for the application of the precautionary principle was relevant for decision-making beyond the EPA Act. The following section examines how the Court has

---

[245] *Warkworth v Bulga* (n 91) [296]–[303].
[246] *Telstra* (n 8) [121].

progressed its ESD doctrine within other statutory decision-making frameworks that refer jurisdiction to the Court.

## C. ESD Principles as Legally Relevant Considerations under Legislation that 'Adopts' Principles: ESD Beyond the EPA Act

The third progressive aspect of NSWLEC ESD reasoning is found in cases in which the Court employs ESD principles as mandatory relevant considerations for decision-making under statutes that 'adopt' ESD principles. This progressive step in the Court's reasoning broadens the doctrinal relevance of ESD principles in NSWLEC case law, engaging ESD principles in a range of different regulatory contexts to which they must adapt (and find marginal meanings), at the same time as painting an overall picture of their fundamental role in NSWLEC case law.

The critical doctrinal step for this expansion of ESD reasoning in NSWLEC cases, involving a statutory framework outside the EPA Act's planning context, was set out in the judicial review decision in *Murrumbidgee Ground-Water Preservation Association v Minister for Natural Resources*, which concerned powers exercised under the Water Management Act 2000 (NSW) ('WMA').[247] In this 2004 case, which preceded both *BGP* and *Telstra*, McClellan CJ held that ESD principles are to be applied 'when decisions are being made under … any … Act which adopts the principles'.[248] McClellan CJ made this finding by explicitly rejecting the view that the precautionary principle, argued to be relevant in the case, was a 'merely a political aspiration'.[249] This was due to the widespread inclusion of ESD principles, or ESD defined by reference to ESD principles, in the objects clauses of many environmental and planning statutes that refer jurisdiction to the Court and which 'adopted' ESD principles through their objects. In McClellan CJ's view, this common ESD purpose was of such significance across these statutory frameworks that ESD principles were relevant considerations in decisions made under any such Act, in the common law administrative law sense.

Although there were other statutory objects of these Acts,[250] which might otherwise balance the calculation of matters a decision-maker was obliged to take into

---

[247] *Murrumbidgee* (n 77).

[248] ibid [178]. The NSWLEC's previous (merits appeal) decision in *Keech v Western Lands Commissioner* [2003] NSWLEC 215; (2003) 132 LGERA 23 had applied similar doctrinal reasoning, without setting it out in general terms, requiring the application of the precautionary principle in relation to a merits appeal under s 18DA(10)(a) of the Western Lands Act 1901, which included in s 2(e) an object of ensuring that the land covered by the Act was used in accordance with ESD principles, as defined by s 6(2) POEA Act.

[249] *Murrumbidgee* (n 77).

[250] eg another statutory object of the Water Management Act 2000 (NSW) ('WMA'), at issue in *Murrumbidgee* (ibid), is to 'recognise and foster the significant social and economic benefits to the State that result from the sustainable and efficient use of water', including 'benefits to urban communities, agriculture, fisheries, industry and recreation' as well as environmental benefits: s 3(c). Similarly, the EPA Act has other, less environmentally-focused objects, such as promoting the 'orderly and economic use and development of land' and 'the proper management, development and conservation of natural

account at common law, the Court was focused on promoting ESD as central to its doctrine. Thus, in *Murrumbidgee*, the Minister was obliged to take into account ESD principles in drawing up a water allocation plan for a particular region under the WMA, which had as an object 'to apply the principles of ecologically sustainable development'.[251] In this case, the Minister had adopted a plan under the Act that significantly reduced water entitlements in order to prevent the depletion of groundwater aquifers, as had been occurring in this area. McClellan CJ found that the Minister had not failed to take into account mandatory relevant considerations in adopting this plan, since the Minister was required to act according to the precautionary principle 'which required a regime to be put in place which was likely to sustain the water source' despite scientific uncertainty concerning the operation of the aquifer in light of water extraction.[252] In this way, the Court also prescribed a marginal application of the principle on the facts.

Following the ESD reasoning in *Murrumbidgee* was a series of NSWLEC cases concerning the NPWA (National Parks and Wildlife Act 1974 (NSW)). These cases involved decisions made under sections 87 and 90 of the Act by which the Director-General of National Parks and Wildlife can permit the disturbance of land for the purpose of discovering an Aboriginal object, or the removal or destruction of such an object.[253] Despite a 2005 Court of Appeal decision suggesting that too much could be read into the obligation under the Act to 'give effect to' the objects of the Act,[254] which included applying ESD principles,[255] subsequent NSWLEC cases went on to find that consents made by the Director-General under sections 87 and 90 were legally invalid if they failed to take into consideration the principle of intergenerational equity.

Thus, in *Anderson v Director-General, Department of the Environment and Conservation*,[256] a judicial review action successfully challenging consent given by the Director-General to destroy Aboriginal objects during the course of a residential sub-division development, Pain J held that the principle of intergenerational equity was a mandatory relevant consideration that had not been taken into account. To determine whether the principle had properly been taken into account, Pain J had

---

and artificial resources … for the purpose of promoting the social and economic welfare of the community and a better environment': EPA Act, s 5(a)(ii). Jagot J points out the doctrinal problems in favouring ESD as mandatory relevant considerations above other statutory objects: *Drake-Brockman* (n 123) [132], whilst Pain J indicates that the 'integration principle' can be a device for reconciling ESD principles with the other objects of the EPA Act in s 5: *Hunter Environment Lobby* (n 240) [164].

[251] Defined by reference to s 6(2) of the POEA Act: WMA, s 3(a). ESD principles also appear in a different form in the overall object of the Act 'to provide for the sustainable and integrated management of the water sources of the State for the benefit of both present and future generations': WMA, s 3. Note there was no merits appeal available in respect of the plan under the WMA.

[252] *Murrumbidgee* (n 77) [186].

[253] No merits appeals are available from these decisions.

[254] *Country Energy v Williams; Williams v Director-General National Parks and Wildlife* [2005] NSWCA 318; (2005) 141 LGERA 426 [65].

[255] NPWA, s 2A.

[256] *Anderson* (n 77).

to define the principle marginally on the facts. Pain J first defined the principle generally by reference to section 6(2) POEA Act—the present generation should ensure that the health, diversity and productivity of the environment be maintained or enhanced for the benefit of future generations—and then more particularly by reference to the facts in this case. The evidence showed that Aboriginal people place considerable cultural importance on ancestral sites where Aboriginal objects are located. As such sites diminish, so does the opportunity for future generations of Aboriginal people to maintain their cultural heritage, in contravention of the principle of intergenerational equity. In properly considering the principle, the Director-General was required to take into account 'the cumulative impact of destruction of Aboriginal objects of significance to Aboriginal traditional owners' in making any decision under section 90, and he had failed to do so.[257]

After this case, the Department of Environment and Climate Change commissioned a 'cumulative impact assessment' of the Aboriginal objects on the proposed development site, and concluded that there was a large number of other sites of similar Aboriginal significance in the vicinity and that the Aboriginal archeological material on the subject site had already been highly compromised.[258] When the Director-General then granted a second consent to destroy Aboriginal objects under the NPWA, a subsequent judicial review challenge was unsuccessful, as the Director-General had properly taken into account the principle of intergenerational equity, as defined and applied on these facts.[259]

In this third mapping category, ESD principles have been employed in the NSWLEC's evolving doctrine to justify decisions by operating as mandatory relevant considerations in relation to decision-making under environmental statutes beyond the EPA Act that 'adopt' ESD principles through their objects clauses. Through this reasoning, the Court broadens the doctrinal reach of ESD principles in its case law, giving rise to a body of increasingly connected environmental law doctrine centred on ESD principles, which is significant in light of the widespread incorporation of ESD principles as objects of legislation that refers jurisdiction to the Court. In the following section, this trend of progressive doctrinal reasoning continues, with the relevance and importance of ESD principles as mandatory matters for consideration being further entrenched in the Court's reasoning.

## D. ESD Principles as Legally Relevant Considerations Beyond Legislative Frameworks Altogether

This mapping category includes cases in which the NSWLEC employs ESD principles as mandatory relevant considerations for no reason other than the force of the

---

[257] ibid [200].

[258] ibid.

[259] *Anderson v Director-General of the Department of Environment and Climate Change* [2008] NSWLEC 182 [46].

Court's own reasoning. Rather than linking such reasoning to an applicable statutory framework, ESD principles are found to have an independent doctrinal role in these NSWLEC decisions. ESD principles are maxims that are drawn on to justify NSWLEC decisions in various ways, where applicable on the facts, giving them an inherent doctrinal role in NSWLEC reasoning. This represents another way in which the NSWLEC engages in progressive doctrinal reasoning involving ESD principles, and highlights that ESD doctrine has become increasingly ingrained in the Court's environmental law.

Seeds of this implicit doctrinal reasoning involving ESD principles can be seen in early merits appeals involving the precautionary principle. In cases such as *Greenpeace* and *Lend Lease*,[260] the Court did not engage in detailed reasoning interpreting section 79C EPA Act to find that the precautionary principle was a required relevant consideration. Rather, the Court used no reasoning technique other than relying on its own case law—in particular, the early case of *Leatch*—to accept counsel's arguments that the principle should apply in deciding the case before it.[261] This classic common law technique, deriving legal reasoning from previous case law, illustrates how the Court develops its own doctrine, including in its merits review jurisdiction.

A more recent case that highlights the entrenched nature of ESD doctrinal reasoning in NSWLEC case law is *Taralga Landscape Guardians v Minister for Planning*.[262] This was a merits appeal from a Minister's decision to approve a wind farm, brought by a group of community objectors. Preston CJ found that the wind farm should be approved, particularly on the basis of the principle of intergenerational equity. He explained the implicit doctrinal relevance of this principle in the following way: '[the] principles of sustainable development are central to any decision-making process concerning the development of new energy resources'.[263] No longer was there any reference to the particular statutory framework, as required to determine mandatory relevant considerations in administrative law doctrine; rather it was the issue before the Court that justified its reliance on ESD principles.[264] Preston CJ discussed various policy developments and papers on climate change and wind energy to conclude that the 'broader public good of

---

[260] *Greenpeace* (n 138); *Lend Lease Development v Manly Council* [1998] NSWLEC 136. See also *Our Firm Facility v Wyong Shire Council* [2001] NSWLEC 243 and the discussion in ch 3(IV)(C)(i).

[261] This was despite the sceptical judicial attitudes in both these cases as to how the principle should apply on the facts.

[262] *Taralga Landscape Guardians Inc v Minister for Planning* [2007] NSWLEC 59; (2007) 161 LGERA 1. See also *Hamilton v Sutherland Shire Council* (n 170) (precautionary principle applied in a merits appeal under the Local Government Act 1993, without any explicit link to a statutory basis for the principle, other than setting out the applicable local environmental plan that included ESD principles by way of background).

[263] ibid.

[264] However, it is still an appeal under the EPA Act, in relation to which ESD principles have been confirmed as doctrinally relevant for a number of reasons, as seen in other mapping categories: see above Sections III(A) & (B).

increasing the supply of renewable energy' justified granting planning approval for the scheme under consideration.[265]

In relation to the principle of intergenerational equity, Preston CJ defined it and used it to justify the planning consent decision. He found that intergenerational equity, in this context of energy production, involved meeting two requirements. First, the 'mining of and their subsequent use in the production of energy of finite, fossil fuel resources need to be sustainable', both in terms of the exploitation of the resource and the maintenance of the ecological environment.[266] Second, as far as practicable, intergenerational equity requires the substitution of energy sources that result in fewer GHG emissions for energy sources that result in more GHG emissions, 'thereby reducing the cumulative and long-term effects caused by anthropogenic climate change'.[267] By these two requirements, the 'present generation reduces the adverse consequences to future generations'.[268] This highly prescriptive statement of energy policy is the 'definition' of the principle of intergenerational equity in this case, which was marginal in that was specific to the facts and decision at issue, and which was applied to decide the appeal as a relevant matter for consideration.

*Taralga* demonstrates the implicit doctrinal relevance, and importance, of ESD principles in NSWLEC reasoning. As the ESD case law of the Court has built over time, so has the confidence of the Court in applying the principles to justify its reasoning and decisions. This confidence is confirmed in the next section, which sets out the final mapping category.

## E.  ESD Principles as Legally Relevant Considerations in All Aspects of NSWLEC Jurisdiction

The final mapping category includes cases in which ESD principles are employed as legally relevant considerations in a looser doctrinal sense—beyond cases of administrative law (merits or judicial review)—to justify decisions in all aspects of NSWLEC jurisdiction. This is particularly evident in the other major aspect of NSWLEC jurisdiction—its jurisdiction to hear trials in respect of criminal offences and criminal appeals.[269] This reasoning is progressive not only in expanding ESD doctrine in NSWLEC case law, but also in its use of ESD principles to inform common law sentencing principles.

An early sentencing case in which the Court used ESD principles was *EPA v Transgrid*.[270] The defendant was being sentenced for an offence under section 120

---

[265] *Taralga* (n 262) [3]; [67]–[81].
[266] ibid [74].
[267] ibid.
[268] ibid.
[269] See above n 47. Note ESD principles have also been relevant in determining costs decisions, although in relation to a prior merits appeal: *Miltonbrook v Kiama Municipal Council* [1998] NSWLEC 281.
[270] *Environment Protection Authority v TransGrid* [2003] NSWLEC 18.

Protection of the Environment Operations Act for causing water pollution.[271] Lloyd J found that ESD principles, included in the Act's objects,[272] along with the defendant's status as a state-owned corporation, imposed on the defendant a 'special obligation' to comply with the environmental law at issue, such that its conduct amounted to an 'aggravating factor' for sentencing purposes.[273] ESD principles accentuated the gravity of the offence and weighed in favour of a tougher sentence.

Similar but more detailed reasoning involving ESD principles is found in two later cases arising out of one set of facts: *Bentley v Gordon*[274] and *Bentley v BGP Properties*.[275] These cases involved an offence under section 118A(2) NPWA relating to clearing an endangered species of vegetation on a site planned for development by the second defendant, BGP Properties. The first defendant, Mr Gordon, was the project manager of the site (for BGP Properties), who carried out the clearing operation. In sentencing Mr Gordon, Preston CJ used the principle of conservation of biological diversity to inform a basic common law sentencing principle—determining the gravity of the crime in light of its 'objective circumstances'.[276] Of those circumstances, it was the 'seriousness of the harm' that was relevantly informed by the ESD principle in this case, resulting in a sentence at the higher end of the scale. This was because the vegetation unlawfully cleared in this case was a threatened species and also a sub-population that was key to the genetic diversity of the species—a 'critical component' for the conservation of biological diversity.[277] The criminal offence in this case offended this ESD principle, so defined and applied on the facts, thereby magnifying the seriousness of the harm caused and justifying a harsher sentence.

In the subsequent criminal case of *Bentley v BGP Properties*, a year later, the progressive ESD agenda of the Court is starkly obvious. In sentencing BGP Properties, Preston CJ engaged in much more extensive reasoning and doctrinal employment of ESD principles—the precautionary principle, principle of intergenerational equity, conservation of biological diversity and ecological integrity, polluter pays principle (and internalisation of environmental costs) and integration principle. All these principles were variously used to inform the 'objective circumstances' of the same offence as in the previous case, including the objective seriousness of the offence, as well as the seriousness of the harm caused.

In terms of the seriousness of the offence, Preston CJ found that the statutory framework of the offence, including its ESD objects,[278] made this a serious

---

[271] Protection of the Environment Operations Act 1997 (NSW).
[272] ibid, s 3(a).
[273] *Transgrid* (n 270) [117]–[118].
[274] *Bentley v Gordon* [2005] NSWLEC 695.
[275] *Bentley v BGP Properties* [2006] NSWLEC 34; (2006) 145 LGERA 234.
[276] *Hoare v R* (1989) 167 CLR 348 [7].
[277] *Bentley v Gordon* (n 274) [73]–[75].
[278] The objects of both the NPWA and the TSC Act were relevant to this offence and both included promotion of ESD, defined by reference to ESD principles.

offence,[279] as in *Transgrid*.[280] His Honour also concluded that the circumstances of the offence made it serious since clearing the threatened species of vegetation thwarted the attainment of ESD. Preston CJ went through each ESD principle and showed how the principles were all undermined on the facts by the defendant's actions.[281] As for the seriousness of the harm caused, Preston CJ adopted similar reasoning to that in *Bentley v Gordon*.

In the result, the Court's use of the 'pillars' of ESD justified a harsh sentence in this case.[282] Preston CJ put this reasoning and outcome into a broader context of sentencing for environmental crime. His Honour was concerned that environmental crime should generally be taken more seriously and punished severely, particularly in light of the recent history of environmentalism amongst the 'informed and responsible public' at state, national and international levels.[283] Accordingly, the Court has continued to rely on ESD principles to inform the culpability of offenders in sentencing environmental crime.[284] Further, Preston CJ explicitly drew on ESD reasoning from other Classes of the Court's jurisdiction, displaying an agenda to promote not just environmentalism, but also a unified ESD doctrine in pursuit of that aim in the reasoning of the Court.[285] ESD and its principles were drawn on as a 'touchstone, a central element in decision-making relating to planning for and development of the environment and the natural resources that are the bounty of this environment'.[286] It is within this grand and ambitious doctrinal narrative that ESD principles now sit in the reasoning of the Court.[287] The progressive judicial reasoning in the final mapping category exposes the central, and centralising, importance of ESD principles in the reasoning of the Court across all aspects of its jurisdiction, demonstrating that ESD principles are at the core of the NSWLEC's developing environmental law doctrine.

# IV. Conclusion

This chapter has shown that the NSWLEC is a unique legal institution with an evolving legal culture that finds particular expression in its treatment of ESD

---

[279] *Bentley v BGP* (n 275) [52]–[63].

[280] See also *Minister for Planning v Moolarben Coal Mines* [2010] NSWLEC 147; (2010) 175 LGERA 93 [73].

[281] *Bentley v BGP* (n 275) [171].

[282] *Bentley v BGP* (n 275) [71], [171].

[283] ibid [145].

[284] *Director-General, Department of Environment and Climate Change v Rae* [2009] NSWLEC 137; (2009) 168 LGERA 121; *Plath v Rawson* [2009] NSWLEC 178; (2009) 170 LGERA 253.

[285] eg in *Bentley v BGP* (n 275), Preston J drew on *Murrumbidgee* (n 77), a judicial review action, to find that ESD principles were central to informing common law sentencing principles.

[286] *Bentley v BGP* (n 275) [57].

[287] The polluter pays principle has now been used to inform reasoning of the court in a range of ways, including by informing the application of a civil remedy, in imposing a remediation order

principles. The Court embraces the principles as concepts that inform the evolving doctrine and identity of the Court, in a way that is intended to promote environmental protection and the goals of sustainable development. While the Court is conscious to be part of an institutional, and international, solution for dealing with pressing environment problems, the map of NSWLEC cases in this chapter shows that environmental principles take on doctrinal roles in NSW law that are highly dependent on the legal culture in which they are employed.

This legal culture is shaped by the unique institutional identity of the Court. This identity includes the rationalising and pragmatic reasons for its distinctive creation as a specialist environmental court; its uniquely fragmented but interlinked statutory exclusive jurisdiction; its progressive ESD agenda; its openness to transnational sources and legal influences; and the nature of the administrative law doctrine that it applies, using and developing it as a springboard for the implicit and pervasive doctrinal use of ESD principles across all aspects of its jurisdiction. Accordingly, ESD principles have become central to the Court's reasoning—they are a touchstone for the Court's evolving doctrine, and themselves shape the legal culture of the Court.

In developing this fundamental doctrinal status for ESD principles, the Court has engaged them in its reasoning by a variety of progressive techniques, as mapped in the chapter. In particular, the doctrine of mandatory relevant considerations in administrative law has instigated lines of progressive reasoning leading to the Court's innovation to consider, and require consideration of, ESD principles in justifying decisions across all aspects of its jurisdictions. This was supported by appealing to transnational legal developments concerning environmental principles—both in the international legal sphere and in other jurisdictions—to lend authority to the Court's doctrinal innovation.

What then are the implications of NSWLEC reasoning involving ESD principles for environmental law scholarship more broadly? It seems that some of the legal hopes for environmental principles set out in Chapter Two have come to pass in NSWLEC case law: that environmental principles might bring coherence to environmental law, that they might act as the basis of a new form of law, and that they might assist in solving environmental problems. In the first instance, it can be concluded that ESD principles do unify environmental law in NSW. In fact, this has been a deliberate aim of the Court throughout the progressive doctrinal reasoning outlined in Part III. Preston CJ, in *Hub Action Group*, implicitly used ESD principles to justify his reasoning,[288] in an explicit effort to 'institutionalise'

---

on a defendant who had engaged in dumping of waste in contravention of the NPWA: *Director-General, Department of Environment, Climate Change and Water v Venn* [2011] NSWLEC 118; (2011) 210 LGERA 300. See Brian Preston, 'Sustainable Development Law in the Courts: The Polluter Pays Principle' (2009) 26 *EPLJ* 257.

[288] Albeit in obiter dicta (arguably there is such a thing in precedent-generating merits appeals that contain doctrinal reasoning).

ESD principles and translate their 'grand strategy' into action.[289] However, this is not to say that environmental principles provide general foundations for environmental law universally, despite the Court's appeal to environmental principles in other jurisdictions to give authority to its innovative reasoning in key cases. Rather, the Court has drawn inspiration from transnational developments to build a body of law in which ESD principles unify environmental law in the particular jurisdictional environment of the Court, and in the context of its distinctive judicial architecture and agenda. In particular, this chapter saw how there is a tension between ESD principles and the doctrines of judicial review that are relied on to determine their lawful consideration in some cases. This tension reflects the legal culture of the Court and the legal constraints within which ESD principles can 'unify' its body of environmental law.

Equally, ESD principles do not give environmental law legitimacy as a legal discipline by acting as legal principles in the common law Dworkinian sense, conventionally and properly guiding judicial decision-making. On the contrary, ESD principles, as employed by the Court might be seen as constituting 'policy' in some instances and thus impermissibly used as doctrine by the Court on constitutional grounds.[290] This is particularly the case with respect to planning principles,[291] and in merits appeals in which the Court is robust in prescribing how collective environmental interests ought to be pursued.[292]

The fate of other scholarly hopes for environmental principles is even more dubious in the case of ESD principles in NSWLEC reasoning. For one thing, while the NSWLEC's ESD doctrine is innovative and progressive, it falls short of generating a new form of law altogether (which, for example, rewrites the basic rules of property and land use). This is because the Court still operates within statutory frameworks and the doctrinal limitations of the Australian common law. The Court's treatment of ESD principles thus reflects jurisdictional constraints and common law connections as well as the novel opportunities of its unique legal setting.

In terms of how ESD principles might solve environmental problems, the resulting picture from this chapter's mapping exercise is again mixed. Preston CJ's ambition is that the Court's case law might do just this—address pressing environmental problems[293]—particularly in light of its jurisdiction to decide cases on the merits and its progressive environmentalist agenda. However, two issues remain. First, the predictability of any solutions to environmental problems provided by environmental principles is undermined by the fact-specific application of ESD principles, once found legally relevant. Marginal application and definition of environmental principles were consistently observed throughout the mapping

---

[289] *Hub* (n 1) [2].
[290] See ch 2, text accompanying nn 186–187.
[291] Williams, 'Land and Environment Court's Planning Principles' (n 106).
[292] eg *Taralga* (n 262); *Hub* (n 1).
[293] See above, text accompanying n 70.

exercise of this chapter. Second, it is very difficult (and certainly legally impossible) to determine whether a particular application of an ESD principle constitutes a 'solution' to an environmental problem. Not only is this determination primarily dependent on scientific rather than legal appraisal, but, as seen in some NSWLEC cases, ESD principles might point in different directions as to the environmentally protective, or sustainability-promoting, outcome required on the facts.[294] In this respect, Preston CJ has emphasised that the ESD principles are to be seen as 'part of a package', which will sometimes reinforce each other and sometimes 'tug in different directions and may need to be weighed against one another'.[295] Some applications of ESD principles by the Court certainly do operationalise a progressive understanding of environmental principles as sustainability goals,[296] but this kind of application is not guaranteed or always obvious on the facts.

In sum, the NSWLEC is an excellent example of a legal context in which environmental principles might have significant and transformative legal roles. In the NSWLEC case law mapped in this chapter, ESD principles are central to a novel body of environmental law and doctrine developed by the Court through progressive and innovative reasoning. At the same time, the legal roles for ESD principles in this body of law remain intertwined with, and dependent on, the distinctive legal culture of the Court and the law it applies. This legal setting is unique and, while it may be inspirational to legal scholars, lawyers and systems elsewhere,[297] it has no legal equivalent internationally. Accordingly, nor do its environmental principles.

---

[294] eg *Greenpeace* (n 138); *Gerroa* (n 236); *Taralga* (n 262); *Hub* (n 1).

[295] Preston, 'The Judicial Development of Ecologically Sustainable Development' (n 5). See also *Telstra* (n 8) [182] (where possible, ESD principles should work together, in a complementary fashion to justify a particular decision).

[296] Consider eg *Bulga v Warkworth* (n 242) and *Taralga* (n 262).

[297] Harry Woolf, 'Judicial Review: A Possible Programme for Reform' [1992] *PL* 221, 228–229; Robert Carnwath, 'Environmental Enforcement: The Need for a Specialist Court' [1992] *JPEL* 799, 808; Cowdroy, 'Land and Environment Court of New South Wales' (n 40); Grant Report (n 68).

# 6

## Conclusions

This book has explored an important, emergent and unstable phenomenon in environmental law—environmental principles. It is a difficult book to conclude, since any last word is made at an arbitrary moment in an evolving legal story. This story started from the position that environmental principles are not well-established doctrinal concepts legally; they do not have pre-determined or in-built meanings, roles and legal effects. Nor are they typical forms of 'transnational' regulation that represent emerging common standards beyond and across legal orders.[1] Rather, environmental principles are generally formulated phrases, representing policy ideas, and their versatility means they have been developing increasing roles in judicial reasoning as well as in other legal and non-legal fora. In their legal form, they are novel concepts and this book has started to identify that novel legal form. It has shown that courts play a critical role in shaping and accommodating the legal potential of environmental principles within the structure of discrete legal systems. In doing so, they are sites for doctrinal evolution involving environmental principles within legal systems. In light of the hopes for environmental principles as legal ideas, understanding this evolution has broader implications for environmental law scholarship.

## I. Environmental Principles and Doctrinal Evolution

This book has shown that, in certain legal settings, environmental principles can be important concepts in the evolution of legal doctrine. With ambiguous meanings and unpredictable legal roles, environmental principles are flexible and potentially powerful concepts in diverse legal contexts. Chapters Four and Five showed how environmental principles are used, in legally idiosyncratic ways, to build different normative frameworks for environmental protection and sustainable development into the fabric of different jurisdictions. These frameworks are not simply instrumental vehicles for achieving environmental outcomes. The legal roles and impact of environmental principles are dependent on the legal culture

---

[1] cf Peer Zumbansen, 'Defining the Space of Transnational Law: Legal Theory, Global Governance and Legal Pluralism' (2012) 21 *Transnat'l L & Contemp Probs* 305; Gregory Shaffer and Terence C Halliday (eds), *Transnational Legal Orders* (CUP 2015).

of the jurisdictions in which they are employed. Environmental principles are defined by, and come to life within, existing legal frameworks, whilst also agitating new developments within them. This was seen in both jurisdictional contexts examined in the book—the EU and NSWLEC—in which environmental principles have a highly contingent and evolving legal character.

In EU law, Chapter Four showed that environmental principles are employed (or not) by the EU Courts in three ways. In policy cases, environmental principles play no doctrinal role, reflecting the essential character of environmental principles as drivers of substantive environmental policy. In interpretive cases, environmental principles manifest their substance legally by informing the interpretation of legal provisions. In cases in which environmental principles inform legal tests, they inform the application of established tests for reviewing the boundaries and exercise of EU environmental competence. In so doing, the precautionary principle in particular also generates new tests of administrative review, which in turn inform EU administrative law doctrine. In informing legal review tests, environmental principles are not being directly implemented by courts to produce prescribed environmental outcomes; rather, they are shaping lawful exercises of discretion in relation to environmental and public health matters. The contours and contents of these treatment categories are shaped by distinctive features of EU legal culture, in particular the jurisdiction of the EU courts and legal questions they address, their evolving and open doctrine (particularly in developing tests of EU administrative law), and their style of reasoning.

Furthermore, the constitutional role of the EU courts, and the proper limits of their review of decision-making by EU and Member State institutions, critically determines the doctrinal roles of environmental principles in EU case law. It is only when EU and Member State (legislative and administrative) institutions first exercise EU environmental competence, on the basis of environmental principles, that EU courts employ those principles doctrinally in their reasoning, either to interpret or test the legality of the policy discretion so exercised. This constitutional limit of EU doctrine involving environmental principles both limits legal roles for environmental principles—as seen in policy cases—and provides an opportunity for the CJEU to be progressive in its review of institutional action. It is in the latter sense that the Court has developed detailed and intensive tests of review in relation to action taken on the basis of the precautionary principle, albeit that these tests are formulated and applied differently in reviewing action by EU institutions compared with Member State institutions. This reflects a further layer of the constitutional architecture that defines the use of environmental principles in the EU context.

In terms of the legal potential of EU environmental principles, it is notable that the CJEU has, in some cases, expanded the range of EU institutional decision-making that might be subject to legal scrutiny as informed by environmental principles. This expansion of EU environmental competence has been catalysed particularly by the integration principle. This principle has a distinctive role in EU case law, expanding and defining the size and shape of the map of cases in which a range of EU environmental principles have doctrinal roles, demonstrating how environmental protection considerations can infiltrate other EU policy domains by the legal integration of environmental principles through an expanding scope of EU environmental competence.

In NSWLEC case law, by contrast, environmental principles have fundamentally different legal roles. The group of relevant 'ESD principles' is differently constituted, having been formulated through a deliberative and well-documented Australian policy-making process, influenced by both national political and legal issues and the simultaneously evolving international sustainable development agenda. The Court employs these ESD principles as legally relevant considerations in relation to the full range of questions before it, thereby developing its novel administrative law doctrine and imbuing its case law with ESD principles in a range of progressive ways. ESD principles are now so doctrinally entrenched in NSWLEC reasoning that they have an inherent legal relevance in many NSWLEC cases. The doctrinal map of ESD principles in NSWLEC case law, set out in Chapter Five, looks very different from that in EU law, reflecting the different legal culture of the NSWLEC, and particularly its jurisdictional reach into quasi-administrative decision-making. Rather than simply waiting for judicial review challenges based on ESD principles to be brought, the Court, in its merits review role, can establish legal reasons justifying the application of ESD principles in administrative decision-making as a matter of course. This is done, not through judicial oversight but by way of judicially transparent example. In so doing, the Court has been developing a body of administrative law doctrine that has not traditionally been seen as 'legal' in the Australian common law context.

Another critical element of the NSWLEC's legal culture is its environmentalist or 'ESD' agenda which, amongst other things, unites the disparate classes of the Court's statutory jurisdiction, and influences its developing body of distinctive NSW environmental law. As a result, the ESD doctrine of the Court is expansive and intentionally progressive, to an extent where ESD principles are themselves shaping the identity of the Court as a judicial institution. Unlike the EU courts, where implicit and self-imposed limits on their constitutional role constrain the doctrinal roles of environmental principles; in NSW law, the NSWLEC has more jurisdictional freedom in how it can apply ESD principles. Thus ESD principles inform and justify decisions across all elements of its jurisdiction—from judicial review to merits review to sentencing decisions—with a view to pursuing an agenda of sustainable development and environmental protection. However, the NSWLEC is not without legal constraints in how it can use ESD principles legally. It sits within a hierarchy of courts and within a common law system, which establish a framework of administrative law principles that bind the court. This background of administrative law doctrine blends with the novel jurisdictional remit of the Court to generate a legal culture in which the doctrinal roles for ESD principles are both progressive but also shaped by the legal traditions that bind the Court. Particularly in its judicial review jurisdiction, as compared with its developing body of merits appeals involving ESD principles, there is limited scope to 'operationalise' ESD principles by applying them to the facts where they are seen to be relevant. In such cases, the Court is required to conduct a difficult balance between judicial restraint and giving sufficient legal meaning to the principles where their roles as legally relevant considerations are under review.

In short, the maps in Chapters Four and Five illustrate how environmental principles are not programmatic legal tools to achieve certain environmental outcomes. Rather, environmental principles take on varying and contingent legal roles that are expressions of the legal cultures of which the principles form part.

## II. Environmental Principles in Environmental Law Scholarship

Environmental law scholars have given environmental principles a high profile in environmental law scholarship, highlighting what these principles might do as legal concepts to solve both environmental problems and legal problems in environmental law. As a result of the mapping exercises in Chapters Four and Five, it can be concluded that environmental principles are not so much about solving problems in environmental law as representing and generating new legal developments within legal systems, often co-evolving with the development of norms of public law. Environmental principles act as normative vehicles for moving legal doctrine on, both to inculcate the policy ideas embodied in environmental principles within existing doctrinal frameworks, and to agitate the development of those frameworks in their own doctrinal terms. In that light, there are at least four conclusions that can be drawn for environmental law scholarship from the legal treatment of environmental principles analysed in this book.

First, claims that environmental principles are universal, by virtue of their similar nomenclature across jurisdictions and assumed common international law derivation, cannot be supported. In particular, salient lessons of comparative law are often ignored if one assumes environmental principles to be universal legal concepts. This was seen initially in Chapter Three through the distinctive historical evolution of environmental principles and their varying groupings in different legal systems. The mapping of evolving EU and NSWLEC doctrine involving environmental principles in Chapters Four and Five further demonstrated how widely the legal identities of environmental principles may vary. Not only are different groups of environmental principles employed doctrinally in each jurisdiction, but they take on doctrinal roles that are contingent on the history, jurisdiction and constitutional roles of the different courts, their reasoning style and judicial attitude, and the openness of their pre-existing doctrine to influence by environmental principles. Environmental principles are not universal and equivalent legal concepts that are (or can be) simply translated across legal contexts.

Even when there are legal connections between environmental principles across jurisdictions—either through judicial cross-referral or similar patterns of doctrinal reasoning (as with the precautionary principle and its generation of a similar legal test or decision-making step in EU and NSWLEC cases)—these do not give rise to doctrinal convergence. As indicated above, the distinctive doctrinal frameworks in each jurisdiction, involving different legal questions, different administrative law doctrine and different jurisdictional remits, mean that similar patterns of reasoning still present different legal pictures in each body of law. Having said that, claims of universality for environmental principles might be a convenient shorthand for indicating how the global sustainable development agenda, incorporating a particular set of environmental principles, can act as a spur for individual jurisdictions to generate jurisprudence around their own sets of environmental principles, and might give innovative judicial reasoning involving environmental principles a legitimising foothold (as in the NSWLEC). The transnational turn relating to environmental principles is one of normative inspiration rather than cascading legalisation.

Second, any suggestion that law works instrumentally to deliver good environmental outcomes through its normative force, including through legal environmental principles, again fails to appreciate the complexity of legal frameworks and contexts in which legal principles might have a role, and the real world outcomes to which such roles might be causally connected. As seen in EU law, environmental principles do not act as free-standing legal grounds or standards that may be called in aid to ground legal actions in response to perceived environmental problems. Even in the NSWLEC, where the Court has professed an intention to contribute to solving environmental problems through its ESD case law, the picture is not so simple. In its merits review jurisdiction, the Court certainly has the power to implement ESD principles to sets of facts and bring about certain outcomes—which it has exercised to overturn the consent of coal mining projects, approve wind farm development, and so on. However, ESD principles, as legally required considerations, may also point in more than one direction in relation to an environmental problem; environmental principles do not generate predictable and general responses to environmental problems. It is also not possible to determine through legal appraisal the (scientific) consequences of a particular legal decision for an environmental problem in order to determine how ESD principles are promoting 'environmental outcomes'. Rather, the maps of both EU and NSWLEC case law in Chapters Four and Five demonstrated that environmental principles give rise to marginal definitions or applications of the principles that are specific to the particular regulatory frameworks or (often complex) facts involved. There is no neat translation of environmental principles as policy ideas into predictable legal concepts that drive discrete solutions to environmental problems, with the imprimatur of the law to back them up.

Third, environmental law is a fragmented body of law (along jurisdictional, regulatory, doctrinal and subject matter lines) that cannot easily be unified through the simple legal construction of foundational principles for the subject. As seen in

Chapter Four, for example, EU environmental law is an evolving and widespread body of EU jurisprudence that has both discrete aspects and elements that overlap with other areas of EU law, whether involving a range of areas of EU competence and regulatory subject matters, different elements of EU law doctrine, or various actions before EU courts. In addition, issues of multi-level governance, when Member State action is legally implicated, complicate the legal picture. In part, this fragmented picture of EU environmental law is also driven by the varying roles of environmental principles themselves, as seen with the principles of sustainable development and integration and their distinctive doctrinal roles, and the selective use of some environmental principles more frequently as interpretive aids. Rather than unifying EU environmental law, environmental principles are better understood as critical components of its evolution that are worthy of close legal analysis to determine and appraise the current state of EU environmental law.

The picture in NSWLEC case law is different. While ESD principles do, through the deliberate doctrinal efforts of the NSWLEC, unify its environmental law, the coherence this brings is specific to the unique jurisdiction and culture of this environmental court. It cannot be said that environmental principles universally or generically provide unifying foundations for environmental law; the precise legal context must be taken into account. In NSW law, it has taken concerted action by the NSWLEC, legislature and academics to place ESD principles at the heart of NSW environmental law. Even then, their central role does not overcome the wide variations in regulatory and factual scenarios with which the Court must deal—ESD principles provide a symbolically unifying core that drives and justifies the Court's progressive reasoning, but they manifest in many different decision-making outcomes and applications on the facts, reinforcing the disparate nature of environmental law. Further, despite the existence of transnational connections between some courts in developing doctrine around environmental principles, the principles do not provide universal foundations for unifying environmental law across jurisdictions, as the very different roles environmental principles in EU and NSWLEC case law demonstrate.

Fourth, pre-existing understandings of 'legal principles' from other areas of legal scholarship are not generally helpful in analysing environmental principles. Such existing frameworks do not accommodate the novel and policy-based nature of environmental principles, or the distinct nature of environmental law as a legal discipline. This is seen in EU law in relation to the easy elision made by the General Court and some scholars between environmental principles and 'general principles of EU law'. The doctrinal analysis in Chapter Four showed that, while there are some overlapping doctrinal features (for example, both act as interpretive aids), the doctrinal picture of environmental principles is more nuanced, and likely in a state of evolution. This is particularly evident in light of the complex ways in which environmental principles are employed to inform other EU review tests, including general principles of EU law such as proportionality, within the circumscribed scope of EU environmental competence first exercised by EU and Member State institutions on the basis of EU environmental principles.

In relation to jurisprudential understandings of 'legal principles', in particular the Dworkinian account, the maps in Chapters Four and Five again demonstrate the limitations of such theoretical ideas for environmental law. Not only are the legal roles of environmental principles across jurisdictions inconsistent, negating any general theoretical account of them, but the judicial use of environmental principles as 'policy' ideas to justify reasoning infringes a central postulate of Dworkin's model of proper judicial reasoning involving legal principles. While such authoritative jurisprudential accounts are tempting territory for scholars to explore in analysing new environmental law developments and legitimising environmental law scholarship, they are methodologically inappropriate in this context.

Further, environmental law scholarship does not need such well-established but ill-suited intellectual contributions to give it legitimacy. It needs methodological rigour on its own terms to meet the deep analytical challenges of the discipline and thus to establish its scholarly legitimacy.[2] Environmental law must grapple with problems of multi-jurisdictionality, interdisciplinarity (including legal interdisciplinarity), and a diverse subject-matter; a background of often pressing and controversial public policy problems to which it relates; and a raft of novel legal and regulatory concepts for which there are no pre-established or obvious analytical frameworks.[3] The study of environmental principles in environmental law involves all these challenges. This book has shown that a doctrinal analysis of environmental principles within, and on the terms of, individual legal cultures exposes the legal forms of specific principles within the evolving legal landscapes of which they are part. This is a conclusion and lesson for environmental law and its scholarship more broadly—environmental law is a rapidly evolving discipline, and its evolution in doctrinal terms involves navigating new legal terrain within frameworks that have well established foundations and histories. Environmental law often agitates but it remains part of the existing legal order. Making sense of environmental law developments often involves walking an intellectual tightrope between the old and the new in legal terms and environmental principles are no exception in this respect.

[2] Elizabeth Fisher, Bettina Lange, Eloise Scotford & Cinnamon Carlarne, 'Maturity and Methodology: Starting a Debate about Environmental Law Scholarship' (2009) 21(2) *JEL* 213.
[3] ibid.

# INDEX